WELCOME TO WESTMINSTER ABBEY

OVER THE CENTURIES Westminster Abbey has meant many things to many people. Founded as a large Benedictine monastery, it continues today to reflect something of that tradition through a disciplined life of prayer, work and study. The abbey has also served as the coronation church of kings and queens for over a thousand years, and we still regularly welcome members of the royal family to services throughout the year. At the heart of the nation and standing alongside the Houses of Parliament, Supreme Court and the offices of government, the abbey is a symbol of the connection between Church and State. In serving the nation, we welcome visiting heads of state and other distinguished visitors, and we hold many special services to mark occasions of national celebration and mourning.

Every day we welcome people from all over the world. Some come to take part in our worship, others to explore and wonder at this unique house of God and kings where many of the most significant figures in British history are buried and memorialised. We look back to the past with pride and to the future with hope as we seek to engage with society in the many issues that face us today. Whatever your background and for whatever reason you have come, you are welcome. We hope that you will enjoy your visit.

RIGHT: A view of the quire, looking east towards the high altar and the lofty vaulting above.

THE HISTORY OF WESTMINSTER ABBEY

NO ONE KNOWS EXACTLY when the first church was built on this site, but it was well over a thousand years ago. At that time this area was a swampy and inhospitable place on the outskirts of London. The church stood on an island called Thorney Island, surrounded by tributaries of the Thames. There are various myths and legends to explain its origin. One story says that King Sebert (died AD 616), king of the East Saxons, founded the church in 604. The monks in the fourteenth century were so impressed with this idea that they exhumed what they thought were Sebert's bones from the cloisters and reburied them in a place of honour by the high altar. However, in 2003 archaeologists found what they now believe is the king's grave miles away in Essex! A lot of these stories claiming ancient origin were embellished by the monks partly to establish that their abbey – the west minster, or church – was older than St Paul's Cathedral – the east minster.

Legends apart, in 960 Dunstan, the bishop of London, brought twelve Benedictine monks from Glastonbury to found a monastery at Westminster.

One hundred years later King Edward, who was known as 'the Confessor' because he led a particularly holy life, and to distinguish him from Edward the Martyr, who had died in 978, founded his church on the site, and from then on we are certain of its history.

ABOVE: The coronation of Edward the Confessor from *Flores Historiarum*, a fourteenth-century manuscript in the Abbey Library.

Edward had been born in about 1005 but was driven from England by the Danes. It was said that during his exile in Normandy, Edward vowed that, if his kingdom was restored to him, he would make a pilgrimage to Rome. When he did eventually reclaim his throne in 1042, there was so much unrest in the kingdom that he was advised not to make the perilous journey in case a coup occurred while he was away. The Pope absolved him of his vow on condition that he raise or restore a church in honour of St Peter. Edward's abbey was consecrated on 28 December 1065, but the king was too ill to attend. He died a few days later and was buried before the high altar, which in those days was several metres east of where it is today. The Bayeux Tapestry depicts Edward's body being carried into the abbey for burial. It also shows us what the abbey looked like: it had a central

tower and transepts, heavy pillars and rounded arches. A workman is seen placing a weathervane on the roof, indicating that the abbey had just been finished. Archaeologists have found remains of Edward's church beneath the floor of the abbey and have concluded that Edward's abbey was nearly as big as the present one.

After Edward's death his reputation as a holy man grew. Miracles were said to have occurred at his tomb, and in 1161 he was made a saint. King Henry III (1207–72) held the Confessor in such reverence that he resolved to build a new shrine for him in a yet more glorious church in the Gothic style, with slender, pointed arches and larger windows. Work started in 1245. At the east end the new Lady Chapel, which had been built only twenty years earlier, was left intact and the new Abbey was built on to it, with Edward's

RIGHT: The great rose window in the south transept depicts religious and other figures and was dedicated in 1902.

OPPOSITE: The Bayeux Tapestry shows Edward the Confessor's body being carried into his newly finished abbey for burial.

church being demolished as work progressed westwards. Henry's architect was Henry of Reyns, who was either a Frenchman or an Englishman trained in France – his work reflects many French influences, including the flying buttresses, the radiating chapels in the apse and the rose windows in each transept. The church was consecrated on 13 October 1269, when the body of St Edward the Confessor was translated to its present position behind the high altar. By 1272 the sanctuary, quire and the first bay of the nave had been completed, but in that year King Henry died and work stopped.

During most of the fourteenth century the Abbey must have been a strange sight, with the Gothic building attached to the Norman nave of Edward's church. Then in 1376 the foundation stone was laid for the new nave, and over the next 140 years, with money from rich benefactors including Cardinal Simon Langham, a former abbot of Westminster, and with help from Richard II and Henry V, the nave was completed. In 1503, at the east end, Henry III's Lady Chapel was pulled down, and a new Lady Chapel was begun by Henry VII (reigned 1485–1509). It was consecrated in 1519, but just twenty years later England's monasteries faced a crisis. Henry VIII had fallen out with the Pope because the Pope had refused to annul the king's marriage to his first wife, Catherine of Aragon. Henry proclaimed himself supreme head of the Church of England and in 1540 dissolved the monasteries and seized their assets. Westminster Abbey fared better than most religious houses, perhaps because of its royal connections, and instead of being stripped and abandoned was re-founded as a cathedral, with a bishop and a dean.

The Abbey's new constitution, established by Henry VIII, was not to last, because in 1553 Queen Mary succeeded Henry's son, Edward VI, and Roman Catholicism became once more the approved religion. She made the Abbey a monastery again, and the monks returned. The upheavals were to continue because her successor, Queen Elizabeth I,

who came to the throne just five years later, in 1558, reversed Mary's changes and re-founded the Abbey yet again, this time as the Collegiate Church of St Peter in Westminster, once more with a Dean and Chapter. The dean was answerable to no one but herself as sovereign, and it is in this form that the Abbey survives today, not subject to the jurisdiction of a bishop, as are most churches, but as a special church under The Queen – an institution known as a Royal Peculiar.

Constitutionally the Abbey has not changed since the time of Elizabeth I, but physically it has faced many changes. During the Civil War, which culminated in the execution of Charles I and the establishment in 1649 of Oliver Cromwell's Commonwealth, the Abbey was damaged when Puritans smashed altars, destroyed religious images and the organ, and seized the crown jewels. They were keen to rid the Abbey of all symbols of religious 'superstition'. Although the Abbey escaped wanton destruction better than many churches, it still bears the scars to this day. During this period the Westminster Assembly, a gathering of

LEFT: The fourteenth-century painting of Richard II is the earliest portrait of an English sovereign.

churchmen and others that formulated
the Presbyterian Confession of Faith, met
at the Abbey.

Architecturally the next major
milestone came in 1745, when the two
west towers were built to a design by Sir
Christopher Wren's pupil, Nicholas
Hawksmoor. The Abbey looked much as
we know it today, except for the façade of
the north front, which was remodelled at
the beginning of the eighteenth century,
when the ancient porch was destroyed,
and again in Victorian times, when the
triple portico was built and the rose
window redesigned.

The Abbey faced new peril during the
Second World War. It miraculously
survived, although bombs destroyed the
roof over the crossing, much of the
Deanery, several houses in Little Cloister
and the Westminster School hall (part of
the old monks' dormitory). After the war
the interior of the Abbey was dark and
dirty, and it was only in the 1960s that
the whole of the interior was cleaned to
reveal the true pale-honey colour of the
stonework.

In 1995 a major restoration of the
exterior stonework of the Abbey was
completed, and new statues were added
to the west front, including those of ten
twentieth-century martyrs.

THE NORTH TRANSEPT, QUIRE AND SANCTUARY

Edward the Confessor's church was the first in England to be built in the shape of a cross, with the north and south transepts forming its arms. Most visitors enter the Abbey via the north transept. Their first impression is of the soaring height of the vaulting. At 102 feet, it is the highest in Britain. The rose window above the entrance dates from 1722 and depicts the Apostles, excluding Judas Iscariot. The rose window in the opposite transept depicts a variety of religious and other figures and was re-dedicated in 1902.

The link between the Abbey and the State is immediately obvious in this transept, which contains several larger-than-life statues of eighteenth- and nineteenth-century prime ministers, including Viscount Palmerston (1784–1865), Robert Peel (1788–1850), Benjamin Disraeli (1804–81) and William Gladstone (1809–98), who is buried nearby. A statue of Prime Minister William Pitt, Earl of Chatham (1708–78), is featured in his thirty-foot memorial. He is also buried nearby, together with his son William Pitt the Younger (1759–1806), who became prime minister at the age of just twenty-four and whose monument is over the Abbey's west door.

The north transept leads down to the crossing – effectively the centre of the church. To the west is the quire – an intimate space forming effectively a church within a church. This was where the monks worshipped, though not in these stalls, which are Victorian, and here is where the choir sit for the eight regular choral services each week. The choir consists of twelve men, known as lay vicars, and twenty-four boys, who come from the Abbey's own choir school, now the only school in the country exclusively for the education of choristers.

In the Middle Ages the quire was the

LEFT: The 'statesmen's aisle' in the north transept contains statues of several prime ministers.

ABOVE: The quire – a 'church within a church' – was where the monks once worshipped.

OVERLEAF: The lantern roof, restored after the Second World War, was designed by the Abbey's surveyor, Stephen Dykes Bower.

scene of a horrible murder. In those days criminals could seek sanctuary in the Abbey. Once they were within the precincts, the law could not reach them. But in 1378 fifty of the king's men, ignoring the right of sanctuary, chased a prisoner into the quire. According to a contemporary account, one of the soldiers 'clove his head to the very brains' and also dispatched a monk who tried to rescue the poor man.

Leading up from the crossing to the east are the steps to the high altar, in front of which is one of the Abbey's most precious possessions – a medieval pavement designed and laid in 1268. The abbot of the monastery, Richard de Ware, had seen the remarkable pavements being laid in Italian churches by mosaic workers in the Cosmati style, and he invited them to England to lay a similar pavement in the Abbey. It consists of about 80,000 pieces of porphyry, glass and onyx set into Purbeck marble. The

swirling patterns were designed to encourage the monks in their contemplation. It also incorporated an inscription in brass letters, which seemed to foretell when the universe would end – calculated as the year 19,683 after the Creation. The 700-year-old pavement was recently cleaned and restored – a two-year project completed just before the wedding of the Duke and Duchess of Cambridge in April 2011.

On the north side of the sanctuary is an important group of medieval tombs. Nearest the steps is the tomb of Aveline, Countess of Lancaster. In 1269, aged just twelve, she was married to Edmund Crouchback, the youngest son of Henry III, in what is thought to have been the Abbey's first royal wedding in Henry III's re-built Abbey. She lived only five more years and died in 1274. Nearest the altar screen is the tomb of Edmund Crouchback himself, who outlived his child bride by twenty-two years, before

ABOVE: A detail from 'The Feeding of the Five Thousand' – one of the miracles depicted in the Abbey's original altarpiece, or 'retable', now in the Museum.

OPPOSITE: The 'Cosmati' pavement in front of the high altar was laid in the thirteenth century.

dying in 1296. Between husband and wife is the tomb of Edmund's cousin Aymer de Valence, the Earl of Pembroke, who died in 1324. These three tombs were originally beautifully coloured and decorated, so that in the candlelight they must have shimmered with an extraordinary luminescence impossible to replicate today.

The Abbey is not preserved in aspic as a museum; it is constantly evolving. So it is that the elaborate gilded screen behind the high altar is relatively recent. It was designed and constructed in Victorian times and fully gilded only in the 1960s. The façade was superimposed on a fifteenth-century screen, which can be seen in its original form from the other side. Henry III's original altarpiece, or 'retable', dating from about 1270, is the oldest oil painting in Britain and is now on display in the Abbey's museum. It is an exceptionally important work, and although the centuries have treated it

harshly, there is enough painting left to give a tantalising insight into what it must once have been like.

To the south of the altar are the medieval sedilia, or seats, for the priests. Above them are paintings of two early kings, thought to be Henry III (nearest the altar) and Edward I. The blank panels next to them originally pictured saints, but during the Commonwealth period they were planed off by order of Parliament, which wanted no 'idolatry' in the Abbey. To the west of the sedilia is the flat-topped tomb of Anne of Cleves, the fourth wife of Henry VIII. Above is a picture by a sixteenth-century Florentine artist, Bicci di Lorenzo, now identified as the 'lost' altarpiece from a church in Florence. When the Abbey is prepared for a coronation, the royal box is installed in this bay, and it was from here that the four-year-old Prince Charles, the current heir to the throne, watched his mother, Elizabeth II, being crowned Queen in 1953.

THE CORONATION CHURCH

THIRTY-NINE MONARCHS have been crowned in Westminster Abbey. Indeed, Henry III re-built the Abbey specifically as a coronation church, with long transepts, so that as many people as possible could witness such events. Before the coronation of Elizabeth II the Abbey was closed for many months while the inside was transformed. Tiers of extra seats were built in the nave, quire and transepts to increase the seating capacity from about 2,000 to 8,000. An annexe was built on to the west front of the Abbey, where the entry processions assembled.

Though the coronation service has obviously changed since that of King Edgar in 973, the essential ingredients are the same, as exemplified at The Queen's coronation in 1953. She was first presented to the people by the Archbishop of Canterbury and was acclaimed by fanfares and shouts of 'God Save the Queen'. Next, she signed the oath to govern her people properly, and then, in the context of the Eucharist and sitting in the Coronation Chair, she was anointed with holy oil, invested with the symbols of monarchy and crowned with St Edward's Crown. Finally she moved to the throne, which was on a dais at the crossing, where she received the homage of her subjects, starting with the Archbishop of Canterbury and The Duke of Edinburgh. The Eucharist completed, and having exchanged St Edward's Crown for the lighter Imperial State Crown, The Queen processed to the west end of the Abbey, where she retired for lunch in the annexe before setting off in the golden coronation coach on her triumphant procession back to Buckingham Palace.

The Queen's coronation service went perfectly, but at previous coronations things often went very wrong. At the coronation of William I in 1066, for example, when the congregation shouted their acclamations, the soldiers outside thought a riot had broken out and set fire to the surrounding houses. William trembled with fright and urged the Archbishop of York to complete the ceremony as quickly as possible. At the coronation of George II the choir sang Handel's anthem *Zadok the Priest* at the wrong point, and at the coronation of George IV the crowds outside the Abbey had great sport when the king's estranged wife, Caroline, tried to enter the Abbey and was locked out. At Queen Victoria's coronation the archbishop tried to force the ring on to the wrong finger, making her wince in pain.

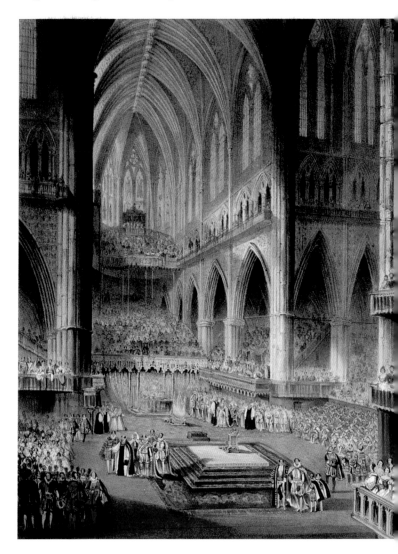

BELOW: A contemporary print showing Queen Victoria's coronation in 1838.

ABOVE: The artist Sir Henry Rushbury recorded the structural preparations for the last coronation, which increased the Abbey's seating capacity from about 2,000 to 8,000.

BELOW: Newly crowned, Queen Elizabeth II sits in the Coronation Chair.

To avoid any such problems, Queen Elizabeth II's coronation was fully rehearsed. Television showed the ceremony for the first time, and the whole occasion was a triumph.

The Coronation Chair, now on display in St George's Chapel at the west end of the Abbey, is one of its most famous artefacts. It was made in about 1297, on the orders of Edward I, to house the Stone of Destiny (also known as the Stone of Scone), which the king had captured in Scotland. For centuries Scottish kings had been inaugurated sitting on the Stone, and Edward took it to prevent Scotland having its own kings in future. The Stone was sent back to Scotland in 1996, although it will return to the Abbey for future coronations.

Every crowned sovereign since Henry IV, and possibly even since Edward II, has been crowned and anointed sitting in the chair, except the Roman Catholic Queen Mary, who had a separate chair made so that she could avoid being crowned in the chair her Protestant half-brother had used. Originally it was sumptuously decorated and gilded with images of vine leaves, animals and kings, including an image believed to be of St Edward the Confessor. The lions around the base date from 1727.

Over the centuries the chair has been badly abused. The original shields that once decorated the compartment housing the Stone gradually disappeared, possibly wrenched off as souvenirs. For some coronations cloth was nailed to it. Vergers used to charge visitors a fee for allowing them to sit in it, and boys from Westminster School and others are responsible for much of the carved graffiti. One piece of graffiti reads, 'P Abbott slept here 5/6 July 1800'. For the coronation of George IV the pinnacles were sawn off, but they were afterwards put back when the weight of history pricked someone's conscience. Perhaps the worst damage was caused when, for Queen Victoria's Golden Jubilee service, it was darkened and varnished, much to the dismay of the House of Commons, which demanded an explanation. Further damage was done when the varnish was cleaned off.

In 1914 one of the pinnacles was smashed when a bomb, hung there by suffragettes, exploded. The chair has left the Abbey only three times: once when it was taken to Westminster Hall for the installation of Oliver Cromwell as Lord Protector in 1657, the second time for the Victorian makeover, and the third time during the Second World War, when it was taken to Gloucester Cathedral for safe keeping. It has recently been cleaned and conserved.

OPPOSITE: The coronation of a king and queen from a fourteenth-century manuscript, the *Liber Regalis*, in the Abbey Library.

RIGHT: The Coronation Chair, commissioned in 1297, is the oldest piece of furniture in Britain still used for its original purpose.

ST EDWARD THE CONFESSOR'S CHAPEL

THE CHAPEL OF ST EDWARD the Confessor is the spiritual heart of the Abbey. It was here in 2010 that Pope Benedict XVI, making the first ever visit of a Pope to the Abbey, prayed alongside the Archbishop of Canterbury. Around the shrine in the centre, which contains the saint's body, lie five kings and four queens.

When Edward died in 1066, he was buried in front of the Abbey's high altar, which in Edward's church was several feet east of the present high altar. Recent research using ground-penetrating radar has discovered what is thought to have been Edward's original burial vault beneath the floor of this chapel. But Edward was not to 'rest in peace'. Such has been the fascination with his remains that he has been moved several times.

Edward's remains were said to be responsible for miracles. In 1102, some thirty-six years after his death, the grave was opened, and the body was found to be in very good condition, with the joints flexible, as if he was only asleep. This was taken as yet another sign that Edward was greatly favoured by God. When he was canonised in 1161, work started on building a glorious new shrine for him. St Edward's body was eventually moved, or 'translated', into it on 13 October 1163, in the presence of Henry II.

One hundred years later St Edward's body was moved again, into the magnificent new shrine that Henry III had built. This was encrusted with gold and jewels and would have shone like a beacon in the candlelit abbey. The shrine remained secure until 1540, when Henry VIII dissolved the monasteries. The monks, fearing they might lose their saint, hid his body, and the shrine was dismantled. Seventeen years later, when Queen Mary had re-established Roman Catholic practice, the monks rebuilt the shrine, rather inexpertly, and put the saint's body back – where it remains to

OPPOSITE: The shrine of St Edward the Confessor, completed in 1269, was at the heart of Henry III's rebuilding of the Abbey.

BELOW: Effigies of Richard II and his queen, Anne of Bohemia.

this day. However, St Edward was still not allowed to rest undisturbed, because during the preparations for the coronation of James II in 1685 one of the workmen put a scaffolding pole through the coffin. A curious choirman, Charles Taylour, investigated and pulled out a cross on a chain. It was given to the king, who gave it to the Pope, but its whereabouts today are unknown. King James had the coffin properly secured with iron clamps, and it now lies at head height in the shrine, covered with the wooden canopy.

Episodes from St Edward's life are depicted in the frieze along the top of the fifteenth-century screen on the west side of the chapel. These include his birth, illustrated towards the south end, and the building of his abbey, at the opposite end.

On the south side of St Edward the Confessor's Chapel are two kings and two queens. Nearest the screen is the double tomb of King Richard II (1367–99) and his queen, Anne of Bohemia (1366–94), who were married in the Abbey in 1382. Richard was one of the Abbey's great benefactors. After he was deposed by his cousin Henry IV he was imprisoned, murdered in Pontefract Castle and then buried in Langley in Hertfordshire. Thirteen years later Henry V brought Richard's body to the Abbey to lie beside his beloved first wife.

Unfortunately, like the Confessor's, Richard's body was not allowed to rest in peace. In the eighteenth century a hole appeared on the ambulatory side of his tomb, through which visitors could put their hand, and a number of bones went missing, including Richard's jawbone, taken by a Westminster School boy. It became a family heirloom until 1906, when it came into the possession of a

ABOVE: Henry III's gilt-bronze effigy, by master goldsmith William Torel, is said to be an idealised portrait of the king.

RIGHT: Edward III's effigy is thought to have been modelled on a death mask.

BELOW: The beautiful effigy of Edward I's queen, Eleanor of Castile, was cast in 1291 and is also by Torel.

descendant who was a priest. He decided it was time the king had his jawbone back, and in a simple ceremony the dean of Westminster carefully replaced it in the tomb. East of Richard's tomb are those of King Edward III (1312–77) and his wife Philippa (1310–69).

Directly to the north of St Edward the Confessor's shrine is the tomb of his great devotee, King Henry III (1207–72). Henry's body was originally placed in the empty vault that the Confessor's body had occupied. Nineteen years later Edward I moved his father's body to its final resting place, a tomb beautifully decorated with mosaic and raised up, as befitted the man who had built this part of the Abbey. Henry's splendid effigy, difficult to see because it is so high, is cast in bronze and gilt and was said to be 'in the likeness of King Henry'. The mosaic has long since been picked out by souvenir hunters – except on the far side, where it was out of reach.

East of Henry III is the tomb of Queen Eleanor of Castile (1241–90), first wife of Edward I. After her death in Harby, Nottinghamshire, her body was brought to Westminster in state. Wherever the cortège stopped for the night on the journey, Edward raised a memorial cross.

On the ambulatory side of the tomb is a curved iron grille with spikes on top. Grilles like this probably once protected all the chapel tombs, deterring intruders from climbing into the chapel to steal the precious relics that were kept here.

West of Henry III's tomb is that of his son Edward I (1239–1307). It was he who, in 1296, captured the Stone of Scone, on which, for centuries, Scottish kings had been inaugurated. This is the only tomb in the chapel with no effigy on it, because at the time there was no money for one. It used to have a tester, or wooden canopy, over it like the other tombs, but that collapsed in 1764, when an unruly mob climbed on to it to get a better view of a funeral taking place in the ambulatory below. In 1774 Edward's tomb was opened, and the king was seen, lying in a Purbeck marble coffin, wrapped in a waxed linen cloth, his head covered with a cloth of crimson sarcenet, a fine soft fabric. In his right hand was a sceptre, in his left a rod decorated with green enamel oak leaves and with a dove at the top. On his head was a gilt crown. He was measured and found to be 6 feet 2 inches, which was very tall for those days – hence his nickname, Edward Longshanks.

BELOW: A modern head of Henry V, cast in polyester resin, replaced the original solid silver head, which was stolen in 1546.

Directly east of the shrine, and lying under the chantry chapel he had ordered to be built, is the tomb of Henry V (1387–1422). Plates of silver originally covered his effigy, but these and the silver regalia he once held, together with the effigy's solid silver head, were stolen in 1546. It was not until 1971 that the king was made whole again by the addition of new hands and head, cast in polyester resin. His wife, Catherine de Valois, who outlived him and died in 1437, was initially buried in the Lady Chapel, but when Henry VII pulled down that chapel to build a new one, her coffin was exhumed and placed on the floor beside Henry's tomb. There it remained in full view for centuries. The diarist Samuel Pepys, on a visit to the Abbey in 1669, kissed her leathery lips. He wrote: 'This was my birthday, thirty-six years old and I did first kiss a queen.' The queen now lies under the altar in the chantry chapel above Henry's tomb.

THE NORTH AMBULATORY

MORE THAN 3,000 PEOPLE are buried or memorialised in the Abbey, and there are more than 600 tombs and monuments, some of them quite massive. Many people commemorated here are remembered because of their distinguished careers, but quite a few owe their presence in the Abbey more to their wealth or social position. Today distinguished figures are still commemorated in the Abbey, although our tributes are rather muted compared with the flamboyance of previous centuries.

The huge monument in the north ambulatory to General James Wolfe (1727–59) reflects the eighteenth and nineteenth centuries' glorification of military figures, especially when they have died at the moment of victory. Wolfe was killed, aged thirty-two, while fighting on the Plains of Abraham above Quebec in order to capture the city from the French. Behind Wolfe's monument is one of the most remarkable in the Abbey. Designed by Louis François Roubiliac, it shows Lady Elizabeth Nightingale (1704–31), who died in childbirth, being protected by her husband as he fends off the spear aimed at her by the skeletal figure of death emerging from a tomb. It transfixes many a young visitor.

Further along the north ambulatory is the two-story chantry the Chapel of the Holy Name, furnished by Abbot John Islip (1464–1532). There are medieval puns on his name along the frieze above the entrance and in the stained glass, which show an eye and a boy falling out of a tree – 'eye-slip'. The upper chapel, called the Nightingale Chapel after Florence Nightingale, is dedicated to the nurses and midwives killed during the Second World War.

Next to Islip is the Chapel of our Lady of the Pew. It is the Abbey's smallest chapel ('pew' meaning a small enclosure) and is cut into one of the flying buttresses. The alabaster statue of the Virgin Mary is modern, but the chapel has many original fourteenth-century features, including the outer doorway with its painted wooden half-gates. A few feet further along is the tomb of Bishop Thomas Ruthall, who died in 1532. Ruthall was one of Henry VIII's Privy Counsellors and a wealthy man. Unfortunately, by mistake he sent an inventory of his wealth to the king instead of some state papers and was so horrified when he realised what he had done that he had a heart attack and died.

BELOW: The striking Nightingale monument transfixes many visitors.

ABOVE: The effigy of Sir Francis Vere, a military commander, lies beneath a marble slab on which is a set of armour in alabaster.

LEFT: Abbot John Islip's mortuary roll depicts his tomb in the chapel that bears his name.

RIGHT: The tiny Chapel of Our Lady of the Pew with its modern alabaster carving of the Virgin and Child.

HENRY VII'S LADY CHAPEL

BEYOND THE CONFESSOR'S CHAPEL, at the east end of the Abbey, is one of its principal glories – the Lady Chapel of King Henry VII (1457–1509). The chapel was begun in 1503 and consecrated in 1519. It is one of the most astounding architectural achievements of the Tudor age. It was probably designed by Robert Janyns and built by Robert Vertue, who had worked on the Abbey's nave as a mason, and his brother William. Henry's claim to the throne was tenuous, and he hoped to consolidate his position by seeking sainthood for his dead uncle, Henry VI (1421–71), and burying him in his glorious new chapel at the Abbey, which would also serve as a mausoleum for himself and his wife. However, the fee demanded by the Pope for elevating Henry VI to sainthood was too high; Henry VI was never canonised, and his body remained at Windsor. The chapel became Henry VII's own resting place. His magnificent Renaissance tomb and that of his wife, Elizabeth of York, lie within the grille behind the altar. In fact, the king and queen are buried in a vault beneath the tomb. The effigies are the work of Pietro Torrigiano, an Italian sculptor who fled to England to escape the authorities after he had a fight with Michelangelo and broke his nose. Also buried in the same vault, but with no monument above, is the body of King James I (1566–1625).

Around the chapel walls, in niches high up and partially concealed behind the banners, are 95 out of an original 107 medieval statues of saints, which miraculously survived the depredations of the Puritans in the seventeenth century, probably because they were out of reach. Beautiful though the chapel is today, it was originally even more glorious as Henry lavished many gifts on it, including plate and tapestries and crucifixes. The small apse chapels have long since lost their altars and become repositories for memorials to distinguished men and women.

At the far east end is the RAF Chapel, dedicated in 1947. The window is a memorial to those who died in the Battle of Britain in 1940, at a crucial phase of the Second World War. A small hole in the wall, now covered in glass, was made by a bomb that fell just outside the chapel. Oliver Cromwell (1599–1658) and

ABOVE: The effigies of Henry VII and his queen, Elizabeth of York, are by Pietro Torrigiano.

OPPOSITE The spectacular fan vaulting in the Lady Chapel.

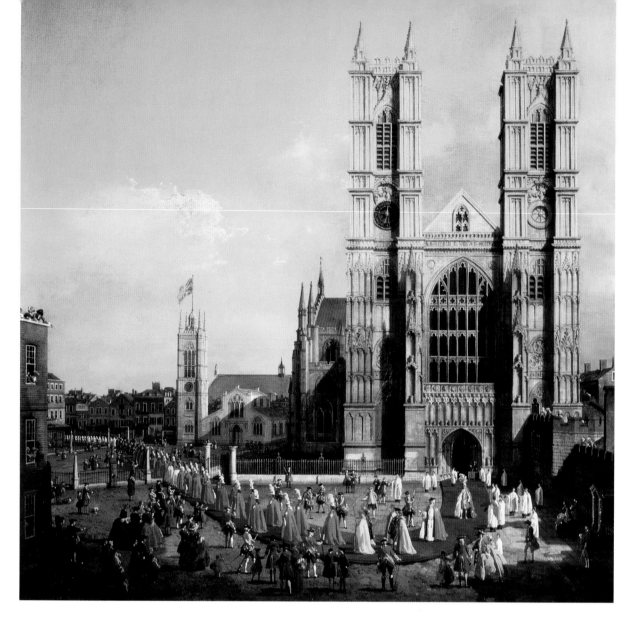

several of his colleagues, who were responsible for trying and beheading Charles I in 1649, were also buried in this area, but their bodies were thrown out after the monarchy was restored in 1660.

Henry VII's chapel is the chapel of the Most Honourable Order of the Bath – an ancient order of knighthood, revived in 1725, the name of which derives from the medieval tradition that newly appointed knights took a bath of purification, analogous to baptism, when appointed. Every four years new knights are installed in a colourful ceremony attended by the order's Great Master – currently The Prince of Wales. Newly appointed knights often have to wait for many years before a stall becomes vacant with the death of its previous incumbent. The knight's banner is hung above his stall together with his

LEFT: Stall plate of Admiral Lord Nelson on the south side of the chapel.

specially carved crest, and an enamelled plate is fastened to the back of the stall. After his death his banner and crest are given to his family, but his stall plate remains as a perpetual memorial. Lord Nelson's stall plate is on the south side, at the east end.

The oak stalls retain the carved misericords – small seats on which the monks could perch while standing during the long services. The stalls extend the whole length of the nave, cutting off access to the side aisles, which have to be entered from small doorways west of the chapel.

The beautiful altar was given to the Abbey in 1935 by members of the Order of the Bath and is based on the Renaissance

RIGHT: The altar, given to the Abbey in 1935, is based on the Renaissance design of the original, which was destroyed in 1644.

design of the original altar, which was destroyed in 1644 by the Puritans at the start of the Civil War. The altarpiece is a fifteenth-century picture of the Madonna and Child by Bartolommeo Vivarini, presented when the new altar was installed by Viscount Lee of Fareham, a Knight Grand Cross of the Order of the Bath.

Vaults beneath the nave contain the remains of two more kings. Beneath the altar lie the remains of the boy king Edward VI (1537–53), son of Henry VIII and Jane Seymour. At his funeral the burial service of the English Prayer Book was used for the first time. In a second vault is a black marble sarcophagus containing the remains of George II (1683–1760) and his wife, Caroline of Ansbach (1683–1737). When their coffins were placed in the same sarcophagus, the adjacent sides of the coffins were removed because the king wanted

nothing to separate them after death.

Although George II was the last monarch to be buried in Westminster Abbey, royal funeral services are still held in the church, notably those of Diana, Princess of Wales, in 1997 and of Her Majesty Queen Elizabeth The Queen Mother in 2002. Hers was the thirteenth funeral of a queen consort to have taken place in the Abbey, the previous one being the funeral of King Edward VII's queen, Alexandra, in 1923, and the first one being that of Queen Edith, wife of Edward the Confessor, in 1075.

In the north aisle of the Lady Chapel is the ornate tomb of Queen Elizabeth I (1533–1603). In the vault beneath, her coffin rests directly on that of her half-sister, Mary I (1516–58), who preceded her on the throne, and in whose reign some 300 'heretics' who refused to recant the Protestant faith were put to death.

The east end of the north aisle is

ABOVE: A white marble effigy of Queen Elizabeth I rests on her ornate tomb where her half-sister, Queen Mary I, is also buried.

known as 'Innocents' Corner'. Here lie two daughters of James I, three-day-old Sophia (died 1606) and two-year-old Mary (died 1607), in unusual and beautifully crafted tombs. In a casket designed by Sir Christopher Wren and set into the wall are thought to be the remains of the 'Princes in the Tower', thirteen-year-old Edward V (1470–83) and eleven-year-old Richard, Duke of York (1472–83). Twice their mother, Elizabeth Woodville, wife of Edward IV, sought sanctuary in the abbot's house (now the Deanery), and it was here that she was persuaded to give up Richard, so that he could join his brother Edward V in the Tower of London, where their uncle Richard III had confined him. Later that year Richard is said to have murdered both children. What are thought to be their bones were discovered beneath a staircase in the Tower of London in 1674 and were placed in the Abbey on the orders of Charles II.

Queen Elizabeth's tomb is large – but not quite as grand as that of her rival for the throne, Mary, Queen of Scots (1542–87), who was eventually executed on Elizabeth's orders. Mary's tomb, erected by her son James I, lies in the south side of the chapel. Also in the south aisle is the tomb of Henry VII's mother – the hugely wealthy and thrice-married Lady Margaret Beaufort, Countess of Richmond (1443–1509) – whose bronze effigy, designed by Pietro Torrigiano, shows her in old age. She is said to have died in a room in the Deanery.

In another vault beneath the eastern end of the south aisle lie members of the Stuart dynasty, including Charles II, the joint sovereigns William III and Mary II, and Queen Anne. This vault was last entered in 1976, when the Abbey suspected a leak from a gas main. No leak was found, but the entry did produce one surprise. The coffin of Charles II had collapsed, and it was possible to see some of his funeral clothes, including his buckled shoes and the ring he wore on his little finger.

BELOW: Mary, Queen of Scots, lies in a magnificent tomb in the south aisle of the Lady Chapel.

THE SOUTH AMBULATORY AND TRANSEPT

OFF THE SOUTH AMBULATORY leading from the Lady Chapel are three chapels, each containing elaborate and impressive tombs and monuments. The first, St Nicholas's Chapel, contains a vault constructed in 1776 in which members of the Percy family (the dukes of Northumberland) are buried. At the funeral of the first member of the family to be buried here, Elizabeth, Duchess of Northumberland (died 1776), a crowd of onlookers climbed on to the canopy over Prince John of Eltham's alabaster tomb nearby and broke it. Several people were injured, and such was the confusion that the funeral had to be suspended until order was restored. Among the other large, brightly coloured monuments here is one erected by Lord Burghley, the immensely powerful Secretary of State to Elizabeth I, in honour of his second wife, Mildred Cecil (died 1589), and their daughter Anne, Countess of Oxford (died 1588), which is made of many different coloured marbles. There is another to two other seventeenth-century worthies, Sir George and Lady Fane (she died in 1618).

Against the south wall of the ambulatory is a small tomb said to contain the bodies of nine royal children. The first to be buried was Katherine, daughter of Henry III, who died at the age

LEFT: Medieval wall paintings in the south transept depict the incredulity of St Thomas (left) and St Christopher carrying the infant Christ.

OPPOSITE: Ornate monument to Sir George and Lady Fane.

DÑA
ELIZABETH FANE
antiquo NOBILITATA natalitiis
probris VIRTVTE, clarior,
FILIA Rob: Baró SPENCER de wormleighton
præn̄ob GEORGII FANE de Buftoñ
Com: Cancellarii VXOR
CASTA PVDICA
PIA
Spiritum Redemptori suo, ardentissimis votis
voces, forti æquo que iterato
Commendat

An° Dom 1618   Magna Fama
An° Ætat 34   Superstite
Conjug 10   prole Nulla

Moestissimus Coniux   Qui sui corporis negatam
Coniugi incomparabili   recipiam fri Mortuæ sint
PLM   Coniuct Oras ænotiatu que ila

ROBERT SOUTHEY.
BORN AUGUST 12T 1774. DIED MARCH 21T 1843.

KEATS
1795-1821

SHELLEY
1792-1822

GVLIELMO SHAKSPEARE
ANNO POST MORTEM CCXIV
AMOR PVBLICVS POSVIT

JOHNSON

JANE
AUSTEN

1775
1817

WILLIAM SHAKESPEARE 1564-1616
BURIED AT STRATFORD-ON-AVON

THOMAS CAMPBELL
BORN JULY XXVII. MDCCLXXVII.
DIED JUNE XV. MDCCCXLIV.

OPPOSITE: Shakespeare rests on his elbow among the monuments in Poets' Corner.

LEFT: As space has become more limited in Poets' Corner, names of newly honored writers are placed in its stained glass.

BELOW: George Frederick Handel's memorial is said to have been modelled from a death mask.

of just five. Henry was grief-stricken and ordered this tomb to be made and decorated with Cosmati mosaic work. Four more of the same king's children are also here, together with four children of Edward I. The wall behind the tomb was once richly painted, but this decoration has long since gone.

The ambulatory leads into the south transept, on the south wall of which are two important medieval paintings. They were discovered in 1936 behind two eighteenth-century monuments, since moved to the triforium. The paintings depict *St Christopher with the Christ Child* and *The Incredulity of St Thomas*. In the Chapel of St Faith, beyond, is another medieval wall painting showing St Faith holding the gridiron on which she was martyred by being roasted alive. This chapel's atmosphere is ideally suited for private prayer.

In the south transept is Poets' Corner, where men and women of letters have been buried or commemorated for centuries. The tradition began almost by accident, with Geoffrey Chaucer (1343–1400), who was buried in the Abbey not because he was a poet but because he was Clerk of the King's Works at Westminster Palace, just over the road. When, some 200 years after Chaucer's death, Edmund Spenser (1553–99) died and, according to his wishes, was laid to rest close by Chaucer, the precedent was set.

Among the graves of distinguished poets such as Alfred, Lord Tennyson (1809–92), and Robert Browning (1812–89) are others to figures long forgotten – few have now heard of Connop Thirlwall or

ABOVE: The actor David Garrick is buried in front of Shakespeare's monument. Garrick's monument was erected in 1797.

Byron (1788–1824) was not honoured with an Abbey memorial until 1969. Oscar Wilde (1854–1900), whose homosexuality scandalised society and led to his eventual imprisonment, is commemorated in a window overlooking Poets' Corner that was dedicated in 1995 – further evidence of time being a healer. Surprisingly, William Shakespeare (1564–1616), who wanted to be buried in his home town of Stratford upon Avon, did not get his memorial until 1741.

Prominent in the centre of the transept is the grave of the novelist Charles Dickens (1812–70). After a private funeral thousands filed past his grave. When eventually it came to be closed, it was found to be filled with floral tributes, some wrapped in rags – gifts from the poor who had come to honour their hero. The lexicographer Dr Samuel Johnson (1709–84), whose famous dictionary contains some barbed definitions, is also buried here. After a quarrel with his intended patron the Earl of Chesterfield, Johnson defined a 'patron' as 'commonly a wretch who supports with insolence, and is paid with flattery'. His near-namesake the dramatist and poet Ben Jonson (1573–1637) has a monument here but is buried in the nave upright (but, it is thought, head down), because he is said to have begged only 18 inches of ground in the Abbey from Charles I.

It is not only literary giants who are buried or commemorated in Poets' Corner. Actors have gathered around Shakespeare's monument, including David Garrick (1717–79), Henry Irving (1838–1905) and, more recently, Laurence Olivier (1907–89). The memorial to Dame Peggy Ashcroft (1907–91) was unveiled in 2005.

On the wall opposite Shakespeare's monument is a life-size statue of the composer George Frederick Handel (1685–1759), whose grave lies just beneath. His face was modelled from a death mask, although when someone objected that his ears were too large they were remodelled on a smaller scale.

The grave of a man said to be the oldest ever to have lived in Britain, Thomas Parr, is close by Dickens's grave. According to his gravestone, Parr died in 1635, at the

Thomas Triplet. Some poets lived unconventional lives and thus forfeited their place in the Abbey. It was only when a later, more tolerant age forgave them that they were found room. John Milton (1608–74), for example, was a strong supporter of the Cromwellian cause during the period of the Commonwealth and was denied his place in the Abbey by the strength of Royalist feeling until 1737. Because of his profligate lifestyle Lord age of 152. He had lived in Shropshire and was brought to London by the Earl of Arundel. The crowds flocked to see him, but the change of air, or perhaps the germs to which he was exposed, soon caused his demise, and Charles I ordered his burial in the Abbey. In fact his legendary age is a myth, as it is thought his birth date was mixed up with that of his grandfather.

Sixteen poets of the First World War are remembered in the first 'collective' memorial in Poets' Corner. Among them is Laurence Binyon, author of the lines:

They shall grow not old,
*   as we that are left grow old:*
Age shall not weary them,
*   nor the years condemn.*
At the going down of the sun
*   and in the morning*
We will remember them.

These words are spoken at every Remembrance Day service throughout the country.

BELOW: The First World War poets are commemorated in a collective memorial that was dedicated in 1985.

THE NAVE

WHILE THE EASTERN HALF of the church was heavily influenced by French architecture, the long nave is typically English. During its construction in the late fourteenth century Cardinal Simon Langham, a former abbot, was anxious to see faster progress and urged the use of cheaper stone for the pillars. We have Abbot Nicholas Litlyngton to thank for resisting such pressure and insisting that the more expensive Purbeck marble should be used throughout. It gave the Abbey its architectural continuity, so that visually it is not obvious that its construction spanned four centuries.

In the same way that Poets' Corner has evolved as a hallowed place for remembering men and women of letters, so other parts of the Abbey have been adopted as places for honouring people of other callings. Set against the west side of the organ screen, facing the nave, is J.M. Rysbrack's monument to Sir Isaac Newton (1642–1727), the philosopher and mathematician. Newton is best known for his conception of the law of gravity, but his other discoveries and inventions in the fields of optics, mechanics and astronomy made him one of the world's leading scientists. His interests and discoveries are reflected in the sculpture, which features optical and mathematical instruments, his books and a globe showing the signs of the zodiac and of the constellations. He is buried just in front of the monument. Other leading scientists and engineers have since been buried or commemorated here, including Michael Faraday (1791–1867), who worked on electricity and magnetism, and Ernest Rutherford (1871–1937), who studied atomic structure. Charles Darwin (1809–82) is buried nearby and is commemorated in the north quire aisle, just around the corner from Newton's monument, with a medallion portrait on the wall beneath

the organ case. Alongside his portrait are those of other scientists, including Joseph Lister (1827–1912), who pioneered antiseptics, and the botanist Sir Joseph Hooker (1817–1911), a friend of Darwin. Engineers commemorated in the nave include the famous clock-makers Thomas

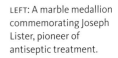

LEFT: A marble medallion commemorating Joseph Lister, pioneer of antiseptic treatment.

LEFT: Sir Joseph Hooker, botanist, explorer and close friend of Charles Darwin.

LEFT: Charles Darwin is buried close by his memorial medallion.

OPPOSITE: The quire screen viewed from the nave, with Isaac Newton's monument by J.M. Rysbrack on the left.

OPPOSITE: A view of
the nave, looking
west from high up
in the organ loft.

Tompion (1638–1713), George Graham (1673–1751) and John Harrison (1693–1776), who found a way to determine longitude at sea by inventing a seagoing clock. His memorial was unveiled in 2006.

In the centre of the nave is the grave of the famous explorer and missionary David Livingstone (1813–73), who died in Africa. His heart was buried where he died, but, eleven months later and borne by faithful servants, his body eventually arrived at the Abbey for burial.

At the west end, in the centre of the nave, is a large green marble stone commemorating Sir Winston Churchill (1874–1965), whose inspired leadership during the Second Word War helped secure victory for the Allies. It was unveiled by The Queen on 19 September 1965 – twenty-five years after the Battle of Britain.

The most famous grave in the Abbey is that of the Unknown Warrior. Situated at the west end of the nave and surrounded by a border of red silk poppies, it has come to symbolise the dead of not just

the First World War but of all wars. Every official visit by a foreign head of state starts with the laying of a wreath at the grave, and each year on Remembrance Sunday the grave is the focus for the Abbey's Act of Remembrance.

The idea that a British soldier of no known name or rank should be buried among the kings and princes in Westminster Abbey is credited to a young army chaplain, David Railton, who first had the idea in 1916, when serving on the Western Front during the First World War. Returning to his billet one night, Railton saw a simple wooden cross over a grave on which were the words 'An Unknown British Soldier'. Two years after the war had ended he wrote to the Dean of Westminster suggesting an Abbey burial for an unknown soldier. Although the Dean was enthusiastic, King George V was at first doubtful, wondering whether such a funeral so long after the war might be considered belated. However, the idea gained support from the government and the public and was finally approved.

With great ceremony the body of a soldier was brought to Britain from France, carried on a warship escorted by six destroyers. On the morning of 11 November 1920 it was borne on a gun carriage to the Abbey via Whitehall, where the procession paused while the king unveiled the Cenotaph. It entered the Abbey via the north door and was carried through the nave, which was lined by 100 holders of the Victoria Cross – the nation's highest award for valour. The body was laid to rest in earth brought from a battlefield in France so that it should lie in soil on which so many of Britain's troops had given up their lives. The flag that had covered the coffin on its last journey hangs on a pillar nearby. It had belonged to David Railton, who had often used it to cover makeshift altars when celebrating Holy Communion for the troops. On other pillars are the bell from HMS *Verdun*, the ship that had brought the body to Britain, and the Congressional Medal of Honor, awarded to the Warrior by the government of the USA.

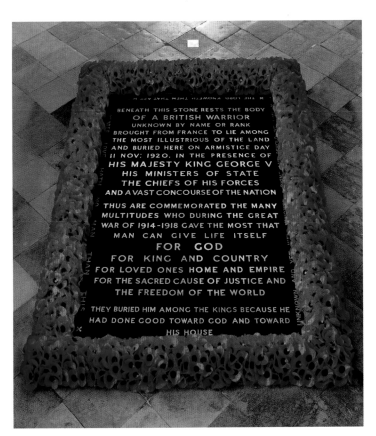

BELOW: The grave of
the Unknown Warrior
who was buried in the
Abbey in 1920.

THE MUSICIANS' AISLE

JUST AS POETS AND SCIENTISTS are gathered together, so musicians have their own special place in the Abbey, in the north quire aisle close to the place where Henry Purcell (1659–95) was buried. Purcell, who was organist of the Abbey from 1679 until his death, was probably one of Britain's greatest composers. He was such a gifted musician that it is said his predecessor as Abbey organist, John Blow (1649–1708), resigned to allow Purcell to take his place. After Purcell's death at the young age of thirty-six, Blow resumed the organist's seat. Purcell wrote music for many state occasions, including the coronations of James II and of William and Mary. When Purcell died, the Dean and Chapter asked his widow, Frances, where in the Abbey she would like him buried. She chose a spot at the foot of the steps leading up to the organ loft, which, in those days, was over the north quire aisle. On the pillar close by is a cartouche commemorating the great man with the words:

> *Here lyes Henry Purcell Esq.*
> *Who left this Life*
> *And is gone to that Blessed Place*
> *Where only his Harmony*
> *Can be exceeded.*

Among the other musicians commemorated is Orlando Gibbons (1583–1625), a former organist at the Abbey, who died in Canterbury. His bust is a duplicate of that in Canterbury Cathedral, where he is buried. John Blow lies here, as does Charles Burney (1726–1814), who wrote a celebrated *History of Music*. The ashes of Charles Villiers Stanford (1852–1924) and Ralph Vaughan Williams (1872–1958) are buried here, while Edward Elgar (1857–1934), Benjamin Britten (1913–76) and William Walton (1902–83) are honoured with memorial stones.

Further east along this aisle is the seated figure of the anti-slavery MP

ABOVE: The Abbey's organ, one of the largest in the country, has grown from one built in 1727 for the coronation of George II and Queen Caroline.

OPPOSITE: The 'musician's aisle', where Henry Purcell is buried.

William Wilberforce (1759–1833), who is buried in the north transept nearby. At his feet is a memorial to Thomas Clarkson (1760–1846), who also played a key role in the anti-slavery campaign. It was Clarkson who first recruited Wilberforce to raise the matter in Parliament. The two men, both devout Christians, worked together for twenty years until the British slave trade was abolished in March 1807. Although widely recognised at the time, Clarkson was rather left in the shadows when the biography of Wilberforce written by his sons failed to give him due credit. The statue of Wilberforce was installed in 1840; Clarkson's name was inscribed below in 1996.

THE CLOISTERS
AND PRECINCTS

ON THE SOUTH SIDE of the Abbey are extensive precincts where the monks once lived and worked. Many of the buildings they knew have gone, but some survive. The cloisters date from the thirteenth and fourteenth centuries, the original Norman cloisters having been destroyed by fire. The monks' refectory used to open off the south cloister walk. Now the position is occupied by the Abbey's Song School – the practice room for the choir.

Off the east cloister, which dates from the middle of the thirteenth century, is the vestibule leading to the Chapter House. In the corner on the south side is a rather insignificant-looking wooden door, now identified as the oldest surviving door in England, dating from about 1050. It may have formed the door to Edward the Confessor's original Chapter House

and was clearly of special significance to Henry III, for he re-used it in his own church. The door was originally larger, but at some stage it was reduced in size. Today it forms the entrance to an office, but originally this was the entrance to the Pyx Chamber.

The thirteenth-century Chapter House, with its medieval tiled floor, is one of the largest in Britain, measuring some 60 feet across. Here the monks would meet each morning to listen to a reading from the Rule of St Benedict and to get their orders for the day from the abbot. Some of its medieval paintings still survive on the walls. For several years, in the second half of the fourteenth century, the Chapter House became the parliament building where the Commons met, further testimony to the importance of the Abbey in the life of the country. A wooden floor

BELOW: The south cloister walk, built in the fourteenth century, includes several military memorials.

ABOVE: The oldest door in England, in the Chapter House vestibule, dates from about 1050.

once covered the tiles when the Chapter House was used to store public records. The floor and other fittings were removed in 1863, and the building restored. Underneath the Chapter House is a small crypt, now used to store vestments but which in the thirteenth century housed the regalia and the royal money chests. In 1303 it was broken into when Edward I was away on a campaign, and the treasure was stolen. It was thought to be an 'inside job', and about fifty monks were sent to the Tower, although after a lengthy trial they were released. The regalia were found hidden in the precincts and transferred to the Pyx Chamber, where they remained until the Commonwealth period.

The Pyx Chamber, off the south-east corner of the cloisters, dates from between 1065 and 1090. It has a rare pre-Reformation stone altar, one of the few to escape destruction at the Reformation, and a medieval tiled floor dating from the thirteenth century. When used as the royal treasury, it was fitted with two doors

ABOVE: The eleventh-century Pyx Chamber with its rare original stone altar.

and six locks, which remain. The Pyx Chamber held the nation's standard gold and silver coinage, against which other coinage would be compared once a year in what was called 'the trial of the pyx'.

The Pyx Chamber and the occupies a vaulted lower storey beneath the former monks' dormitory, now the Abbey Library and the main hall of Westminster School, one of the best known of Britain's independent schools. Walk a little further through the barrel-vaulted 'dark cloister', which leads off the south-east corner of the cloisters, and you come to Little Cloister, where the monks had their infirmary and the more senior monks their houses. Today this is where the Abbey's clergy and lay officers live.

Beyond the Little Cloister is the 900-year-old College Garden, the oldest garden in England. It was here the monks would grow their herbs, which were used to make medicines for the sick monks. There were also fish ponds and targets for archery practice. The garden is now open to the public on certain days of the week. Just outside the garden and towering over it is the Victoria Tower, part of the Palace of Westminster, where parliamentary bills are stored. Elizabeth Tower, which houses Big Ben, the great bell of the clock at the north end of the Palace of Westminster, is also clearly visible.

When the Abbey was a Benedictine monastery one of its functions was to offer hospitality to visitors. The same tradition continues today in the Abbey's café sited near the south-west corner of the cloisters in the fourteenth-century Cellarium buildings, which is where the monks stored their food and wine.

RIGHT: College Garden, one of the oldest cultivated gardens in England.

OPPOSITE: The thirteenth-century Chapter House where the monks gathered daily to conduct their business.

ST MARGARET'S CHURCH

CLOSE TO THE ABBEY, and administered by it, is the church of St Margaret. In the Abbey the public were not allowed into the quire area, which was reserved for the monks, so the monks built St Margaret's for public use. The abbot appointed one of the monks to take the services there.

The present church was built between 1482 and 1523. In 1614 it became the 'parish church of the House of Commons'. The front pew on the south side is reserved for the exclusive use of the Speaker.

In 1655 Samuel Pepys was married here, and in the last century St Margaret's became a fashionable place for many society weddings. Winston Churchill was married here, as were other members of the aristocracy.

The stained-glass windows are of interest. The east window was made in the Netherlands around 1526 but not placed here until 1758. It commemorates the marriage of Henry VIII to his first wife,

OPPOSITE: St Margaret's Church was built by the monks for the use of the local people.

RIGHT: Sir Walter Raleigh and Queen Elizabeth I from the west window.

OPPOSITE: The chancel, with the high altar, reredos and east window beyond.

Catherine of Aragon. At the other end of the church over the west door is a window commemorating Sir Walter Raleigh, who was buried beneath the altar.

A few parishioners have been commemorated both in St Margaret's and in the Abbey. The poet John Milton worshipped in the church, and there is a window to his memory at the west end in addition to his memorial in the Abbey. And William Caxton (c.1422–c.1492), who set up the first printing press in England close by, has a memorial plaque here as well as a plaque on the outside of the

Abbey by the door to Poets' Corner. In the south aisle is a plaque commemorating Phillips Brooks (1835–93), bishop of Massachusetts, a celebrated preacher best known today for his poem beginning 'O Little Town of Bethlehem', now a popular Christmas carol.

Just inside the west door on the south side is a board containing the names of those who donated money towards the restoration of St Margaret's at the end of the twentieth century. Among the names is that of a man familiar around the world for his music – Frank Sinatra.

SERVICE TIMES

SUNDAYS
08.00 Holy Communion
10.00 Matins
11.00 Sung Eucharist
(in St Margaret's Church)
11.15 Sung Eucharist
15.00 Evensong
18.30 Evening Service

WEEKDAYS
07.30 Matins (09.00 on
Bank Holidays)
08.00 Holy Communion
12.30 Holy Communion
17.00 Evensong (said service
on Wednesdays)

SATURDAYS
08.00 Holy Communion
09.00 Matins
15.00 Evensong (17.00 during
the summer months)

Visitors are always welcome at these services. The above times may alter when other events take place. Please check the Abbey's website or telephone for the latest information.

Westminster Abbey
London SW1P 3PA
Email: info@westminster-abbey.org
www.westminster-abbey.org
Tel.: (020) 7222 5152

FRONT COVER: The west towers of Westminster Abbey.

BACK COVER: The interior of Henry VII's Lady Chapel.

FRONT COVER FLAP: The exterior of the north transept.

INSIDE FRONT COVER/BACK COVER FLAP: The wedding of the Duke and Duchess of Cambridge, 2011.

ABOVE RIGHT: The Very Reverend Dr John Hall, Dean of Westminster.

This edition © Scala Arts & Heritage Publishers Ltd, 2016
Photography © Westminster Abbey Enterprises Ltd, 2016, except: back cover flap © Press Association, 2016; inside front cover © Clara Molden / The Daily Telegraph; p.2 (below) © Musee de la Tapisserie, Bayeux, France / The Bridgeman Art Library
Text © Dean and Chapter of Westminster, 2016

First published in 2013 by
Scala Arts & Heritage Publishers Ltd
10 Lion Yard
Tremadoc Road
London SW4 7NQ

The text is a revised and updated version of an original text first published under the same title in 2006.

ISBN: 978 1 85759 821 6

Text: James Wilkinson
Editor: Esme West
Proofreader: Julie Pickard
Designer: Nigel Soper
Produced by Scala Arts & Heritage Publishers Ltd
Printed and bound in China

Advice from the Presidents

Advice from the Presidents

The Student's Guide to Reaching the Top in Business and Politics

G. Scott Thomas

GREENWOOD PRESS
Westport, Connecticut · London

Library of Congress Cataloging-in-Publication Data

Thomas, G. Scott.
  Advice from the presidents : the student's guide to reaching the top in business and politics / G. Scott Thomas.
    p. cm.
  Includes bibliographical references and index.
  ISBN 978-0-313-35662-9 (alk. paper)
  1. Executive ability. 2. Leadership. I. Title.
  HD38.2.T46 2008
  658.4′09—dc22   2008010184

British Library Cataloguing in Publication Data is available.

Library of Congress Catalog Card Number: 2008010184
ISBN: 978-0-313-35662-9

First published in 2008

Greenwood Press, 88 Post Road West, Westport, CT 06881
An imprint of Greenwood Publishing Group, Inc.
www.greenwood.com

Printed in the United States of America

The paper used in this book complies with the Permanent Paper Standard issued by the National Information Standards Organization (Z39.48–1984).

10 9 8 7 6 5 4 3 2 1

For my mom, who introduced me to the presidents way back when

Contents

Preface

Molly Ivins, the late syndicated columnist, never had much use for George W. Bush. His successes, she believed, were not of his making. The Ivy League education, the enormous wealth, the governorship of Texas, the presidency—those, to her mind, all resulted from Bush's fortunate birth and family connections, not from personal skill or intense effort. She nicknamed him Shrub.

Ivins was an unrelenting critic. She accused Bush of lacking compassion. She suggested he was unintelligent. She insisted he was simply marking time, failing to advance a constructive agenda of any kind. "This is not a man," she sighed, "who is terribly interested in policy or cares about it deeply."

But her antipathy did not cloud her political judgment. George W. Bush, whatever his faults, was undeniably a success in his chosen field. He was very good at running for public office.

"This is a man with real political skills," Ivins admitted to an interviewer in early 2000, as Bush's first presidential campaign gathered steam. "Do not underestimate George W. Bush. And sometimes when people say, oh, he's a good politician, they do it in a way that's contemptuous or denigrating. I admire people with real political skills. And you know, I think they're needed, whether in a contentious family, or to lead a country or anything else, and W. has real political skills."

Everyday life and politics, as Ivins understood, are intertwined. But most people fail to see the relationship. They mock politicians and deny the value of political skills. There is nothing political, these average Americans say, in the way they conduct their own personal or professional lives.

They're as wrong as they can be. "Politics is a part of the life of every institution, be it corporation, school, church, or union," contended John Gardner in his classic book, *On Leadership*. Gardner backed his words with decades of experience in both the private and public sectors, as president of the Carnegie Corporation, founder of Common Cause, and member of Lyndon Johnson's cabinet.

"The connotations of the word politics are decidedly negative," Gardner conceded. Yet he went on: "To say of one's organization, 'We don't have any politics around here,' is considered by some to be a high compliment. But it is almost certainly untrue."

LESSONS THAT ARE UNIVERSAL

The typical politician starts small, seeking a local office, perhaps a seat on the city council. Do an effective job there, make some friends, get a little publicity, and the young councilman might move up to a berth in the state legislature. Which, in turn, could set the stage for an even bigger step—governor of the state or United States senator. And then, with enough friends and enough publicity and a very healthy dose of luck, perhaps a shot at the biggest prize of all. The White House itself.

How does that differ from the corporate world, where a young sales representative toils on nights and weekends, builds alliances and friendships in other departments, and works like crazy to impress the higher-ups—all with the goal of eventually becoming sales manager and then vice president of marketing and then, who knows, maybe even chief executive officer a couple of decades down the road?

It isn't different at all.

The blunt truth is that the same skills, tactics, and strategies will help you rise in any organization, be it the Herbert Hoover Elementary School PTA, the Podunk High Student Council, the Acme Xylophone Corporation, or the government of the United States of America. The PTA president may be an unpaid volunteer, and the Acme CEO may bark out orders in an office that is predictably rectangular, not oval. But the paths that lead to those positions are remarkably similar to the trail that ends so gloriously at the front door of the White House.

Thousands of men (and a handful of women) have pursued the American presidency since the late 1700s—dreaming, scheming, and laboring ceaselessly toward their common objective. Only 150 or so of these political hopefuls ever received enough support to be labeled serious contenders. Just forty-two, as of this writing, managed to grab the prize they lusted after so feverishly.

This book examines the lives of these presidential candidates—winners and losers, famous and obscure—with an eye for the qualities and tactics that served their careers well or damaged them beyond repair.

Here's your chance to observe the politicians who pursued the ultimate goal of their profession, seeking to become leader of the world's most powerful nation. Which strategies for advancement are effective and which are doomed to fail? Which personal traits should be emulated and which should be cast off? America's presidential hopefuls have learned the answers the hard way, earning the education of a lifetime in the gritty, cutthroat arena of national politics, an industry that's as competitive as any in corporate America.

Many of their stories offer a hopeful message. You don't need to come from a big city or a fancy suburb to be successful. Bill Clinton was born in Hope, Arkansas; Ronald Reagan in Tampico, Illinois; and Jimmy Carter in Plains, Georgia. Nor do you need to possess an Ivy League degree. Lyndon Johnson passed through the unhallowed halls of Southwest Texas State Teachers College. Harry Truman's highest credential was his high-school diploma. "I've always been sorry I did not get a university education in the regular way," Truman said. "But I got it in the army the hard way—and it stuck."

Ah, you ask, but what advice could these political masters possibly give to women and minorities climbing the corporate ladder? The deed to the White House has been entrusted exclusively to white men since the ink dried on the Constitution, has it not? That's a fact, just as it's true that nearly all *Fortune* 500 companies to this day are run by white males.

But women, blacks, and Hispanics gained footholds in the political power structure long before doing so in the business world. Margaret Chase Smith was a serious presidential candidate in 1964, hailed by the male senator who nominated her at the Republican convention as "one of the most capable persons I have ever known." Jesse Jackson blazed the trail for minorities, drawing substantial support from white voters in his 1984 and 1988 campaigns. "We've shown that we're able to run the race," he declared to black audiences. "We've shown that we're able to debate the case. We may or may not win, but our doubts and our fears have been removed."

The doors to the Oval Office will swing open for female and minority presidents in the coming decades, as will the doors to corner offices at the nation's largest corporations. The pioneers who cross those thresholds will possess the same attributes and use the same tactics that served their white male predecessors so well—the attributes and tactics, indeed, that allowed Smith and Jackson to rise as far as they did in the face of staunch opposition. The lessons in this book are universal.

THE SEVEN STEPS

Morris Udall, an Arizona congressman who mounted a joyous (though ineffectual) presidential campaign in 1976, quipped famously that White House fever was "a disease that can only be cured with embalming fluid." The same could be said of the desire for success in the private sector. It's human nature to hunger for the next promotion and to dream of ultimate victory.

This book offers a blueprint for the upward mobility you crave, distilling more than two centuries of presidential politics into a plan that can transform a young adult into a chief executive. Here's a sneak preview of the seven time-tested steps that will be discussed in the chapters that follow.

1. Deciding upon your long-term goal

American mythology tells us that Abraham Lincoln was a humble small-town lawyer who mysteriously and fortuitously attained the presidency on the eve of the Civil War. His law partner, William Herndon, scoffed at the very idea. "That man who thinks Lincoln calmly gathered his robes about him, waiting for the people to call him, has a very erroneous knowledge of Lincoln," Herndon wrote. "He was always calculating and planning ahead. His ambition was a little engine that knew no rest."

The first step toward success in any field, as Lincoln understood, is simply making the decision to pursue excellence. He intended to be ready if opportunity beckoned, so he built alliances and lined up supporters throughout the 1840s and 1850s, preparing for a presidential campaign that might never occur. It did in 1860.

It may seem bold to establish such a lofty goal, but audacity is precisely what you need. Don't be overly cautious. Don't be awed by the competition. And prepare to work hard. If you're a woman or a member of a minority group, get set to work even harder.

2. Developing your skills and interests

Impatience is the foe of any up-and-coming executive. Don't rush up the career ladder. Take the time to develop yourself thoroughly, beginning with a solid education. As Theodore Roosevelt so colorfully put it: "A man who has never gone to school may steal from a freight car. But if he has a university education, he may steal the whole railroad."

It's equally important to develop leadership skills, empathy (sometimes called "emotional intelligence"), and a broad range of interests and abilities. Specialists rarely attain key positions in any line of work. The corner office usually goes to a generalist.

3. Polishing your image and your people skills

Self-promotion may be vaguely distasteful, but it's essential. You can't become successful without shining up your image and improving the way you deal with people. So break out of your shell. Learn how to speak in public. ("Of all the talents bestowed upon men, none is so precious as the gift of oratory," said Winston Churchill, who was neither a president nor an American, but surely was a political master.) Develop your sense of humor. Dress as if you wish to be taken seriously.

A touch of stagecraft is required of any effective leader, as the presidency of Ronald Reagan proved so well. "There have been times," Reagan laughed, "when I've wondered in this office how you could do this job if you hadn't been an actor."

4. Organizing a network of mentors and helpers

Don't leave a step to chance. Devise a plan to reach your short- and long-term career goals, and seek as much assistance as you can along the way.

Build a solid network of mentors, staff members, and allies. Lyndon Johnson was especially adept at organizational work of this type. He began to weave his web in the 1930s, when he was a young congressional aide and then a fledgling congressman. Edward Clark, Texas's secretary of state during that era, marveled at LBJ's precocious skills. "Nothing was too much trouble for him to do for someone who might be able to help him someday," Clark recalled. His friends eventually helped Johnson reach the White House.

5. Controlling yourself and your opponents

If you want to succeed, you must maintain an even keel. Keep your inner demons in check. Stay cool, remain humble, and speak only when necessary. Never forget that excuses and complaints are for losers.

A controlled approach can be equally effective with your rivals. Stay as friendly with them as possible, but don't offer a prospective opponent a helping hand. Adlai Stevenson, a two-time Democratic presidential nominee, made the latter mistake when he helped bring John Kennedy to national attention in 1956. JFK vaulted past Stevenson to win the 1960 election, and the two men had a rocky relationship thereafter. Stevenson always regretted facilitating their role reversal. "This young man had risen so rapidly and passed him by," his son, Adlai III, would recall sadly.

6. Maneuvering to improve your position

No one becomes a top executive without executing a wide range of maneuvers. If a deal has to be made, make it. If things aren't going well, give your story a positive spin, even if you have to, well, shade the truth from time to time. ("The American people like being lied to. Hence Ronald Reagan," wrote humorist Roy Blount Jr. "But even for a president who is not a professional actor, misrepresentation is part of the job.") And if an opponent has a weakness, by all means exploit it.

Lyndon Johnson used the latter tactic to portray conservative Barry Goldwater as a trigger-happy fanatic, which led to Johnson's landslide victory in 1964. "The whole campaign was run on fear of me," Goldwater would later reflect. "In fact, if I hadn't known Goldwater, I'd have voted against the son of a bitch myself."

7. Succeeding with grace and serenity

If you suffer a defeat, don't give up. Ronald Reagan won the presidency on his third try, Richard Nixon and the elder George Bush on their second. They never stopped believing in themselves, no matter how dark their prospects may have seemed.

Be aware that your fortunes will ebb and flow. Self-help books tend to gloss over the importance of luck, but its impact is significant. It can derail your plans—or put you on the fast track. Theodore Roosevelt soared from assistant cabinet secretary in 1898 to commander-in-chief three years later, and he had no doubt why. "As regards the extraordinary prizes," he wrote, "the element of luck is the determining factor."

The key, of course, is to be ready when fortune strikes, to be primed when luck glances your way—and to maintain your sense of grace and serenity, regardless of what the final outcome may be.

Franklin Roosevelt was a master at keeping things in perspective. Issues of monumental importance landed on his desk with great frequency—economic and military questions that affected the entire world—yet he ended each day at peace with the decisions he had made. "I say to myself—well, I have done the best I could," FDR said, "and turn over and go to sleep."

LEARNING FROM THE BEST TEACHERS

American presidents have come in all shapes, sizes, and temperaments.

John Kennedy blended charisma and family money to reach the White House on his first try. Richard Nixon—decidedly uncharismatic and unwealthy—doggedly pursued the same goal despite setbacks that would have discouraged most people. Both men became the nation's chief executive, as did a reluctant George Washington, a combative Andrew Jackson, a manipulative Martin Van Buren, a scholarly Woodrow Wilson, and a truly confused Warren Harding. (Harding himself laughed at early suggestions that he run for president. "I should like it said, since this question has been raised, that I think too well of my country to wish one of such incapacity in so exalted a position," he declared on the floor of the Senate. A colleague delightedly replied, "The humility of the senator doth most become him.")

There have been smart presidents and unintelligent ones, honest and dishonest ones, diligent and lazy ones. But all of these men—remarkably different in skills and personality—had one thing in common. They all made use of the seven-step career plan that's detailed on the following pages.

And you can follow in their footsteps, no matter what your chosen field might be. This book may have a political theme, but its lessons apply to people in all walks of life.

"You should learn from the best teachers," John Connally always advised. That's certainly what he did, rising from poverty to become Lyndon Johnson's protégé, then governor of Texas (sharing a car with John Kennedy on that fateful day in Dallas), a cabinet secretary under Richard Nixon, and a presidential candidate in his own right. "I try to associate myself with successful people," Connally said. "Not rich people. But many of them are rich. Many of these people are smarter than I am. You don't learn much from a tennis player you can beat six-love."

Connally never achieved his ultimate goal, the presidency, but he went much farther in life than any son of a tenant farmer could have dared to dream. Now it's your turn. Follow his advice and learn, as he did, from the best teachers available. Who better to start you on your way than the men and women who pursued the very highest executive position in the land?

Cast of Candidates

You don't need a history degree to read this book, nor do you need to be familiar with the more obscure men and women who traipse through these pages. Everybody is introduced and described in the text itself.

But, if you're curious, the following list provides additional information about all presidents and presidential candidates mentioned within. This roster includes only those people who actually ran for the White House. It leaves out those who considered running or were pushed to do so, but never actually did, such as Mario Cuomo and Patricia Schroeder.

THE CANDIDATES

CANDIDATE (LIFESPAN), party-state, years ran for president (positions)

JOHN ADAMS (1735–1826), F-Massachusetts, 1796** (vice president) and 1800* (president)

JOHN QUINCY ADAMS (1767–1848), DR/NR-Massachusetts, 1824** (secretary of state) and 1828* (president)

JOHN ANDERSON (1922–), R/NU-Illinois, 1980 (congressman)

CHESTER ARTHUR (1830–1886), R-New York, 1884 (president)

REUBIN ASKEW (1928–), D-Florida, 1984 (former governor)

BRUCE BABBITT (1938–), D-Arizona, 1988 (former governor)

EDWARD BATES (1793–1869), R-Missouri, 1860 (former congressman)

BIRCH BAYH (1928–), D-Indiana, 1976 (senator)

LLOYD BENTSEN (1921–), D-Texas, 1976 (senator)

JOSEPH BIDEN (1942–), D-Delaware, 1988 and 2008 (senator)

JOHN BIDWELL (1819–1900), PROH-California, 1892 (former congressman)

JAMES BIRNEY (1792–1857), LTY-New York and Michigan, 1840 and 1844 (abolition movement leader)

JAMES BLAINE (1830–1893), R-Maine, 1876 (congressman), 1880 (senator), 1884* (former secretary of state), 1888, and 1892 (former nominee)

WILLIAM BORAH (1865–1940), R-Idaho, 1936 (senator)

BILL BRADLEY (1943–), D-New Jersey, 2000 (former senator)

CAROL MOSELEY BRAUN (1947–), D-Illinois, 2004 (former senator)

JERRY BROWN (1938–), D-California, 1976, 1980 (governor), and 1992 (former governor)

WILLIAM JENNINGS BRYAN (1860–1925), D-Nebraska, 1896* (former congressman), 1900*, and 1908* (former nominee)

JAMES BUCHANAN (1791–1868), D-Pennsylvania, 1848 (secretary of state), 1852 (former secretary of state), and 1856** (former ambassador)

AARON BURR (1756–1836), DR-New York, 1800 (former senator)

GEORGE H.W. BUSH (1924–), R-Texas, 1980 (former ambassador), 1988** (vice president), and 1992* (president)

GEORGE W. BUSH (1946–), R-Texas, 2000** (governor) and 2004** (president)

NICHOLAS MURRAY BUTLER (1862–1947), R-New York, 1920 (college president)

JOHN CALHOUN (1782–1850), DR/D-South Carolina, 1824 (secretary of war) and 1844 (former senator)

SIMON CAMERON (1799–1889), R-Pennsylvania, 1860 (senator)

JIMMY CARTER (1924–), D-Georgia, 1976** (former governor) and 1980* (president)

SALMON CHASE (1808–1873), R/D/LR-Ohio, 1860 (former governor), 1864 (secretary of the treasury), 1868, and 1872 (Supreme Court justice)

SHIRLEY CHISHOLM (1924–2005), D-New York, 1972 (congresswoman)

FRANK CHURCH (1924–1984), D-Idaho, 1976 (senator)

CHAMP CLARK (1850–1921), D-Missouri, 1912 (congressman)

WESLEY CLARK (1944–), D-Arkansas, 2004 (former general)

HENRY CLAY (1777–1852), DR/NR/W-Kentucky, 1824 (congressman), 1832*, 1840 (senator), 1844*, and 1848 (former nominee)

GROVER CLEVELAND (1837–1908), D-New York, 1884** (governor), 1888* (president), and 1892** (former president)

BILL CLINTON (1946–), D-Arkansas, 1992** (governor) and 1996** (president)

DeWitt Clinton (1769–1828), F/I-New York, 1812* (mayor)

Hillary Clinton (1947–), D-New York, 2008 (senator)

Roscoe Conkling (1829–1888), R-New York, 1876 (senator)

John Connally (1917–1993), R-Texas, 1980 (former secretary of the treasury)

Calvin Coolidge (1872–1933), R-Massachusetts, 1924** (president)

James Cox (1870–1957), D-Ohio, 1920* (governor) and 1924 (former nominee)

William Crawford (1772–1834), DR-Georgia, 1816 (secretary of war) and 1824 (secretary of the treasury)

John Davis (1873–1955), D-West Virginia, 1924* (former ambassador)

Howard Dean (1948–), D-Vermont, 2004 (former governor)

Thomas Dewey (1902–1971), R-New York, 1940 (district attorney), 1944*, and 1948* (governor)

Elizabeth Dole (1936–), R-North Carolina, 2000 (nonprofit agency president)

Robert Dole (1923–), R-Kansas, 1980, 1988, and 1996* (senator)

Stephen Douglas (1813–1861), D-Illinois, 1852, 1856, and 1860* (senator)

Michael Dukakis (1933–), D-Massachusetts, 1988* (governor)

Pierre Du pont IV (1935–), R-Delaware, 1988 (former governor)

John Edwards (1953–), D-North Carolina, 2004 (senator) and 2008 (former senator)

Dwight Eisenhower (1890–1969), R-New York and Pennsylvania, 1952** (former general) and 1956** (president)

James Farley (1888–1976), D-New York, 1940 (postmaster general)

Millard Fillmore (1800–1874), W/AM-New York, 1852 (president) and 1856 (former president)

Steve Forbes (1947–), R-New Jersey, 1996 and 2000 (magazine publisher)

Gerald Ford (1913–2006), R-Michigan, 1976* (president)

James Garfield (1831–1881), R-Ohio, 1880** (congressman)

John Nance Garner (1868–1967), D-Texas, 1932 (congressman) and 1940 (vice president)

Richard Gephardt (1941–), D-Missouri, 1988 and 2004 (congressman)

John Glenn (1921–), D-Ohio, 1984 (senator)

Barry Goldwater (1909–1998), R-Arizona, 1964* (senator)

Al Gore (1948–), D-Tennessee, 1988 (senator) and 2000* (vice president)

Ulysses Grant (1822–1885), R-Illinois, 1868** (general), 1872** (president), and 1880 (former president)

Horace Greeley (1811–1872), D/LR-New York, 1872* (newspaper editor)

WARREN HARDING (1865–1923), R-Ohio, 1920** (senator)

FRED HARRIS (1930–), D-Oklahoma, 1972 (senator) and 1976 (former senator)

BENJAMIN HARRISON (1833–1901), R-Indiana, 1888** (former senator) and 1892* (president)

WILLIAM HENRY HARRISON (1773–1841), W-Ohio, 1836 and 1840** (former general)

GARY HART (1937–), D-Colorado, 1984 (senator) and 1988 (former senator)

VANCE HARTKE (1919–2003), D-Indiana, 1972 (senator)

RUTHERFORD HAYES (1822–1893), R-Ohio, 1876** (governor)

ERNEST HOLLINGS (1922–), D-South Carolina, 1984 (senator)

HERBERT HOOVER (1874–1964), R-California, 1920 (former relief administrator), 1928** (secretary of commerce), and 1932* (president)

CHARLES EVANS HUGHES (1862–1948), R-New York, 1908 (governor) and 1916* (Supreme Court justice)

HUBERT HUMPHREY (1911–1978), D-Minnesota, 1960 (senator), 1968* (vice president), and 1972 (senator)

ANDREW JACKSON (1767–1845), DR/D-Tennessee, 1824, 1828** (former general), and 1832** (president)

HENRY JACKSON (1912–1983), D-Washington, 1972 and 1976 (senator)

JESSE JACKSON (1941–), D-Illinois, 1984 and 1988 (civil rights activist)

THOMAS JEFFERSON (1743–1826), DR-Virginia, 1796* (former secretary of state), 1800** (vice president), and 1804** (president)

ANDREW JOHNSON (1808–1875), D-Tennessee, 1868 (president)

HIRAM JOHNSON (1866–1945), R-California, 1920 and 1924 (senator)

LYNDON JOHNSON (1908–1973), D-Texas, 1956, 1960 (senator), and 1964** (president)

ESTES KEFAUVER (1903–1963), D-Tennessee, 1952 and 1956 (senator)

EDWARD KENNEDY (1932–), D-Massachusetts, 1980 (senator)

JOHN KENNEDY (1917–1963), D-Massachusetts, 1960** (senator)

ROBERT KENNEDY (1925–1968), D-New York, 1968 (senator)

BOB KERREY (1943–), D-Nebraska, 1992 (senator)

JOHN KERRY (1943–), D-Massachusetts, 2004* (senator)

RUFUS KING (1755–1827), F-New York, 1816* (senator)

DENNIS KUCINICH (1946–), D-Ohio, 2004 and 2008 (congressman)

ROBERT LA FOLLETTE (1855–1925), R/P-Wisconsin, 1912, 1916, and 1924 (senator)

ALFRED LANDON (1887–1987), R-Kansas, 1936* (governor)

JOSEPH LIEBERMAN (1942–), D-Connecticut, 2004 (senator)

ABRAHAM LINCOLN (1809–1865), R-Illinois, 1860** (former congressman) and 1864** (president)

JOHN LINDSAY (1921–2000), D-New York, 1972 (mayor)

HENRY CABOT LODGE JR. (1902–1985), R-Massachusetts, 1964 (ambassador)

DOUGLAS MACARTHUR (1880–1964), R-Wisconsin, 1944 and 1948 (general)

JAMES MADISON (1751–1836), DR-Virginia, 1808** (secretary of state) and 1812** (president)

WILLIAM GIBBS MCADOO (1863–1941), D-New York and California, 1920 and 1924 (former secretary of the treasury)

JOHN MCCAIN (1936–), R-Arizona, 2000 and 2008 (senator)

EUGENE MCCARTHY (1916–2005), D/I-Minnesota, 1968 (senator), 1972 and 1976 (former senator)

GEORGE MCCLELLAN (1826–1885), D-New York, 1864* (general)

GEORGE MCGOVERN (1922–), D-South Dakota, 1968, 1972* (senator), and 1984 (former nominee)

WILLIAM MCKINLEY (1843–1901), R-Ohio, 1892 (governor), 1896** (former governor), and 1900** (president)

WALTER MONDALE (1928–), D-Minnesota, 1984* (former vice president)

JAMES MONROE (1758–1831), DR-Virginia, 1808 (former ambassador), 1816** (secretary of state), and 1820** (president)

LEVI MORTON (1824–1920), R-New York, 1896 (governor)

EDMUND MUSKIE (1914–1996), D-Maine, 1972 (senator)

RICHARD NIXON (1913–1994), R-California and New York, 1960* (vice president), 1968** (former vice president), and 1972** (president)

BARACK OBAMA (1961–), D-Illinois, 2008 (senator)

ALTON PARKER (1852–1926), D-New York, 1904* (state judge)

ROSS PEROT (1930–), I/REF-Texas, 1992 and 1996 (company president)

FRANKLIN PIERCE (1804–1869), D-New Hampshire, 1852** (former senator) and 1856 (president)

JAMES POLK (1795–1849), D-Tennessee, 1844** (former governor)

DAN QUAYLE (1947–), R-Indiana, 2000 (former vice president)

RONALD REAGAN (1911–2004), R-California, 1968 (governor), 1976, 1980** (former governor), and 1984** (president)

THOMAS REED (1839–1902), R-Maine, 1896 (congressman)

NELSON ROCKEFELLER (1908–1979), R-New York, 1964 and 1968 (governor)

FRANKLIN ROOSEVELT (1882–1945), D-New York, 1932** (governor), 1936**, 1940**, and 1944** (president)

THEODORE ROOSEVELT (1858–1919), R/P-New York, 1904** (president) and 1912 (former president)

RICHARD RUSSELL (1897–1971), D-Georgia, 1948 and 1952 (senator)

TERRY SANFORD (1917–1998), D-North Carolina, 1972 and 1976 (former governor)

WINFIELD SCOTT (1786–1866), W-New Jersey, 1840, 1848, and 1852* (general)

WILLIAM SCRANTON (1917–), R-Pennsylvania, 1964 (governor)

WILLIAM SEWARD (1801–1872), R-New York, 1860 (senator)

HORATIO SEYMOUR (1810–1886), D-New York, 1864 (governor) and 1868* (former governor)

AL SHARPTON (1954–), D-New York, 2004 (civil rights activist)

JOHN SHERMAN (1823–1900), R-Ohio, 1880 (secretary of the treasury) and 1888 (senator)

PAUL SIMON (1928–2003), D-Illinois, 1988 (senator)

ALFRED SMITH (1873–1944), D-New York, 1920, 1924, 1928* (governor), and 1932 (former nominee)

MARGARET CHASE SMITH (1897–1995), R-Maine, 1964 (senator)

HAROLD STASSEN (1907–2001), R-Minnesota, Pennsylvania, and New York, 1948 (former governor), 1952 (college president), 1964, 1968, 1976, 1980, 1984, 1988, and 1992 (former governor)

ADLAI STEVENSON (1900–1965), D-Illinois, 1952* (governor), 1956*, and 1960 (former nominee)

STUART SYMINGTON (1901–1988), D-Missouri, 1960 (senator)

ROBERT TAFT (1889–1953), R-Ohio, 1940, 1948, and 1952 (senator)

WILLIAM HOWARD TAFT (1857–1930), R-Ohio, 1908** (secretary of war) and 1912* (president)

ZACHARY TAYLOR (1784–1850), W-Louisiana, 1848** (general)

SAMUEL TILDEN (1814–1886), D-New York, 1876* (governor)

HARRY TRUMAN (1884–1972), D-Missouri, 1948** (president)

PAUL TSONGAS (1941–1997), D-Massachusetts, 1992 (former senator)

JOHN TYLER (1790–1862), D-Virginia, 1844 (president)

MORRIS UDALL (1922–1998), D-Arizona, 1976 (congressman)

OSCAR UNDERWOOD (1862–1929), D-Alabama, 1912 (congressman) and 1924 (senator)

MARTIN VAN BUREN (1782–1862), D/FS-New York, 1836** (vice president), 1840* (president), 1844, and 1848 (former president)

ARTHUR VANDENBERG (1884–1951), R-Michigan, 1940 and 1948 (senator)

GEORGE WALLACE (1919–1998), D/AI-Alabama, 1964 (governor), 1968 (former governor), 1972, and 1976 (governor)

HENRY WALLACE (1888–1965), P-Iowa, 1948 (former vice president)

EARL WARREN (1891–1974), R-California, 1948 and 1952 (governor)

GEORGE WASHINGTON (1732–1799), F-Virginia, 1789** (former general) and 1792** (president)

DANIEL WEBSTER (1782–1852), W-Massachusetts, 1836, 1848 (senator), and 1852 (secretary of state)

WENDELL WILLKIE (1892–1944), R-New York, 1940* (utility president) and 1944 (former nominee)

WOODROW WILSON (1856–1924), D-New Jersey, 1912** (governor) and 1916** (president)

LEONARD WOOD (1860–1927), R-New Hampshire, 1920 (general)

Explanations

Parties: Al-American Independent, AM-American, D-Democratic, DR-Democratic-Republican, F-Federalist, FS-Free Soil, I-Independent, LR-Liberal Republican, LTY-Liberty, NR-National Republican, NU-National Unity, P-Progressive, POP-Populist, PROH-Prohibition, R-Republican, REF-Reform, W-Whig.

Years ran for president: The years listed are those when the person was an announced candidate for president or received significant support in primary elections and/or party conventions.

Positions: The positions listed are those by which the candidate was identified at the time of each campaign. If a candidate sought the presidency more than once, each specified position encompasses all the years to its left, up to any prior position that might be noted.

Results: *-Nominee of major party, **-Elected president.

1

Deciding

William Jennings Bryan and Jimmy Carter shared two qualities in common. Both men knew precisely what they wanted, and they didn't care if others thought they wanted too much.

The flamboyant Bryan showed real skill as a public speaker at an early age. His resonant voice and dramatic flair captivated the voters of Nebraska, who elected him to the House of Representatives in 1890 and again two years later. He became known as the Great Commoner, eloquent defender of the rural Midwest against the moneyed classes of America's big cities.

But not everyone was impressed by the young orator from the prairies. Many Easterners dismissed Bryan as nothing more than a windbag, accusing him of putting little thought behind his heated rhetoric. "He is in one sense scripturally formidable, for he is unquestionably armed with the jawbone of an ass," barked Charles Francis Adams, one of the famous Adamses of Massachusetts. "He can talk longer, and say less, than any man in Christendom."

The verbal torrent would not last long, ceasing in just four years. Bryan overestimated his popularity, abandoning the House in 1894 to pursue the greater prestige of a Senate seat. He lost the Senate election and was forced to return to Nebraska as a newspaper editor, seemingly washed up at the ripe, old age of thirty-four.

The typical politician would have proceeded cautiously after such a defeat. He might have run for his old House seat a couple of years down the line, or perhaps he would have nursed his wounds, waiting a half-decade or more before daring to face the voters again.

But William Jennings Bryan was anything but typical. His best course, he decided, was to aim much, much higher than the Senate. He believed he was destined to be president someday, so why delay the inevitable? He would run for the White House in 1896.

It was a crazy idea, but Bryan would not be deterred. He had made his decision and was determined to follow through. He began corresponding with hundreds of Democratic Party leaders, tenaciously seeking their support. Charles Thomas, a senator from Colorado, reacted as most top Democrats did. "Here was a young man, barely thirty-six, living in a comparatively unimportant Republican state west of the Mississippi River, audaciously announcing his probable candidacy for the presidential nomination," Thomas later wrote. "The very seriousness of the suggestion emphasized its absurdity."

Bryan eventually converted the naysayers. He whipped the 20,000 delegates and onlookers in the Democratic convention hall into a frenzy with his dramatic attack on the gold standard, the most controversial topic of all in 1896. "You shall not press down upon the brow of labor this crown of thorns. You shall not crucify mankind upon a cross of gold," he boomed. His speech "brought tears to the eyes of men and caused women in the gallery to become hysterical," recalled Mark Sullivan, one of the journalists in attendance. The Democratic nomination, against all odds, went to Bryan shortly thereafter.

The Great Commoner would never become president. He lost to Republican William McKinley in 1896 and set his heart on a rematch in 1900, pledging to "stand just where I stood" on gold and other key issues. "Sit down, Mr. Bryan. You must be awfully tired," the *New York Press* sighed. He lost to McKinley again and also fell short with a third presidential campaign against William Howard Taft in 1908. Yet his audacity and determination had paid off in a very real sense, establishing William Jennings Bryan as a world figure for the final three decades of his life. It sure beat editing a newspaper in Nebraska.

Jimmy Carter, on the surface, seemed to be Bryan's polar opposite. He was highly educated, mild-mannered, and nothing special as a public speaker. His clipped Southern drawl and flat delivery lacked the power to stir a mass audience.

Yet Carter was Bryan's twin in the most important way of all. He, too, would not be dissuaded once he had decided upon a goal. Political observers laughed when he launched his campaign for governor of Georgia in 1966. It was insane, they said. He had served just four years in the State Senate. No one knew who he was. But Carter outworked the field of Democratic contenders and finished third in the primary election, a truly impressive showing for a political novice.

Everyone else took the next three years off, resting up for the 1970 campaign. Carter never stopped working, not even for a day. He followed a regimen that drove aides and reporters to exhaustion, rising at 4:30 or 5 A.M., not stopping until midnight or even later. As he would say during another campaign a few years later, "I can get up at nine and be rested, or I can get up at six and be president." Such steely dedication brought him the governorship on his second try.

Carter's 1971 inaugural address as governor earned national acclaim for its repudiation of the South's sordid past. "I say to you quite frankly that the time for racial discrimination is over," he asserted. It was a brave declaration to make, less than a decade after the bombings in Birmingham and the race riots at the University of Mississippi. He was hailed as a leader of the New South, a man clearly worth watching.

But no one suggested that Carter was presidential material. No Southerner had reached the White House by election since Zachary Taylor in 1848. (There *had* been two Southern presidents since Taylor, it was true, though they came with asterisks attached. Woodrow Wilson, a native of Virginia, had spent his adulthood in the North, and Lyndon Johnson of Texas was elevated by the assassination of John Kennedy.) It was absolutely unthinkable that the governor of Georgia might someday be commander-in-chief.

Carter had different ideas, as he hinted toward the end of his brief address in Atlanta. He subtly acknowledged his similarity to Bryan, quoting the old master on the subject of ambition: "Destiny is not a matter of chance. It is a matter of choice. Destiny is not a thing to be waited for. It is a thing to be achieved." Reporters paid no attention. William Jennings Bryan was a political fossil. Why would anyone cite him in a speech?

They eventually learned why. Carter believed the White House was his destiny. He ripped a page from Bryan's book and decided to run for president in 1976, even though he seemed certain to fail. Early polls put his support at less than 1 percent. The prospective presidential candidate appeared on a TV show, *What's My Line*, where panelists tried to guess the identity of mystery guests. They didn't have a clue who he was.

But two years of dawn-to-midnight campaigning changed all that. Jimmy Carter delivered another inaugural address in Washington in 1977, just six years after taking the oath as governor. He hadn't waited for his destiny. He had achieved it.

Bryan and Carter both understood that the first step toward ultimate success must occur within your own mind. You, and you alone, must decide which long-term goal will fulfill your ambitions, quench your thirst for attention, and satisfy your ego. Everything else—all the upcoming years of planning, organizing, and just plain hard work—will stem from whatever decision you make.

It's not a simple process. Your personal calculations will be affected by a broad range of factors. If you're going to reach the best decision for your future, you'll have to gain a deeper understanding of your basic urges, ward off distractions, overcome potential barriers, and prepare yourself for all of the hard work ahead. This chapter deals with each of these points in depth:

Basic urges

- Ambition, when under control, is a good impulse.
- There's nothing wrong with wanting recognition.
- A healthy ego is fine, but egomania is dangerous.

Distractions

- Don't shape your career to please someone else.
- Excessive caution can destroy your chances.
- Your competitors are only human, so don't be awed.

Potential barriers

- Women must work harder and be tougher.
- Minorities must work harder and be tougher.
- Health problems don't have to be impediments.
- It doesn't really matter where you grew up.

Hard work

- If you want the top job, make the top effort.

That last point is especially important. Reaching your ultimate goal will require intense exertion and steadfast determination. Never waver in your commitment to the choice you've made.

Jimmy Carter certainly didn't. Winning the presidency in 1976 wasn't good enough for him. He resolved to validate his original decision with another victory in 1980. The biggest challenge to his reelection, it seemed, would come from Edward Kennedy, the Massachusetts senator with an immense fortune, movie-star looks, and impeccable liberal pedigree. (Ronald Reagan, of course, would prove to be a more formidable obstacle in 1980, though it didn't seem that way at first.) Kennedy announced in 1979 that he would oppose President Carter for the Democratic nomination the following year. Early polls showed Kennedy ahead by a two-to-one margin. It seemed to be in the bag.

But Carter wasn't worried, or so he said. He met with a group of Democratic congressmen in the White House and promised them he would defy the odds once again. One of his guests wondered aloud how the president could possibly prevent a candidate as powerful as Kennedy from winning the nomination. Polite, soft-spoken Jimmy Carter smiled and replied, "I'll whip his ass."

And that's exactly what he did.

AMBITION, WHEN UNDER CONTROL, IS A GOOD IMPULSE

Edward Bates's fortunes seemed bright during the summer of 1859. Journalists and political insiders were beginning to speak of him as a serious contender for the Republican presidential nomination the following year. They believed he had a reasonable—and growing—chance of capping his career by winning America's highest office.

So Bates did what came naturally. He worried. "I must try to resist the temptation, and not allow my thoughts to be drawn off from the common channels of business and domestic cares," he wrote. "Ambition is a passion, at once strong and insidious, and is very apt to cheat a man out of his happiness and his true respectability of character."

Those might appear to be noble sentiments, yet they were based on two serious miscalculations. Ambition, despite the nasty side effects that troubled Bates, can be a positive force. It has been the driving engine behind countless accomplishments and inventions that have benefited mankind.

Believing that ambition can be tamed was Bates's second error. He proved to be as powerless against it as most mortals, eventually entering the 1860 Republican battle and pushing hard until the bitter end. A fellow Missourian noted approvingly, "The mania has bitten old Bates very seriously." He finished third behind Abraham Lincoln and William Seward at the party's convention, then accepted the post of attorney general that Lincoln offered.

What else could have been expected? Politicians—and indeed, ambitious executives in every field—are always on the lookout for the next opportunity. This fever for advancement was epitomized by Lincoln, the relentless striver who was Bates's new boss. "It was in the world of politics that he lived," wrote Lincoln's former law partner, William Herndon. "Politics were his life, newspapers his food, and his great ambition his motive power." It was also Herndon who famously compared Old Abe's ambition with "a little engine that knew no rest."

Lincoln was constantly refiguring his personal geometry, "always calculating and planning ahead," as his ex-partner put it. Step A might lead to Job B, which perhaps would create Opportunity C, which might yield Job D, and on and on. He never stopped weighing the odds and considering the possibilities.

Rutherford Hayes, running for governor of Ohio in 1875, indulged in the same type of forward thinking. His mind wandered into the future as he awaited the statewide returns with his wife. "We both knew well enough that victory meant the chance for the presidency—the certainty that Ohio would present my name. Defeat meant retirement and obscurity," he later wrote. Hayes read the signs correctly. He was elected governor by a small margin, then moved on to the White House a year and a half later.

Modern consultants would say that Lincoln and Hayes weren't blindly ambitious, but were engaging in self-visualization. It's an effective technique. Imagining yourself in a position of greater power and responsibility is the first step toward attaining it.

But ambition can be an effective force only when leavened with a personal vision, common sense, and a healthy dose of moderation.

It was Richard Nixon, of all people, who recognized the importance of vision. He said that presidential candidates could be divided into two categories—those who want to do big things, and those who merely want to be big. Nixon put himself in the former camp, and indeed, he entered the Oval

Office with impressive plans to reorganize the federal government and normalize relations with China and the Soviet Union. He sabotaged himself, of course, with another big idea that involved the Watergate Hotel.

Yet his point remains valid. If you strive for solid accomplishments, not only will you leave a legacy that you can be proud of, but you'll be ideally poised for the next promotion. If all you're seeking is a better title and a key to the executive washroom, you'll squander a terrific opportunity and undoubtedly hit a corporate dead end.

Common sense is equally important. It's rare to encounter a politician who doubts his capacity for higher office, even when the facts suggest otherwise. John McCain, himself a presidential aspirant, joked that among the hundred senators at any given time, the only ones who don't envision themselves in the White House are the few under indictment or in rehab centers. One of McCain's colleagues, John Chafee, agreed. "It's only crossed the minds of maybe ninety-eight senators," he laughed.

It certainly entered the cranium of Vance Hartke, a senator from Indiana, though there was no plausible reason it should have. Hartke lacked charisma and had accomplished virtually nothing worth discussing. Indiana's other senator, Birch Bayh, may have been considered presidential timber during the 1970s, but Hartke most definitely was not. Critics insisted that he was more interested in serving special interests than the public interest. Indiana's two senators, they scoffed, were Bayh and Bought.

Yet Hartke's ambition got the better of him. He couldn't stop imagining himself in the Oval Office, so he announced his candidacy in 1972. Commentators hooted and voters yawned, yet Hartke doggedly pursued his dream. Reality slapped him in the face when he received a mere 2,417 votes in the New Hampshire primary, leaving him no choice but to drop out. This bizarre interlude confused some of his colleagues. What, they later asked, had he been thinking of? "Politics," Hartke could only reply, "is a disease with no cure."

And yet, it must be admitted, a few candidates *have* successfully bucked the rule of common sense. It defied logic, as already noted, for an unknown governor of Georgia to aim for the White House. "President of *what*?" Jimmy Carter's mother asked when her son confided his next career goal. She was astounded by his answer, yet he made it come true. Howard Dean, the ex-governor of Vermont, was an equally improbable candidate, yet he spent a few heady months as the frontrunner for the 2004 Democratic nomination before melting down.

The final quality that makes ambition tolerable—moderation—was totally lacking in Salmon Chase, Henry Clay, and James Blaine, three men who pursued the presidency with a frequency that was as remarkable as their lack of success. Chase was "a little insane" on the subject, in the opinion of Abraham Lincoln. He formally sought the Republican nomination in 1860 and surreptitiously maneuvered for Republican or Democratic endorsements— either was fine with him—in the following three elections. Clay and Blaine ran five times each. "When I want a thing, I want it dreadfully," Blaine admitted. All of these men were urged to abandon their presidential dreams as the losses piled up, but they couldn't, totally consumed as they were by ambition.

That concept was foreign to Mario Cuomo, New York's eloquent governor during the 1980s and early 1990s. Journalists touted Cuomo as a presidential contender in 1988 and 1992, yet he shied away. "Show me a guy with fire in his belly to be president, and I want to spritz him seltzer," he shot back. "What makes you so consumed by it? What would give you fire in the belly? Were you inspired by God? Were you inspired by vanity?"

Columnists dubbed Cuomo the "Hamlet of Albany," citing his unwillingness to seek the presidency as proof that he was terminally indecisive. They ignored the alternate possibility that Cuomo possessed the self-awareness that is essential to any successful executive. He didn't want to be president, and he knew it. He wisely channeled his ambition in directions that were more interesting and important to him.

Walter Mondale demonstrated the same sense of balance. Mondale spent half a decade gearing up for the 1976 presidential campaign, but began to wonder why. He found that he didn't enjoy the campaigning or the pressure. He was running solely for ambition's sake, he thought. So Mondale withdrew in 1974, two years before the election. He quipped famously that he was dropping out because he didn't want to spend the next two years in Holiday Inns. "How lucky I am to be out of presidential politics," he exulted to a friend. "I'm alive. I'm free."

Mondale eventually found a less painful way to test the presidential waters. He served as Jimmy Carter's vice president, then mounted his own campaign in 1984, a full decade after his original withdrawal. It was admirable that he had demonstrated such self-control, that he had waited until he was certain of what he wanted. But the press was suspicious of his reemergence, badgering him when he was announced as Carter's running mate. Mondale had a response all set.

"What I said at the time was that I did not want to spend most of my life in Holiday Inns," he joked. "But I checked and found they've all been redecorated. They're marvelous places to stay, and I've thought it over, and that's where I'd like to be."

THERE'S NOTHING WRONG WITH WANTING RECOGNITION

George McGovern grew to appreciate the warm feeling that comes when people pay attention. The unassuming, mild-mannered senator rose quickly in the Democratic Party, shocking its old-line leaders by snatching away the 1972 nomination. McGovern was on top of the world. He was idolized by millions of Americans, especially the young. His every word was reported and analyzed.

But his fortunes turned for the worse that November, when Richard Nixon buried him in one of the biggest landslides in American political history. McGovern was suddenly branded a loser. His fans moved on to candidates with fresher faces and unsullied records. Fewer and fewer reporters listened when he spoke. The voters of his native South Dakota even tossed him out of the Senate in 1980.

McGovern, a self-described "soft-spoken egomaniac," found the silence maddening. He began seeking a way to recapture the public's attention, eventually deciding to run for the Democratic presidential nomination in 1984, despite his lack of a political base. "As a non-officeholder, not running for anything, it doesn't command network attention," he explained. "I would walk down the street here (in Washington) on Connecticut Avenue, and people would say, 'Jesus, I never hear anything about you anymore.'"

They flocked back in the early months of 1984, just as McGovern had hoped. He enjoyed a brief flurry of media coverage before his campaign reached its inevitable end with another defeat. "The gratifying thing," he concluded, "has been the sense that what I'm saying is getting out to people."

McGovern had much in common with Harold Stassen, a former Minnesota governor who ran for president nine times between 1948 and 1992. Both men were careful to stress that vanity was not their motivation. It was about the issues, they said. It was all about exposing their views to a wider audience.

The sentiment may have been admirable, but it wasn't exactly truthful. Neither man was pushing unusual issues or advocating stands that were advanced for their times. Stassen was a fairly orthodox Republican. McGovern was a liberal Democrat running against several other liberal Democrats in 1984. What both wanted, most of all, was simply to be in the spotlight.

And there was no shame in that. Everybody craves attention, a need that actually has several positive aspects, as psychiatrist Anna Fels has noted. "Far from being a pleasant but largely inessential response, it is one of the most basic of human requirements," she wrote in the *Harvard Business Review*. "We all want our efforts and accomplishments to be acknowledged."

This desire inspires most people to acquire new skills and enhance the ones they already have. What better way to attract even more attention, after all, than to develop expertise and attain success? It's unlikely that Stassen would have become Minnesota's "boy governor" or McGovern would have galvanized the movement against the Vietnam War without their strong needs for recognition. Your own career will likewise receive a boost from your desire to impress people and gain their admiration.

So don't be concerned about your thirst for attention. If you keep it in perspective, if you make sure it isn't the sole motivating force in your life, you will find it to be more of a positive factor than a negative.

But don't forget this corollary piece of advice: The tide will turn against you, as it does against everyone. The day will come when people lose interest in you, even if you're the most high-powered figure in your line of work. It might be overexposure or a terrible annual report or simply your decision to retire, but something will cause the world to stop paying attention. Try to handle the inevitable blackout more gracefully than Stassen and McGovern did.

Fred Harris, a former senator from Oklahoma, kept his sense of humor when the darkness descended. Harris ran for president in 1972 and 1976, quickly falling to the rear of the Democratic pack both times. He had been a rising star in the party—even serving as chairman of the Democratic National Committee—but sank from view after his second presidential loss. He settled into a quiet life as a professor of political science.

A lecture tour in the early 1990s took him to London, where he entertained students with tales of his life as a presidential contender. An American in the crowd, a young Iowan who was studying overseas, was so astounded that she had to interrupt.

"You ran for president?" she asked.

"Yes, I did," Harris replied.

"President of what?"

"President of the United States."

"Really?"

"Yes," he said, "and I can also tell you that I was not elected."

Harris found it all amusing, both the episode itself and the extent to which he had disappeared from the public eye in a relatively short period of time. "And she wrote it down," he laughed. "That's what I like about teaching. Students write down what you say. They take you seriously. She was probably afraid it would be a question on the final exam."

"As Long as God Gives Me Breath"

Harold Stassen always liked having an audience.

"There are only three ways you can get any attention for your positions," he said. "Number One is to throw a brick through a window on Main Street with advance notice. Number Two is to take somebody hostage. Number Three is to run for something."

Stassen preferred the latter. He ran for governor of Minnesota in 1938 at age thirty-one—and won—sparking a lifelong affair with politics. He mounted a serious campaign for the Republican presidential nomination in 1948, spending a few heady weeks as the frontrunner. It seemed logical that he try again in 1952. But he lost to Dwight Eisenhower, and the pundits assumed they would hear no more from Harold Stassen.

They were wrong. Stassen sought the presidency in seven elections to come, the last in 1992. He also ran for Congress, governor of Pennsylvania, mayor of Philadelphia, and his old job, governor of Minnesota. He lost every single time.

But that was okay with him. Stassen never seemed discouraged by defeat. He simply enjoyed having a reason to give speeches, to be interviewed by reporters, to be remembered by the public. He refused to rise for the bait whenever anyone asked if his latest campaign would be his last. "I never think in those terms," he would say. "I'm going to be active as long as God gives me breath."

A HEALTHY EGO IS FINE, BUT EGOMANIA IS DANGEROUS

A person clearly needs a large ego to even think about running for president or seeking any kind of leadership role. Yours is big enough, or you wouldn't be reading this book. Why deny it?

John Anderson didn't. Anderson was a mild-mannered, grandfatherly congressman who unsuccessfully sought the Republican presidential nomination in the spring of 1980 and then pushed on with an equally unsuccessful independent candidacy in the fall. He seemed the antithesis of a self-centered politician, yet confessed that a healthy ego burned beneath his placid exterior. "It's not a tiny one," he said. "Let's say it's presidential. Anyone who's been in political life as long as I have, who has enjoyed the smell of the greasepaint and the roar of the crowd, would have to have some degree of egotism."

But Anderson knew the importance of self-restraint. "When a man's ambition is so intense it mutes his voice," he said, "that's not worth doing." An unbridled ego, in fact, can eventually destroy a leader, as two twentieth-century presidents learned to their sorrow.

Woodrow Wilson was one of the most intelligent men ever to reach the White House. He certainly was the most highly educated president in American history, the only one to earn a Ph.D. But his brainpower, to his misfortune, was linked with arrogance of titanic proportions.

Wilson's ego surfaced in an ugly manner shortly after he won the 1912 Democratic nomination. His victory had been far from a sure thing. Another contender, Champ Clark, had led the early ballots at the convention. Wilson wasn't chosen until the forty-sixth roll call, bitterly opposed by Clark's diehard supporters even then.

But the nominee behaved as if he had been divinely anointed. "I wish it clearly understood that I owe you nothing," he lectured one of his top aides. "Remember that God ordained that I should be the next president of the United States. Neither you nor any other mortal could have prevented that."

Few people can match such egotism, but Lyndon Johnson was equal to the challenge. West Germany's chancellor, Ludwig Erhard, visited LBJ's ranch during his presidency. Johnson loved to take guests on long tours of the countryside, so he guided Erhard to his car and announced that they were off to see his birthplace. "I understand you were born in a log cabin," said Erhard, trying to imagine the rustic Texas of 1908, the year of Johnson's birth.

"No, no," LBJ replied with a laugh. "You have me confused with Abe Lincoln. I was born in a manger."

Great egos can produce great works. Wilson and Johnson were remarkably successful during the early years of their administrations. The former created the Federal Reserve System and cracked down on business monopolies. The latter declared war on poverty and crafted the Great Society, a wide-ranging package of social legislation.

But egomania was their undoing. Both presidents made bitter, lasting enemies with their stubborn, self-righteous behavior. Wilson steadfastly refused
to compromise with the senators who disliked the peace treaty he signed after
World War I. Johnson persisted with the Vietnam War despite massive public unrest. (These were two of the four worst blunders ever committed by a
president, according to a survey of historians by the University of Louisville
in 2006.) Both men, as a result, ended their terms with the nation in turmoil
and their reputations badly soiled.

"He Has Been Acting Strangely"

No discussion of egotistical behavior would be complete without mentioning Nicholas Murray Butler, perhaps the most self-
centered person to run for the White House.

Butler was an educator by profession, serving as president of
Columbia University from 1902 until 1945. But he dreamed of
higher power, believing that he was undoubtedly the best-
qualified person to run the country. He flirted with politics a
couple of times—receiving electoral votes for vice president in
1912 and seeking the Republican presidential nomination eight
years later—yet he never came remotely close to victory.

Butler was a fine orator, always in search of an audience.
Columnist Heywood Broun insisted that he had a brass pole in
his house and slid down immediately upon any speaking invita-
tion. But it was his ego that made him so memorable. Butler
took great care with his entry in each new edition of *Who's
Who in America*, stuffing in every award, every board member-
ship, every article he had written. His goal was to have the longest biography in the entire book, and he always did,
eventually stretching his listing to a full column and a half of
very small type.

Conceit of such magnitude inevitably became fodder for
humor. A joke began making the rounds in Butler's later years.
It seemed that Sigmund Freud had arrived at the pearly gates,
where he was met by angels who implored him to hurry.
"Come with us quickly," they said. "We want you to see God
professionally. He has been acting strangely. He has hallucina-
tions. He thinks he is Nicholas Murray Butler."

DON'T SHAPE YOUR CAREER TO PLEASE SOMEONE ELSE

John Quincy Adams didn't have much choice about running for president.
His father, John Adams, himself the nation's second president, groomed him
for the position from adolescence. John began showing John Quincy the
ropes at age fifteen—employing the boy as his personal secretary—and
closely monitored his progress ever after. The old man could be severe and

demanding. "If you do not rise to the head of your country," he admonished his son, "it will be owing to your own laziness and slovenliness."

John Quincy showed promise. He was an intelligent, diligent student who blossomed into a skillful diplomat. But the White House didn't hold the same appeal for him as it did for the elder Adams. "I have indeed long known that my father is far more ambitious for my advancement ... than I ever have been or shall be," the young man confided to his diary.

But there was a score to be settled. The voters had evicted John Adams from the White House in 1800, and he looked to the next generation for vindication. "John Adams took his defeat for reelection very hard, which his son was most aware of," said David McCullough, the father's Pulitzer Prize–winning biographer. "And John Adams saw the rise of his son with nothing but pleasure. Although he worried about the strain of the presidency on him, it seems pretty apparent he saw his son as redeeming his defeat."

The strain was considerable. John Quincy Adams was elected president in 1824, but was badly suited for the position. He was annoyed by the ceaseless demands of office seekers, sickened by political campaigning, and horrified by the controversy that inevitably swirls around a high-profile leader. "I subject myself to so much toil and so much enmity, with so very little apparent fruit," he wrote, "that I sometimes ask myself whether I do not mistake my own motives. The best actions of my life make me nothing but enemies." He seemed almost relieved to depart the White House after Andrew Jackson defeated him for reelection in 1828.

The tale of John Quincy Adams shows how misguided it can be to plot your career in line with a parent's wishes. It's just as unwise to allow a spouse, close friend, or anyone else to dictate your future.

The hefty William Howard Taft was pushed toward the presidency by his wife. He had little interest in the job. "Politics, when I am in it, makes me sick," he complained. What would be ideal, he thought, would be the sedate life of a judge.

But fate—and Nellie Taft—had other plans. President Theodore Roosevelt, who had already announced that he would not seek reelection in 1908, invited the Tafts over for dinner one night. He took them up to his library after the meal.

"I am the seventh son of a seventh daughter and I have clairvoyant powers," Roosevelt intoned, closing his eyes. "I see a man weighing 350 pounds. There is something hanging over his head. I cannot make out what it is. At one time, it looks like the presidency. Then again, it looks like the chief justiceship."

"Make it the presidency," said Nellie eagerly.

"Make it the chief justiceship," urged Will.

It was the former, much to Mrs. Taft's delight. Roosevelt revealed that he wanted her husband to be his successor. Taft dutifully followed the wishes of his benefactor and his wife, running for president in 1908 and being elected with ease.

Warren Harding followed a similar route to the White House twelve years later. Harding mounted a halfhearted campaign in 1920, barely winning the Republican primary in his home state of Ohio and then getting trounced in neighboring Indiana.

His logical course after the Indiana defeat was to drop out of the presidential race immediately, hustling home to seek reelection to the Senate while he still had time. The filing deadline was close at hand, so Harding picked up a phone in Indianapolis to make the necessary arrangements. But his domineering wife, Florence, snatched the receiver from his hand. "Warren Harding," she huffed. "What are you doing? Give up? Not until the convention is over. Think of your friends in Ohio!"

Harding backed down from his wife, as he usually did, though he certainly wasn't optimistic about his chances. He was as shocked as anyone when the Republican convention turned his way that summer and he won the general election that fall.

It should come as no surprise that Taft and Harding, who never really wanted to be president in the first place, didn't enjoy their time in the White House. "I'm in jail, and I can't get out," Harding would complain. He was even more explicit when a senator, Frank Brandegee, asked him how he liked his new job. "Frank, it is hell," the reluctant commander-in-chief snapped. "No other word can describe it."

Men who had no real motivation to seek the presidency, it also could have been predicted, weren't likely to handle their duties very well. Taft is generally rated by historians as having been of average to below-average quality. Harding, in the opinion of many, was the worst president ever.

The moral is obvious: Follow your heart. If you want to be hugely successful, pursue your goal with energy and enthusiasm. If the idea doesn't excite you, find something else to do.

But don't be swayed by others. Don't be like Horatio Seymour, who truly didn't want to be president, yet was bullied into accepting the Democratic nomination in 1868.

Seymour, a former governor of New York, was a solid administrator and good public speaker, but he loved private life considerably more than public office. He was known as "the great decliner" for all of the political positions he had spurned over the years.

That tendency was in full flower in 1868. The Democratic Party had no clear frontrunner that year, and for good reason. General Ulysses Grant, the Civil War hero, had already been chosen as the Republican candidate. It was difficult to imagine anyone defeating him for the presidency. Few men wanted to try.

Rumors began to fly that the Democrats would draft Seymour for the nomination. He persistently denied any interest in being president, issuing five separate statements to that effect. And it appeared the convention was taking him at his word, ignoring him for the first twenty-one ballots.

That's when an Ohio delegate, George McCook, rose on the floor. "Let us vote for a man whom the presidency has sought, but has not sought the presidency," he thundered. The landslide was suddenly on, with state after state switching to Seymour. He tried valiantly to stem the tide. "May God bless you for your kindness to me," he told the delegates, "but your candidate I cannot be." It made no difference. He received every single vote on the twenty-second ballot.

Seymour wavered, but finally consented to carry the Democratic banner against Grant. The campaign was everything he had expected it to be— lengthy, bitter, and ultimately unsuccessful. Accepting the nomination against his own wishes and better judgment, he would say in later years, was "the mistake of my life."

EXCESSIVE CAUTION CAN DESTROY YOUR CHANCES

Al Gore was always a cautious politician. He liked to take his time— studying every angle, considering every option. Supporters praised him for being thorough and detail-oriented. Critics lampooned him as obsessive and stiff. They tagged him with unflattering nicknames like "Al Bore" and "Analytical Al." Late-night TV hosts likened his mechanical personality to that of a space alien.

That's why it seemed out of character when Gore dived into the 1988 presidential pool at the age of thirty-nine. People who didn't know any better assumed him to be brash and impulsive, a young man on the make. They didn't realize how much thought the candidate had put into his decision. A *Washington Post* reporter, Helen Dewar, showed up to inspect the Gore campaign for traces of spontaneity, but found none. "His approach," she concluded, "is cerebral, analytical, cautious."

Gore won a few primaries in 1988, yet eventually was flattened by Michael Dukakis, who rolled to the Democratic nomination. Some candidates might have reacted to this defeat by loosening up, adopting a more open, appealing style. Gore reached the opposite conclusion. "If I had to do it over again, I would have started a year earlier than I did," he said, contending that a longer campaign would have given him the opportunity to do even more planning.

It wasn't that Gore was unaware of his cautious nature. He admitted in a 1991 book that he had a tendency to be a "finger in the wind" politician. He expanded on that theme two years later, after being elected vice president: "I grew up in a determinedly political family, in which I learned at an early age to be very sensitive—too sensitive, perhaps—to what others were thinking, and to notice carefully—maybe too carefully—the similarities and differences between my way of thinking and that of the society around me."

Gore sought the presidency again in 2000, losing or not losing to George W. Bush, depending on your interpretation of Florida's votes. But experts agreed that it never should have come down to a recount. Gore was running as the representative of a generally popular administration during a time of economic prosperity. He should have defeated Bush easily, yet seemed unable to inspire the nation. "He ran a pretty lousy campaign. It was his to lose," said Robert Reich, a former member of Bill Clinton's cabinet. Polls showed that a substantial percentage of Americans considered Gore to be too cautious—bordering on indecisive—and certainly not much of a leader.

No executive should ever make an important decision impulsively or without weighing the facts. But paralysis by analysis can be equally damaging, as Gore's story demonstrates. If you waffle and agonize over every matter that reaches your desk—especially those that might alter the course of your career—you risk being branded as an executive who lacks the ability to lead.

William Scranton eventually picked up precisely that image. Scranton had an attractive personality and real skill as a campaigner, yet always seemed reluctant to pull the trigger. He had to be coaxed into all three political races of his life. The Republican Party cajoled him into running for the House of Representatives in 1960 and governor of Pennsylvania in 1962. He declined both times, but eventually consented and won.

Pressure began to build on Scranton to seek the presidency in 1964. The loudest clamor came from moderate Republicans who hoped to prevent conservative Barry Goldwater from seizing control of their party. Scranton thought about it, then thought some more. Reporters began to call him the "Hamlet of Harrisburg." He delayed for months before finally agreeing to make the race.

His announcement, though, was strangely equivocal. Scranton didn't make a grand entrance. He tiptoed into the campaign. "I don't plan to go out to try and defeat Senator Goldwater," he told a national TV audience. "I have no such intention. I do think it is important ... that the party keep to its sound footing."

The governor of New York, Nelson Rockefeller, himself a moderate, watched in disbelief. A reporter asked if he thought that Scranton would be an effective candidate. Rockefeller smirked. "Did you see him on television?" he asked. The determined Goldwater pulverized the ambivalent Scranton, who soon began expressing doubts about ever seeking elective office again. He was true to his word.

Excessive caution will usually destroy your chances of becoming the boss, but it can be especially harmful if, by some miracle, you actually find yourself in charge of a company or government office.

James Buchanan, one of the champion fence straddlers of all time, had the great misfortune of being elected president in 1856. These were three of his vapid pronouncements as the storm clouds of the Civil War grew larger and darker overhead:

- "It is better to bear the ills we have than to fly to others we know not of."
- "What is right and what is practicable are two different things."
- "All that is necessary to (abolish slavery), and all for which the slave states have ever contended, is to be let alone and permitted to manage their domestic institutions in their own way."

Real leaders make decisions and take risks. The overly cautious Buchanan did neither, allowing the nation to drift toward the worst conflict in its history. "Buchanan fiddled while Rome burned," said presidential scholar Michael Genovese. "He saw the breakup of the republic, but believed his hands were tied and thus watched the union break." All of America paid the price.

YOUR COMPETITORS ARE ONLY HUMAN, SO DON'T BE AWED

No one ever accused Hiram Johnson of being timid or modest. Business monopolies—the railroads foremost among them—ruled California with an iron fist at the dawn of the twentieth century, but they couldn't scare Johnson, who was then a little-known prosecutor. He ran for governor in 1910, vowing to battle "against the interests and the system, and for true democracy." The young upstart unseated the old robber barons, dismantled their plutocracy, and instituted an impressive series of political, social, and economic reforms.

Johnson moved on to the Senate in 1916 and emerged as one of its dominant members. He brooked no opposition to his progressive ideals, a decidedly unlegislative trait that shocked a fellow senator, William Borah. "When a man opposes me, I do not become angry at him," Borah said. "On the next issue, he may agree with me. When a man opposes Johnson, he hates him."

It was only natural that a politician of such prominence and spirit would come to be considered presidential material. Johnson was touted as a frontrunner for the Republican nomination in 1920, which promised to be a very favorable year indeed for the Republicans, but he hesitated to run. He couldn't shake a nagging sense of awe. It seemed presumptuous for someone like him—just a decade removed from the obscurity of a California legal practice—to seek the exalted office once held by George Washington and Abraham Lincoln.

Johnson overcame his doubts, but not easily. "I'd dream of the past of the nation, of the great grown greater in the mist of history, and I'd feel a real humility that I dared to try for the place they had occupied," he confessed. But then he assessed the rest of the Republican field for 1920, which included a charming nonentity from Ohio, Warren Harding. "And then suddenly I'd recall the other candidates," Johnson went on, "and a decent self-respect enabled me to recover my equanimity."

Johnson had come to an important realization: Great men and women are, after all, just men and women. They appear to be giants when viewed at a distance, but they're all too human at close range. There is no logical reason for you to sit in awe of them, or to fear them.

Johnson's only problem was that the voters did not inspect his challengers as closely as he had. "I like Harding," the California senator sputtered as the nomination slipped from his fingers to those of his amiable colleague. "I like him very much, but I can't conceive of his being president of the United States." The nation had no such trouble, electing Harding in a landslide.

Jimmy Carter faced a mental barrier similar to Hiram Johnson's. Carter began moving in rarefied circles after being elected governor of Georgia in

1970. He visited the president, Richard Nixon. He was courted by the Democratic candidates who hoped to unseat Nixon in 1972. The small-town boy from Plains, Georgia, was both excited and intimidated by this opportunity to meet the political stars of his generation.

His sense of wonder didn't last long. "I lost my feeling of awe about presidents," Carter admitted. Nixon and his challengers weren't as dynamic or intelligent or clever as he had expected. They were surprisingly like the politicians Carter knew—and had defeated—in Georgia.

Peter Bourne, one of the governor's close advisers, traced his boss's new attitude to a 1971 Senate committee hearing. Carter testified before the panel, which was headed by Edmund Muskie, then the leading candidate for the Democratic presidential nomination. Bourne and Carter discussed Muskie's qualities as they flew back from Washington to Atlanta.

"He was interested that Muskie was the frontrunner at the time," Bourne remembered. "It surprised Carter because he was most unimpressed with Muskie, who just didn't strike him as that presidential. It was part of the process of realizing his own talent and building his self-confidence. He thought that if this guy can get to be president that it was not too far-fetched for him."

Carter's wife, Rosalynn, remembered this period of discovery more bluntly. "Jimmy knew a lot more about a lot of things than did these men who were running for president," she said. That realization marked the beginning of a most improbable rise to the White House.

WOMEN MUST WORK HARDER AND BE TOUGHER

Margaret Chase Smith thought the question was crazy when she first heard it a few years after World War II.

Harry Truman had surprised the experts by winning another term as president, and Smith was settling in as the new senator from Maine, the lone woman among the Senate's ninety-five men. A reporter asked if she had given any thought to the next step in her political career. What would she do, he wondered, if she woke up in the White House one day?

That was an easy one. "Apologize to Mrs. Truman and then go home," she laughed.

It was a good joke at the time—women, after all, simply didn't run for president in the 1940s—but Smith saw less humor in it as time went by. She was a skillful politician, the first woman elected to both houses of Congress. And she was tough, too. Most of her male colleagues cowered when Joe McCarthy embarked on his infamous witch hunts of alleged Communists. The lady from Maine did not.

She encountered McCarthy one spring morning in 1950 on the underground train that ran between the Senate Office Building and the Capitol.

"Margaret," McCarthy said, "you look like you've got something on your mind."

"Yes, Joe, I have," she said, looking straight ahead in the small car. "I think I'm going to make a speech, and I don't think you're going to like it."

She made a speech all right, condemning McCarthy in no uncertain terms. "I speak as a Republican," she said. "I speak as a woman. I speak as a United States senator. I speak as an American. I don't want to see the Republican Party ride to political victory on the four horsemen of calumny—fear, ignorance, bigotry, and smear." Four years would pass before the Senate followed her lead and censured McCarthy for his excesses.

So why couldn't a woman seek higher office, especially a woman as successful and hardworking and tough as Margaret Chase Smith? A few visionaries in the Republican Party began whispering that, yes, she might make a good *vice*-presidential candidate in 1964. Smith had a better idea. She announced for president.

The odds were against her. She came from a small state, had little money, and insisted on giving first priority to her Senate duties, not her national campaign. But she was unmistakably in the race, the first woman ever to seek a major-party presidential nomination.

Thruston Morton, the head of the Republican Party, officially welcomed her candidacy, but his subsequent words weren't especially friendly. "We want to win," he said. "If she proves in the primary she can bring us the suffragettes and the old maids, she's in." Smith reminded Morton that she had served in Congress twelve years longer than the Republican frontrunner, Barry Goldwater.

She didn't seem to mind the putdowns, saying toward the end of her life, "Sometimes I've been badly mistreated. So what?" She pushed on. Her campaign picked up speed in the Illinois primary, where she won a quarter of the votes, but it ran out of gas long before the convention. "After a bit, you know, you men are going to have a woman for president," sighed Frances Bolton, a congresswoman from Ohio. "It's just too bad you didn't take this one."

Yet there were signs of hope. Smith liked to say that she was "pioneering the way for a woman of the future," and some in the next generation were indeed paying attention. An envelope containing a single dollar bill arrived at her headquarters during the waning days of the primary season. The accompanying note was from a ten-year-old girl. "This," she wrote, "is my *own* money that I saved for you."

Women have made considerable progress—both in politics and business—since that young lady entrusted her personal fortune to Smith's campaign. The number of female senators climbed to fourteen by 2006, and the number of female governors was up to eight, each a record high. Women actually held both Senate seats and the governorship in Washington state that year, the first such sweep in American history. There was progress in the private sector, too, with nearly a quarter of a million women serving as CEOs of businesses, big and small. Eleven major corporations—all large enough to make the *Fortune* 500—were led by female presidents in 2006, including such behemoths as Archer Daniels Midland, Sara Lee, Rite Aid, and Xerox.

Yet, despite these gains, parity is a long way off. Men still dominate the government and the economy. More than 80 percent of all senators and governors were male as of 2006, as were 77 percent of all CEOs. The *Fortune* 500 remains the most exclusive club of all, with 489 corporate giants being run by men, a fraction short of 98 percent.

The reasons for this imbalance are varied. Women bear some of the responsibility. They tend to be less driven and goal-oriented than men, partly because that's what society expects, according to researchers. "None of them would admit to being ambitious," wrote psychiatrist Anna Fels of the female executives she studied for a 2004 report. "Instead, the constant refrain was, 'It's not me; it's the work.' 'It's not about me; it's about helping children.' 'I hate to promote myself; I'd rather be in my workshop alone.'"

Biology is also a factor. Female executives who start families in their twenties or thirties often step away from their jobs, sometimes for years, increasing the odds against them ever becoming CEOs. A 2004 study by the Center for Work-Life Policy focused on 2,400 highly qualified women, all of whom held advanced degrees or high-honors undergraduate degrees. Thirty-seven percent said they had left work voluntarily at some point in their careers, a process known as "off-ramping." The study estimated that the typical off-ramper suffered a decline of 18 percent in earning power.

And then, of course, there's the matter of bias. Shirley Chisholm, a black congresswoman from New York, encountered it on two fronts when she sought the Democratic presidential nomination in 1972, but considered one type worse than the other. "I met far more discrimination because I am a woman than because I am black," she said. What struck her was the quiet way that male politicians—both white and black—opposed her candidacy. "Their response was ridicule—in private, not in public," she said, "because a gentleman doesn't make fun of a lady, and a politician doesn't want to risk losing the black vote."

Bias has become subtler since Chisholm's day, but it continues to exist, sometimes in innocuous ways. Carol Moseley Braun was puzzled by the reaction to her brief presidential campaign in 2004, feeling that she was somehow taken less seriously. "I'm still trying to figure out why people hug me more," she said. "They give the men handshakes, but me, they have to hug."

A reporter suggested that Braun could short-circuit the huggers by sticking her hand out first.

"I do," she said. "And they still hug me! I'm always interested in why that happens, and I can't figure it out." But she really could. Braun, like Chisholm, was a black woman, and she heard the same whispers in 2004 that had dogged her predecessor three decades before. "The notion," said Braun, "is that nobody thinks that a woman who is black can win the presidency." (The same thought held true, at the time, for one who was white. No woman of any race mounted a credible campaign for a major-party nomination until Hillary Clinton in 2008.)

It may be unfair, but a female contender must work harder and be tougher than her male competitors, whether in politics or in business. That's typically how it is for underdogs, a role that women play in both arenas.

Hard work is essential, though not sufficient by itself. If it were, Patricia Schroeder might have become president in the late 1980s. The congresswoman from Colorado had a flair for attracting attention—it was she who nicknamed Ronald Reagan the "Teflon president"—and certainly wasn't shy about putting in the long hours that were necessary. She traveled 75,000 miles in 1987 alone, laying the groundwork for a full-scale presidential campaign the following year.

But, in the end, she opted to remain on the sidelines, announcing her decision in what the *Washington Post* called an "artless, teary performance." Schroeder came off as helpless and weak, reinforcing the stereotype that women were ill-equipped for the presidency. "I could not figure out how to run," she told reporters. "There must be a way, but I haven't figured it out yet."

Others *are* figuring it out. A growing number of women are rising in the executive ranks, successfully juggling their personal and professional lives. And they're proving to be as strong as their male counterparts, without sacrificing such "feminine" characteristics as compassion and tenderness. "A person can be high on both—directive and caring, warm and assertive," said psychologist D. Anthony Butterfield, co-author of a study that compared the leadership traits of male and female politicians.

That's precisely the balance that Margaret Chase Smith was able to strike in 1964, making her a female pioneer in the men's world of presidential politics—and a role model to this day. "You didn't take Mrs. Smith for granted," admitted John Stennis, an arch-conservative senator from Mississippi who was no fan of the feminist movement. "No one controlled her. We tended to treat her as a man, without ceasing to treat her as a woman."

MINORITIES MUST WORK HARDER AND BE TOUGHER

Shirley Chisholm blazed two trails simultaneously in 1972, as noted above. She was the second woman to mount a formal campaign for a major-party presidential nomination—and the first member of a minority group ever to do so.

The tiny Chisholm—five-foot-four, occasionally as light as ninety-six pounds—came off as supremely confident, even defiant, in her public appearances that year. "Other kinds of people can steer the ship of state besides white men," she declared. But she knew in her heart that America wasn't ready to install a black woman in the Oval Office. "Of course, my candidacy had no chance," she admitted later. "I had little money and no way of raising the funds it takes to run for high office. I had no big party figures supporting me."

Her gender, she thought, was the reason why male politicians of all races scorned her efforts. "If anyone thinks white men are sexist," she snapped, "let them check out black men sometime." But she also blamed the racial barriers that continue to hinder minority candidates—male and female—in today's campaigns. "That I am a national figure because I was the first person in 192 years to be at once a congressman, black, and a woman proves, I think, that our society is not yet either just or free," she said.

A few black politicians have followed in Chisholm's presidential footsteps since 1972. (No Hispanics, Asian-Americans, or American Indians did so before 2008.) The first one to emerge as a serious contender was Jesse Jackson, who shocked the media twice—finishing third in the scramble for the 1984 Democratic nomination and climbing to second place four years later. Jackson never had a realistic chance of winning at either convention, but believed he had scored a lasting breakthrough. "Blacks will never again be taken for granted," he crowed as his initial campaign began to catch fire. "Politics in America is quite different tonight from what it was a year ago. Quite different."

It wasn't that simple. Jackson was a unique candidate—charismatic, indefatigable, and battle-hardened from his years in the civil rights movement. Other black candidates before 2008 failed to duplicate his energy or his success. Carol Moseley Braun and Al Sharpton both tried in 2004, but flamed out in the early stages. Eric Easter, a political consultant who once worked for Jackson, was unimpressed as he surveyed the wreckage of their campaigns. "You have to work a whole lot harder," he said. "You can't just say, 'Vote for me because I'm the black candidate.'"

There's no point in belaboring the parallels between women and minorities. Almost everything that was said in the previous section applies here as well. It's difficult for either group to make significant progress in public and private sectors that remain dominated by white men, but victories *are* coming more frequently these days, especially for up-and-coming executives willing to work as hard as Jesse Jackson and keep the faith like Shirley Chisholm.

And, make no mistake, rising stars of that sort *are* out there. Barack Obama was anointed the great black hope after winning one of Illinois's Senate seats in 2004. Obama, then forty-three years old, was the first African-American male ever elected to the Senate as a Democrat and the only black in that body when he was sworn in. "I don't think I have a place in history yet," he cautioned. "I got elected to the U.S. Senate. I haven't done anything yet." But that didn't stop the media from heralding him as a good bet to someday become America's first nonwhite president—a prediction that Obama sought to fulfill in the 2008 campaign.

Minority leaders are also emerging in the private sector. Three of the nation's one hundred largest corporations were headed by blacks by 2005, disproportionately low for a racial group that encompasses 12 percent of all Americans, but better than its traditional total of zero top-level CEOs. Bruce Gordon, the president of the NAACP, predicted that those ranks will swell in the future. "The best thing is when it's not even a topic of conversation," he said. "Today, you don't even think about how many black quarterbacks there are. We can still count up the black CEOs. But at some point in time, they will not be a matter of discussion."

HEALTH PROBLEMS DON'T HAVE TO BE IMPEDIMENTS

The Franklin Roosevelt who went upstairs to bed on August 10, 1921, was a weary man who felt a "slight case of lumbago" coming on, yet otherwise had no reason for complaint. He was wealthy, normally full of energy, indisputably well-connected. Roosevelt had been the Democratic Party's vice-presidential candidate the year before at the age of thirty-eight. He and his running mate, James Cox, may have been buried in a Republican landslide, but it was easy to imagine FDR becoming president in his own right someday.

Roosevelt awoke to a much grimmer reality. One of his legs felt unaccountably weak on the morning of the eleventh and would be lifeless by afternoon. The paralysis spread quickly, claiming his entire body from the chest down within two days. His doctors were baffled at first, but eventually agreed that he had contracted polio.

Roosevelt faced the prospect of being confined to a wheelchair for the rest of his days. He eventually would be able to hobble on crutches and heavy leg braces for short distances, but would never walk unaided again. It seemed obvious that his political career was over.

We know differently, of course. Roosevelt fought valiantly to regain his strength and restore his political profile. He reentered the fray by making the nominating speeches for Al Smith at the Democratic conventions of 1924 and 1928. Observers were impressed by his courage and spirit. Will Durant, a journalist and historian, wrote in the latter year that Roosevelt was "beyond comparison the finest man that has appeared at either convention."

Smith liked what he saw, too, and insisted that Roosevelt succeed him as governor of New York in 1928. The thought of a paraplegic governor horrified the *New York Herald Tribune*. "The nomination is unfair to Mr. Roosevelt," the paper sputtered. "It is equally unfair to the people of the state who, under other conditions, would welcome Mr. Roosevelt's candidacy for any office." Smith rose eloquently to his friend's defense. "We do not elect him for his ability to do a double backflip or a handspring," he retorted. "The work of the governorship is brain work. Ninety-five percent of it is accomplished sitting at a desk. There is no doubt about his ability to do it."

The voters came to agree, electing Roosevelt to two terms as governor, followed by four in the White House. FDR guided the nation through two of its greatest trials, the Depression and World War II. And he did all this at a time when employment opportunities and legal protections for the disabled were virtually nonexistent. Today's historians generally rank him as one of the three greatest presidents of all time, along with George Washington and Abraham Lincoln. His story proves that, if at all possible, you must not allow an illness or disability to prevent you from pursuing your ultimate goal.

Many observers, in fact, believed that Roosevelt benefited from his struggle with polio. They thought it made him more patient and more willing to think deeply. Frances Perkins, who knew him in his younger days and who served in his Cabinet, said, "The man emerged completely warm-hearted, with new humility of spirit and a firmer understanding of philosophical concepts."

Perhaps. But it's worth noting that another person who knew him well, his son, Elliott, could detect no change at all. "Throughout his adult life, his was the same, consistent personality, the mixture of ... lion and fox," Elliott wrote after his father's death. "There was just one purely physical difference: After 1921, he could not walk."

Serious illness has affected other presidential hopefuls in markedly different ways.

It spurred Frank Church, whose political career seemed over before it began. Church was struck by cancer in 1948 at the age of twenty-four. The prognosis was dark. He had less than six months to live, the doctors said.

But Church defied the odds. "When I found out I wasn't going to die, I thought I'd take all the chances that came my way," he said later. "As a result, I was much more inclined to gamble." Taking a slow approach no longer made any sense. Church announced his candidacy for the Senate at the age of thirty-two. Naysayers scoffed that he was inexperienced and, even worse, he was a Democrat in heavily Republican Idaho. But he beat the odds again, becoming the youngest member of the Senate in 1956. He eventually emerged as a leader of the anti–Vietnam War movement and a candidate for the Democratic presidential nomination in 1976.

A brush with serious illness had the opposite effect on Joe Biden, the quintessential man in a hurry. Biden was even more audacious than Frank Church. He ran for one of Delaware's Senate seats at thirty—the youngest age the Constitution allows—and somehow defeated an entrenched incumbent. Everyone, Biden included, assumed his victory was merely one step up the ladder. It came as no surprise when he launched a presidential campaign in early 1987, still only forty-five.

But Biden's luck turned sour. Allegations of plagiarism forced him out of the race long before the Democratic convention. His loss seemed devastating until it was put in perspective by a blow that was much worse, the discovery of a potentially fatal pair of aneurysms. The young senator was to endure three operations and seven long months of recuperation.

The Joe Biden who returned to the Senate seemed to be a changed man. He insisted that he no longer felt a "sense of urgency" about his career, even saying he had been lucky to lose the presidency because it allowed him to focus solely on regaining his health. "In a strange way, it saved my life," he said a year later. "My doctors told me point-blank that I would not be alive today had I stayed in the race."

Any ill will toward his opponents, he said, "dissipated somewhere between the first aneurysm and the blood clot." And yet, Joe Biden found it impossible to completely abandon his dream of sitting behind that massive desk in the Oval Office. It might happen later rather than sooner, but he retained a glimmer of hope.

His unquenchable spirit was evident even when his illness was at its very worst, as the orderlies prepared to wheel him in for his first operation. The brain surgeons, so the story goes, assured Biden that no matter how dark things might seem, they were optimistic that he would pull through. They would do whatever they could.

The senator had no doubts about the outcome. His thoughts were already far in the future. "Do a good job, boys," Joe Biden told his surgeons, "because someday I'm going to be president."

IT DOESN'T REALLY MATTER WHERE YOU GREW UP

Carter Glass was fed up. The Senate was supposed to be tending to other business that day in 1928, but William Cabell Bruce of Maryland had steered the debate to the racial situation in the South, including Glass's home state of Virginia.

Glass asked for a chance to reply. "I want to assert for Virginia that the laws there apply with perfect equality between the whites and blacks," he declared. Bruce shot back that he deplored the political situation in Virginia and was disgusted by racial prejudice.

Carter Glass would not stand for being called a bigot, no matter how indirectly. He glared at Bruce. "Let me ask the senator how long it has been since the end of the Civil War," he heatedly inquired. "Let me ask the senator if he believes that a Southern man could be nominated for president of the United States. He is talking about prejudice."

Bruce did not hesitate in his response: "Certainly I think so."

"Why has not one been nominated in the last sixty-five years? That is not prejudice, is it?"

"I think," replied Bruce, "that we will have a Southern man in the White House again in the future."

"Yes," Glass agreed, feeling he had won the argument. "But the senator's great-great-grandchildren will not live to see it."

The Virginian's prediction didn't hold for all four generations, but another forty-eight years would pass before a Southern candidate won the presidency on his own. Jimmy Carter's breakthrough in 1976 would have surprised Carter Glass, and the South's subsequent power would have stunned him. The region—led by native son Bill Clinton and two New-Englanders-turned-Texans named Bush—would win every presidential election but two between 1976 and 2004. (The two exceptions were victories by a Westerner, Ronald Reagan.)

Such hot and cold streaks have always been part of national politics, though they aren't as permanent or powerful as many politicians think they are. It seems that a particular state or region enjoys the upper hand for awhile, then fades away.

Virginia was so dominant after America's birth that early politicians spoke darkly of a "Virginia Dynasty." John Adams, the only non-Virginian among the first five presidents, moaned that his son, John Quincy, couldn't possibly win "till all Virginians shall be extinct." But the dynasty wasn't quite as durable as it seemed. Not a single resident of Virginia has been elected to the White House since John Quincy Adams finally gained admission in 1824.

The magic eventually passed to Ohio, birthplace of seven presidents. "Between the Civil War and the 1920s," wrote historian Andrew Sinclair, "the White House was every Ohio politician's retirement plan. It seemed the natural reward for a lifetime of service to the Grand Old Party in the Buckeye State." New York also enjoyed a lengthy roll, capped by Franklin Roosevelt's unprecedented four terms as president. But all streaks come to an end, and Ohio and New York have been on the outside ever since.

Corporate America has also known its share of regional dynasties. There was a time when most CEOs were upper-crust New Englanders, well-bred New Yorkers, or rock-solid Midwesterners. Southerners and Westerners were generally dismissed, the former presumed to be too hotheaded and prejudiced, the latter too undisciplined and independent.

But that streak has ended, too, and for the same reason that the South and West have recently been so successful in presidential politics: They finally have the votes. The influence of those two regions has grown in step with their populations and economic strength. Almost half of the nation's 1,000 largest corporations are now based in the South and West. California (110) and Texas (102) boasted more headquarters of *Fortune* 1,000 companies in 2006 than New York (ninety-two) and Ohio (sixty-two) did.

Carter Glass would have no reason for complaint today. The East and Midwest no longer have a stranglehold on the best jobs in politics or business. If you're interested in becoming a high-powered official, it matters little which region or state you hail from.

But let's narrow our focus to your hometown. Your chances of success would logically seem to be better if you come from a major city or affluent suburb than from some sleepy small town or farming community. It stands to reason, doesn't it?

The best answer is to present this list of the birthplaces of the eleven presidents since World War II:

Harry Truman: Lamar, Missouri
Dwight Eisenhower: Denison, Texas
John Kennedy: Brookline, Massachusetts
Lyndon Johnson: Stonewall, Texas
Richard Nixon: Yorba Linda, California
Gerald Ford: Omaha, Nebraska
Jimmy Carter: Plains, Georgia
Ronald Reagan: Tampico, Illinois
George H.W. Bush: Milton, Massachusetts
Bill Clinton: Hope, Arkansas
George W. Bush: New Haven, Connecticut

This isn't exactly a list of high-profile communities. The *combined* population of the eleven presidential birthplaces, as of the 2000 census, was 695,000, which is less than one-tenth the population of New York City. Omaha and New Haven are the only cities on the list with more than one hundred thousand residents today. Three—the birthplaces of Johnson, Carter, and Reagan—still have fewer than one thousand people each.

Here's another way of looking at it. The odds, based on current populations, are 35-to-1 that any given president would be a native of New York City, but 26,500-to-1 that he would come from Hope, Arkansas. If you were a betting person, you'd have to put your money on New York. Yet the nation's largest city has produced only one president (Theodore Roosevelt), precisely matching the small town in Arkansas. It truly doesn't matter where you're from.

This fact amazed no one more than Bill Clinton, the self-proclaimed Man from Hope, as he confessed to a crowd in Little Rock on the night of his reelection in 1996. "Fifty years ago, when I was born in a summer storm to a widowed mother in a small town in the southwest part of our state, it was unimaginable that someone like me could have ever become president of the greatest country in human history," he said, his voice catching briefly. "It has been, for me, a remarkable journey."

IF YOU WANT THE TOP JOB, MAKE THE TOP EFFORT

Chester Arthur knew a great opportunity when he saw it.

Arthur was an obscure New York official, one of the hundreds of faceless delegates attending the 1880 Republican convention. But he had just received a breathtaking proposal that promised to elevate his status considerably. An emissary from James Garfield, the party's new presidential candidate, had offered Arthur the vice-presidential slot on the Republican ticket.

He seemed to be a bizarre choice. Why give such an elevated post to someone as little known as Arthur? But Garfield's logic was sound. The Ohio congressman had been shocked when the weary, bitterly divided convention turned to him as its compromise candidate for president. Choosing the right running mate would help him to inspire confidence and begin healing the party's wounds.

Garfield had two factors to consider. The first was geographic. He was a Midwesterner, so it made sense to balance the ticket with a vice president from the East, the only other region with any clout in the Republican Party of 1880.

The second factor was deeply personal. The convention had nominated Garfield after being deadlocked between two frontrunners—James Blaine, a charismatic senator from Maine, and Ulysses Grant, a former president who hoped for a comeback. Grant's campaign had been managed by Roscoe Conkling, a vain, imperious senator from New York. He and Blaine hated each other. Theirs was the great political feud of the age.

Garfield got along well with Blaine. It was the latter's supporters, in fact, who had started the rush to Garfield on the convention floor. But Conkling? He would almost certainly be a problem.

The obvious solution was to appease him by picking someone—anyone—from New York for the ticket. Garfield first offered the spot to Levi Morton, who dutifully trotted to his leader for approval. But Conkling angrily ordered Morton to turn it down, which he did. So the call went out to Arthur, another of Conkling's lieutenants. He, too, went to see his master.

"The Ohio men have offered me the vice presidency," he reported.

Conkling glared at his subordinate. "Well, sir," he replied, "you should drop it as you would a red-hot shoe from the forge."

Arthur pondered this advice, but did not back down, undoubtedly to his boss's surprise. "The office of the vice president is a greater honor than I ever dreamed of attaining," he said. "A barren nomination would be a great honor. In a calmer moment, you will look at this differently."

"If you wish for my favor and my respect," Conkling huffed, "you will contemptuously decline it." He stormed off.

But Chet Arthur could hear opportunity knocking, and he decided to answer. This unusual act of independence became profoundly significant when Garfield was assassinated in 1881 by a Conkling supporter who shouted, "Arthur is president now." Indeed he was. He had risen from a minor role in New York's Republican machine to the nation's highest office in a single year, all because he had the good sense to take advantage of a break that came his way.

Levi Morton, who could have been Garfield's successor, cooled his heels instead as minister to France. He was given a second chance in 1888—once again being offered the Republican vice-presidential nomination—and this time accepted with alacrity. But his new job didn't bring the unexpected promotion that Arthur had received. Morton served an undistinguished term under an all-too-healthy president, Benjamin Harrison, then quietly slipped out of Washington.

The ability to recognize and seize upon an opportunity is critical to making the best decisions about your future. Study your situation thoroughly, consider all of the available options, and then have the courage to make the choice that's best for you and your family, no matter what outsiders might think.

The willingness to work hard is equally important.

We've already noted how Jimmy Carter outlasted his opponents. Up at 4:30, to bed after midnight, day after day after day. He set a brutal pace that the other candidates simply were unable to match, bringing him a victory that had once seemed highly improbable.

Hard work, indeed, can sometimes perform miracles. John Kerry's presidential campaign was in disarray in December 2003, less than two months before the critical New Hampshire primary. Polls pegged his support at 12 percent, thirty points behind the leader, Howard Dean. If a well-known senator from the neighboring state of Massachusetts could do no better than 12 percent in New Hampshire, said the experts, it obviously was time to strike the tents.

But Kerry refused to quit. He reorganized his staff, personally borrowed money to keep his campaign afloat, and promised an all-out blitz to turn his fortunes around. "I need to campaign like a bandit over the course of the next weeks and make sure people are clear about my candidacy," Kerry said, "and I intend to make them clear." His comeback victories in Iowa and New Hampshire in January put him on the road to winning the Democratic nomination.

Kerry's vigor stood in stark contrast to Bill Bradley's lackluster perform- ance in New Hampshire four years before. The former senator from New Jersey had achieved fame as a National Basketball Association star and was widely admired as one of the Democratic Party's young leaders. But he was strangely subdued as a presidential candidate. "I feel I'm ready," he would say, "and all I can do is offer myself to my country when I am ready, and it's up to the country to see whether or not they want to accept." Bradley didn't seem willing to fight or even to make much of an effort. It was no sur- prise when Al Gore easily defeated him in New Hampshire and all subse- quent primaries.

But it took a man who actually reached the White House, John Quincy Adams, to raise diffidence to a political art form. Adams, as we've already seen, was never particularly enthusiastic about seeking the presidency. The job itself had some appeal, but the thought of actively pursuing it was abhor- rent to him.

Adams's friends and supporters begged him to make efforts in his own behalf. He bowed to their wishes to a slight extent in 1824, winning a strange four-way race because of his apparent willingness to cut a deal with one of his opponents, Henry Clay. But he was back to his intransi- gent ways by 1828, when he faced an imposing challenger, Andrew Jackson.

Adams steadfastly refused to campaign for reelection. He would not give speeches or otherwise "exhibit" himself to the people. He would not corre- spond with prospective supporters. "I write no letters upon what is called politics," he sniffed. "That is electioneering." He would not engage in pa- tronage, the time-honored practice of appointing people to government jobs simply to secure their loyalty. Enough was enough.

Adams preferred to leave everything to fate. It seemed more dignified, more gentlemanly. He liked to quote Macbeth, "If chance will have me king, why, chance may crown me, without my stir."

Real life, however, didn't work that way in 1828, when the vigorous Jack- son proceeded to rout the passive Adams in the general election. And it most certainly doesn't work that way today.

"Every Job I've Had Is Bigger Than I Am"

Lyndon Johnson always demonstrated a capacity for hard work, but he shifted into overdrive after becoming president.

Johnson began his typical day in the White House at 6:30, reading several newspapers in bed and watching the morning news shows on three side-by-side TVs. His aides soon assembled at his bedside, awaiting their first orders. Lady Bird Johnson, the covers pulled to her chin, would eventually say, "Now, you boys look the other way," and leave for her dressing room. But the flow of presidential commands never stopped. Johnson continued barking at his assistants while he showered, even while he used the toilet.

Then he was off on a dizzying round of meetings, business lunches, more meetings, public appearances, and dozens and dozens of phone calls. It wasn't unusual to see the lights burning past midnight in the Oval Office. Johnson knew no other way. "Every job I've had is bigger than I am," he said with uncharacteristic modesty, "and I have to work twice as hard as the next man to do it."

2

Developing

John Kennedy tried to stay warm as he wandered through a windswept Wisconsin town. It was early in the 1960 presidential campaign, and the locals were about as welcoming as the bitterly cold weather.

The youthful candidate approached an elderly woman, who made no effort to hide her skepticism. "You're too soon, my boy, too soon," she told him. Kennedy, three months shy of his forty-third birthday, had heard it before. He smiled at the old lady. "No, this is my time," he replied. "My time is now."

The voters gradually came to agree. Kennedy won enough votes in Wisconsin and other primary elections to emerge as the frontrunner for the Democratic nomination. But party leaders continued to resist. It wasn't right, a man this young seeking the top office in the land. Harry Truman felt so strongly about it that he convened a press conference. "Senator, are you certain that you're quite ready for the country," he asked, "or the country is ready for you in the role of president?"

It was one thing for an old woman to express doubts, quite another for a former president to do so. His response, Kennedy knew, must be quick and emphatic. He called his own press conference, where he spoke for every young adult who ever sought a promotion that his elders believed was beyond his grasp. "To exclude from positions of trust and command all those below the age of forty-four," he declared, "would have kept Thomas Jefferson from writing the Declaration of Independence, George Washington from commanding the Continental Army, James Madison from fathering the Constitution, Alexander Hamilton from serving as secretary of the treasury, Henry Clay from being elected speaker of the House, and Christopher Columbus from even discovering America."

True enough, yet the naysayers had a point. There is a rhythm to professional advancement that rarely can be disturbed without harm. It takes decades for aspiring executives to blossom into effective leaders. They need time to develop self-control, learn how to make decisions under pressure, and gather a wide range of experience. The process shouldn't be rushed. "Delaying a promotion can sometimes be the best thing a senior executive can do for a junior manager," concluded a 2002 study by researchers from Boston University and the Center for Creative Leadership.

The stereotypical man (or woman) in a hurry often pays the price. Kennedy, in a sense, was right about 1960 being his time, since he narrowly won the election that November. But he stumbled badly just weeks after taking office in January 1961. He approved a CIA-backed invasion of Cuba by a ragtag band of political exiles, which was easily (and embarrassingly) repulsed by Fidel Castro's troops at the Bay of Pigs. The young president's first venture in high-level diplomacy ended much the same way. Nikita Khrushchev, the Soviet premier, bullied Kennedy during their summit meeting in Vienna in June. "Worst thing in my life. He savaged me," JFK admitted to James Reston, the legendary *New York Times* columnist, shortly after the final session with Khrushchev. Reston thought that Kennedy was almost in shock.

Bill Clinton was nearly as young—forty-six—when he entered the White House in 1993, and he too suffered a shaky initiation. Clinton seemed to lose his focus immediately after taking the oath of office. He became bogged down in a fruitless controversy over the role of gays in the military, abandoned his promise of an immediate tax cut, and churned out a plan for health-care reform that was notable only for its mind-boggling complexity. Americans punished him by handing control of Congress to the Republicans in 1994. "Reflecting on his presidency, I believe Clinton was elected too early for his own good," concluded David Gergen, one of his former aides.

Kennedy and Clinton eventually learned the ropes. Their solid accomplishments later in their terms—Kennedy's cool command during the Cuban missile crisis, Clinton's deft handling of a booming economy—proved they had the necessary ability. But observers couldn't help wondering how much better their administrations might have been if they had arrived at the Oval Office with greater maturity and experience.

The ages of victorious presidential candidates have been remarkably constant—from George Washington (fifty-seven when elected in 1789) to George W. Bush (fifty-eight when reelected in 2004)—with the median for all winners of presidential elections pegged at fifty-six years old. Just eight presidents have been voted into office before reaching fifty; only two of those youngsters (Kennedy and Clinton) entered the White House by election during the past hundred years.

So that's generally the dividing line—fifty years old. Consider it the threshold for top executive positions.

Those who try to break the fifty barrier often come to regret it. That certainly was true of Thomas Dewey, who entered America's consciousness during the 1930s as a brisk, no-nonsense prosecutor who fearlessly grappled with the toughest figures in the underworld—mobsters like Lucky Luciano and Dutch Schultz—and usually sent them to prison. "If you don't think Dewey is Public Hero Number One," the *Philadelphia Inquirer* wrote, "listen to the applause he gets every time he is shown in a newsreel."

Dewey, like any ambitious person, hoped to capitalize on his sudden popularity. His plan was audacious. He would skip the traditional rung-by-rung climb up the career ladder, seeking instead to land on the roof with a single vault. He would run for the Republican presidential nomination in 1940.

Two factors made this task even more formidable than it first appeared. Tom Dewey didn't have a typical political base. He wasn't a governor or a senator, just the district attorney of Manhattan. Would people really vote for a DA for president? And then there was the question of age. The famed gangbuster was only thirty-eight. Harold Ickes, a member of Franklin Roosevelt's cabinet, spoke for established politicians everywhere when he cracked that Dewey had "thrown his diaper in the ring" by entering the race.

The campaign went better than the skeptics expected. Dewey emerged as the Republican frontrunner, tailing off only after the Nazis invaded France in May 1940. Americans, it seemed, didn't believe a candidate in his late thirties should be entrusted with a problem as serious as World War II. Wendell Willkie—older and more worldly—grabbed the nomination at the convention.

Dewey dusted himself off, won the governorship of New York in 1942, then secured the next two Republican presidential nominations with ease. The odds were against him in the autumn of 1944, when he challenged a popular incumbent, Franklin Roosevelt, as the Allies rolled toward Berlin and a long-awaited military victory. But 1948 was to be his year. The new president, Harry Truman, was decidedly unpopular. Voters seemed ready to opt for any alternative. Tom Dewey was absolutely certain to become president. It was in the bag.

The only problem was, he lost.

His was a stunning, demoralizing, incomprehensible defeat. Dewey would serve another six years as governor, but would never seek the presidency again. He was, in effect, washed up at the youthful age of forty-six, destined to slip into the shadows after soaring too far too fast and failing to hit his target. "Everything came too early for me," he would admit ruefully toward the end of his life.

Most of the blame was his. Tom Dewey channeled his youthful energies into pursuing his goals, not to developing his personal qualities and abilities. If he had slowed his pace, broadened his base of knowledge, improved his leadership skills, and allowed some sunshine to warm his chilly personality, he undoubtedly could have won the presidency in 1952—a Republican year if ever there were one—instead of preparing for his political retirement.

You may face the same temptation to race ahead at all costs. Avoid it. Prepare yourself thoroughly for the challenges ahead, and have confidence that your time will come. The key is to be ready when opportunity knocks.

That's easier said than done. You'll have to devote considerable time and effort to developing the foundation on which your career will be based, as well as the good personal habits that will harbor your energy and protect your sanity. If you have any built-in advantages, such as family connections or inherited wealth, by all means take advantage of them as you begin your climb. This chapter touches on each of these points:

Laying the foundation

- A college education (Ivy League or not) is essential.
- Emotional intelligence is as important as IQ.
- Get out and experience all that life has to offer.
- Develop and demonstrate leadership qualities.

Good habits

- Don't become a dull and dreary workaholic.
- Learn the blessings of patience.

Built-in advantages

- If your family gives you a leg up, say thanks.
- Personal wealth can certainly come in handy.

Beginning the climb

- Assume jobs of greater and greater responsibility.
- Always keep your bandwagon on the move.

Ignore these rules at your peril. Your goal, after all, is to build a legacy of success, not to become a flash in the pan like George McClellan, a young, obscure general who won a few battles at the outbreak of the Civil War.

Cynics insisted that his victories were more like skirmishes than battles, and they were way out in the mountains of Virginia (soon to be the new state of West Virginia), not in the main theater of action. But the war had started badly for the North, and any win was better than the defeats that well-known generals were suffering. So McClellan suddenly found himself elevated to command of the whole Union army at the tender age of thirty-five. "By some strange operation of magic," he marveled, "I seem to have become the power of the land."

McClellan, it turned out, was not ready for his new duties. He drilled and drilled his men, yet hesitated to lead them into battle. Abraham Lincoln quietly fumed as his general-in-chief dawdled. Lincoln's attorney general, Edward Bates, was more caustic in his dissatisfaction: "Never before was there such a grand army, composed of truly excellent materials, and yet, so poorly commanded." McClellan, said Bates, had "but one of the three Roman requisites for a general. He is young, I fear not brave, and surely not fortunate." Lincoln endured McClellan's stalling until the end of 1862, when he finally sacked him.

That's where the story truly grew strange. The Democrats, searching for an anti-Lincoln candidate in 1864, turned to the army's ex-commander. McClellan, an unknown engineer just a half-decade previously, was named the Democratic presidential nominee at the age of thirty-eight, entrusted with the incongruous task of criticizing a war effort that he had once led. He was even less prepared for a political campaign than he had been for the military kind. Lincoln pummeled him in the general election.

The war years left George McClellan in a daze. He later reflected that everything—the military command, the national prominence, the presidential nomination—had arrived much too quickly. "It probably would have been better for me personally," he wrote, "had my promotion been delayed a year or more."

A COLLEGE EDUCATION (IVY LEAGUE OR NOT) IS ESSENTIAL

Theodore Roosevelt was wonderfully concise. Others might prefer to flutter around a topic without ever landing on it, but Roosevelt scorned such nonsense. He stressed the importance of a college degree in typically blunt terms, avoiding any esoteric references to the broadening qualities of the liberal arts. The whole matter, as he saw it, could be reduced to a simple equation.

"A man who has never gone to school may steal from a freight car," Roosevelt said. "But if he has a university education, he may steal the whole railroad."

The Census Bureau has reinforced his argument in a manner that is both more genteel and more precise. A worker with a graduate degree earns 45 percent more, on average, than a colleague with a bachelor's degree, and 167 percent more than someone who never progressed beyond high school, according to a study released by the bureau in 2005.

If the typical high-school grad in your town earns $30,000 a year, for instance, that means you could boost your annual pay to $55,200 with a four-year degree and to $80,100 with a master's, doctorate, or professional degree. A university education, as Roosevelt suggested, will indeed improve your bottom line.

And it's important in another way that is even more basic. A college diploma has become an unspoken requirement for anyone who aspires to a high position in government or the private sector. Every U.S. president since 1953 has held a bachelor's degree, and several have completed graduate work as well. It's impossible to imagine anyone being elected to the White House these days without having passed through college.

The last president who lacked a degree was Harry Truman, and it wasn't by choice. "I've always been sorry I did not get a university education in the regular way," he said in later life. But Truman's family simply didn't have the money to send him to college. He sought an appointment to West Point, where the government would pay his tuition, but his eyesight wasn't good enough for him to be admitted. He drifted off to a few odd jobs, then returned to the family farm for several years before an improbable series of events elevated him to the presidency.

That, then, is the first rule of career development. You must graduate from a four-year college. No ifs, ands, or buts.

Does it matter, though, which school you attend? Conventional wisdom insists that it certainly does. Ivy League schools such as Harvard, Yale, and Princeton receive top billing in the rating guides that annually flood newsstands. Tens of thousands of high-school seniors battle furiously to gain admission to these elite institutions each fall.

Their motivation was best expressed in Richard Ben Cramer's fascinating 1992 book, *What It Takes*, which examined the personal lives of the presidential candidates who ran four years earlier. Cramer described a backyard party in Wilmington, Delaware, where one of the state's senators, Joe Biden, was holding forth on a favorite topic, the value of an Ivy League diploma.

"There's a river of power that flows through this country," Biden began. His friends, who knew what was coming, rolled their eyes. Their kids, the senator's two boys included, were all in grade school. It was several years too early for this conversation, but Biden would not be deterred.

"Some people—most people—don't even know the river is there. But it's there. Some people know about the river, but they can't get in. They only stand at the edge. And some people, a few, get to swim in the river. All the time. They get to swim their whole lives—anywhere they want to go—always in the river of power."

"And that river," Biden concluded, "flows from the Ivy League."

If his monologue betrayed a hint of envy, it was only natural. Joe Biden had attended two distinctly non-Ivy colleges, the University of Delaware (bachelor's degree) and Syracuse University (law degree). Dozens of his Senate colleagues displayed Ivy League diplomas on their office walls. Who could blame him if he felt inadequate by comparison?

But Biden was ignoring the lesson of his own career. He had emerged as a senatorial leader and presidential candidate despite his lack of Ivy League credentials. It didn't matter *where* he had gone to college, only that he had graduated and moved onward and upward. He was swimming in the river of power just like the boys and girls from Harvard and Yale.

Biden's story is being duplicated all over the country, as two recent studies have confirmed:

- Researchers Peter Cappelli and Monika Hamori compared the men and women who held 1,000 top executive positions at America's one hundred largest companies in 1980 and 2001, and found a distinct shift in educational backgrounds. The number of execs with Ivy League degrees dropped by 30 percent during that span, while the number who graduated from public universities grew by 50 percent.

- Harvard had long owned the distinction of producing the most CEOs on Standard & Poor's list of five hundred major corporations. But it yielded that title in 2004, according to Spencer Stuart, an executive search firm. Harvard was passed up by a very large, very public school—the University of Wisconsin.

The trend is clear. Ivy League institutions still provide an excellent brand of education, but they aren't the only gateway to executive achievement.

"The Ivies and other A-league schools have a lot of prestige because they're supposed to open doors and lead to successful careers. But people who believe that are fighting the last war," said Loren Pope, author of *Colleges that Change Lives*, a guide to small liberal-arts schools. "Parents who expect the Ivies to ensure their kids' success are going to be disappointed. The old-boy network isn't much good in an economy like this. It's competence that counts."

But that has always been the case, hasn't it? Lyndon Johnson is a classic example of competence trumping an alma mater. He was always somewhat ashamed of his diploma from a truly inferior school, Southwest Texas State Teachers College, yet he evolved into a master politician and president of the United States.

Johnson demonstrated his envy of the Ivy League elite in a couple of conflicting ways. He would grouse about the "overbred smart alecks" on his staff, derisively referring to them as "the Harvards," yet he would try to hire as many of those New England Ph.D.'s as he could. He secretly admired them, as historian Robert Dallek put it, "for having obtained something he valued and craved."

It was ironic that at least one distinguished Ivy League graduate thought Johnson's background was equally admirable. Franklin Roosevelt followed young LBJ's congressional career closely and once confessed his admiration to a cabinet member, Harold Ickes. The aging president was impressed with Johnson's political dexterity and energy. Roosevelt considered him, as Ickes recalled, "the kind of uninhibited young pro he would have liked to have been as a young man"—the kind that FDR believed he could have become himself "if he hadn't gone to Harvard."

EMOTIONAL INTELLIGENCE IS AS IMPORTANT AS IQ

John Quincy Adams was a bright man, possibly the brightest ever to become president. His mind was so quick that he mastered five foreign languages—Latin, Greek, French, Dutch, and Spanish—before turning eighteen. His father marveled at John Quincy's precociousness as a college student. "The oldest (son) has given decided proofs of great talents," boasted John Adams, himself the second president, "and there is not a youth his age whose reputation is higher for abilities."

But intelligence doesn't always translate into professional success. John Quincy Adams was remarkably skilled as a diplomat—many historians consider him America's best secretary of state ever—but he was a disappointing president. He reached the White House inauspiciously, seeming to trade off a cabinet post in exchange for Henry Clay's support, an accusation from which he never recovered. His cold manner and inability to connect with average Americans doomed his 1828 reelection campaign to defeat.

Nor was he alone. Several other highly intelligent men have been overmatched by the presidency. William Howard Taft, Herbert Hoover, Richard Nixon, and Jimmy Carter, to name four from the past century, brought superior brainpower to the job, but left the White House as defeated men.

The blunt truth is that smart people don't necessarily get the glory—in politics or in business. "Unless you are a moron, there is zero correlation between grades or IQ and success in life," concluded Warren Bennis, author of several bestselling books about leadership. There is plenty of evidence to support his assertion.

Franklin Roosevelt was no intellectual, despite his degree from Harvard, yet he typically ranks with George Washington and Abraham Lincoln as one of the three greatest presidents of all time. Oliver Wendell Holmes Jr., a former Supreme Court justice, met FDR shortly after the latter's inauguration in 1933, and quickly grasped his essential quality. "A second-class intellect," said Holmes, "but a first-class temperament."

Similar judgments would later be made about Ronald Reagan, regarded by many as the best president since World War II (and so named in a national poll conducted in May 2006 by Quinnipiac University).

Critics were frustrated by Reagan's breezy disregard for facts and his aversion to hard work. "Most of the time, he was an actor reading lines," sputtered Tip O'Neill, the speaker of the House. But Reagan's skills as a leader and orator counterbalanced his deficiencies as an administrator. O'Neill freely conceded that the president had a winning personality. The speaker once prefaced an attack with a semi-apology: "I hate to say it about such an agreeable man." Then he laced into Reagan once again.

David Gergen, who served as an aide to four presidents, was won over by Reagan's spirit and his ability to sell his conservative philosophy. "Reagan changed my mind about the qualities we need in a president," Gergen later wrote. "We no more need an Einstein in the Oval Office than a Mother Teresa. What we need is someone who has a good grasp of public affairs and an excellent temperament." (That word again.)

Reporters make a great production of unearthing the IQ scores and college report cards of presidential candidates. They discovered in 2004 that George W. Bush and John Kerry both had IQs in the 120s—well above average, though short of the genius level—and both had struggled in a few courses at Yale. Bush received a D in astronomy, while Kerry picked up D's in geology, history, and political science.

The candidates treated the story with the seriousness it deserved. Kerry joked about his deficient grades: "I always told my dad that D stood for distinction." And Bush famously addressed Yale's graduating class in 2001: "To those of you who've received honors, awards, and distinctions, I say well done. And to the C students, I say you can be president of the United States."

Many experts agree that IQs and SAT scores say little about a person's leadership ability or prospects for success. "The SAT is a remarkable judge of how well a student will perform in college, but nothing beyond that," conceded Gaston Caperton, the president of the College Board, which administers that particular test.

Caperton knew a good bit about the political world, having served two terms as governor of West Virginia, and he saw no linkage between grades and professional accomplishment. He himself had overcome dyslexia to graduate from college and eventually reach the governor's office. "The skills that really help you in politics," he said, "are having a huge amount of energy and knowing how to get along with people."

That sounds remarkably like the "first-class temperament" ascribed to Roosevelt and Reagan, which in turn has much in common with "emotional intelligence" (sometimes incongruously abbreviated as EQ), a concept advanced by psychologist Daniel Goleman. He argued in a 1995 book that several qualities are more important than IQ, including self-awareness, self-discipline, persistence, and empathy. "The art of sustained leadership is getting others to produce superior work," he wrote, "and high IQ alone is insufficient to that task."

The ability to work effectively with others is an essential component of EQ, yet was sadly deficient in one of history's smartest presidents, Woodrow Wilson, the only man in the bunch to have a Ph.D. An unbending stubbornness offset his impressive mental abilities. "He finds great difficulty in conferring with men against whom, for some reason, he has a prejudice and in whom he can find nothing good," noted a close adviser, Colonel Edward House.

Wilson's willful nature severely damaged his administration in the aftermath of World War I. The president insisted that the United States join the League of Nations, a forerunner of the United Nations. A small cadre of congressional Republicans vowed to block him at any cost, but a larger group merely wanted a few modifications made in the peace treaty. Wilson turned a deaf ear to the pleas of his advisers and adamantly refused to make a deal of any kind. It would be dishonorable, he said.

The president paid a heavy price for his obstinacy. Congress rejected the treaty and the League of Nations, the nation descended into postwar disillusionment, and the voters tossed the Democrats out of the White House at the earliest opportunity. Wilson's shining reputation for cool, intellectual leadership lay in shambles, leaving the president's loyal secretary, Joseph Tumulty, aghast at the unexpectedly decisive end to his boss's career. "It wasn't a landslide," Tumulty gasped as the dust cleared from the election of 1920. "It was an earthquake."

"I Don't Know What to Do or Where to Turn"

Don't get the impression that brainpower is completely unimportant to an executive. Profound ignorance is never a desirable alternative. Consider the case of Warren Harding, commonly considered one of the least intelligent presidents in history, an unhappy distinction that he might not have disputed. "I don't know what to do or where to turn on this taxation matter," he once wailed to an aide. "Somewhere there must be a book that tells all about it, where I could go to straighten it out in my mind. But I don't know where the book is, and maybe I couldn't read it if I found it!"

Harding was clearly out of his element and deservedly ranks among the worst presidents. But how much damage did he really do? America was at peace during his administration. The economy was on an upswing when he died in 1923. Teapot Dome, the scandal that broke after his death, produced no lasting scars. Harding may not have been up to the job, but he left the country in moderately better shape, all in all, than he had found it in 1921.

"What really matters in a leader is not being smart, but being right," said Gregory Cochran, a present-day evolutionary biologist. "Who was smarter, Warren G. Harding or V.I. Lenin? I'm sure Lenin could have beaten Harding in chess, but I definitely would rather have lived under Harding than Lenin. Harding was kind of a dumb bunny, but his prejudices and instincts were much more reasonable than Lenin's, who was wrong about everything."

GET OUT AND EXPERIENCE ALL THAT LIFE HAS TO OFFER

Rutherford Hayes came of age in the 1840s, a decade that offered several appealing options to young men lusting for fame and fortune. They could enlist in the army, marching off to glory in the Mexican War. They could set out for the West, joining the scramble for California gold. Or they could move to an urban center, blending into the throngs that would boost the population of New York City, Boston, and Baltimore by more than 45 percent between 1840 and 1850.

But Hayes spurned these opportunities. His doctor advised him not to volunteer for service in Mexico. Nor did California have any allure. "There is neither romance nor glory in digging for gold," he scoffed. He opted to remain a small-town lawyer in Ohio, safely isolated from the tumultuous outside world.

Hayes's primary objective was domestic. He wrote at age twenty-four: "Uppermost in the medley of ideas that are rolling about under my hair is that before a year rolls around, I'll get me a wifey, or at least a sweetheart, if I can find one who agrees with me that I am one of the sunniest fellows in the world."

But his romantic life was restricted by his unadventurous spirit. Hayes proposed to Fanny Perkins, a Connecticut woman whom he met while she was visiting relatives in Ohio. She was inclined to accept, but insisted that they live in her home state. Hayes refused. "I could not get her without more feeling and trouble than was to my taste," he sniffed. He turned thirty before settling down with Lucy Webb, a woman who was considerably more compliant.

Calvin Coolidge also preferred the path most traveled. He graduated from Amherst College and opened a law office a few miles away in Northampton, Massachusetts, where he and his family lived in a duplex and shared a party-line telephone. He entered politics—partly to stir up business for his legal practice—and plodded through a succession of incrementally higher positions: city council, mayor, both houses of the state legislature, lieutenant governor, and at long last, governor. His climb through the ranks was methodical and thoroughly unexciting.

All of which was fine with Coolidge. "What we need in politics," he said primly, "is more of the office desk and less of the show window." But his critics wished that he had stepped away from his desk and experienced more of life during his formative years. Henry Cabot Lodge, the senior senator from Coolidge's state, was shocked by the suggestion that his one-dimensional governor might be presidential material. "Nominate a man who lives in a two-family house?" Lodge shrieked. "Never! Massachusetts is not for him!"

Hayes and Coolidge reached the White House, of course, but they were poorly prepared for it. Both men lacked the necessary fire and creativity. Hayes was essentially a caretaker president, pledging from the start that he would not seek reelection. Coolidge seemed to take a perverse pleasure in his reputation for inaction and taciturnity. "If you don't say anything," he would advise, "you won't be called on to repeat it." Not exactly words to inspire the troops.

These stories point to a common failing. Hayes and Coolidge frittered away their early adult years in quiet, dusty law offices or behind closed doors with fellow politicians. They became increasingly skilled in their narrow field—eventually reaching the pinnacle of their profession—but learned little of the world along the way. They didn't live in a variety of cities and towns, or work unusual jobs, or become acquainted with a wide circle of people, or learn how to view life from different perspectives. They never built the personal base that is essential to the successful leader of any organization, and as a result, they fumbled their opportunity to inspire the nation and develop positive, lasting reputations.

Rutherford Hayes and Calvin Coolidge might have made great corporation counsels, but they definitely weren't CEO material.

Your goal, after all, isn't merely to reach the top, but to take charge and establish yourself as a star once you get there. You can succeed only if you know how things really work, if you have a broad understanding of life, not a narrow grasp of minutiae.

"Leaders have always been generalists," leadership guru John Gardner insisted. "Tomorrow's leaders will, very likely, have begun life as trained specialists, but to mature as leaders, they must sooner or later climb out of the trenches of specialization and rise above the boundaries that separate the various segments of society."

Theodore Roosevelt epitomized Gardner's vision of the leader as generalist. He was, if you will, the ultimate anti-specialist. He wanted to do *everything*. "A mere life of ease," he insisted, "is not a very satisfactory life."

Roosevelt built a very broad base, indeed. He authored a dozen books. ("I should like to write some book that would really take rank as in the very first class.") He was a boxer, sometimes sparring with professionals. He was a rancher out West. ("I felt as absolutely free as a man could feel.") He was assistant secretary of the navy. He led a famous cavalry charge up Cuba's San Juan Hill in the Spanish-American War. ("San Juan was the great day of my life.") He served as police commissioner of New York City, governor of New York State, and vice president of the United States.

And he did all of these things before becoming president in 1901 at the age of forty-two, the youngest person ever to hold the office.

Roosevelt's vast array of experiences helped him develop the supreme self-confidence for which he was noted. And it won him an enormous number of friends, acquaintances, and supporters. He might never have become vice president or president, for example, if not for his seemingly innocuous stint as a rancher fifteen years before. "It was believed," Roosevelt confessed to a friend, "that I would greatly strengthen the ticket in the West, where they regard me as a fellow barbarian and like me much."

It's no coincidence that today's historians rate Theodore Roosevelt among the very best of all presidents, considerably higher than Hayes and Coolidge. Nor is it a surprise that the two men at the very top of those rankings developed their leadership abilities in similar ways.

George Washington began his working life as the surveyor of Culpeper County, Virginia. He went on to serve as a major in the state militia during the French and Indian War, rising to the rank of colonel. The deaths of his half-brother, Lawrence, and Lawrence's daughter brought him the title to Mount Vernon, saddling him in his twenties with the responsibility for developing and expanding the plantation. And he was elected to Virginia's colonial legislature at the age of twenty-six.

Washington, as a result, had amassed a wealth of military, business, and government experience by his mid-thirties. It proved to be perfect training for the future commander-in-chief and president of a new nation.

Abraham Lincoln's rise to the White House was as circuitous as it was improbable. He worked as a farmer, laborer, surveyor, rail-splitter, militia member, store clerk, postmaster, state legislator, congressman, lawyer, and lecturer before reaching the presidency.

Others saw weakness in Lincoln's checkered career. He saw only strength. "I am not ashamed to confess that twenty-five years ago, I was a hired laborer, mauling rails, at work on a flatboat—just what might happen to any poor man's son," he freely admitted. He knew how much he owed to that background. It was the source of his unbreakable bond with everyday Americans, his fabled sense of humor, his amazing energy—"work, work, work is the main thing"—and his remarkable resilience.

It was, in short, what made him the greatest president in American history.

DEVELOP AND DEMONSTRATE LEADERSHIP QUALITIES

Presidential candidates have a mystical faith in "the issues." They make speeches, write position papers, and participate in debates—always hammering home their views on the important matters of the day.

They behave as attorneys do before a jury, which should be no surprise, given that so many politicians are lawyers. They speak with great passion, flatter their listeners, and occasionally beg for support. If they somehow can persuade the voters to agree with them on Social Security or crime prevention or the Middle East, they have a better chance of winning the office of their dreams. So goes the conventional wisdom.

NBC put this belief to the test on election day in 1984, surveying more than 11,000 voters as they left polling places in all fifty states. "Which one characteristic of the presidential candidate for whom you just voted," the network asked, "was most important in helping you decide how to vote today?"

These were the top two answers:

- Leadership qualities, 41 percent
- Positions on issues, 40 percent

So the politicians are partially correct. A candidate *does* benefit from lining up with the majority of voters on key issues, though that's not the only path to victory. An opponent perceived by those same voters to be a strong leader has at least an equal chance of winning, as proved by the election that very day in 1984. NBC's poll found Walter Mondale closer to the prevailing national mood on several domestic issues, but Ronald Reagan received a much higher score on the question of leadership.

Everybody knows which candidate won the election—and by one of the widest margins in American history.

Leadership is equally important in the business world. You, as a rising executive, certainly need to know the ins and outs of your chosen field, but you also must exude the confidence, determination, and energy that will convince others to follow you. There's no better time to start developing those qualities than now.

So what's involved? Let's begin by harkening back to the two decades that preceded the Civil War. That was a contentious time, marked by bitter disagreement between North and South on several issues, slavery being the most prominent. The gap between the two regions widened slowly throughout the 1840s, and much more rapidly as the 1850s progressed. If ever an era cried out for presidential leadership, this was it.

The seven men who served between 1841 and 1861 were generally unequal to the task. We can safely ignore William Henry Harrison, who died just a month after taking the oath of office in '41. And we can make an exception for James Polk, who literally worked himself to death during a single energetic term from 1845 to 1849. But the other five are all ranked as below-average or poor presidents by historians today. Each reached the pinnacle of his profession, to be sure, but none brought with him the necessary leadership skills to save the country from disaster or to establish a positive legacy. Here's a quick look at each:

John Tyler (1841–1845) was a waffler, always seeking to compromise divergent interests, but never quite sure of which way to go. John Calhoun, a former vice president, scoffed that Tyler was "essentially a man for the middle ground, and (he) will attempt a middle position now when there is none."

Zachary Taylor (1849–1850) spent only a year and a half in the White House, long enough to prove that the career military officer had no ability for political leadership. Henry Clay, a prominent figure in Taylor's Whig Party, complained that the president was "wholly incompetent to the office."

Millard Fillmore (1850–1853) was a not a strong executive, nor did he have a commanding presence. "Fillmore lacks pluck," wrote journalist Horace Greeley. "He wants backbone. He means well, but he is timid, irresolute, uncertain, and loves to lean."

Franklin Pierce (1853–1857) was a great believer in "harmony"—a word that appeared frequently in his speeches—but he had no idea how to attain it. Theodore Roosevelt, donning his historian's hat, judged Pierce to be "a small politician, of low capacity and mean surroundings, proud to act as the servile tool of men worse than himself."

James Buchanan (1857–1861) was perhaps the weakest of the lot. He sought to minimize or even ignore the issue of slavery, despite the fact that the nation was veering dangerously toward open warfare. Critics and many of his friends considered him to be fussy and skittish. "He is an able man," James Polk had written years earlier, "but sometimes he acts like an old maid."

What can we say about these five men who were so ill-suited for the presidency? They were passive. They lacked confidence in themselves and their fellow Americans. They were incapable of making tough decisions. They were afraid of taking unpopular positions. They could not stand up to pressure.

They were not leaders.

You can learn from the poor examples they set, even if you're in a mid-level corporate position or just starting out. Approach every task with great energy. Try to appear confident, especially if you harbor secret doubts. Force yourself to make decisions and speak out on business-related issues. Stand fast in the face of any pressure you might face.

This advice may seem simple in theory, yet it can be extremely difficult to implement. Confronting one's fears is never easy, but an aspiring executive must develop the habits of leadership at a young age to prepare for his or her eventual opportunity. John Gardner, writing in *On Leadership*, recalled seeing a senior partner speak to the young attorneys in a law firm. The partner stressed the importance of winning a client's trust. An ambitious young lawyer, naturally enough, wanted to know the shortcut. How, he asked, could he gain someone's trust? What was the secret? The partner smiled. "Try being trustworthy," he replied.

The same here. How can you prepare for leadership? Try being a leader.

Trust, by the way, is a key part of the equation. People won't follow you unless they trust you. And they won't trust you unless they believe that you're a person of competence and integrity. Jimmy Carter and both George Bushes eventually failed the first test, Richard Nixon and Bill Clinton the latter. Their loss of trust was reflected in their deteriorating images, declining popularity scores, and in some cases, eviction from the White House.

The great presidential leaders were those who maintained the public's trust, and at the same time, inspired Americans to believe in themselves and their common destiny. Abraham Lincoln and Franklin Roosevelt both understood this to be their primary role, one they played with unsurpassed skill.

"With public sentiment, nothing can fail. Without it, nothing can succeed," Lincoln said with characteristic grace. Roosevelt, as was his style, made the same point in a more informal way. He admitted to speechwriter Samuel Rosenman that even the greatest leader can't get the people to go faster than they're willing to go. His job, he said, was to help them to realize their own potential and to coax them to keep moving. "It's a terrible thing," said FDR, "to look over your shoulder when you are trying to lead, and find no one there."

DON'T BECOME A DULL AND DREARY WORKAHOLIC

John Adams wasn't what you would call a fun guy. He possessed a fiery temper, for one thing. "It is a fact that he is often liable to paroxysms of anger which deprive him of self-command and produce very outrageous behavior," contended Alexander Hamilton, one of his great rivals. Even grandson Charles Francis Adams admitted that his grandfather's temper could be "extremely violent."

Then there was his intense thirst for accomplishment. John Adams was consumed by his own career and exceedingly ambitious for his family.

Nothing ever seemed good enough for him. He was elected the first vice president of the United States, but ridiculed it as "the most insignificant office that ever the invention of man contrived or his imagination conceived." He finally moved up to the presidency in 1797, yet complained that his inaugural guests were more intent on bidding farewell to George Washington than on congratulating him. He relentlessly pushed his son, John Quincy, to become president in his own right, admonishing the younger man that only his "own laziness and slovenliness" could keep him from winning the job.

But John Adams had a firmer grasp on reality than it seemed. He was a great believer in education and strenuous work, it's true, but he understood that both could be carried to extremes. Leisure activities were equally important to him.

Adams enjoyed ice skating, both for its athletic requirements and artistic qualities. "It is not simple velocity or agility that constitutes the perfection of it, but grace," he wrote. He also approved of horseback riding, fencing, and dancing. "Everything in life," he said, "should be done with reflection."

He passed this philosophy along to John Quincy, perhaps confusing his son by imploring him not to study too much at Harvard. "The smell of the midnight lamp is very unwholesome," the elder Adams wrote. "Never defraud yourself of sleep, nor your walk. You need not now be in a hurry."

That, of course, is a recurring theme in this book. You cannot build a career—or a life—in haste.

Do your absolute best to avoid becoming a dreary, boring workaholic. Cultivate hobbies and other leisure activities, and set aside enough time to pursue them. Outside interests will replenish your energy and contribute to a well-rounded personal base, both of which will benefit you at work. But this advice isn't primarily about your career. It's about your life, and the importance of enjoying it while you can.

Several presidents have understood the value of leisure, Thomas Jefferson foremost among them. His range of interests was tremendously broad, beginning with his enthusiasm for the natural sciences. "Not a sprig of grass shoots uninteresting to me," he wrote. He delved into everything from epistemology to the mechanical arts in his spare time. He invented such things as a dumbwaiter, a leather buggy top, and a swivel chair. He ran Monticello as a large working farm. He was an architect. He kept detailed records of the weather. Jefferson surely never knew a boring day.

James Garfield agreed that a life dedicated solely to politics could "fossilize" a person. His great love was literature. He read voraciously—novels, plays, biographies, it didn't matter what. Garfield's home in Ohio featured an enormous library that ran twenty-five by fourteen feet, yet was far too small for his collection. "You can go nowhere in the general's home without coming face to face with books," wrote a visitor. "They confront you in the hall when you enter, in the parlor and sitting room, in the dining room and even in the bathroom, where documents and speeches are corded up like firewood."

Other presidential passions have run the gamut from convivial (Warren Harding and poker) and briskly athletic (John Kennedy and touch football) to quietly competitive (Dwight Eisenhower and golf) and solitary (Franklin Roosevelt and stamp collecting). Each of these hobbies allowed a harried executive to slip away from his professional responsibilities for a few hours. Winston Churchill recalled watching FDR with his stamps "as he stuck them in, each in its proper place, and so forgot the cares of state."

But not every politician has pursued a balanced life. Grover Cleveland, an affable bachelor during his early adulthood in Buffalo, evolved into a presidential drudge. He toiled at least fourteen hours a day, often past midnight. "Well, I guess we'll quit and call it half a day," he would lamely joke to his secretary as they wrapped up another marathon. Cleveland's routine was easy to describe. The president "eats and works, eats and works, and works and eats," one journalist wrote.

Cleveland left office in 1897 badly in need of a rest, though not as fatigued as one of his predecessors, James Polk, whose austere view of life encompassed little more than work. "For four years, there would be no rest for James Knox Polk," wrote his biographer, John Seigenthaler. "He was an obsessed workaholic, a perfectionist, a micromanager, whose commitment to what he saw as his responsibility led him to virtually incarcerate himself in the White House for the full tenure of his presidency."

Polk would take a walk on occasion, perhaps even a horseback ride. But he figuratively chained himself to his desk the rest of the time. His presidency was considered successful, yet it exacted a terrible toll. Polk left the White House in March 1849 a shell of the man who had entered four years earlier. "He was spent, wan, and appeared much older than his fifty-three years," wrote Seigenthaler. The ex-president would be dead by June.

Polk's mistake was one that workaholics commonly make. He believed that if he lengthened his workday, he was certain to be more successful. Several modern presidents have operated under the same delusion.

Jimmy Carter has already been praised in this book for his ability to outwork his opponents. "I can get up at nine and be rested, or I can get up at six and be president," was his famous quote. Yet Carter overdid it. He continued working eighteen-hour days after reaching the White House, often plowing through 300 pages of reading in a single evening.

The president began to look haggard. His temper grew short. He aged rapidly, his hair turning snow white even though he was in his mid-fifties. "An even more important consideration is your own health and peace of mind," Carter's chief of staff, Hamilton Jordan, wrote him in a memo. "You badly need rest and the opportunity to rejuvenate. . . . You don't look good."

Bill Clinton would receive similar advice from his aides in 1993. Clinton's presidency began with high hopes that quickly dissipated in confusion. The new commander-in-chief seemed unable to concentrate. He tackled several major problems at once, but couldn't bring any to a successful conclusion. "I was watching from afar, and the harried man on television bore little resemblance to the confident, relaxed leader I had known," said David Gergen, soon to become a Clinton aide. "Coming to the White House early that summer, I concluded that he was almost too tired to think straight."

The remedy, it turned out, was sleep. Clinton went on summer vacation in Martha's Vineyard and suddenly hit his stride. He became a different man—rested, confident, and finally ready to do his job. "It is no coincidence," Gergen concluded, "that the weeks that followed were among the most productive of his presidency."

LEARN THE BLESSINGS OF PATIENCE

John Adams's letter to his college-age son still resonates from the previous section. "You need not now be in a hurry," he wrote. It's sage advice.

Patience is an attribute worth cultivating in politics or business. Your career, so the saying goes, is a marathon, not a sprint. You're certain to spend years and years cruising with the pack, looking for an opening to dart through and leave the competition behind. It's essential that you wait for the widest possible hole, the very best opportunity. Don't force the issue too quickly. Don't be in a hurry.

Two of the most successful men in American history, Abraham Lincoln and Dwight Eisenhower, counted patience among the greatest virtues. Both endured lengthy professional dry spells—Lincoln when he lost two Senate races in the 1850s, Eisenhower when he plodded through a series of uninspiring military assignments in the 1920s and 1930s. Their big breaks wouldn't come until the age of fifty-one, when each suddenly vaulted into national prominence—Lincoln as the Republican presidential nominee, Eisenhower as the commanding general of Allied forces in the European theater.

Both men learned the importance of remaining calm and collected, even when it seemed their chances for advancement were rapidly dwindling.

Eisenhower always counseled against acting in haste. "Make no mistakes in a hurry," he liked to say. Listeners were often surprised by his definition of leadership. They expected him to stress military attributes—boldness, courage, strength—but he insisted that quieter nouns had greater impact. "I'll tell you what leadership is," he once said. "It's persuasion, and conciliation, and education, and patience."

Lincoln would have agreed. He saw no need to rush, preferring to study a matter thoroughly before committing himself. His law partner, William Herndon, noted that Lincoln refused to express an opinion on any issue until he knew it "inside and outside, upside and downside." And Lincoln himself admitted to another friend: "I am slow to learn and slow to forget that which I have learned. My mind is like a piece of steel, very hard to scratch anything on it and almost impossible after you get it there to rub it out."

His gift for patience would serve Lincoln well. His political career—stagnant for nearly a decade—seemed reborn when Illinois Republicans chose him to run against Stephen Douglas, a true giant of the Senate, in the 1858 election.

Douglas considered him a formidable opponent. "I shall have my hands full," the senator said of Lincoln. "He is the strong man of his party—full of wit, facts, dates—and the best stump speaker, with his droll ways and dry jokes, in the West." But Douglas managed to win another term, and it seemed that Lincoln's best chance to become a national figure had passed him by.

That, however, wasn't the way he saw it. His loss to Douglas, Lincoln maintained, was "a slip and not a fall." He thought he still might have a chance to be president someday. Only time—and more hard work—would tell.

"A man watches his pear tree day after day, impatient for the ripening of the fruit," Lincoln liked to tell his friends. "Let him attempt to force the process, and he may spoil both fruit and tree. But let him patiently wait, and the ripe pear at length falls into his lap."

Lincoln kept the faith. The presidential pear dropped into his lap just two years after he lost that Senate race to Stephen Douglas.

IF YOUR FAMILY GIVES YOU A LEG UP, SAY THANKS

Americans have always had a fondness for self-made men and women. It's a feeling that can be traced back to the Revolutionary War, when two of the most celebrated founding fathers were go-getters who had blazed their own trails since adolescence.

Alexander Hamilton arrived in New York as a teenaged orphan from the West Indies. He was destined to be America's first secretary of the treasury, the father of the new nation's financial system. Benjamin Franklin straggled into Philadelphia at age seventeen. He found his fortune in a myriad of ways, as a printer, inventor, humorist, diplomat, and philosopher. Franklin achieved international fame during his lifetime and remained popular into the twenty-first century, becoming the featured attraction of a 2002 PBS documentary series. "He was a can-do person," exclaimed Catherine Allan, the show's executive producer. "I love that quality about him."

That's what we all love, isn't it? Franklin and Hamilton overcame imposing odds and truly made something of themselves. We're always much more impressed by a can-do guy who builds a successful company from nothing, like Bill Gates, than by a CEO who simply inherits his job, like Bill Ford.

But let's not go overboard. America is a democratic country, to be sure, and it's certainly possible for you or any American to climb the career ladder from the bottommost rung to the very top. It's much easier, though, if your family gives you a boost.

Franklin and Hamilton were exceptions in their day. Most of the Founding Fathers were "well-bred, well-fed, well-read, well-led, and well-wed," to use the felicitous phrase of historian James MacGregor Burns. George Washington had inherited Mount Vernon in his twenties. Thomas Jefferson had been born into a prosperous Virginia family. Several other signers of the

Declaration of Independence and the Constitution, though not as well-known today, were among the wealthiest heirs of their time.

And thus the pattern was established. The United States has never had a royal family, but family ties have always been extremely important. It's difficult to imagine John Quincy Adams reaching the White House in 1824 without the benefit of his presidential father's fame and name. The same with George W. Bush in 2000.

Such connections can remain strong for several generations. Twenty-three-year-old Theodore Roosevelt won his first political office, a seat in New York's state legislature, almost totally because of his father, an influential philanthropist. "Mr. Roosevelt has hereditary claims to the confidence and hopefulness of the voters of this city, for his father was in his day one of the most useful and public-spirited men in the community," claimed the *New York Post* in its endorsement of the young candidate.

Franklin Roosevelt was only distantly related to Teddy—they were fifth cousins—but he profited greatly from their common surname. It was the key factor when the Democratic Party tapped a still-obscure FDR as its vice-presidential nominee in 1920. Confused citizens would shout, "I voted for your father," at every campaign stop that fall. Another successful political career was under way.

The power of family brand names has been proven over and over again in recent decades, with the Kennedys as Exhibit A. John Kennedy used father Joseph's wealth and connections to win the presidency in 1960. Old Joe then insisted that John's thirty-five-year-old brother, Robert, be named attorney general. Advisers gingerly warned against such blatant nepotism, especially involving a man so young and inexperienced. "Nepotism, my foot," Joe snarled back. "Why should anybody think that Bobby needs a job?"

His orders were followed, though the president-elect would have avoided a formal announcement if possible. "Well, I think I'll open the front door of the house some morning about two A.M., look up and down the street," said John Kennedy, "and if there's no one there, I'll whisper, 'It's Bobby.'" The new attorney general also flashed a sense of humor when asked to explain his meteoric rise. "I worked hard, I was ambitious, I studied, I applied myself," he laughed, "and then my brother was elected president."

Now it was the youngest brother's turn. Joe decreed that Edward Kennedy should fill the Senate seat that John had just vacated. This command was even more improbable than Bobby's appointment. Teddy wouldn't turn thirty, the threshold age for the Senate, until 1962, and he had no record of public service in Massachusetts. The old man didn't care. "Whatever he wants," Joe said of Teddy, "I'm going to see he gets it." He supposedly added, "I spent a lot of money for that Senate seat. It belongs in the family."

The result, of course, was another Kennedy victory. "If your name was simply Edward Moore instead of Edward Moore Kennedy, your candidacy would be a joke," carped an opponent. But it didn't matter to voters bedazzled by the Kennedy name. Teddy was campaigning at a factory gate one morning when an old worker shuffled up. "My boy, I hear you've never done a day's work in your life," the laborer barked. Teddy searched for a suitably earnest reply, but the man cut him off. "Let me tell you something, lad," he said. "You haven't missed a thing."

So youthful Ted Kennedy became a member of the Senate, one of the most exclusive clubs in America. He and Bobby were firmly on track to run for president themselves one day, just as their big brother had.

It's not unusual for a young man or woman to join a family business or follow in a parent's line of work. Business executives beget executives, doctors beget doctors, and plumbers beget plumbers. Nor is it unusual for a parent to help a child get started in the adult world, offering a tip here, an introduction there.

The Roosevelt, Kennedy, and Bush children weren't embarrassed by the head starts they received. They capitalized. If you're lucky enough to be part of a family that has an influential name and rock-solid connections, follow their lead. Somebody, you can be sure, will be outraged by the "undemocratic" advantages you're receiving. Let them stew.

"It Made My Life"

The Kennedys weren't the only New England family to spawn an electoral dynasty. The Bushes followed in their footsteps— and eventually blazed a new trail of their own.

George H. W. Bush's father, a senator from Connecticut, eased his son's entrance into Republican politics. The younger Bush twice ran unsuccessfully for the Senate in Texas, his adopted state, then filled a series of appointed positions, which eventually led to the presidency in 1988.

Two members of the next generation, George W. and Jeb, won the governorships of Texas and Florida, respectively, in the 1990s. Rumors of another Bush presidential campaign began floating as early as 1997. Author Doug Wead asked George W. if he planned to carry the family standard in the national election three years hence.

"I'm not going to run," Bush answered.

"And why not?" Wead countered. "You're at the head of the pack."

"Because of the girls (twin daughters Barbara and Jenna). They would be in college then, and it would ruin their lives."

"Did it ruin your life?" Wead asked.

"No," Bush paused. "It made my life."

It made his career, too. A change of heart took George W. Bush to the White House, where he surrounded himself with his father's key advisers, even choosing his dad's secretary of defense, Richard Cheney, as his vice president.

Jim Hightower, once the agriculture commissioner of Texas, was known for his feisty personality and strong populist leanings, which made him the direct opposite of placid, conservative George H. W. Bush, his political contemporary. Hightower fought his way through the ranks, but higher offices like governor or senator always seemed beyond his reach. It irritated him that Bush's climb was so easy by comparison. "He's a man," Hightower moaned, "who was born on third base and thinks he hit a triple."

Perhaps he was correct, but it was clear which man had the brighter future, like it or not. Hightower was still swinging wildly at the plate, while Bush was already taking his lead off of third.

PERSONAL WEALTH CAN CERTAINLY COME IN HANDY

Michael Dukakis was far from a wealthy man. The governor of Massachusetts lived in a typical middle-class home in the Boston area. He often took the trolley to his office in the state capitol. No mansions or limousines for him.

But Dukakis knew how important money was to a political campaign. He assembled a high-powered machine in 1988, raising cash more quickly than any other contender for the Democratic presidential nomination. It made him very difficult to beat. "Whatever mistakes the Dukakis campaign made, they had the funds to recover from," marveled Richard Gephardt, one of his opponents. Dukakis locked up the Democratic race weeks before the convention.

Money, as we all know, makes life easier. It buys us independence. It allows us to survive errors that would destroy someone who lacks a cash reserve. It provides us opportunities that otherwise would never exist, as the story of the Forbes family demonstrates.

Malcolm Forbes was one of the true eccentrics of American publishing, renowned for his joyful, magnetic personality. He exulted in the wealth generated by the magazine that carries his family's name. Forbes loved to throw lavish parties. He collected fine art, yachts, and Harley-Davidson motorcycles. He bought a Boeing 727 and renamed it *The Capitalist Tool*.

Malcolm's lifelong celebration came to an abrupt end in 1990. Control of *Forbes* magazine passed upon his death to son Steve, who was a much different type of person. Steve was quiet, even shy. He was more interested in discussing public policy than pursuing a jet-set lifestyle.

It somehow crossed Steve's mind in the mid-1990s that he should get off the sidelines and enter politics. His decision stunned friends and casual observers alike. Forbes didn't have a political organization or allies. He was unknown by American voters. And his personality seemed ill-suited—to say the least—to life on the campaign trail.

Aides suggested that Forbes cut his teeth at the state level in New Jersey, running for governor or senator. But he waved them off. It was the presidency or nothing, and Steve had the money to make his fantasy come true. He sold some of his stock holdings, a chateau, and even an island in the South Pacific to underwrite races for the Republican nomination in 1996 and 2000.

Forbes, as predicted, was a horrible campaigner—awkward, devoid of humor, fixated on sleep-inducing topics like federal taxation policy. He was so stiff that filmmaker Michael Moore once asked a Forbes supporter on camera, "Is your candidate an alien?" It didn't matter. Steve Forbes had plenty of cash. He even managed to win a couple of primaries before his political career reached its inevitable demise.

If you're blessed with a personal fortune—regardless of whether it's self-made or inherited—you should rejoice. Don't be reticent about throwing your money around. Take advantage of your freedom the way Steve Forbes did. Purchase a company and install yourself as CEO. Donate to nonprofit organizations and raise your profile in the community. Bankroll candidates for public office and boost your political influence.

Money has been a powerful factor from George Washington's time to the present day. Washington's holdings, when converted to twenty-first-century dollars, would probably make him a billionaire today. The 2004 election pitted George W. Bush, one of the ten richest presidents of all time, against a contender who would have ranked third on that list if he had won, John Kerry.

"One thing is clear, the popular assumption that most of the presidents were of humble birth is wrong," concluded Edward Pessen in his 1984 book, *The Log Cabin Myth*. At least half of the presidents, in his estimation, belonged to the upper 3 percent of American society in terms of wealth and class origins. A dozen were probably in the top 1 percent.

Money tipped the career balance for several of these men. John Kennedy, for example, wouldn't have won the presidency without his family's millions. JFK faced a crucial primary election in West Virginia in May 1960. If he won, he would become the frontrunner for the Democratic nomination. If he lost to Hubert Humphrey, he might have to withdraw.

Kennedy pulled out all the stops. His team saturated West Virginia with radio and television advertising, assembled an extensive network of local organizers, and distributed "walking around" money to thousands of prospective voters. Humphrey knew he was licked. "I don't have any daddy who can pay the bills for me," he lamented. "I can't afford to run around this state with a little black bag and a checkbook." It was Humphrey who had to withdraw after a shattering defeat.

Kennedy was able to joke about the West Virginia mismatch. He got up at a fundraising dinner after the crucial primary, brandishing a telegram. It was from his father, he said. "Dear Jack," he read to the crowd. "Don't buy one more vote than necessary. I'll be damned if I'll pay for a landslide."

The audience roared with laughter. Old Joe, though, was definitely not amused.

ASSUME JOBS OF GREATER AND GREATER RESPONSIBILITY

Lyndon Johnson always kept his eyes on the ultimate prize. He arrived in Washington in 1931 to serve as an aide to a Texas congressman, another anonymous paper-shuffler in a town that was full of them. But his ambitions ran much higher, beginning with his own election to the House of Representatives in 1937 at the age of twenty-nine. "From the day he got here, he wanted to be president," recalled James Rowe, then a rising star in Franklin Roosevelt's administration.

LBJ, even with his titanic ego, knew that a presidential campaign lay decades in his future. There were dues to be paid, alliances to be formed, and a political ladder to be climbed in the meantime. "As soon as he got a job," remembered a college friend, "he thought, 'Now that I'm in this, how can I use this job for the next step?'"

That would remain Johnson's operating principle for the next quarter-century. He cultivated powerful Texas contractors and developed an unusually close relationship with President Roosevelt while still a junior member of the House. The former provided the funds he needed to run effective campaigns; the latter gave him instant political credibility. LBJ advanced to the Senate in 1948, still just forty years of age, and so charmed his new colleagues that they chose him in 1953 to be the Democratic floor leader. He was the youngest person ever to hold the post.

Johnson emerged as the dominant force in the Democratic Party as the 1950s rolled on, perhaps the nation's most powerful politician besides President Dwight Eisenhower. It was Johnson who set the agenda for Congress and determined his party's response to Ike's policies. His next step, it seemed, was to succeed Eisenhower as commander-in-chief.

John Kennedy had other ideas. He introduced LBJ to a Boston audience in 1959 with a mild joke: "Some people say our speaker might be president in 1960, but frankly, I don't see why he should take a demotion." A few political pundits suggested that Johnson could end up as Kennedy's running mate, though the Senate leader insisted that JFK was better suited for a subordinate role. "The vice presidency," Johnson scoffed, "is a good place for a young man who needs experience, a young man who needs training."

It was Johnson, of course, who accepted the Number Two job after Kennedy beat him for the Democratic presidential nomination. JFK supposedly said, "I didn't offer the vice presidency to him. I just held it out like this"—Kennedy moved his hands an inch or two from his body—"and he grabbed at it." Johnson's sudden eagerness proved to be fortunate in two ways. He hated being vice president, but the position put the final sheen on his career, completing his transformation from Texas neophyte to national leader. And it elevated him to the presidency when Kennedy was assassinated.

Lyndon Johnson's story is a classic tale of step-by-step career advancement—congressional aide, congressman, junior senator, Senate leader, vice president, president. It's precisely the course that experts recommend to aspiring business executives.

"The very best preparation for CEOs is progression through positions with responsibility for steadily larger and more complex profit-and-loss centers," wrote Ram Charan, a renowned business consultant and author. "A candidate might start by managing a single product, then a customer segment, then a country, then several product lines, then a business unit, and then a division."

Steady advancement of this sort, according to leadership guru John Gardner, not only develops a budding executive's abilities, but also widens his or her perspective. "Young people benefit by periodic shifts to tasks that pose new challenges, hone new skills, and broaden their experience," he wrote. "This is particularly important for young potential leaders who need exposure to many constituencies and must end up as generalists."

Your mission is to derive the most from each step along the way. Learn whatever you can, make as many professional acquaintances as possible, and always exceed your employer's expectations. If you make your boss look good, Dwight Eisenhower liked to say, your career is bound to keep moving. "My ambition in the army," he said, "was to make everybody I worked for regretful when I was ordered to other duty." Lyndon Johnson also understood the importance of keeping his superiors happy and his own ego in check. He was a dutiful vice president, beginning with the telegram he sent Kennedy after their showdown at the 1960 Democratic convention. "LBJ," he wrote, "now means Let's Back Jack."

This career plan—gradually assuming jobs of greater and greater responsibility—offers an additional benefit. It's flexible. No single path is guaranteed to take you to the chief executive's office. Several positions within your company may prove to be equally good as launching pads. Moving from job to job will give you the best chance to assess the possibilities.

Consider the parallel in the field of politics. Six positions have supplied most of the presidential nominees in American history (ignoring, for the moment, the thirty-two presidents who were renominated by their political parties). Here's the breakdown of major-party nominations in the fifty-five elections from 1789 through 2004:

- Governors, eighteen
- Senators, fifteen
- Military officers, thirteen
- Vice presidents, nine
- Cabinet members, eight
- Congressmen, five

What's striking is how competitive these standings are. Governors, senators, and military officers are tightly bunched, with vice presidents close behind. None of these positions has a clear advantage over the others when it comes to presidential advancement.

Three additional points are suggested by the numbers above:

1. It's no surprise that governors have fared so well. They've won eighteen nominations and nine presidential elections, leading all other positions in both categories. Four of the five presidents since 1976—Jimmy Carter,

Ronald Reagan, Bill Clinton, and George W. Bush—were governors before reaching the White House.

Governors, in effect, are mini-presidents. They make policy decisions, lay out budgets, and assume the ultimate responsibility at the state level—precisely what the president does on a national scale. "I don't mean to minimize or downgrade the importance of the presidency," Reagan once said. "But my biggest surprise was how quickly I got used to it. It had to do with being governor. Except for the foreign policy dimension, the jobs are really very similar. The governorships are a good training ground for the presidency. The buck stops there."

Governors are similar to the heads of small companies. They learn the ropes in an environment that can be demanding, yet isn't too large in scale. Several years of such intensive training prepares talented executives to jump to the big time. If your goal is a corporate presidency, you might want to follow their lead by starting with a smaller firm.

2. You would assume that a vice president—just a heartbeat away from the top job—would have a big advantage over outsiders like governors and military officers. But it hasn't worked that way. Just four sitting vice presidents have been directly elected to the presidency, with George H.W. Bush the only one since 1836.

Dozens of men, to their bitter disappointment, have found the vice presidency to be a dead end. John Nance Garner, who served under Franklin Roosevelt, said the job wasn't worth "a warm barrel of piss." Thomas Marshall, who was Woodrow Wilson's subordinate, vented his frustration in a tall tale. "Once upon a time, there was a farmer who had two sons," he said. "One of them ran away to sea. The other was elected vice president of the United States. Nothing was heard of either of them again."

If you're the second-in-command for your current or future employer, consider this a warning. It's tough to assert your personality or take credit for your successes as a vice president or an assistant manager, which in turn can make it very difficult to win the top job when it comes open.

Richard Nixon learned that the hard way in 1960. He claimed that his eight years as Dwight Eisenhower's vice president had given him broad experience as an executive, preparing him well for the presidency. Reporters wanted details. They asked Eisenhower to name a key decision that Nixon had been involved in. "If you give me a week," Ike replied, "I might think of one."

3. Senators and congressmen love to run for president, but their record has been nothing special. These classic insiders have received twenty nominations since 1789—fifteen for senators, five for congressmen. That's just slightly better than the eighteen won by governors, who operate far outside the Washington power structure.

The results in general elections have been considerably worse. Governors regularly win the presidency these days, as we've noted. But no president has been directly elected from the Senate since John Kennedy in 1960. Nor has there been a winner from the House since James Garfield in 1880.

Legislators, to be blunt, don't have any executive responsibilities. They give speeches and debate the merits of bills, but their ability to make decisions is rarely tested in a serious way. If you find yourself in a similar position in the business world—like chief of research, corporate spokesman, or executive adviser—you've been derailed from the fast track.

Jobs that involve talking don't lead to jobs that require action, as Roscoe Conkling noted more than a century ago. Conkling, a New York senator who himself ran for the White House in 1876, spoke contemptuously of the "hothouse air in the Senate which breeds candidates for the presidency, but makes them past bearing, and kills them off before they get their growth."

Bill Bradley was another senator who couldn't resist the temptation of a presidential campaign, even though he knew the two positions have little in common. "The job of legislator is different from the job of president," he said. "It's to find consensus, common ground, take positions that have smooth edges, that are not too bold. A legislator running for president often shows the smooth edges, not bold direction. In a country in need of leadership, that's not what people want."

ALWAYS KEEP YOUR BANDWAGON ON THE MOVE

People will latch onto anyone who appears to be on the way up. If you become the hot ticket in your company—by snagging the promotion everybody wanted, say, or by landing the biggest account of the year—you'll have no shortage of friends. Your bandwagon will be full.

This desire to be associated with a winner is wired into human nature. Why else would millions of fans support the New York Yankees? They're certainly not attracted by George Steinbrenner's charm and sparkling wit. The Yankees have won more World Series than any other team, and they always have more money to spend than any of their competitors. There used to be a joke, back when America was the world's industrial powerhouse, that rooting for the Yankees was like rooting for U.S. Steel. A bit boring, perhaps, but as close to a sure thing as you could get. Substitute Microsoft for U.S. Steel, and the sentiment still holds true today.

Ross Perot discovered exactly how much Americans love to be connected with winners. Perot, a somewhat eccentric businessman from Texas, ran for president in 1992, and his message of reform resonated with voters to a surprising degree. He even led the major-party nominees, George H.W. Bush and Bill Clinton, in the early polls, something that was unprecedented for a third-party candidate. But he slipped badly for several reasons, not the least being the repeated warnings issued by Bush and Clinton that Perot couldn't possibly win. It became, just as they hoped, a self-fulfilling prophecy. "Because if we know anything," Perot said later with the slightest touch of sarcasm, "the American people want to vote for a winner, right?"

Precisely. This bandwagon effect is evident in most aspects of life, but it attains its purest form in presidential politics. If you keep winning primary elections week after week, you will inevitably gather more and more supporters, raise more and more money, and lock up more and more delegate votes. That's the proven way to win a presidential nomination and, after that, the White House itself.

But it only works if you steer your bandwagon with a steady hand, which is not easily done.

Consider the cautionary tale of the elder George Bush, who surprised observers in 1980 by winning the Iowa caucuses, the first contest in the long race for the Republican nomination. Bush crowed that he now had "Big Mo"—his folksy nickname for momentum—firmly on his side. "There will be absolutely no stopping me," he declared. He was, in fact, quite easily stopped by Ronald Reagan in the very next contest, the New Hampshire primary. Bush had to settle for the consolation prize of being Reagan's vice president.

Bush didn't understand that a single victory does not give the winner "Big Mo" or any other kind of momentum. What it does bring are more publicity and increased scrutiny. The key is what the candidate does under the glare of this spotlight. If he projects an image of competence and self-assurance, if he continues to connect with the voters, he can keep rolling toward his goal. If he lacks a compelling message or if he flubs his public appearances—both of which were true of Bush in New Hampshire—his campaign will screech to a halt.

John McCain, who won the 2000 Republican primary in New Hampshire, had a better understanding of this phenomenon. That single victory, he said, gave him a megaphone, not a bandwagon. But McCain was unable to convert this knowledge into the desired result. He was soon pushed off the road by George W. Bush, who had learned a thing or two about "Big Mo" by watching his father.

The same principle holds in business. One big success will not necessarily lead to another. That glamorous promotion or lucrative account will win you new corporate friends, to be sure, but it doesn't guarantee that you'll continue to rise in the years to come. What it will do is increase your profile. More people will be watching. If you continue to develop your abilities and handle yourself well, they'll be impressed. If not, you'll be like Gary Hart, who won the 1984 Democratic primary in New Hampshire, then found he wasn't ready for the next step.

Hart burst from obscurity to ubiquity overnight. He could be seen everywhere—on the cover of newsmagazines, at the top of network newscasts. Pundits were sure he would win the nomination. But he couldn't control a campaign that, in his words, expanded rapidly from "a mom-and-pop" store before New Hampshire to "a national retail chain" afterward. Critics began carping that Hart was disorganized and lacked substance. He quickly lost momentum and careened to defeat at the Democratic convention.

And that's the dark side of the bandwagon effect. If you suffer a serious defeat, you're going down by yourself. You can be sure that your newfound friends and supporters will jump off the wagon as it accelerates downhill.

John Kennedy was never more popular than the day he took the oath of office, a vital, young president who declared himself ready to lead America into the space age. But he stood alone three months later, after dispatching a U.S.-backed invasion force of Cuban exiles to a bloody defeat at the Bay of Pigs. The military operation had been poorly conceived by everyone involved, he saw in retrospect, but he knew that only one person could shoulder the blame. And *he* was that person.

"Victory has a hundred fathers," Kennedy told his aides, "and defeat is an orphan." He had the math exactly right.

3

Polishing

The afternoon of April 12, 1945, was slipping toward evening. It had been an uneventful day for Vice President Harry Truman, who was thinking about heading home from the Capitol. But a telephone call from Eleanor Roosevelt changed his plans. She insisted upon seeing him as quickly as possible, though she didn't say why.

Truman suspected that the news wouldn't be good. The color drained from his face as he hung up the phone. "Jesus Christ and General Jackson," he muttered. He grabbed his hat, summoned his driver, and hustled toward his rendezvous with destiny.

The vice president arrived a few minutes later at the White House, where Mrs. Roosevelt informed him that her husband, Franklin, had died that afternoon at his Georgia retreat. Truman was now the president of the United States. He suddenly was burdened with new, frightening responsibilities, yet his first instinct was to express his condolences to the widow and inquire what he could do for her.

"Is there anything we can do for *you*?" Mrs. Roosevelt asked in reply. "For you are the one in trouble now."

She was right. Truman appeared to be colossally unprepared for the presidency. He didn't have a college degree, his political career had been masterminded by a shady Democratic boss in Missouri, and he had been the vice president for just twelve weeks. Roosevelt had told him virtually nothing about the inner workings of his administration. Truman had never even heard of the atomic bomb that was being assembled in New Mexico.

The new president's doubts surfaced the next day. "I don't know whether you fellows ever had a load of hay fall on you," he said to a group of reporters. "But when they told me what had happened, I felt like the moon, the stars, and all the planets had fallen on me." The rest of the world had similar feelings about the abrupt transition from Roosevelt, the amiable patrician, to Truman, the former haberdasher from Kansas City. "I must confess, sir, I held you in very low regard," Winston Churchill admitted years later. "I loathed your taking the place of Franklin Roosevelt."

It certainly didn't help that Truman lacked FDR's smooth grasp of the social graces. He often seemed so undignified, so *unpresidential*. Vice President Truman had planned to attend the 1945 Missouri state convention of the American Legion, and President Truman kept the date. He swapped stories with fellow legionnaires in the hotel lobby, soloed on the piano in the dining room, rooted for the winners at the horse track, and played hours of poker with the boys. "Mr. Truman did everything except have himself shot from the mouth of a cannon," groaned a *Washington Post* reporter.

Truman's popularity declined rapidly once World War II ended in September 1945. Most Americans considered him an accidental president who didn't have a clue how to lead the nation to postwar prosperity. It seemed a joke that he held the same office once occupied by Roosevelt. Voters turned control of Congress over to the Republicans in 1946, and were almost certain to do the same with the White House two years later. "I became quite used to being vilified," Truman later reflected. "It has its stimulating aspects and, for all I know, it may even be good for the liver."

A run-of-the-mill politician would have reacted to this disheartening state of affairs by desperately scrambling to change his image, seeking to become more statesmanlike, more Rooseveltian. Such a transformation rarely works, as Truman was aware, and he wasn't interested in trying. "He knew who he was, and liked who he was," wrote biographer David McCullough. "He liked being Harry Truman. He enjoyed being Harry Truman."

That worked to the president's favor in the long run. Truman wasn't Franklin Roosevelt, to be sure, but he did have his own distinctive style. He possessed the ability to express himself simply and emphatically. And he projected a clear, positive image—that of a feisty, independent Midwesterner unafraid of bucking the odds. He simply needed time for FDR's shadow to recede and his own qualities to be recognized.

Truman finally came into his own in 1948, even though early polls showed two leading Republicans, Thomas Dewey and Robert Taft, defeating him easily. "I will win this election and make these Republicans like it, don't you forget that," the president insisted. He repeatedly promised to "give 'em hell," and audiences began to respond in kind. A man listening to one of his speeches in Washington State yelled, "Pour it on, Harry!" He shot back, "I'm going to, I'm going to." Another man shouted, "What about throwing eggs at Taft?" Truman laughed in reply, "I wouldn't throw *fresh* eggs at Taft." Americans warmed to Truman's combative style, his sure sense of self. They rewarded him in November with an upset victory for the ages.

Today's historians categorize Truman as a near-great president, a testament to his decisive administrative style and superior skills as a campaigner. His example has inspired generations of presidential contenders, among them Paul Simon, an Illinois senator who was never in danger of being named one of Washington's best-dressed men. "To become fashionable, some people tell me to get rid of my bow tie and my horned-rimmed glasses, and most of all to change my views," Simon said in announcing his candidacy for the 1988 Democratic nomination. "Well, Harry Truman wore a bow tie and horned-rimmed glasses, and he didn't knuckle under to pressure."

And that was the key. So what if Give 'Em Hell Harry had created an image entirely different from Roosevelt's? His style connected with the voters in a positive way, helping him to win the highest position in his chosen field. *That* was what mattered.

Anyone seeking a starring role in business or politics must follow Truman's lead and begin developing an attractive persona at an early age. Brainpower and professional expertise are always useful, of course, but a comfortable manner and an appealing reputation are equally essential for any young person on the rise.

Why is style so important? Because emotional responses often dictate who wins and loses in competitive situations, as psychologists Robert Abelson and Donald Kinder discovered when studying the presidential races of 1980 and 1984. They found that voters tended to pay less attention to the issues than to the candidates' personalities. Abelson, far from condemning this focus on individual traits, described it as "a much more natural response than rational reflections on policy choices."

Voters considered Jimmy Carter to be vague and indecisive in 1980, while Ronald Reagan was seen as firm. Reagan's leadership rating in 1984 far outweighed Walter Mondale's higher scores for competence and empathy. The ability to inspire hope and pride among voters also worked in Reagan's favor. "If a candidate can make you feel good, or avoid making you feel bad," concluded Abelson, "the odds are he'll win."

Your chances of winning the next promotion at work—and eventually reaching the top of the career ladder—clearly depend on how well you polish your people skills and your image. You must communicate effectively in any setting, whether it's an intimate conversation or a speech to a large group. And you need to craft an effective message and a strong, attractive image. This chapter addresses each of these requirements:

Communicating

- Break out of your shell, but don't go too far.
- A good (or bad) speech makes a lasting impression.
- Invigorate your career with a touch of stagecraft.
- Reach people through their funny bones.

Spreading the word

- Don't be shy about blowing your own horn.
- Write for publication, or have someone do it for you.

Establishing an image

* Looks do matter, so spiff up your appearance.
* Establish a positive reputation, and keep it.
* If you want to be a leader, you must exude strength.

The importance of an appealing, well-defined personal style was dramatized by two men who lacked that valuable quality, the very same Republican candidates who had seemed so formidable at the dawn of 1948.

Robert Taft was undeniably intelligent. He graduated first in his class at Yale and repeated that feat at Harvard Law School. A teacher said that he "stored facts in his mind as if it were a filing cabinet." The presidency didn't intimidate him in the least.

But Taft was extremely limited in other ways. He was a cold and impatient man. If another senator—even a fellow Republican—dared to disagree with him, he would instantly snap, "Why, that's nonsense!" A Wisconsin politician once thanked Taft for sending a congratulatory telegram. "Oh, that," the senator scoffed. "Never saw that wire myself, you know. My staff sends those things out by the dozen."

Thomas Dewey was more relaxed than Taft in private, but suppressed any spontaneous impulse in public, coming across as prim, proper, and very dull. Theodore Roosevelt's daughter, the acerbic Alice Roosevelt Longworth, famously asked about Dewey, "How can you vote for a man who looks like a bridegroom on a wedding cake?" But no amount of ridicule could push Dewey to loosen his self-imposed restraints. He defeated Taft for the Republican nomination in 1948, then played it safe during the fall campaign, refusing to respond to any of Truman's attacks. "I will not get down into the gutter with that fellow," he sniffed.

Dewey's election to the White House was generally treated as a foregone conclusion, though author John Gunther admitted to a few doubts. He had warned a year earlier that Dewey's lack of warmth might derail his career. "Many people do not like him," Gunther wrote. "He is, unfortunately, one of the least seductive personalities in public life." This observation was punctuated by Truman's astounding triumph.

Tom Dewey had anticipated a busy post-election period. There would be a legislative program to prepare, a White House staff to recruit, a cabinet to fill. But he found himself, instead, with time on his hands. Life was so unhurried that he spent one lazy evening pitching pennies with his sons. Dewey's wife, always conscious of her husband's image, suggested that he stop before any photographers saw him, but Dewey ruefully shook his head. "Maybe if I had done this during the campaign," he sighed, "I would have won."

BREAK OUT OF YOUR SHELL, BUT DON'T GO TOO FAR

Success is not for the shy.

George McGovern learned this unhappy fact as a quiet, timid boy in Mitchell, South Dakota. His childhood, he later wrote, was marked by "painful bashfulness." Speaking to adults was often difficult for him. Getting up in front of a large group was unthinkable.

This intense shyness created an inner conflict for McGovern, who believed he had the talent to accomplish big things, perhaps as a professor, maybe even as a politician. Both of those occupations, though, required constant interaction with other people, and young George wasn't sure he could muster the courage to fulfill his potential.

Ambition eventually won out. "My friends," the adult McGovern would joke, "say I'm the most soft-spoken egomaniac they know." That ego pushed him to tackle challenges of increasing difficulty. He joined the high-school debate team, moved up to college, enlisted as a bomber pilot during World War II, went back to earn his Ph.D. in history, became a professor, and started working as an organizer for the South Dakota Democratic Party. His shyness melted away in the process.

McGovern said he learned "the enormous value—not only in politics, but in diplomacy, in anything—of personal contact. By getting out and meeting people face to face, just by working hard at it, you could overcome a lot of disadvantages." He began considering a career in politics, not as a behind-the-scenes organizer, but as a candidate himself. It was a shift that propelled him to three terms in the Senate and the 1972 Democratic presidential nomination.

But not everybody is as determined as McGovern was. Tony Filson, the president of a New York City recruitment firm, said he knew dozens of talented executives whose careers had been damaged by shyness. These men and women were unable to make formal presentations to professional organizations or to chat casually with corporate officers—and they paid the price. "It can be hard for the shy," Filson said, "because they can't be forceful and obnoxious enough to get to the front of the line."

Overcoming shyness may not be easy, but it's clearly essential for anyone who dreams of succeeding in businesses. A variety of remedies are available. You can join a group, such as Toastmasters, that teaches members how to communicate with any type of audience, large or small. You can seek professional help from counselors, therapy programs, and support groups. Or you can decide to confront your fears on your own, as George McGovern did.

It's surprising how many presidents have been afflicted with social anxiety disorder, the clinical name for shyness. James Polk was an extreme introvert, but he wanted a political life above all else, so he forced himself to mingle and develop other social skills. He worked mightily to improve his memory. "I don't think I was ever introduced to a man and talked with him ten minutes, that I ever afterwards forgot him," he boasted. Polk grew to be an effective public speaker, though never a fiery one. His election to the presidency in 1844 was a tribute to his intense willpower.

Woodrow Wilson, Calvin Coolidge, and Richard Nixon were other men who reached the White House despite an inclination toward shyness. Coolidge's story was especially heartrending. "When I was a little fellow, as long ago as I can remember, I would go into a panic if I heard strange voices in the kitchen," he recalled. "I felt I just couldn't meet the people and shake hands with them.... I was almost ten before I realized I couldn't go on that way. And by fighting hard, I used to go through that door. I'm all right with old friends, but every time I meet a stranger, I've got to go through the old kitchen door—and it's not easy."

Coolidge never grew comfortable with the rituals of politics, but he learned to play the game well enough. He even managed to become a folk hero of sorts. Comedians nicknamed him "Silent Cal." Stories about his reticence abounded, like the one involving a woman who bet her husband she could entice Coolidge to say more than two words at a White House luncheon. She confided her wager to the president after they were seated. "You lose," he replied.

If you're a rising executive, you must defeat or at least suppress your shyness, as Coolidge did. But his success proves it isn't necessary to cross to the other extreme and become an uninhibited chatterbox. An extrovert, in fact, can have just as much difficulty as an introvert when it comes to snagging a promotion. Showboating can kill a career as effectively as silence.

James Blaine slowly learned this lesson during the latter half of the nineteenth century. Blaine was blessed with an outgoing nature and a flair for the dramatic. His expansive personality was so attractive that he was nicknamed the "Magnetic Man." An acquaintance once said, "I defy anyone, Republican or Democrat, to be in his company half an hour and go away from him anything less than a personal friend."

Blaine's problem was that he never left the stage; he always seemed to be performing. He was constantly in the public eye as speaker of the House of Representatives, senator, and secretary of state under three presidents. The White House was his perpetual goal. "When I want a thing," he admitted, "I want it dreadfully." He ran in every presidential election between 1876 and 1892—mounting five serious challenges in all, tying the record held by Henry Clay. He was at the center of every national campaign, debate, and dispute for nearly three decades.

Blaine was a colorful exception to a drab political era. Yet he remained outside the White House gates as Americans elected a series of bland presidents—men like Rutherford Hayes, Grover Cleveland, and Benjamin Harrison. They somehow seemed sturdier and more dependable than Blaine, who was developing a reputation for being too eager and way too glib. One critic contended that he had become precisely the sort of politician who would promise to "paint the moon pink, and the first cloudy night, he would take the voter out of doors and say, 'There, can't you see that I have done the job?'"

Blaine's final presidential campaign in 1892 was a pitiful affair. Almost everyone knew it was hopeless, yet he seemed unable to stay out of the spotlight. A Wisconsin congressman was shocked at his appearance: "His countenance is that of a man standing in the shadow of death, the face ... flabby and wrinkled, is the face of a broken-down old man." The Republicans nominated the stolid Harrison instead. Blaine died the following year.

> ## "People Tire of Seeing the Same Name"
>
> It's always wise to show a little restraint and maintain a bit of mystery. Franklin Roosevelt never lost sight of this rule during his twelve years as president. FDR was one of the greatest communicators in American history, partly because he chose his opportunities so wisely. "The one thing I dread," he confessed, "is that my talks should be so frequent as to lose their effectiveness."
>
> Roosevelt is justly famous for his fireside chats, in which he casually unraveled complicated issues for a national radio audience. The common impression today is that he gave hundreds of these talks, certainly at least one per month. But he was too smart for that. His actual count was less than three fireside chats per year. "People tire of seeing the same name day after day in the important headlines of the papers, and the same voice night after night over the radio," Roosevelt explained. "Individual psychology cannot, because of human weakness, be attuned for long periods of time to constant repetition of the highest note in the scale."

A GOOD (OR BAD) SPEECH MAKES A LASTING IMPRESSION

Ours may be a high-tech age, but today's politicians still place great stock in the low-tech art of public speaking. Their reverence for the podium borders on the mystical, as Bill Carrick, a consultant to Democratic candidates, noted in 2004. "Politicians," he said, "always put a greater importance on what they say in speeches than in their ads."

And why not? Speeches have been making or breaking careers since the beginning of American history. Consider these five snapshots:

The early years: Several presidential contenders earned widespread acclaim prior to the Civil War for their speaking skills, an honor not easily won in a rural nation before the invention of broadcasting. Henry Clay had a style that was remarkably intimate and effective. Historian George Bancroft wrote that Clay's voice "was music itself, and yet penetrating and far-reaching, enchanting the listener." Daniel Webster, on the other hand, was the great classical orator of the period, employing grand words and broad gestures. Webster saved his own admiration for Rufus King, who carried the presidential banner of the Federalist Party in 1816. "You never heard such a speaker," Webster marveled. "In strength and dignity and gesture as well as in matter, he is unequaled."

Abraham Lincoln: Lincoln probably couldn't have been elected president without the speech he delivered at New York City's Cooper Union in February 1860. It was passionate at times—"let us have faith that right makes might"—and eloquent throughout. Many in the audience had been drawn by curiosity, expecting to see a backwoodsman at the podium. They were stunned by Lincoln's grace and powers of persuasion. "No man ever before made such an impression on his first appeal to a New York audience," raved the *New York Tribune* the next day. The Cooper Union speech was reprinted throughout the country, elevating Lincoln to celebrity status, an unexpected dividend from an engagement that earned him only two hundred dollars. "I (wish) that it were $200,000," wrote one of the event's sponsors, "for you are worthy of it."

William Jennings Bryan: The Bryan who arrived at the 1896 Democratic convention was a young has-been, a thirty-six-year-old ex-congressman. The one who departed was the party's presidential nominee. This amazing transformation was the result of his "Cross of Gold" speech, a blazing attack on the gold standard that galvanized the twenty thousand people in the convention hall. "They believed that Bryan was a young David with his sling, who had come to slay the giants that oppressed the people, and they felt that a new day had come and, with it, a new leader," wrote Josephus Daniels, a future cabinet secretary who was in the crowd that day. Awestruck delegates stampeded to Bryan when it came time to choose a nominee, though many soon wondered if there was any substance behind his powerful words. "I have been thinking over Bryan's speech," John Peter Altgeld, the governor of Illinois, admitted to a friend. "What did he say, anyhow?"

Ronald Reagan: Reagan spent his adult life in front of an audience. He was a broadcaster before Warner Brothers snapped him up in 1937. He appeared in more than fifty films and TV series, supplementing his income on the lecture circuit as a conservative spokesman. It was a 1964 fundraising speech for Barry Goldwater, in fact, that convinced Republican leaders of Reagan's political abilities, paving the way for his election as governor of California two years later. A performance of similar virtuosity won him the White House in 1980. Polls showed a tight race between Reagan and President Jimmy Carter, but Reagan broke it open with two memorable lines in their televised debate. He chuckled, "There you go again," when Carter attacked him, those four short words planting the impression that the president was a loose cannon. And he closed with a piercing question: "Are *you* better off than you were four years ago?" Voters answered in Reagan's favor on election day.

Bill Clinton: Clinton experienced both failure and success as a public speaker. His nominating speech for Michael Dukakis at the 1988 Democratic convention was a disaster—long, boring, and full of platitudes. The audience watched in horrified silence, stirring only when Clinton said, "In closing...." Then it broke out in mock applause. Johnny Carson drew raucous laughter when he began his next *Tonight Show* monologue with the same two words. Clinton was a national laughingstock. "It was the worst hour of my life. No, make that hour and a half," he later joked. But a 1991 speech to a group of Democratic Party state chairmen did much to resuscitate his career. Clinton blended policy recommendations with a stirring call for America to reclaim its greatness, outshining the other party leaders on the dais. "He was aggressive and confident, but not cocky," said Wisconsin's Democratic chairman. "(He was) all the things you'd want in a candidate for president."

Those also are the qualities that any corporation would desire in a CEO, which is why public-speaking skills carry the same importance in business as in politics. A rising executive needs the ability to convey competence and confidence to the board of directors or a group of employees, just as a candidate must be able to connect with the voters.

But that's easier said than done, isn't it? If the very thought of getting up in front of an audience sends shivers down your spine, you're not alone. A 2001 Gallup Poll asked Americans to identify the things they feared. These were the top five:

- Snakes, 51 percent
- Public speaking, 40 percent
- Heights, 36 percent
- Being closed in small spaces, 34 percent
- Spiders and insects, 27 percent

The happy news is that your corporate position is unlikely to require you to handle snakes. (You'll probably meet a few along the way, but that's another chapter.) The not-so-happy news is that you have no choice but to confront your Number Two fear, public speaking.

The stakes are simply too high. Why remain mute at a committee meeting when you could preside over it? Why merely attend an industry convention when you could deliver an address at it? Speaking to an audience of your peers will stamp you as someone to be reckoned with, an expert, a leader. It will make you stand out from the crowd. Think of all the contacts—not to mention all the job offers—that increased visibility could bring.

The key is to begin gathering experience as soon as you can. If you're still in school, sign up for a public-speaking course. If you're older, join a community organization that provides opportunities to speak to small groups. It may not be pleasant at first, and you may not be very good. But you'll improve with repetition.

Bruce Babbitt, the former governor of Arizona, had problems at the podium, too. His wife always laughed about his first race for state attorney general, remembering him as "a tall, skinny ectomorph without any public-speaking ability." Babbitt somehow won that election in 1974 and eventually saw the need to polish his act. He kept giving speeches on a regular basis, working in the meantime with teachers and consultants to put some zip into his delivery. "If they can teach Mr. Ed to talk," he laughed, "they can teach me." They eventually succeeded in bringing out the folksy humor that distinguished Babbitt's campaign for the Democratic presidential nomination in 1988. "I think I came from hopeless to passable," he said of his speaking style, "and that's a small victory."

It's essential that you view every speaking engagement as an opportunity to seize an audience's attention and advance your career. Prepare thoroughly for each one, whether it's an hour-long address or a two-minute introduction. Outline your remarks carefully, and make sure that you offer new and useful information to your listeners. Don't waste their time with platitudes. Meaningless phrases and bureaucratic lingo won't impress anyone.

Richard Nixon had a useful rule of thumb for measuring a speech's effectiveness. The finished text, he said, should contain three cogent, memorable lines that reporters would find irresistibly quotable. These sentences would summarize the points that Nixon wanted to make and drive them home in a colorful way. Each had to be a line "that not only snaps, but advances the story," recalled David Gergen, a young presidential speechwriter at the time. If a speech didn't have three of them, Nixon thought, it would be a failure.

Polishing your text, of course, is only half the battle. Practicing is equally important. Deliver your speech again and again—to your mirror, your spouse, anyone who will listen. Franklin Roosevelt may have been one of the greatest orators in American history, but he never skimped on rehearsal. He typically spent four or five days preparing each fireside chat, drilling tirelessly until he felt he had mastered his material.

You're unlikely to match Roosevelt's skill in front of a massive audience—few men or women ever have—but there's no reason why you can't become an effective speaker at meetings and conventions. The benefits can be great. "Of all the talents bestowed upon men, none is so precious as the gift of oratory," said one of FDR's contemporaries, Winston Churchill. "He who enjoys it wields a power more durable than that of a great king. He is an independent force in the world."

And who knows? If you keep getting up in front of crowds, you might even come to like it. Adlai Stevenson, a two-time Democratic presidential nominee in the 1950s, was engaged in conversation one day with a young woman who was describing her first speech. It had gone well, the audience had risen to applaud, and she had been thrilled.

Stevenson, himself a renowned public speaker, listened to her eagerly. He sensed an instant kinship. "You've felt it, too, then, haven't you?" he replied with a broad grin. "You know how it is."

INVIGORATE YOUR CAREER WITH A TOUCH OF STAGECRAFT

Franklin Roosevelt and Orson Welles were household figures in the early 1940s. Roosevelt was one of the most controversial presidents of all time, either hailed as the conqueror of the Depression or reviled as the destroyer of capitalism. Welles had rocketed to fame as the youthful auteur of the film *Citizen Kane* and provocateur of *War of the Worlds*, the radio play that frightened and thrilled Americans the night before Halloween in 1938.

They met on at least one occasion. Roosevelt broke the ice by suggesting that he and his guest had something in common besides their success, which caused Welles to wonder aloud what their shared quality might be. It was obvious, the president replied. The two of them, he laughed, were the finest actors in America.

He may have been right. The Roosevelt presidency was distinguished by its strong element of stagecraft. FDR could be disarming and congenial, as when he delivered one of his legendary fireside chats on radio. Or he could unleash an intense, confrontational side, as when he attacked rich Republicans as "economic royalists" and declared that he welcomed their hatred. Perhaps his greatest acting performance occurred on his very first day in the White House, when he pledged his undying confidence—"the only thing we have to fear is fear itself"—in a nation that had plummeted to its lowest point in seventy years.

Any corporate leader must be able to put a positive spin on his company's latest quarterly report, especially if the bottom line is bathed in red ink. And he or she must exude the necessary confidence to inspire the troops, even if layoff rumors are in the wind. "Being a politician is something like being an actor," mused Henry Cabot Lodge Jr., the 1960 Republican vice-presidential nominee. He could have said the same about any executive position.

A few people, Franklin Roosevelt among them, are blessed with natural acting ability. They can shift personas with ease—friendly one moment, gruff the next. But most of us lack that gift. If you're among this majority, you would be wise to polish your thespian skills. Think about auditing a drama course at a nearby college, signing up for an improvisation workshop, or even getting involved with your local theater company.

You may consider this to be absurd advice for a budding executive. Well, think again. Consider what happened to a onetime radio announcer who detoured into drama. "There have been times when I've wondered in this office how you could do this job if you hadn't been an actor," laughed the old radio man, Ronald Reagan, as his presidency reached its final days.

Some leaders lack Reagan's understanding of the value of stagecraft. Jimmy Carter made it plain that any form of acting was beneath him, and refused to indulge in it.

Carter was scheduled one day to announce the elimination of thousands of pages of regulations, a key step toward fulfilling his promise to streamline the federal government. Staffers wanted to punch up the announcement, so they assembled a huge stack of paper. Maybe the president could throw it in the garbage, they suggested. Or he could sweep it off the table, with pages fluttering all over the room. It would look great on the evening news.

Here's what Carter chose to say: "This is a prop prepared by my staff. It's supposed to represent the thousands of pages of regulations. Actually, it's just a pile of blank sheets of paper." He let it sit there. The press, unsurprisingly, didn't devote much attention to his important announcement.

There are limits, of course. Acting ability may help you sell almost anything in the short term, but it wears thin in the long run unless it's backed by solid belief. Roosevelt *believed* he could turn the economy around and, later, that he could defeat the Nazis. Reagan *believed* he could effect a conservative revolution. They combined showmanship and core values to become two of the most successful presidents of the twentieth century.

If you don't believe, no amount of dramatic ability can propel you to your ultimate goal, as demonstrated by General Douglas MacArthur's story. MacArthur was not content with his chestful of military honors. He desperately wanted to be president, not to implement any particular philosophy, but simply to possess America's highest office.

MacArthur's acting skills were never in doubt. Everything about him was flamboyant—the signature sunglasses, the corncob pipe, the bold exclamations ("I shall return"), the supreme confidence that crossed the line into arrogance. One of his longtime aides scoffed, "I studied dramatics under him for five years in Washington and four years in the Philippines." But the voters wanted more than drama. They never took the general seriously as a presidential contender.

It turned out that MacArthur's aide, a fellow by the name of Dwight Eisenhower, also knew a thing or two about acting, as he later proved in World War II. But Ike's humility wore better with the American people. Both political parties began pushing him to enter the presidential race in 1948. Eisenhower was sincerely hesitant (and indeed, would not run until 1952). He confessed his ambivalence during a private meeting with his old boss.

MacArthur merely nodded. "That's the way to play it, Ike," he replied approvingly.

REACH PEOPLE THROUGH THEIR FUNNY BONES

The first few months of 1976 were painful for Morris Udall. The Arizona congressman lost a series of primary elections to Jimmy Carter, several by agonizingly close margins. His defeats piled up week after week after week. Carter established himself as the frontrunner for the Democratic presidential nomination, while the frustrated Udall received nothing for his efforts except a new nickname. Reporters started calling him "Second Place Mo."

The Wisconsin primary in early April promised to be different. Udall entered it with high hopes. He believed he could pick up some badly needed momentum by beating Carter in Wisconsin, and the early returns on election night confirmed his expectations. NBC soon projected him the winner, as did ABC.

Udall finally had a chance to enjoy one of the happy rituals of politics. He went down to the ballroom of his headquarters hotel to declare victory and bask in the cheers of his supporters. "It looks like we are winners tonight," he crowed. "How good it is."

It didn't bother Udall that the other major network, CBS, had not yet projected a winner in Wisconsin, or that officials in hundreds of small towns and villages kept tabulating votes as he and his fans celebrated past midnight. All that mattered was that he had won at last. He had derailed Jimmy Carter's express train to the nomination.

Except that he hadn't. Carter inched ahead during the predawn hours and eventually won by a single percentage point. Udall awoke to the awful reality that he had finished second yet again, an embarrassing second in light of his revelry the previous night.

An aide gingerly suggested that he speak to the press. The reporters filed in, wondering if Udall might claim a moral victory in Wisconsin or simply erupt with a burst of anger. He did neither. "You may amend my statement of last night," he simply told them with a smile. "Insert the word 'losers' where I had 'winners.'"

It was classic Mo Udall. His legislative and political skills were highly respected in Washington, but his sense of humor was perhaps more famous. "Let's turn inflation over to the post office. That'll slow it down," he once suggested in a congressional debate. His 1969 campaign to become majority leader of the House of Representatives ended in failure, yet he couldn't resist a laugh at his own expense. He marked that defeat by turning his "MO" button upside down. It read "OW."

Udall never got back on track in 1976 after his Wisconsin debacle, a failure he noted in the title of his autobiography, *Too Funny to Be President*. But he always contended that humor was essential in his line of work. "Politics is a people business—and people crave laughter," he wrote. "Other things being equal, a droll politician will have an easier time than a dour one getting elected. Wit is an essential element of charisma, of leadership." There is plenty of evidence to support his point. John Kennedy and Ronald Reagan, both blessed with sparkling wit, remain popular to this day. Richard Nixon and Jimmy Carter, both deficient in the comedy department, saw their bases crumble during their final years in the White House.

Humor is just as valuable in business as in politics, in the opinion of Jeffrey Gitomer, an author, syndicated columnist, and sales consultant. If you get a customer to laugh, Gitomer maintained, your chances of completing a deal will skyrocket. A light touch can enliven the mundane aspects of your job, turning a dreary PowerPoint presentation into an effective sales tool. "Count the laughs," Gitomer advised. "Your goal is at least one laugh for every five slides. If there's at least one laugh every five slides, you can count on one other thing: money."

So get out there and tickle people's funny bones. But keep it light. Stay away from sarcasm, which doesn't sell well at all. A sarcastic streak, in fact, may have prevented Thomas Reed from becoming president in the late nineteenth century. Reed was an imposing man—six-foot-three and almost three hundred pounds—who rose to become Speaker of the House. His barbed wit was both his distinctive characteristic and his greatest weakness.

Reed once congratulated Theodore Roosevelt on his "original discovery of the Ten Commandments." He ridiculed a colleague who protested that he would rather be right than be president. "The gentleman need not be disturbed," Reed snapped back. "He will never be either." Reed very much wanted to be president himself in the 1890s, but most of his fellow

Republicans so feared him that they desperately sought alternatives. "They might do worse," he concluded, "and I think they will." The kindly William McKinley defeated Reed for the 1896 nomination.

It's obviously a good career move to ditch the Don Rickles act, which shouldn't be difficult to do. But what if you have a bigger problem? What if you're simply not a funny person?

The good news is that comedy is like any other form of public speaking. If you work at it, you will improve. "Just remember that there are few 'natural' comedians," wrote Udall. "Being funny isn't some mysterious, arcane black art like, say, defrosting a turkey in a microwave. Being humorous is a *skill*, which you can learn and develop through practice."

Udall was blessed with natural wit, yet he never stopped honing his act. He collected jokes during his travels, jotting the ones he liked in large notebooks that were carefully divided by subject headings: Aging and Death, Lawyers, Vices (Including Drinking), and so on. He cheerfully blended this new material into his speeches. "The first two times you use a joke, give your source credit," he recommended. "From then on, to hell with it! Be shameless—claim it as your own. After all, your source undoubtedly stole it from someone else."

"Oh, Excuse Me, Jerry"

The effective use of humor requires practice. If you're not comedically gifted, you should practice a lot.

Henry "Scoop" Jackson, to his misfortune, decided to ignore this rule. It would be inaccurate to describe Jackson as a dull speaker. He was worse than that. *Newsweek* insisted that his oratorical monotone "would put a No-Doz addict to sleep." Yet he somehow developed into a formidable politician, running high-profile campaigns for the Democratic presidential nomination in 1972 and again four years later.

Jackson decided in 1976 to spice up his standard speech with topical humor. His writers suggested that he have some fun with the pardon that Gerald Ford had granted to Richard Nixon after the latter's resignation. They wrote a joke about Nixon coming back to the Oval Office, where he tripped and fell into the new president. "Oh, pardon me, Jerry," Nixon said. Ford replied, "I already did, Dick."

Not exactly belly-laugh material, but pretty good for Scoop Jackson. The only problem was that he never worked on his delivery. He decided to wing it, changing the joke just a bit as he told it. The penultimate line—Nixon's apology—came out as, "Oh, excuse me, Jerry."

Poor Scoop could never figure out why nobody laughed.

DON'T BE SHY ABOUT BLOWING YOUR OWN HORN

It's nice to be a skillful speaker, equally adept at tugging your audience's heartstrings or tickling its fancy. But it's even nicer if you actually have something to say. A communicator, after all, is truly effective only when he or she has a message to convey.

And what's your message? That's simple. It's *you*.

Our culture frowns on singing your own praises. The whole process seems grubby, egocentric, and immodest. But self-promotion is essential if you have big plans for your future. That's because corporate America, in all honesty, does a lousy job of identifying the CEOs of tomorrow.

Ram Charan, the business consultant and author, has translated this problem into numbers. He created a hypothetical corporation with annual revenues of twenty-five billion dollars and a workforce of seventy thousand. Such a firm, he estimated, might count three thousand potential leaders among its employees. Fifty to a hundred would qualify for jobs just below the top level, while anywhere from two to five might be CEO material.

But which five? That question, in Charan's opinion, is one that most companies can't answer. "Recognizing which five saplings in a 3,000-tree forest are the ones to nurture," he wrote, "requires a degree of discernment that most line managers and HR departments lack and few are developing."

It doesn't help that corporations are thinning their ranks of middle managers, removing the very people who had been ideally positioned to recognize rising stars. "With spans of control increasing from five or six (employees) to twenty or thirty, the odds of a supervisor having enough contact with you to actually know your accomplishments are low," concluded Jeffrey Pfeffer, a professor of organizational behavior at Stanford University's Graduate School of Business.

Politicians have long faced the same problem. There are more than half a million elected officials at the local, state, and national levels in the United States, but fewer than one-tenth of 1 percent reach the top echelon, which consists of a hundred senators, fifty governors, and the president. Those who attain this rarefied level must make the climb on their own. Neither political party does anything to identify, guide, or develop the prospective senators, governors, and presidents of the coming generation.

It's an unfortunate fact that quiet, modest individuals have little hope of rising very far in business or politics. If you wish to be a candidate for a leadership position, you must actively seek recognition, like it or not.

John L. Lewis, a crusty union boss during the decades surrounding World War II, liked to rephrase this rule in quasi-classical terms. "He that tooteth not his own horn," Lewis declared, "the same shall not be tooted." Mario Cuomo, a three-term governor of New York in the 1980s and 1990s, expressed the same sentiment in clearer English. "In this business," he said, "if you don't blow your own horn, there's no music."

But which tune should you play? Modern society rewards self-promotion only if it's seasoned with taste, flair, and restraint. Obnoxious bragging and blatant boasting may draw attention in the short term, but they'll reap nothing but scorn in the long run. Your mission is to define yourself for others in a positive, appealing way.

This is an eternal challenge. Benjamin Franklin, who achieved success in both the private and public sectors, proved to be a whiz at marketing his own talents. Franklin was just twenty-three when he took over the *Pennsylvania Gazette* in 1729. The survival of his newspaper—and, indeed, the course of his career—depended on attracting the support of Philadelphia's elite.

Franklin raised his profile with a couple of ingenious gimmicks. He began making a public show of purchasing newsprint for the next day's *Gazette*. Franklin could have had his supply delivered quietly, but he opted to pick it up himself each evening, pushing it back through the busy city streets in a wheelbarrow. He became known as an industrious young man who was willing to tackle any chore to get ahead. This image was cemented by his second ploy—publishing phony letters to the editor that always praised the *Gazette* for its trustworthiness and Franklin himself for charitably declining to expose "the continual blunders" of his rival publishers. He was on his way.

Franklin would later become famous for the pithy sayings and witticisms that spiced his *Poor Richard's Almanack*. But the same publication also offered serious advice, including this gem that undoubtedly came straight from the author's heart: "Hide not your talents. What's a sundial in the shade?"

Legend has it that one of Franklin's contemporaries, Thomas Jefferson, was a placid, soft-spoken man. He was, in reality, a skilled self-promoter who sought to influence public opinion through newspapers, the dominant medium of his era. Jefferson mailed a steady stream of comments and suggestions to friendly editors. He advised another president-to-be, James Madison, to follow his lead and "set aside a portion of every post day to write what may be proper for the public." Jefferson went so far as to help establish the *National Intelligencer*, a Washington newspaper that trumpeted his point of view.

The elements of successful self-promotion have changed little since Jefferson's day. Starting your own newspaper is certainly beyond your means, but you should find it easy to follow these five basic steps.

1. Don't be heavy-handed about it, but make sure your superiors see that you're hard at work, just as Franklin did with his wheelbarrow. Volunteer for key assignments. Set deadlines for important projects, and then make a small production out of beating them.

2. Plot your personal story line. Presidents are great at this. Ronald Reagan's White House, for example, carefully chose the topics it emphasized. "We would go through the president's schedule day by day and hour by hour, and figure out what we wanted the story to be at the end of each day and at the end of each week," recalled a key Reagan aide, Michael Deaver. This technique can be adapted to your career. Study your schedule for the coming week,

identify the best prospects for success, and ponder ways to increase their visibility.

3. Copy Jefferson's example and make your voice heard. Seek speaking engagements, even if they're only at the Rotary Club. Write articles for publication. (We'll discuss this idea in greater detail in a minute.) Get your name in the company newsletter.

4. Brag about your coworkers and the projects on which you're working together. You'll benefit from the association. Dwight Eisenhower's message to his troops on D-Day began on a glorious note. "You are about to embark upon the Great Crusade," he told the men who would storm the beaches of Normandy. He went on to praise the army's "overwhelming superiority in weapons" and its "great reserves of trained fighting men" before concluding, "I have full confidence in your courage, devotion to duty, and skill in battle." These inspiring words inevitably reflected well on the humble general who had put the Great Crusade into motion.

5. Never brag about yourself, and never exaggerate your accomplishments. Theodore Roosevelt was a master of self-promotion. "President Roosevelt, of all the presidents, best understood the uses of publicity. He had a genius for it," conceded Gus Karger, a veteran Washington reporter. But even TR slipped on occasion. He once claimed to have read twenty thousand books before becoming president. That figure didn't seem as awe-inspiring—or realistic—after a skeptic calculated that Roosevelt would have had to read nine books every week *from birth* to hit it.

This penchant for tall tales sometimes put Roosevelt in danger of becoming a laughingstock. Famed historian Henry Adams eventually reached the point where he simply couldn't take TR seriously. "Theodore is never sober," said Adams. "Only he is drunk with himself and not with rum."

WRITE FOR PUBLICATION, OR HAVE SOMEONE DO IT FOR YOU

Joseph Kennedy suggested to his second-oldest son that he might find it worthwhile to give writing a try. "You would be surprised," he told him, "how a book that really makes the grade with high-class people stands you in good stead for years to come."

It was sound advice, and John Kennedy, much to his good fortune, took his father's words to heart. He became the author of two bestsellers, which established his reputation as a man of intellect and helped to make him a serious presidential candidate.

But did he write those books himself? Ah, that's an interesting question.

Kennedy's first foray into long-form writing came in 1940 with *Appeasement at Munich*, his 148-page Harvard senior thesis. It was intended solely for the eyes of the four faculty members who were to grade it, and their reviews were mixed at best. Two gave thumbs up; two did not. One of the naysayers scrawled, "Fundamental premise never analyzed. Much too long, wordy, repetitious." It was, in other words, a typical student paper.

But Joseph Kennedy thought his son's project had potential, and he used his connections to fulfill it. Joe asked an influential friend, *New York Times* columnist Arthur Krock, to punch up the writing. Krock suggested, too, that the title should be less academic in tone. World War II was dominating the daily headlines, with Nazi Germany securing its hold on France and turning its gaze to Great Britain. Krock scuttled *Appeasement at Munich* for something that was catchier and more relevant—*Why England Slept*.

And, just like that, Jack Kennedy's thesis evolved into a widely circulated book. The young man basked in his new fame, even though a few of his father's friends disapproved. Harold Laski, a prominent British economist, told Joe, "I don't honestly think any publisher would have looked at that book of Jack's if he had not been your son, and if you had not been ambassador (to Great Britain). And those are not the right grounds for publication."

No matter. The young author went to war, returned a hero, and launched a political career. Kennedy was serving in the Senate and daydreaming of the White House when he decided to revisit the success of *Why England Slept*. He instructed an aide, Theodore Sorensen, to dig up past examples of senators "defying constituent pressures."

Rumors circulated around Washington that Sorensen was the true author of the resulting book, *Profiles in Courage*, which hit the bestseller list in 1956. It's indisputable that Sorensen and a Georgetown University professor, Jules Davids, did much of the research and even helped draft chapters. Kennedy simply edited their work and dictated the final version. But it was the senator who received sole credit on the title page.

The gossip might have died down if not for what happened a year later. *Profiles in Courage* won the 1957 Pulitzer Prize under highly unusual circumstances. The Pulitzer jury dutifully read all of that year's nominated books and recommended five finalists to the Pulitzer board, *Profiles in Courage* not among them. But the board rejected all five—something that virtually never happens—and presented the award to JFK. It was whispered that Joe Kennedy had indulged in literary wheeling and dealing to achieve the desired result. There is little doubt that the omnipresent Arthur Krock met with Pulitzer board members shortly before the decisive vote.

Again, no matter. John Kennedy had polished his credentials very nicely. He would run for president three years later, brandishing his Pulitzer Prize as proof that, despite his youth, he had the necessary intelligence and depth to serve as commander-in-chief.

Kennedy's story offers two lessons. The first is that it can be extremely valuable to have your name associated with a respectable publication. A well-written book can establish you as an expert in your field, as an up-and-coming star. If you find a book to be too daunting, you might write an article for a professional journal, or an op-ed column for your local newspaper, or something as simple as a letter to the editor. Or, in this era of the Internet, you might even consider starting your own blog.

Any of these vehicles offers a way to separate yourself from the pack. Write intelligently about your field of work. Explain how any company can serve customers better, take advantage of demographic trends, increase profit margins, or get more involved in its community. You will brand yourself as a rare talent and someone worth listening to.

The second lesson, of course, is that whatever you write, you don't have to write it yourself.

It's taken for granted these days that a presidential candidate must publish a book shortly before the campaign begins. It might be an autobiography or a lengthy essay about important issues or a collection of speeches, but it has to be a *book*.

Almost all of them are ghostwritten. George W. Bush's 1999 screed, *A Charge to Keep*, reportedly was slapped together by Karen Hughes, his communications director. All nine Democratic contenders in 2004 published books, and all had the help of collaborators. Most were kind enough to acknowledge it.

Politicians, of course, are accustomed to having things written for them. No president has regularly penned his own speeches in more than three generations. Senators, congressmen, governors, and even local officials now keep writers on staff, poised to churn out prose at a moment's notice.

You're not likely to have similar access. If you don't require any assistance, so much the better. But there are several ways to get writing help if you need it. Your company might have a public-relations department that could lend a hand. You could link up with a corporate writing consultant. You could approach a local writer, perhaps a freelancer or someone at the daily newspaper or even a high-school English teacher.

The key, whatever you do, is to take credit for the final product—a lesson that James Madison never grasped.

Madison played an important role in drafting the Constitution in 1787. He was an active participant in the debates that shaped the final document, and he wrote many of the *Federalist* essays that subsequently swayed the nation in its favor. He attained fame as the "Father of the Constitution"—perhaps the ultimate author's credit in American history—and went on to win the presidential elections of 1808 and 1812.

But Madison emphatically rejected any praise for his writing prowess. "You give me a credit to which I have no claim in calling me 'the writer of the Constitution of the U.S.,'" he admonished one admirer. "This was not like the fabled goddess of wisdom the offspring of a single brain. It ought to be regarded as the work of many heads and many hands."

Madison was lucky, given his profound humility, that he ever became president at all.

LOOKS DO MATTER, SO SPIFF UP YOUR APPEARANCE

Most of us believe that the way we look has a direct impact on the way we're treated. Researchers have now proven that we're correct.

A team from the Federal Reserve Bank of St. Louis set out in 2005 to look for any possible link between personal appearance and wages. It determined that a worker who is below average on the beauty scale will earn about 9 percent less than a comparable employee who is considered attractive. "If someone looks like Brad Pitt or Julia Roberts, and society values that, that attribute is built into wages," concluded Michael Owyang, an economist who was part of the team.

No surprise there. We all know about the advantages the so-called "beautiful people" enjoy. But it turns out that other aspects of personal appearance can be equally rewarding.

Alexander Todorov, a Princeton University psychology professor, conducted an experiment to see if any connection exists between facial characteristics and political success. He gathered photos of House and Senate candidates from the 2000, 2002, and 2004 campaigns, removed the famous politicians (like Hillary Clinton and John McCain), and put everybody else into an enormous slide show.

Todorov recruited more than eight hundred students for his audience. They watched as he flashed pairs of opposing candidates onto a screen. Photos of a Democrat and a Republican from an obscure Ohio congressional district would suddenly appear, quickly followed by two politicians who had squared off for a Senate seat in Montana, and so on.

The students weren't told the candidates' names, parties, or political philosophies. They were simply given a couple of seconds to make a snap judgment about each race, so they went with what they could see. They based their votes totally on looks.

The results were surprisingly one-sided. Most students selected candidates with jutting chins, furrowed brows, angular noses, and other characteristics that made them appear stronger, more competent, and more mature. Candidates with youthful features, broad cheeks, and big eyes didn't fare nearly as well. These decisions, despite the haste with which they were made, were remarkably similar to the choices of actual voters. Seventy percent of the slide-show winners also won their real-life elections.

Todorov's research was reinforced by a study at Colgate University, where psychologist Caroline Keating digitally altered the photos of well-known politicians. Students rated a youngish version of Bill Clinton as warmer and more honest, but they considered an elderly Clinton to be more powerful. The inner man hadn't changed at all, but perceptions of him differed radically as his appearance evolved.

Height has a strong impact on our preferences, too. Several early presidents were vertically gifted, notably six-foot-four-inch Abraham Lincoln and a pair of six-foot-two founding fathers, George Washington and Thomas Jefferson. The trend continues to this day, with the taller major-party candidate winning ten of the fourteen presidential elections between 1952 and 2004. And the pattern is similar in the private sector. The typical CEO of a *Fortune* 500 company stands nearly six feet tall, putting him three inches above the norm for an American male, according to research by Malcolm Gladwell for *Blink*, his 2005 bestseller.

Why should a stray inch or two make such a difference? Timothy Judge, a management professor at the University of Florida, has called it a self-fulfilling cycle. Taller people are perceived to be authoritative and competent, according to Judge's theory, so they tend to be more self-confident and successful. Edmund Muskie, a senator from Maine who sought the 1972 Democratic presidential nomination, certainly loved the power his six-foot-four frame brought him. "I've always found it useful to be thought of as an intimidating sort of fellow," he said with a grin. "Someone once said that I would intimidate Mount Rushmore."

It would be understandable if this litany of research left you with an empty, helpless feeling. The results don't seem to bode well for the great majority of us, the ones not blessed with stunning beauty, distinguished visages, or Lincolnesque height. But don't despair. It's good to know what you're up against, and it's even more important to be aware that you can counteract any natural disadvantages.

Begin with your wardrobe. Casual dress may be the rage these days, but professional attire is still the best option for anyone who desires professional respect. Wear a suit or a skirt with a jacket, and you will increase your chances of advancement. "People make an assessment about you in the first three seconds. First impressions mean quite a lot. It's about building confidence in the profession and letting people know you're serious," said Marsha Firestone, president of the Women Presidents' Organization, a group of female business owners.

Offering fashion tips is beyond this book's purview, but there are hundreds of manuals, guides, magazines, newspaper columns, and television shows primed with the specific advice you need. Store clerks, family members, friends, and coworkers are undoubtedly eager to chip in with their own opinions.

Only two basic guidelines need to be noted here. If you're an up-and-coming executive, your dress must be appropriate to the occasion, and it must be tasteful. A few politicians have deviated from these rules over the years, and they invariably have paid the price.

Jimmy Carter, for example, was especially fond of sweaters. He even wore a cardigan when delivering a nationally televised address on energy, a terrible miscalculation on his part. Carter's casual dress clashed with his serious speech, sending a mixed message to the public. His image as an authority figure began to erode. "Ordinary Americans didn't have to aspire to the heights of the presidency," Robin Givhan, the *Washington Post*'s fashion editor, wrote of the Carter years. "The presidency had come crashing down to their level. Fashion empathy had arrived."

There are occasions, as well, when formality can be harmful. Leonard Wood, an army general, was a leading contender for the 1920 Republican nomination. He seemed to be an ideal candidate—decisive, well-respected, and a dear friend of Theodore Roosevelt. But Wood alienated war-weary voters by campaigning in full military regalia, a deviation as inappropriate as Carter's colorful sweaters. Wood's managers begged him to wear civilian clothes instead of his uniform, but the general refused. The Republicans decided they were more comfortable with Warren Harding and his sensible suits.

Good taste should be a self-evident requirement, yet some executives and politicians don't immediately grasp its importance. Jesse Jackson was among them. "I used to love wearing diamond pinkie rings," he recalled. "But there was this contradiction. Here we were fighting exploitation in South Africa, and there I was wearing diamonds." Jackson became accepted as a serious political force only after ditching his gaudy jewelry in the 1970s. He ran for president a decade later.

Tasteful restraint is also important when using cosmetics. Makeup, like fashion, is an integral component of a female executive's polished look. We'll leave it to the experts to recommend brand names and application procedures. But take note that men also have makeup issues from time to time. Richard Nixon may have lost the presidency in 1960 because of his pasty appearance during his first televised debate with John Kennedy. And Richard Gephardt, whose reddish-blond brows were virtually invisible, routinely used an eyebrow pencil during his two national campaigns.

The final—and most important—step in your personal beautification plan must occur underneath your skin. It may not be easy to do, but as we've discussed elsewhere in this book, it's essential that you learn how to radiate enthusiasm and carry yourself with confidence. A positive, attractive personality can overcome any physical shortcoming.

Nobody ever proved this point more thoroughly than Stephen Douglas. He was so unusually tiny—various sources place him between four-foot-six and five-foot-four—that a career in public office seemed to be out of the question. A contemporary wrote that Douglas had "a Herculean frame, with the exception of his lower limbs, which were short and small, dwarfing what otherwise would have been a conspicuous figure."

Yet Douglas served in the Senate with distinction during the fourteen tumultuous years that led up to the Civil War. He even ran for president three times. It was his misfortune to finally secure the Democratic nomination in 1860, a year in which the party's Northern and Southern wings were badly polarized, leaving no chance of victory in the general election.

Bravado was one of the keys to Douglas's success. He compensated for his small stature with a booming voice, a fiery attitude, and an unquenchable thirst for political battle. He was a flashy dresser, usually turned out in a sharp blue suit with silver buttons. He believed he was the equal—if not the superior—of any of his taller colleagues, including the towering Lincoln, whom he defeated in a famous Senate campaign in 1858.

His fellow politicians reciprocated by referring to Douglas as the Little Giant, a nickname that expressed their utmost respect.

ESTABLISH A POSITIVE REPUTATION, AND KEEP IT

Bruce Babbitt earned style points for his presidential campaign in 1988. He possessed two qualities—a sharp wit and a willingness to discuss complicated issues—that are both rare in political candidates and highly popular with reporters on the election beat. The latter showered him with favorable coverage.

Those upbeat stories, unfortunately for Babbitt, didn't translate into votes. He withdrew from the race after the early Democratic primaries, yet even at that moment of defeat, he was unable to resist a joke at the media's expense. "I think you engaged in a deliberate conspiracy to destroy my candidacy," he said with heavy irony, "by making me into a kind of house pet and destroying my credibility in the eyes of the American people. Thanks." The press loved it.

But Babbitt also had his earnest side, the half of his brain that delighted in debating fiscal policy and issuing lengthy position papers on conservation. It was this serious candidate who admitted to preparing poorly—"I walked into this thing really pretty naive"—and to confusing the voters. "It's asking an awful lot in the course of a campaign before the American people," he sighed, "to say, 'Consider both a new messenger and a challenging and different message.'" A reporter asked what the correct approach would have been. Babbitt replied that he should have projected an image that the public could have easily comprehended and remembered. Any new candidate, he said, should take a personal inventory and ask, "Where is my bumper sticker?"

Babbitt's advice is equally relevant to up-and-coming executives. Anybody with high hopes and ambitious plans—whether in politics or business—must establish a distinctive, positive reputation. It should be possible to convey your strengths in taut, direct language that will *stick*—not necessarily on the back of a motor vehicle, but certainly in the minds of the people who control your future.

"What are you best at?" asked author and sales consultant Jeffrey Gitomer. "What are you known for? Every magazine publishes a 'best of' issue. What 'best of award' could you win?" Your answers to those questions will be the key to your reputation. They will, in effect, become your bumper sticker.

The most successful presidential candidates in American history were the ones who managed to impress upon the entire country (or most of it, anyway) a strong sense of their skills and personalities. Here are four classic examples:

1. **George Washington:** Washington, of course, had the best bumper sticker in American history. He was the man who won the Revolutionary War, the Father of Our Country. Thomas Jefferson and Alexander Hamilton bickered about politics and nearly everything else, but they agreed that Washington was a military genius and an indispensable chief executive. "Among the legacies of

the Revolution to the new nation, the most widely recognized and admired was a man: George Washington. He had no rivals," wrote historian James Thomas Flexner.

2. **Andrew Jackson:** Old Hickory's spunk caught the nation's attention. His troops repulsed the enemy in the Battle of New Orleans at the close of the War of 1812. "Never before had British veterans quailed," admitted a British officer. "But it would be silly to deny that they did so now." Jackson's later exploits as an Indian fighter added to his reputation for forceful action, making him a hero among farmers, laborers, and other common folk. Everybody had an opinion about him. Aaron Burr, the nation's third vice president, praised Jackson as a "prompt, frank, ardent soul." Thomas Jefferson merely muttered, "He is a dangerous man."

3. **Ulysses Grant:** Never mind that Grant was an ineffectual president. He was successful at the ballot box, thanks to his status as a Civil War hero. Even his Confederate counterpart applauded him. "I have carefully searched the military records of both ancient and modern history," said Robert E. Lee, "and have never found Grant's superior as a general." President Andrew Johnson chimed in, "Grant has treated me badly. But he was the right man in the right place during the war, and no matter what his faults were or are, the whole world can never write him down."

4. **Franklin Roosevelt:** FDR promised a frightened nation that he would relieve the misery of the Depression, whatever tactics might be necessary. "Take a method and try it," he exhorted his aides. "If it fails, admit it frankly and try another. But above all, try *something*." The nation responded to his ingenuity and enthusiasm, the latter epitomized by "Happy Days Are Here Again," the bouncy theme song of his 1932 campaign. Columnist Walter Lippmann, who had dismissed Roosevelt as a lightweight, revised his estimate soon after the inauguration. "In one week, the nation, which had lost confidence in everything and everybody, has regained confidence in the government and in itself," Lippmann marveled.

These four men established impressive reputations before becoming president. Their beliefs and personal qualities were widely known and easily expressed in the terse language of the bumper sticker: Washington—Father of Our Country. Jackson—Fighter for the Common Man. Grant—Defender of the Union. Roosevelt—Happy Days Are Here Again.

Three lived up to their slogans, allowing them to retain their sterling reputations to the present day. Washington, Jackson, and Roosevelt are ranked among the greatest presidents of all time. Grant's administration, on the other hand, was marred by scandal and inaction, sullying the hero's clean, decisive image. Today's historians rate him as one of the worst presidents ever.

Grant's failure raises a key point. A positive image must be carefully protected. If you ever fail to live up to the reputation you've established, it will be difficult—perhaps impossible—to undo the damage.

Woodrow Wilson ran for reelection in 1916 on a slogan—"He Kept Us Out of War"—that resonated with the voters. But Wilson doubted he could fulfill those hopeful words. "I can't keep the country out of war," he privately told Josephus Daniels, his secretary of the navy. And he didn't. The United States entered World War I just five months after the election, the first step toward a period of postwar disillusionment virtually unmatched in American history.

Herbert Hoover established a worldwide reputation as a humanitarian. He directed a charitable organization that fed ten million starving Europeans during World War I, and then distributed twenty million tons of food after the war. Hoover was hailed throughout Europe and America as a savior. "He is certainly a wonder, and I wish we could make him president. There couldn't be a better one," exclaimed an influential New Yorker named Franklin Roosevelt. But Hoover's humanitarian impulses seemed to vanish once he moved into the White House. He did little to combat the ever-deepening Depression.

Lyndon Johnson declared war on poverty a few months after taking the presidential oath in 1963, and he went so far as to guarantee a victory. "It's the time—and it's going to be soon—when nobody in this country is poor," he declared. "It's the time—and there is no point in waiting—when every boy or girl ... has the right to all the education that he can absorb. It's the time when every slum is gone from every city in America, and America is beautiful." Johnson's rhetoric, wonderful though it was, had little substance behind it. Urban riots and the Vietnam War soon submerged the nation in a morass of despair.

Don't make the mistake that Wilson, Hoover, and Johnson did. They were guilty of overpromising. They raised public expectations that they were unable to meet. Their glittering reputations lay in ruins when they left the White House. Hoover put on a stoic front, yet he betrayed the resentment and regret that afflicted all three men in retirement. "I knew from the bitter experience of all public men from George Washington down that democracies are fickle and heartless," he wrote. "When the ultimate bump came, I was well fortified to accept it philosophically and, in fact, to welcome it, for democracy is a harsh employer."

IF YOU WANT TO BE A LEADER, YOU MUST EXUDE STRENGTH

Nobody ever called Lyndon Johnson courageous when he was growing up. Most people considered him a coward.

Young Lyndon protected himself at all costs. He scampered to the sidelines whenever a fight broke out—and kids in rural Texas swung their fists freely a century ago. If his friends decided to roughhouse or dive into a river, he found something else to do.

His aversion to danger continued into his college years. Classmates were shocked by Johnson's reaction when anyone challenged him to a fight. He would immediately drop onto a bed and start agitating his legs wildly. "If you hit me," he'd yell, "I'll kick you!" His instinct for self-preservation was highly developed.

But his thirst for fame and fortune was even stronger. Johnson had been preparing for a political career as long as anybody could remember. He couldn't wait to leave Southwest Texas State Teachers College and immerse himself in the real world. He intended to become president one day, yet he knew that Americans were unlikely to elect a coward as their commander-in-chief.

So LBJ gradually transformed himself into a tough guy—on the surface, at least. He became a fiercely demanding boss who drove his staff relentlessly. He verbally emasculated anyone who differed with him. He had no qualms about saber-rattling. "I am not going to lose Vietnam. I am not going to be the president who saw Southeast Asia go the way China went," he insisted to Henry Cabot Lodge Jr., his ambassador to South Vietnam.

Johnson's bellicose behavior was motivated by fear. If he withdrew American troops from Southeast Asia, he told an aide, he would appear to be "a coward, an unmanly man, a man without a spine." He overcompensated with behavior that was rude and uncouth.

But his actions—offensive as they often were—had logic behind them. Americans may enjoy watching actors like Jimmy Stewart, Alan Alda, and Kevin Kline portray sensitive politicians on the movie screen, but they prefer the real article to be tough. Any demonstration of weakness can doom a candidate to defeat, as Johnson knew.

The lesson here is both simple and obvious. Be courageous. Or, if you lack inner bravery, do your best to *appear* courageous. Strength—real or simulated—is a necessary ingredient for success.

Theodore Roosevelt and Ronald Reagan showed physical courage in surviving assassination attempts. Roosevelt, seeking to regain the presidency as a third-party candidate in 1912, was shot before a speech in Milwaukee. He unbuttoned his coat and felt beneath it, smearing his fingers with blood. "It looks as though I have been hit," he said to the men crowding around him, "but I don't think it's anything serious."

A doctor insisted on an immediate trip to the hospital, but Roosevelt refused. He went instead to the meeting hall, where he dramatically described the shooting to his shocked audience. He showed off his eyeglass case and a folded copy of his speech, both of which had been struck by the bullet and had apparently slowed it. "The bullet is in me now, so that I cannot make a very long speech, but I will do my best," he asserted. He held forth for almost an hour.

Roosevelt finally went to a hospital in Chicago the following morning. X-rays showed that the bullet had stopped less than an inch from his heart, where it stayed harmlessly for the rest of his life. "You were elected last night," insisted the chief surgeon. "It was the turn of the tide in your favor." He was wrong—TR would lose to Woodrow Wilson—but the Roosevelt legend had gained another compelling chapter.

Reagan reacted to his 1981 shooting not with drama, but with humor. "Honey, I forgot to duck," he told his wife. And he greeted the attending physicians by joking, "I hope you're all Republicans." Aide David Gergen considered the attempted assassination to be the defining moment of

Reagan's presidency. "To a great many, especially working people," wrote Gergen, "he was now the president who had taken a bullet—and smiled. He had guts."

You are more likely to be required to show courage in the face of rhetorical fire, standing up to a volley of angry words instead of bullets. Richard Nixon demonstrated this brand of courage—a mixture of defiance and desperate ambition—in the midst of his first national campaign in 1952. The thirty-nine-year-old Nixon had been tapped as Dwight Eisenhower's running mate, a glorious boost to his career, but his future was almost immediately jeopardized by press reports that he was maintaining a slush fund.

Pressure built on Eisenhower to drop Nixon from the ticket. Key advisers suggested to the vice-presidential candidate that he should do the right thing and resign. They hinted that Ike would be truly grateful.

Nixon refused. He went public instead, speaking directly to the voters on national television, a truly innovative concept in 1952. He defended the fund, saying that it was independently audited and that the donations were used for postage, clerical help, travel, and printing costs, nothing more. But he devoted most of the half-hour to himself, talking about his personal debts, his wife Pat's "respectable Republican cloth coat," his three-year-old car, and his daughters' dog, Checkers, whose name would forever be associated with the speech.

Nixon closed on a defiant note. "I am not a quitter," he said. "And, incidentally, Pat is not a quitter. After all, her name was Patricia Ryan, and she was born on St. Patrick's Day, and you know the Irish never quit."

His performance convinced the previously wavering Eisenhower, who told a rally that night: "I have been a warrior, and I like courage. Tonight, I saw an example of courage." Ike met Nixon the next day and insisted that he stay on the ticket. "You're my boy," the old general said.

The three men above—Roosevelt, Reagan, and Nixon—all reacted in a natural way to circumstances that threatened their lives or careers. The toughness they displayed was real and thoroughly impressive.

Overwrought displays of strength, on the other hand, often backfire. The elder George Bush boasted after his 1984 vice-presidential debate with Geraldine Ferraro that he had "tried to kick a little ass" during the telecast. He came off as a childish braggart. Michael Dukakis, the 1988 Democratic nominee, strapped on a helmet and took a well-photographed ride in a tank to demonstrate his readiness to be commander-in-chief. He looked like a wimpy kid playing a war game. Lyndon Johnson and George W. Bush, despite contrary advice from experts, insisted on staying the course in unpopular, unproductive foreign conflicts. Their political bases disintegrated.

A real leader exudes strength in a way that is understated, yet unmistakable. Thomas Dewey seemed to lose the knack as a presidential candidate, running a timid, colorless, and ultimately unsuccessful campaign against Harry Truman in 1948. But there was no doubting his magnetic power as the gang-busting district attorney of Manhattan a decade earlier. "More than any other American of his generation except (Charles) Lindbergh, Dewey became a creature of folklore and a national hero," wrote author John Gunther.

He was no hero to organized crime, which resented his meddling in its affairs. A death threat was received in the DA's mail one morning, followed by a reinforcing phone call in the afternoon. Dewey would be shot that very evening as he headed home from work, warned the caller. Aides considered the threat credible. They advised their boss to alter his routine and proceed with caution.

Dewey knew exactly what to do. He left the office at his habitual time. He walked out the same doors, stepped into the same car, and followed the same route he did every other night.

But the district attorney wasn't totally oblivious to the potential danger. He told his chauffeur to make one important adjustment as they started up Fifth Avenue. Dewey normally rode home in total darkness, but not this time, not with a sniper possibly waiting in the shadows.

He ordered his driver to turn on every light in the car.

"Tell the Truth"

Grover Cleveland showed no taste for combat, paying an immigrant 150 dollars to take his place in the Union army during the Civil War (a legal option at the time). But he repeatedly demonstrated his toughness in political battles.

Cleveland committed a rare act as governor of New York, vetoing an extremely popular bill that would have reduced the cost of riding New York City's elevated railway to a nickel. The state had previously authorized the railroad to set the fare at a dime, and Cleveland argued that it should live up to its word. "The state should not only be strictly just, but should be scrupulously fair," he contended. Cleveland confided to friends that the veto might end his political career, but he didn't care. It turned out to have the opposite effect. The press hailed him as a man of courage.

The same stubbornness surfaced a year later in 1884, when the governor was running for president. A Buffalo newspaper reported that Cleveland, a bachelor, had fathered a child in 1874. There was some doubt about his paternity, but Cleveland had accepted responsibility for the boy's support. The leaders of his campaign anxiously asked if there was any way to finesse the controversy. His three-word response—"tell the truth"—has gone down in the mythology of American politics. And yes, he won the election.

4

Organizing

Wendell Willkie might have been the most improbable presidential nominee of all time.

His job didn't help. Willkie was the CEO of Commonwealth & Southern, the nation's largest supplier of electricity. Americans have never been especially receptive to businessmen in politics, and they've certainly never demonstrated any love for utility executives. Willkie didn't care. "I'm in business and proud of it," he declared. "Nobody can make me soft-pedal any fact in my business career."

Then there was the matter of self-confidence, which Willkie possessed in abundance. His detractors accused him of being dangerously overstocked, and he tended to agree. "I'm the cockiest fellow you ever saw," he conceded. "If you want to vote for me, fine. If you don't, go jump in the lake, and I'm still for you."

And, finally, there was the simple question of timing. Franklin Roosevelt's New Deal was popular with the masses—FDR carried all but two states in the 1936 election—yet Willkie was emerging as one of the president's strongest critics. He wrote articles and made speeches attacking the New Deal, an act of defiance that drew applause from fellow corporate titans. Everyday citizens, on the other hand, seemed unimpressed. Their indifference baffled Willkie, who protested that he too was just a common guy, born and raised in Indiana. Any resemblance was lost on razor-tongued Harold Ickes, a member of Roosevelt's cabinet, who lampooned Willkie as "a simple barefoot Wall Street lawyer."

Here, then, was an unlikely formula for success—a wealthy, headstrong CEO who was swimming against the political tide and proud of it. But Willkie's name nonetheless began to surface in stories previewing the 1940 election. *Fortune* listed him as a potential presidential candidate as early as 1937, and the *New York Times* followed suit in 1939.

Willkie publicly laughed off this early speculation—"it cannot constitute more than a joke"—but he was intrigued. He began to maneuver behind the scenes. Russell Davenport, the managing editor of *Fortune*, quit his magazine job to work full time lining up supporters. Business leaders, including several prominent newspaper and magazine publishers, supplied manpower, funds, and publicity. Willkie stepped up his speaking schedule, appearing on national radio hookups, even quiz shows, to raise his public profile.

This unusual campaign, amazingly enough, caught fire. The Republican Party's other presidential contenders—inexperienced Thomas Dewey, cold Robert Taft, enigmatic Arthur Vandenberg—seemed uninspiring, uncharismatic, and unequal to 1940's daunting challenges, as America teetered on the brink of World War II. The seasoned, energetic Willkie looked to be an attractive alternative. He rose in the polls, which brought more press coverage, which drew more supporters, and on it went. His popularity peaked during the week of the Republican convention, where the galleries endlessly shouted, "We want Willkie," and the delegates gradually came to agree.

The candidate insisted that the whole thing was spontaneous. "All the headquarters I have are under my hat," he said. What about the rumors that Davenport and other professionals were ghostwriting his speeches and articles? "I roll my own," he laughed. What about the galleries, hadn't they deliberately been packed with his supporters? Of course not, said the grinning Willkie, who pulled tickets out of his pocket. "I had only ten tickets myself," he said, "and I have these five left over."

The nomination came on the sixth ballot, with many reporters hailing it as a genuine draft, a rare victory of the popular will. Even H. L. Mencken, the preeminent cynic in American journalism, bought the story. "I am thoroughly convinced that the nomination of Willkie was managed by the Holy Ghost in person," Mencken wrote. "At the moment the sixth ballot was being counted, I saw an angel in the gallery. It wore a Palm Beach suit and was smoking a five-cent cigar, but nevertheless it was palpably an angel."

It was all nonsense. Willkie's campaign may have been unorthodox, but it was definitely not impromptu. Many of his speeches and articles *had* been written by others. The galleries *were* packed. Davenport and his team had been laboring in the shadows for months, lining up delegate support. One of those team members, Fred Smith, scoffed at Willkie's suggestion that he had won without a headquarters. "Neither Willkie's personality, nor the weight of his ideals, could conceivably have produced even a fraction of the phenomenon that we lived through," Smith insisted. "It should never be forgotten that the 'Willkie boom' was one of the best engineered jobs in history."

The same could be said of a nomination often described as the truest example of a spontaneous draft in the history of presidential politics. James Garfield, a congressman from Ohio, served as the floor manager for a cabinet member from the same state, John Sherman, at the 1880 Republican convention. Friends had suggested that he run for president himself, but Garfield refused. "I so much despise a man who blows his own horn," he confessed, "that I go to the extreme of not demanding what is justly my due."

Garfield worked diligently for the colorless, aloof Sherman (appropriately nicknamed "The Ohio Icicle"). The odds, however, were against him. Ulysses Grant, the Civil War hero and former president, was the frontrunner at the convention. Arrayed against him were Sherman, James Blaine (a popular senator from Maine), and a host of minor candidates. Garfield pursued the only realistic course, bringing all of these challengers together in an anti-Grant coalition that deadlocked the convention. Voting droned on for ballot after ballot, with no one making significant headway.

The search inevitably began for an alternative candidate. Garfield protested when he received Wisconsin's votes on the thirty-fourth ballot, but he was ruled out of order. Blaine soon sent a telegram from his home in Washington: "Maine's vote this moment cast for you goes with my hearty concurrence. I hope it will aid in securing your nomination and assuring victory to the Republican Party." Garfield won on the thirty-sixth ballot. He truly seemed shocked at the outcome.

But his victory didn't come as a total surprise. A wealthy Philadelphia banker, Wharton Barker, had been working behind the scenes on Garfield's behalf for a year. Barker, who wanted to stop Grant at all costs, had written Garfield that "the only safety for the Republican Party is in making some man such as yourself our candidate." The two men met in February and April, and Barker subsequently took steps that the Willkie forces would follow sixty years later. He worked to keep Garfield's name in the news, encouraged delegates to consider his man as their second choice, and established a Garfield cheering section in the convention hall. Sherman, when he later learned of these activities, began to wonder about Garfield's loyalty as his floor manager.

Joe Trippi, who managed Howard Dean's briefly incandescent presidential campaign in 2004, liked to say that the formula for victory could be boiled down to three simple words: "Organize, organize, organize." The stories of Wendell Willkie and James Garfield lend weight to his argument that no one can succeed in politics—or in business—without laying the groundwork first.

If you hope to become a commanding figure in the future, you must begin organizing today. John Kennedy often told the story of a French marshal who wanted a rare tree planted on his estate. His gardener delayed. There was no need to hurry, he insisted, since that particular tree wouldn't flower for a hundred years. "In that case," the marshal replied, "plant it this afternoon."

You need the same sense of urgency. Start organizing your career by recruiting mentors and staffers who can provide you with first-rate professional assistance. Make sure that your family and friends are willing to do their part to help you advance. And begin developing a wider circle of relationships. Each of these points will be discussed in this chapter:

Professional assistance

- Find somebody who can teach you the ropes.
- Hire the best staff you can, and get out of its way.

Personal life

- Expect your loved ones to work alongside you.
- Count on friends for help and a fresh perspective.

Developing relationships

- Keep expanding your professional network.
- Collect chits from anyone you can.
- Make alliances with anybody who can help you.

Organizing can be annoying, tedious, time-consuming work. The temptation is to avoid it. Let the others sweat the petty details. You'll win your promotions solely on merit.

The problem is, life doesn't work that way. Even an icon as revered as Abraham Lincoln had to get his hands dirty. It was his organizational skills that allowed Lincoln to rise in the Whig Party, the forerunner of the Republican Party. "Lincoln engaged in every aspect of the political process, from the most visionary to the most mundane," wrote historian Doris Kearns Goodwin. "His experience taught him what every party boss has understood through the ages: the practical machinery of the party organization—the distribution of ballots, the checklists, the rounding up of voters—was as crucial as the broad ideology laid out in the platform."

These insights were completely lost on Lincoln's Republican contemporary, Salmon Chase, who envisioned the party's 1860 presidential nomination coming his way as the result of a spontaneous movement.

Lincoln and William Seward, a senator from New York, ran the Republican race at full speed. They recruited campaign managers and assistants; Chase did not. They accepted speaking engagements around the nation; Chase turned down several key invitations. They worked to line up delegate support from any state they could; Chase didn't even try to get the delegation from his home state, Ohio, wholly behind him.

Chase's friends were exasperated by his inattention to detail. One of his supporters, James Ashley, was disturbed by the contrast. "I now begin to fear," he wrote on one occasion, "that Seward will get a majority of the delegates from Maryland. He and his friends work—*work*. They not only work—*but he works*."

All of their organizing paid off. Lincoln and Seward left Chase far behind when the roll was called at the Republican convention. It was Ohio's votes, in fact, that secured the nomination for Lincoln, setting him squarely on the road to the White House.

FIND SOMEBODY WHO CAN TEACH YOU THE ROPES

Eighteen-year-old Walter Mondale had a few things going for him when he left Minnesota's farm belt for Macalester College in 1946. The minister's son was smarter than most of his fellow freshmen, a pretty good athlete (nicknamed "Crazylegs" for his football prowess), and talented enough as a singer (a self-described "screeching baritone") to win statewide awards and perform at weddings.

But Mondale also had serious deficiencies. He lacked experience, connections, and money. His summers were spent in the fields, where he toiled alongside migrant farm workers to scrape his tuition together. He took whatever odd jobs he could get the rest of the year. "Since childhood, I've always been appalled by poverty," he would recall decades later. "I grew up in the Depression, and I had friends who had absolutely nothing. It always haunted me. It still does." There would be no Kennedy-like head start for Walter Mondale.

But his fortunes changed at Macalester. He met and impressed a former faculty member, Hubert Humphrey, who had become the mayor of Minneapolis. Mondale took charge of the "Diaper Brigade," a team of students who worked for the mayor's reelection in 1947. He was given greater responsibilities the following year, when Humphrey made a successful bid for the United States Senate. And he went on to manage statewide campaigns for one of the new senator's key allies, Orville Freeman.

Mondale learned everything he could from his mentor. He studied Humphrey's style, his way of reaching out to people. He ran political errands for him, eventually becoming a key adviser himself. He adopted Humphrey's causes—civil rights, education, social welfare—as his own. "They were Tweedledum and Tweedledee," a Minnesota congressman recalled. "It would have taken major surgery to separate the two."

Mondale's loyalty and hard work were soon to be rewarded. Minnesota's attorney general resigned in 1960. It was up to Freeman, then the governor, to appoint a replacement, and he tapped his old campaign manager. Mondale twice won reelection. He was on his way.

So was his mentor. Humphrey moved up to the vice presidency in 1964, relinquishing his seat in the Senate. Minnesota's new governor asked for any suggestions on a replacement. Well, said the vice president, it certainly would be nice if his old friend, Fritz Mondale, could be given the appointment. His wish was granted.

Senator Mondale carved out a respectable record in Washington. He was strongly liberal on most issues, though he remained a hawk on the Vietnam War long after most Minnesota Democrats had become doves. The reason was simple. Vice President Humphrey still supported the war, and Mondale couldn't abandon him. "I can't say that wasn't a factor," he later admitted. "I loved Hubert, and I didn't want him hurt."

That type of loyalty was precisely what Jimmy Carter wanted in a running mate in 1976. He chose Mondale—forming the famous "Grits and Fritz" ticket—and never had cause for regret. Vice President Mondale occasionally differed with his new boss's policies in private, but not in public. Some observers frankly thought he overdid it. "Mondale is too loyal. Even Hubert rolled his eyes once in a while," said William Sumner, an editorial writer in Minnesota.

The payoff came in 1984, when Mondale won the Democratic Party's highest honor, its presidential nomination. He couldn't have achieved it without the decades of help from Humphrey, or without the confidence that other men had displayed in appointing him attorney general, senator, and vice president. If not for their assistance, he probably would have been just another Minnesota lawyer.

Mondale's story proves how important it is to find a mentor, someone who can show you the ropes and help you win promotions, no matter what line of work you're in. But don't expect your guru to magically appear. You'll probably have to make the first move, just as Mondale did when he volunteered for Humphrey's mayoral campaign. "While the popular view of mentors is that they seek out younger people to encourage and champion, in fact the reverse is more often true," wrote Warren Bennis, an expert on leadership. "The best mentors are usually recruited, and one mark of a future leader is the ability to identify, woo, and win the mentors who will change his or her life."

This is no recent trend. Mentors have been important since the early days of the republic. Thomas Jefferson groomed his secretary of state, James Madison, to succeed him in the White House in 1808. Madison did the same with *his* secretary of state, James Monroe, who was victorious in 1816.

Martin Van Buren had a similar motivation for cozying up to one of the most popular presidents of all time, Andrew Jackson. The two men seemed to have little in common—Van Buren the suave, manipulative New Yorker, Jackson the blunt, unpretentious Tennessean—but they formed a lasting relationship. Van Buren served Jackson for years as an adviser, secretary of state, and vice president, always hoping that some of the master's political magic would rub off.

His chance finally came in 1836, when the Democrats nominated him to replace their retiring hero. Van Buren, obsequious to the end, pledged to "endeavor to tread generally in the footsteps of President Jackson—happy if I shall be able to perfect the work he has so gloriously begun." The voters fulfilled his presidential dreams in the election that autumn.

We should end, however, with a note of caution. Beware of the heavy-handed mentor who pushes you in a direction contrary to your wishes.

William Howard Taft had no taste for elective office—"politics, when I am in it, makes me sick"—but he was remarkably effective as Theodore Roosevelt's right-hand man. Taft's official title was secretary of war, but TR used him as a troubleshooter, handing him any assignment that required quick results. It gradually dawned on Roosevelt that he had found his ideal successor.

The omens weren't good. Taft wasn't eager for the job, and the Democratic platform accused Roosevelt of plotting "a forced succession to the presidency" in 1908. But TR usually got what he wanted, and this was no exception. He made certain that Taft was elected. "The first letter I wish to write is to you," the new president-elect told Roosevelt, "because you have always been the chief agent in working out the present status of affairs, and my selection and election are chiefly your work."

The whole thing turned out badly. Taft didn't enjoy being president, and he and Roosevelt had a violent falling-out. The reluctant commander-in-chief eventually realized that his biggest mistake had been giving his mentor free rein. "There is no use trying to be William Howard Taft with Roosevelt's ways," he concluded. "Our ways are different."

HIRE THE BEST STAFF YOU CAN, AND GET OUT OF ITS WAY

Robert Shrum was a respected political consultant. He had a good head for strategy and a fluid dexterity with words. The memorable slogan for George McGovern's 1972 presidential campaign ("Come Home, America") was his creation, as was Edward Kennedy's legendary speech to the 1980 Democratic convention ("the work goes on, the cause endures, the hope still lives, and the dream shall never die").

There was just one problem. He never won.

That isn't totally fair. Shrum helped several candidates get elected to the Senate. But it was different at the presidential level. He played key roles in eight national campaigns, and all eight of those clients lost. He came closest to victory when he signed up with Jimmy Carter in 1976, but theirs was a brief, unhappy association. Shrum quit after ten days. "I am not sure what you truly believe in, other than yourself," he told the future president.

That was typical Shrum—brash, supremely self-confident, and ultimately wrong about a presidential contender's prospects. Yet his reputation was undamaged. He remained a political celebrity, a genuine star in his field. Candidates competed for his services every four years, and the successful suitor always crowed about his good fortune. Most high-profile Democrats agreed that having Shrum on your team meant that you had to be taken seriously.

There were, however, a few skeptics, as the winner of the 2004 Shrum sweepstakes discovered. John Kerry and his new consultant headed to South Carolina for one of the first debates of the season. Ernest Hollings, a senator known for his sharp wit, paid them a visit shortly before the cameras came on. "John," Hollings laughed as he pointed at Shrum, "I didn't know you wanted to lose this election." Kerry's speechwriters began to have doubts, too. They thought about printing T-shirts featuring Shrum's photo and the slogan "Reverse the Curse," but they stopped short. They were afraid of angering the master.

The Kerry campaign didn't end well. Shrum eventually lost favor with the candidate and was shuffled to a secondary role. Defeat Number Eight came soon thereafter. "Anybody who says, whether they win or lose, that there weren't mistakes in their campaign is not being very honest," Shrum said. "There are no perfect campaigns."

It was easy to be philosophical. Shrum—like all consultants—was a hired gun, jumping from candidate to candidate every four years. He had no permanent attachment to any single politician. If he chose to work again, he knew that someone would be eager to hire him.

And that may have been the problem. "The successful presidential campaigns have not been run by mercenaries," contended Gerald Rafshoon, who joined Jimmy Carter's team before he was governor of Georgia and stayed through the White House years. "There's a reason there was a Massachusetts mafia with John Kennedy, or a Texas mafia with Bush or Johnson, or a California mafia with Reagan, or a Georgia mafia with Carter. It's always been a small group of people who believe in the candidate, not in promoting themselves or building their businesses."

That's precisely what you need. Not a high-profile business consultant who'll fly in, hand you a report, stick you with an enormous bill, and then jet back out of your life. You need loyal, dedicated staffers who come to work day after day, keeping you and your career foremost in their hearts and minds. You need workers who can run your office smoothly, juggle a thousand tiny details, and make your clients and customers happy, freeing you to concentrate on the big picture—"the vision thing," as the elder George Bush so famously called it.

A tough bill to fill? People like that *can* be found. The White House has witnessed a stream of assistants who selflessly advanced their bosses' careers, becoming famous themselves in the process. Franklin Roosevelt was advised by "brain trusters" such as Raymond Moley and Rexford Tugwell, who put an academic sheen on the New Deal. John Kennedy was blessed with the erudite writing talents of Theodore Sorensen. Richard Nixon was protected—too enthusiastically, to be sure—by his hard-boiled "Prussians," H. R. Haldeman and John Ehrlichman. And George W. Bush benefited from the guidance of his political sage (some would say Svengali), Karl Rove.

These well-known aides had two qualities in common. They signed up for the long haul, and they were fiercely loyal. Jerry Brown, a former California governor who ran for president three times, insisted that an effective candidate needs "a group of people with some continuity and some conviction, a movement that can push opposition out of the way." Those two C words—continuity and conviction—are the key. Those are the qualities you want in your staffers.

There's a catch, of course. You're not likely to have the opportunity to hire many helpers during the early phase of your career. A secretary, perhaps. Maybe an assistant or two.

That's all the more reason to choose wisely. These people—if they're skilled and loyal—will form the core of a staff that will expand as your career takes off. Keep them happy, and the word will spread about your desirability as a boss, which will make it easier to recruit in the future. You can't go wrong by following these four guidelines, no matter how many people work for you:

- Treat them well.
- Pay them well.
- Work as hard as they do (if not harder).
- Don't micromanage.

That last point is crucial. You're hiring intelligent, hard-working staffers—the best people you can possibly find, right? So point them in the proper direction, get out of their way, and let them show their stuff. Don't be afraid to see them shine. They'll be happier, and you'll profit from the quality of their work.

Giving your staff a healthy dose of freedom, as Calvin Coolidge understood, is also the ideal way to stay detached from everyday decisions that might have unpleasant consequences. "There are many things you must not tell me," Coolidge once instructed a subordinate. "If you blunder, you can leave, or I can invite you to leave. But if you draw me into all your department decisions, and something goes wrong, I must stay here. And by involving me, you have lowered the faith of the people in their government."

Major decisions, on the other hand, are your responsibility. Assistants can lay out the options and offer advice, but the final call will always be yours—and yours alone.

A staff will be most effective in this advisory role if it represents a cross-section of society, blending people with different personalities, backgrounds, and skills. Any leader—whether in business or politics—will benefit from exposure to a diversity of opinions. "The team should include a mix," wrote David Gergen, who served on the staffs of four presidents. "People who have known the president a long time to keep the flame alive; veterans of Washington to make sure the flame burns effectively. Youngsters to give the team energy; gray hairs to give it wisdom."

And don't hesitate to include dissenters. Lyndon Johnson always insisted that he didn't want "yes men" on his staff. He wheeled on an aide, Joseph Califano, whom he considered obsequious. "I didn't hire you to 'yes' me," Johnson snapped. "You disagree with me, you let me know it. Don't back off just because I say something." The irony, of course, is that Johnson's administration would be badly damaged because he turned a deaf ear to dissenting views on the Vietnam War.

Melding a cast of opinionated, skilled, self-confident individuals into a cohesive unit may be a daunting challenge, but it's one that any rising executive must meet. "A curious but familiar phenomenon is the leader who does not form a team; that is, one who may hire able subordinates, but never creates the trust and sense of mutual dependence that characterize a team," contended John Gardner, a former Johnson aide who later wrote a classic book about leadership.

The political landscape is littered with campaigns that failed to generate such team spirit and were destroyed by poor staff work. Dozens of examples could be culled from recent history. Let's look at two.

John Glenn seemed the perfect choice for the Democratic presidential nomination in 1984. He was a certified hero, the first American astronaut to orbit the Earth. He was politically experienced, a veteran senator from Ohio. And he was drawing formidable support. Early polls showed him running far ahead of the incumbent president, Ronald Reagan.

But Glenn's campaign dissolved in organizational chaos. His longtime aides and outside consultants battled constantly, forcing a staff shakeup in October 1983 and another just three months later. The campaign's momentum dissipated completely, pushing Glenn out of the race by March. "I thought the problem would straighten itself out," he later admitted. "It never did, but became a wound that drained life from the campaign."

George McGovern advanced further than Glenn, actually winning the Democratic nomination in 1972. But his chances of defeating Richard Nixon in the general election quickly disintegrated, beginning with the misguided selection of a running mate, Thomas Eagleton, whose background had been inadequately researched by McGovern's staff. Eagleton was dropped from the ticket after the press revealed he had been treated for nervous exhaustion.

McGovern's manager, Gary Hart, admitted that his team "lost its direction, if not its soul" after the Eagleton fiasco. Despair infiltrated the headquarters. Staffers began to argue constantly. Some, quite frankly, gave up. Their candidate was buried in a landslide in November, carrying only Massachusetts and the District of Columbia.

McGovern, surprisingly enough, was able to view the ruins of his campaign in good humor. He appeared in early 1973 at Washington's Gridiron Club dinner, an event that placed a premium on comedy, and he met the challenge. McGovern confessed to the crowd that ever since he was a kid, he had wanted to run for president in the worst way. And now, he said, he had.

EXPECT YOUR LOVED ONES TO WORK ALONGSIDE YOU

George W. Bush and John Kerry disagreed about most things during the 2004 campaign, but not on fatherhood. Both men knew how challenging and frustrating kids could be. They had two daughters apiece, all between the ages of twenty-three and thirty-one and all with minds of their own.

The president acknowledged their common ground during his first debate with Kerry. "I admire the fact that he is a great dad," Bush said. "I appreciate the fact that his daughters have been so kind to my daughters in what has been a pretty hard experience for, I guess, young girls seeing their dads out there campaigning."

Kerry replied in the same vein. "I think only if you're doing this—and he's done it more than I have in terms of the presidency—can you begin to get a sense of what it means to your families, and it's tough," he said. "And so I acknowledge his daughters. I've watched them. I've chuckled a few times at some of their comments."

Bush and Kerry both smiled. "I'm trying to put a leash on them," the president said. "Well, I don't know," his challenger replied. "I've learned not to do that, Mr. President."

Both candidates, to be honest, had *unleashed* their offspring in 2004. Barbara and Jenna Bush and Alexandra and Vanessa Kerry made high-profile appearances throughout the year. They delivered speeches at the conventions that nominated their fathers, posed for photo layouts in *Vogue*, and dropped in on the Video Music Awards. They didn't have much to say, but nobody cared. "They don't have to know the briefing book. No one expects the children of the Bushes to stand up and recite why their dad opposes stem-cell research," said Paul Costello, a veteran Democratic aide. "They're there to show that their father has raised them well, and to be a mirror of the family."

Husbands, wives, sons, daughters—everyone in a political family is part of the campaign team, like it or not. Author Doug Wead, who studied the lives of presidential children, found that they had virtually no leeway. Their dads assumed that they, too, would hit the campaign trail. "Most of these presidents were alpha male to the core," Wead wrote. "They saw the whole experience as a great adventure and one that required sacrifices all around, truly a family enterprise. After all, they all had benefited, all had become famous, all had unlimited opportunities."

The same expectations exist in business. Spouses—and, to a lesser extent, children—are often invited to join in work-related activities. Their presence is requested at everything from conventions and formal dinners to cocktail parties and intimate gatherings at the boss's house. Participation is seen as a subtle way to involve them in the corporate culture, to make them feel part of the team.

Are these events optional? Can your loved ones decline? Not if you hope to advance in the company.

Woe to any rebel who plots an independent course. Howard Dean tried to separate his professional and personal lives in 2004. His wife, Judith Steinberg, didn't join him during his campaign for the Democratic presidential nomination. She stayed home in Vermont, where she practiced medicine and raised their teenaged son.

Steinberg's choice was privately ridiculed by reporters and staffers for other candidates. They called her the "absentee wife." Many voters seemed troubled, too, which eventually forced Dean to cave in to the status quo. "People have to know something about Judy to know something about me," he conceded. He asked his wife to join him in Iowa, where she made a positive impression at several events, though it was too late to keep Dean's foundering campaign afloat.

Spouses serve a decorative function at most political and business events, as Steinberg did for her husband, but they can be of far greater assistance in two other roles—social ambassador and adviser.

Calvin Coolidge's wife, Grace, was lively and outgoing, making her a perfect representative for the aloof, taciturn president. "Where he irritated people, she ingratiated herself with them," wrote Donald McCoy, a Coolidge biographer. "Where he turned men sour, she made them smile. Where he chilled women, she warmed them. In short, when he needed help, she supplied it."

Robert Taft, one of the coldest politicians ever to cross the American stage, also benefited from his wife's social skills. The vivacious Martha Taft was a fine public speaker, considerably better than her husband. She could magically convert Bob's weaknesses into strengths, once telling an audience of coal miners, "My husband is not a simple man. He did not start from humble beginnings. He is a very brilliant man. Isn't that what you prefer?" An Ohio newspaper acknowledged the equality of their partnership with its headline after a Senate election: "Bob and Martha Win."

Political spouses have doubled as advisers for more than a century. Theodore Roosevelt always discussed his work with Edith. "Whenever I go against her judgment, I regret it," he admitted. Franklin Roosevelt famously used Eleanor as his personal reporter and sounding board. She occasionally worried about becoming too prominent or outspoken. "Lady," FDR laughed in reply, "it's a free country." Jimmy Carter, Ronald Reagan, and Bill Clinton were recent presidents who depended heavily on their wives' advice. "He thought she had the magic touch," a former aide recalled of Clinton's reliance on Hillary, herself a future senator and presidential candidate.

It may seem unfair to require family members to contribute to your success. They didn't sign up to be symbols, surrogates, or consultants, so why should they be forced into those roles? Because that's what society demands. Not a satisfying answer, but it's the truth.

"You Sort of Step Outside Yourself"

If your loved ones seem willing to participate, invite all of them—parents, siblings, spouse, children, even close friends—to join your personal campaign team. They might enjoy the social opportunities, along with the chance to bask in your growing fame.

Ronald Reagan's two youngest children, Patti and Ron, were in their twenties when their father was elected president in 1980. They made the same rounds that George W. Bush's and John Kerry's kids would come to know a generation later—speeches, interviews, TV appearances.

"It can be kind of fun," Ron told a reporter at the time. "It's kind of fun to do a Barbara Walters interview. Sort of strange. You sort of step outside yourself and see yourself sitting there being interviewed by Walter Cronkite or somebody."

"It's kind of a dream," agreed Patti.

"But on the other hand," said Ron, "it *can* be a pain in the ass."

You must decide whether you and your loved ones can thrive under such expectations. If not, you should delay or even abandon your dream of becoming a leader in business or politics. Find a more reasonable goal to pursue.

Even a politician as driven as Bill Clinton has pondered this dilemma. Mickey Kantor, a California lawyer who had known the Clintons since the 1970s, witnessed a critical moment in 1987. Seven-year-old Chelsea Clinton asked her father, then the governor of Arkansas, if the family would be going on vacation that summer. Maybe not, her dad replied, since there was a good chance he would be running for president by then.

"Well," Chelsea replied, "then Mom and I will go without you."

Bill Clinton announced soon thereafter that he would skip the 1988 presidential race. "I need some family time," he said. "I need some personal time. Politicians are people, too." He eventually refocused on 1992.

COUNT ON FRIENDS FOR HELP AND A FRESH PERSPECTIVE

You might assume that Baltasar Gracian y Morales is beyond the scope of this book. We're focusing on American presidents—primarily from the nineteenth and twentieth centuries—and he was a seventeenth-century Spanish author, philosopher, and theologian.

But Gracian deserves a moment of our time. He summed up the importance of interpersonal relationships in three beautifully crisp sentences. "True friendship multiplies the good in life and divides its evils," he wrote. "Strive to have friends, for life without friends is like life on a desert island. To find one real friend in a lifetime is good fortune; to keep him is a blessing."

Friendship enriches the lives of us all—presidents included—by giving us a chance to laugh, swap tall tales, share secrets, and let off steam. Dwight Eisenhower so enjoyed his military and civilian pals that he devoted a whole book to their get-togethers, *At Ease: Stories I Tell to Friends*. Ronald Reagan was a renowned storyteller himself, happy to pass the time with even the staunchest Democrat in a social setting.

But your interest in this subject is a bit broader, isn't it? You want to be close to other people, of course, but you're also curious whether friends will be able to advance your career.

The answer is yes, as William McKinley learned firsthand. The governor of Ohio was a politician of unusual charm, a man with countless friends across America. "McKinley was more than popular, he was beloved," wrote historian Margaret Leech. "Even his political opponents were attracted by the peculiar sweetness of his personality."

And he was as loyal as he was personable. Robert Walker, a longtime acquaintance who was starting a tin-plate company, needed someone to cosign his bank loan. Anything for a friend, said McKinley. But Walker's business went bankrupt in the depression of 1893, at first glance leaving McKinley on the hook for $17,000, then an enormous amount of money. The accountants kept digging and eventually totaled the debt at $130,000, the equivalent of almost three million dollars today.

McKinley desperately needed cash. His only recourse, he assumed, was to quit as governor, abandon his dreams of becoming president, and return to the practice of law. Mark Hanna, his political patron, begged for a delay to allow McKinley's friends and supporters to handle the matter. Contributions poured in from every corner of the nation, completely retiring the debt.

McKinley, far from being damaged by this affair, emerged with his image enhanced. He had been victimized by the depression—as had so many Americans—yet he had done the right thing. He stood by a man who needed his help, and in turn was helped by others who held him in high esteem. He was elected president three years later.

Another advantage of friendship is that it can provide you with a fresh perspective. Friends can offer advice or even an inside scoop that would be unavailable anywhere else. John Kennedy included journalists in his wide circle of friends, and wasn't above pumping them for information or using them as scouts. Ben Bradlee—then a *Newsweek* correspondent, later the editor of the *Washington Post*—not only covered Kennedy's archrival, Lyndon Johnson, for the magazine, but also kept JFK informed about LBJ's presidential campaign. "The image is poor," Bradlee wrote dismissively of Johnson in a confidential memo to Kennedy. "The accent hurts. He's somebody's gabby cousin from Fort Worth." The memo was considerably more colorful than Bradlee's stories in *Newsweek*.

The sad thing is that many of us are losing the touch for friendship, even though we know how valuable it is. The typical American confides in only two people, including family members. One-quarter of us have no close confidants at all, according to a 2006 study in the *American Sociological Review*.

It's possible—but risky—to pursue a career in business or politics without the gift for friendship. Both professions place a premium on interpersonal skills. If you lack the ability to reach out to others, you should pay special attention to the stories of Woodrow Wilson and Richard Nixon.

Wilson won the presidency in 1912 despite his withdrawn personality. William Allen White, a famous journalist of the time, compared Wilson's handshake unfavorably to "a ten-cent pickled mackerel in brown paper." The new president, despite his exalted office, admitted that he still found it difficult to meet people. "Sometimes, I am a bit ashamed of myself when I think how few friends I have amidst a host of acquaintances," he wrote. "Plenty of people offer me their friendship; but, partly because I am reserved and shy, and partly because I am fastidious and have a narrow, uncatholic taste in friends, I reject the offer in almost every case."

Nixon pursued a political career despite a temperament similar to Wilson's. "I don't think he genuinely liked people," concluded William Ruckelshaus, who was appointed to several positions by Nixon. "I think he was fascinated by them, and interested in them, and tried to understand them, but I don't think he liked them. I marveled at how much he had to control himself—how desirous he was of possessing power—because he overcame this unease."

Both administrations ended badly. Wilson's power and popularity unraveled after World War I, when he refused to compromise with his Senate foes on the terms of the peace treaty. Nixon was forced to resign as the Watergate crisis spiraled out of control. Both men fixated on their enemies. Neither had the ability to widen his circle of supporters.

What Nixon really needed, in the opinion of his Federal Reserve Board chairman, Arthur Burns, was a close personal friend, someone he could talk to during times of trouble. Burns doubted that Nixon had ever known such a person. He certainly didn't in the final months of Watergate, when he spent more and more time alone in his office.

It was all a pity, Burns thought. "A friend like that," he said, "could have saved him."

That doesn't mean you're home free if you have plenty of friends. Warren Harding was an extremely personable man, a great drinking buddy, and the perfect companion at the poker table. But he lacked the ability to discriminate between pure friendship and opportunism.

Many of his acquaintances were guilty of the latter. Harding liberally sprinkled his administration with friends, appointing them to key posts. Several proceeded to loot the government—taking bribes and kickbacks, selling off government supplies to private firms for pennies on the dollar, and virtually giving away federal oil reserves. The president's old friend from Ohio, Attorney General Harry Daugherty, was especially brazen in his thievery. Comedians around Washington suggested that the Department of Justice should be renamed the Department of Easy Virtue.

Harding began to learn of these crimes shortly before his death in 1923. A visitor to the White House that year was shocked to hear loud voices and the sounds of a struggle in the Red Room. He raced in to find the president choking a man against the wall.

"You yellow rat," Harding yelled. "You double-crossing bastard. If you ever...." He saw the startled visitor and released his grip. "I'm sorry," the president said to the onlooker. "You have an appointment. Come into the other room." The man he was choking—the larcenous head of the Veterans Bureau—staggered away.

There is no evidence that Harding took so much as a dime, but his friends—immortalized as the Ohio Gang—made away with millions. Their scandals became public only after Harding's death, but he was plainly a troubled man in his final days. "I have no trouble with my enemies," he confessed to William Allen White. "I can take care of my enemies all right. But my damn friends, my goddamn friends, White, they're the ones that keep me walking the floor nights!"

KEEP EXPANDING YOUR PROFESSIONAL NETWORK

James Farley's political credentials were impeccable. He worked his way up to become chairman of New York's Democratic Party by 1930, emerging as one of Governor Franklin Roosevelt's key advisers. But there was more to his life than politics. He also served as national president of the Benevolent and Protective Order of Elks. His major concern in the summer of 1931 was preparing for that organization's annual meeting in Seattle.

Farley considered the Elks' convention a chance to get out of New York and have some fun. But Roosevelt saw a bigger opportunity. He pushed his aide to turn the trip into a working vacation, perhaps visiting a few Democratic leaders along the way. "At his suggestion," Farley recalled, "I was equipped with a Rand McNally map of the United States, a flock of train schedules, and the latest available list of Democratic National Committee members and state chairmen."

The two men spread out their map and plotted a zigzag route to Seattle. It took Farley three weeks to travel from coast to coast, stopping off to see 1,100 party officials along the way. He remembered the trip as "a sort of graduation from the political minor league." It also marked the informal beginning of the following year's Roosevelt-for-president campaign.

Farley didn't miss a chance to sing his boss's praises, though his real objective was to see and be seen. He hoped to establish contacts that might prove useful in the future. "I was extremely careful to get first and last names correctly," he said, "and, of course, never disputed the views of others if it was at all possible to agree."

The term wasn't used in those days, but Jim Farley was networking. He was widening his circle of professional acquaintances, putting faces to names, and making himself visible. He hoped that his rambling trip to Seattle would pay dividends in 1932, when Roosevelt would need widespread delegate support to win the Democratic presidential nomination. It did. Farley's new friends from distant southern and western states delivered crucial votes to FDR at the convention.

Networking has always been a foundation for success in politics and business. The cliché—"it's not *what* you know; it's *who* you know"—has an element of truth behind it. People naturally are more comfortable with men and women they've already met—and therefore are more likely to vote for them, do business with them, and promote them.

It takes organizational skill to build your own network. The first requirement, as Farley acknowledged, is to get out there and mix. Seize on any pretext to meet prospective clients or helpers. Take note of everybody you meet—and make sure to keep their names straight.

Modern campaign strategists like to believe that they've perfected such recordkeeping. They boast of computer databases that hold millions of names, all cross-filed by street addresses, phone numbers, and political preferences. Their systems are all very impressive, but the truth is that candidates have been keeping lists of potential supporters since the birth of the republic. They've proved that you don't need to go the high-tech route. A pen and a stack of index cards will do just fine.

That's what Woodrow Wilson's campaign used a century ago. His headquarters kept a file on every delegate to the 1912 Democratic convention. The cards were surprisingly comprehensive, as suggested by this sample: "Mayor for sixteen years. For Underwood first, and Wilson as second choice. Very vain. Treat him like a big man, and you can handle him. Has three children. Wonderful children. Likes to talk about them." These cards were given to key Wilson supporters, who used the information to sway wavering delegates. They undoubtedly treated the sixteen-year mayor as a "big man" and asked about his kids. Perhaps he eventually ditched Oscar Underwood for Wilson.

Scores of politicians have built their networks the same way. George McGovern hit the road in 1969 with an improbable dream of winning the presidency three years later. Early polls pegged his support at less than 1 percent, but McGovern persevered. He crisscrossed America, talking to any group that would listen. A few people inevitably came up after each speech to say a kind word and shake his hand. McGovern's aide stood alongside with a handful of three-by-five cards, ready to jot down their names, addresses, and phone numbers. These supporters eventually would be asked to volunteer their services in 1972, and thousands did, creating the powerful organization that rolled to the Democratic nomination.

They responded because McGovern stayed in touch after their initial meeting. He knew that his network would erode without communication, so he and his staff maintained contact with the people in his ever-expanding files. McGovern's efforts were nothing special—a form letter here, a mass-mailed Christmas card there—but they were good enough. The same process of communication should be substantially easier for you in this era of cell phones, fax machines, and e-mail.

If you're diligent, you can greatly expand the number of people you know. The elder George Bush was a master of wholesale networking. His favorite tool was the thank-you note. He wrote them after every campaign appearance, literally thousands over the years, as author Richard Ben Cramer has described: "And after every dinner, every barbecue or picnic, Bush'd get back on his plane, and ask his area chairman: 'Who're the ten people I wanna thank in Pecos?' And he'd do those ten notes before he was halfway home. Back in Houston, he'd do a few dozen more, banging them out on his own machine, with typos and x-outs and other endearing steno foibles, all explained in the top-right corner of the note, where he'd put, 'Self-typed by GB.'"

Bush's wife, Barbara, helped spin this massive web. She took charge of the family's extensive Christmas card list, which gradually spilled over into a box of file cards. The list began with family and friends, of course, and was augmented with people the Bushes met when George was a congressman, United Nations ambassador, CIA director, unsuccessful presidential candidate in 1980, and vice president for eight years.

It contained 4,000 to 5,000 names by the mid-1970s—and kept growing. Volunteers had to be called in to maintain it. A computer database was established in 1983. So many people received Christmas cards from the Bushes that the woman who addressed the envelopes—a lady with exquisite handwriting—had to start the task in the spring.

And still it grew. George and Barbara Bush sent out 30,000 cards by 1986, a few months before he formally launched another national campaign. Their Christmas card list had become the ultimate network, a gift-wrapped package of friends and supporters who were determined to see George H.W. Bush elected president of the United States.

Their wishes came true shortly before Christmas in 1988.

COLLECT CHITS FROM ANYONE YOU CAN

Richard Nixon fell into a slump as he reached middle age. His downward spiral began with a heartbreaking loss to John Kennedy in the 1960 presidential election. The margin may have been narrow, but Nixon's confidence was badly shaken. It was the first defeat of his career.

The best remedy, he eventually decided, was to reenter politics as quickly as possible. Nixon joined the 1962 race for governor of California with high hopes. How difficult could it be for a former vice president to win a mere statewide election? But he lost again, and by a much larger margin than the first time. Frustration poured out when he met reporters. "You won't have Nixon to kick around anymore," he snapped, "because, gentlemen, this is my last press conference." He was washed up at the age of forty-nine.

Nixon fled California within weeks, ostensibly to start a new life outside the spotlight. "I came to New York to practice law and not to practice politics," he insisted to anyone who would listen.

That wasn't the case, of course. Nixon returned to the campaign trail in 1964, making more than 150 public appearances. The difference this time was that he was working for others. He said nothing about his own political future, preferring to boost the Republican ticket headed by presidential nominee Barry Goldwater.

Nixon's diligence was unusual. Most Republican leaders did little or nothing to help Goldwater, whose reputation for extreme opinions and loose talk had stamped him as a certain loser in the general election. But Nixon maintained a veneer of public optimism, predicting a "strong Republican surge." It never occurred.

Goldwater was grateful for the support. He introduced Nixon at a 1965 Republican National Committee meeting as the man "who worked harder than any one person for the ticket." He turned to Nixon and said, "Dick, I will never forget it. I know that you did it in the interests of the Republican Party and not for any selfish reasons. But if there ever comes a time I can turn those into selfish reasons, I'm going to do all I can to see that it comes about."

Nixon's career was clearly on the upswing. He told reporters in 1965 that the next Republican nominee "very probably is not going to be me," but he no longer believed it. He just started working harder, traveling anywhere the party wanted him to go. He spoke to more than 400 Republican groups in forty states during the next two years—still deflecting questions about himself, still insisting he was there only to help the party's candidates for state and local offices.

The payoff came in November 1966, when the Republicans fared surprisingly well in the congressional elections. Nixon was given considerable credit. "We've beaten the hell out of them," he crowed to an aide, "and we're going to kill them in '68." The time for his own campaign was finally at hand.

Reporters were surprised at the smoothness of Nixon's comeback. He sewed up the 1968 Republican presidential nomination fairly easily. The disparate elements of the party fell into line. Goldwater and many of his hard-core conservative supporters pledged their support, as did the Republican National Committee's moderate majority. Hundreds of up-and-coming office-holders were only too glad to repay the man who had helped them get elected.

Nixon affected modesty, denying there had been any master plan. "It was not by dint of my own calculation or efforts," he said of his return to prominence. "No man, not if he combined the wisdom of Lincoln with the connivance of Machiavelli, could have maneuvered or manipulated his way back into the arena."

That was utter nonsense. Nixon's hard work and prowess as a campaigner had put thousands of key Republicans in his debt during the mid-1960s, and he knew it. He had spent those years "collecting chits," the political term for piling up brownie points or pocketing IOUs. The 1968 election was his chance to cash in—and that's exactly what he did.

Many of Nixon's traits and habits shouldn't be emulated—not his isolated lifestyle, his awkward attempts at humor, his persecution complex, or his obsessive need to settle scores with his enemies. But his dexterity in collecting chits is a skill worth noting and imitating.

Any rising politician or business executive can benefit from doing favors for others. Help anyone you can whenever you can—provided, of course, that they aren't your direct rivals. Don't worry where the recipients of your favors fit on the company's organizational chart. Above you, below you—it makes no difference. You never know who might hold the power to advance your career at a critical moment in the future.

Patience is essential, since it might be years before you're able to cash in a chit. Abraham Lincoln slowly built a political network across Illinois in the 1840s and 1850s—making friends, lining up supporters, assessing the opposition. He finally made his move in 1854, declaring his candidacy for a Senate seat. The state legislature, not the voters, elected senators in those days, so he focused his energies on that small group of men in Springfield, the state capital.

Lincoln called in every IOU he could, even contacting people he hadn't seen for years. A letter he wrote to a former law client, Charles Hoyt, was typical. "You used to express a good deal of partiality for me," he wrote, "and if you are still so, now is the time. Some friends here are really for me for the U.S. Senate." Lincoln asked Hoyt to "make a mark for me" with any legislator he might know. His friends tried, but their efforts fell short. Lincoln would lose the 1854 Senate election and another in 1858, yet he persisted in weaving his vast web of supporters. The payoff finally came in the presidential campaign of 1860.

"He Must Have Spent a Fortune on Flowers"

Jimmy Carter faced a dilemma in 1974. Georgia's constitution prohibited him from seeking reelection as governor, yet he needed a political position of some sort to sustain his hopes of running for president two years later. He called Robert Strauss, the chairman of the Democratic National Committee, and asked if there was any way he could help. Strauss, simply to be polite, made Carter the head of the DNC's national campaign, historically an honorary position that required no heavy lifting.

Carter changed the job completely. He traveled the length and breadth of America in 1974, working tirelessly for Democrats in thirty-two states. He didn't seek publicity for himself, but spent as much time as he could with the candidates and their managers. His unspoken hope was that these state and local politicians might reciprocate by endorsing him, an obscure Southern governor, for president in 1976. He courted them assiduously. "He must have spent a fortune in the last two years on flowers," marveled Mark Siegel, then the DNC's executive director. "At every wedding, birth, and funeral in a Democratic family, there were flowers and a card from Jimmy."

Those gestures, as we all know, had the desired effect.

MAKE ALLIANCES WITH ANYBODY WHO CAN HELP YOU

You're the type who doesn't want any help. You're happy to fight your enemies single-handedly. No useless sidekicks, no hangers-on, no excess baggage. Your own wits and abilities are all you need to survive in the corporate wilderness, to win on your own terms.

You're a lone wolf.

Leadership gurus Ronald Heifetz and Marty Linsky understand the temptation: "There's no one to dilute your ideas or share the glory, and it's often just plain exciting." But lone wolfdom, they warn, carries a big downside: "It's also foolish. You need to recruit partners, people who can help protect you from attacks and who can point out potentially fatal flaws in your strategy or initiative."

Let's be clear. Heifetz and Linsky aren't suggesting that you make new friends or turn a quick deal. (Friends and deals are essential, of course, which is why both are discussed elsewhere in this book.) No, they're recommending that you create durable alliances.

Allies are useful in several ways. They can watch your back and offer advice, as Heifetz and Linsky point out. They also can ease your workload, expand your sources of information, and put extra weight behind your decisions. There's strength in numbers, as we all know.

The obvious parallel is the military one. Great Britain, the Soviet Union, and the United States were outmuscled by the Axis powers during the early phase of World War II. Nazi Germany and Imperial Japan seemed destined to rule the world. But the three Allies combined their economic and military strength to turn the tide. The Americans and Russians weren't great buddies—they certainly didn't see eye to eye on the virtues of Karl Marx—but they could agree at least on the necessity of defeating Adolf Hitler.

But, you ask, aren't great leaders individualists at heart? Don't they go it alone whenever possible? Legend would have us believe so, but it's grossly out of sync with reality.

If any political figure ever seemed inclined to be a lone wolf, it was Lyndon Johnson. He wanted everything for himself—all the glory, all the money, all the power. He refused to accept anything less.

LBJ had an obsessive need to one-up people, a compulsion that extended to every aspect of his life. It motivated decisions as minor as his purchase of a mobile telephone in the 1950s, back when they were exceedingly rare. Johnson served as Democratic leader in the Senate, and he loved to conduct Senate business from the backseat of his limousine, always making sure that the person on the other end of the line knew about his newfangled car phone.

Then came the fateful day. A loud bell broke the silence in LBJ's limo. It was the Republican leader, Everett Dirksen, calling from his own car. Dirksen crowed that he had achieved telephonic equality. Johnson had to think fast. He interrupted Dirksen. "Could you hold on a second, Ev?" he asked. "My other phone is ringing."

Anyone with such a desperate need for superiority would seem to be an unlikely alliance-builder, but Lyndon Johnson actually was one of the best of all time. He understood that he couldn't attain his lofty personal goals without plenty of outside help.

This insight came during his years at Southwest Texas State Teachers College, where student politics was dominated by a secret society known as the Black Stars. LBJ, who was already ambitious for political power, made the logical move. He tried to join the in-group. But he was neither an athlete nor a Big Man on Campus, which meant he wasn't Black Star material. The door was slammed in his face.

So Johnson did the next best thing, patching together an alliance of outsiders like himself. He called every shot for the White Stars, as his group became known, though he chose to remain discreetly in the background.

A friend of his ran as the White Stars' candidate for president—and won, thanks to Johnson's organizational skills and tireless support. The White Stars soon controlled student government and campus jobs at Southwest Texas State. The Black Stars found themselves in the unaccustomed position of being without power or influence.

This collegiate triumph guided Johnson's adult career. He built alliances with anyone who could help him, especially Sam Rayburn, the Speaker of the House when LBJ was a congressman, and Richard Russell, a senior and highly influential member of the Senate. He cozied up to a president from the other political party, Dwight Eisenhower, when circumstances warranted. And he linked arms with liberal Democrats whenever it served his purposes, even though he despised much of what they stood for.

Edward Clark, Texas's secretary of state in the 1930s, noted this tendency toward alliances when Johnson was a young congressional aide and then a fledgling congressman. "Nothing was too much trouble for him to do," Clark recalled, "for someone who might be able to help him someday."

LBJ honed this skill to an art by the time he reached the White House in 1963. Political insiders were amazed at President Johnson's ability to form partnerships and coalitions. He pressured, persuaded, and pleaded with congressmen and senators at breakfasts, luncheons, dinners, meetings in the Oval Office, and on innumerable phone calls. He bargained with anyone who might be able to help pass his legislation, from the most powerful committee chairman to a rookie legislator from the minority party.

His touch was golden in the early years of his administration. Few presidents, if any, have rung up legislative successes that were greater than Johnson's in 1964 and 1965. Cynics scoffed that the "Xerox Congress" passed whatever the president told it to pass, whenever he wanted it done.

But LBJ's alliance-building skills rusted badly in later years. Racial unrest and the Vietnam War polarized the nation. Key Democrats turned against the leader of their party. Prominent among these critics was J. William Fulbright, chairman of the influential Senate Foreign Relations Committee, who believed that the president had blundered into an unnecessary war in Southeast Asia.

There was a time when Johnson would have reached out to the likes of Fulbright, seeking common ground on which to form a new partnership, no matter how deeply they disagreed on Vietnam. But the weary, bitter president of 1967 and 1968 settled for ridiculing "Senator Halfbright" as "a revolving son of a bitch." The latter term, he explained, applied to "someone who's a son of a bitch any way you look at him." Relations predictably soured between the administration and Congress. The torrent of legislation slowed to a trickle.

Lyndon Johnson, the master wheeler-dealer, lost control of the country because of his inability—or unwillingness—to do what he had once done best. He acknowledged the irony during his final night in the White House. "Perhaps it would have been different with Fulbright if we had only talked to him more, found some things to agree with him on," he mused to an aide. "We never should have let the fight become so personal."

5

Controlling

Horace Greeley was perfectly suited for his chosen career, and he knew it. The New Hampshire lad signed up as an editor's apprentice at the age of fourteen, his first step toward journalistic stardom. He founded the *New York Tribune* in 1841—when he was still just thirty years old—and established it as the nation's preeminent newspaper by 1860.

The *Tribune* became a must-read prior to the Civil War because of Greeley's trenchant editorials. He led the chorus condemning the Supreme Court's *Dred Scott* decision in 1857. Slaves were property of their masters, not citizens of the United States, said the justices. But Greeley scoffed that the court's ruling was "entitled to just so much moral weight as would be the judgment of a majority of those congregated in any Washington barroom."

Slavery was his greatest hatred, but dozens of other causes stirred him to action. It seemed he had an opinion on *everything*. Greeley wrote in the mid-1840s that women had a "natural right" to vote, seventy-five years before they were allowed to participate in elections. He steadfastly supported labor unions, decades before they began making headway in American society. And he became the foremost proponent of frontier expansion. "Go West, young man, go West," was his most famous saying.

Greeley was proud of the national acclaim that he and his newspaper received. He was "a self-made man who worships his creator," in the amused opinion of Henry Clapp Jr., a *Tribune* reporter. Yet the power of the printed word wasn't enough. Greeley wanted political power, too. He wanted to be president.

John Russell Young, the *Tribune*'s managing editor, worried that his boss was ill-suited for this change in careers. "Mr. Greeley would be the greatest journalist in America," Young sighed, "if he did not aim to be one of the leading politicians in America." The very qualities that made Greeley so successful as an editorialist—eagerness to speak out on any issue, enthusiasm for extreme causes, open disdain for enemies—would serve him badly as an elected official.

But Greeley pushed on, constantly angling to become governor of New York or a member of the Senate. The best he could do was a three-month term in the House of Representatives, where his lack of self-control made him an outcast almost instantly. The rookie boldly charged his fellow congressmen with cheating the federal treasury by filing false expense reports. They responded with unanimous contempt. "I have divided the House into two parties," Greeley confessed, "one that would like to see me extinguished, and the other is one that couldn't be satisfied without a hand in doing it."

Yet he never learned the value of silence. Greeley proceeded to alienate his fellow Republicans by mistakenly abandoning Abraham Lincoln's bandwagon in 1864: "Mr. Lincoln is already beaten. He cannot be elected." And he lashed the other party with equal intensity: "All Democrats may not be rascals, but all rascals are Democrats." Both sides disliked him. Neither wanted to see him in the White House.

A new party eventually came to the rescue. Reformers opposed to the reelection of Ulysses Grant created the Liberal Republican Party in 1872 and, to considerable amazement, tapped Greeley as their presidential nominee. The Democrats, to even greater shock, followed suit. "Six weeks ago," gasped Thurlow Weed, a Republican strategist, "I did not suppose that any considerable number of men, outside of a lunatic asylum, would nominate Greeley for president."

The Republicans couldn't have been happier. All they had to do was turn Greeley's own words against him. They assembled a team to comb through thousands of his editorials and speeches, looking for inflammatory and contradictory statements. It proved to be an easy task. Hundreds of prime examples were slapped into a book of quotations, *What I Know About Politics*, with Greeley's name on the cover. Republicans gleefully distributed it far and wide. Greeley didn't help his cause with a fresh torrent of two hundred campaign speeches that featured a bizarre admission that his prewar opposition to slavery "might have been a mistake."

Greeley's campaign sank under the weight of all the controversial positions he had taken and all the enemies he had made during his lengthy career. "I have been assailed so bitterly," he complained, "that I hardly knew whether I was running for the presidency or the penitentiary." Grant was easily reelected, and the brokenhearted Greeley died just twenty-four days after the election. He was, cynics said, silent at last.

Self-control doesn't come naturally. Most people struggle from cradle to grave to master their impulses and emotions. Horace Greeley never got the hang of it. American icons like George Washington and Abraham Lincoln dealt more effectively with their personal demons, and they reaped the benefits.

Washington was cursed with a titanic temper, which he generally managed to keep under wraps. But there was always the danger that an incident—major or minor—might trigger a fiery outburst. His anger flared up when the Continental Army panicked in an early Revolutionary War battle. Washington swore violently at his troops, flailed at them with his riding crop, and flung his hat to the ground in disgust. "Are these the men with which I am to defend America?" he shouted. His frustration was understandable in the heat of battle, but other explosions seemed trivial. He raged at the commander of his headquarters guard in a dispute over a tent, and let loose again when he couldn't get lumber for a kitchen at the army's winter camp.

Washington mellowed with age, making a conscious effort to hold his temper in check as he shifted from military life to politics. The image he presented as America's first president from 1789 to 1797 was calm, distinguished, and fatherly—precisely what the new nation needed. His occasional tantrums were kept behind closed doors, such as the instance when Thomas Jefferson saw the president in "one of those passions when he cannot command himself." Historian James Thomas Flexner conceded that Washington waged a "lifetime battle for self-control," one that was usually successful.

Abraham Lincoln, despite his kindly demeanor, was also capable of sudden bursts of anger and sarcasm, though they weren't habitual occurrences. His personal burden was depression. "If what I feel were equally distributed to the whole human family," he admitted, "there would not be one cheerful face on the Earth." His law partner, William Herndon, once said, "His melancholy dripped from him as he walked."

Lincoln's depression haunted him in the White House, where he suffered many a sleepless night, yet his miraculous self-control allowed him to offer hope and optimism to a war-torn nation. He brightened meetings with his lively sense of humor and his talents as a storyteller. He inspired the North with the Gettysburg Address and other flights of oratory. And he demonstrated the rare ability to rise above meaningless feuds. "A man has not time to spend half his life in quarrels," he said. "If any man ceases to attack me, I never remember the past against him."

If you hope to be successful in business or politics, you will need similar self-mastery. Conduct your daily affairs with restraint and an air of detachment. Fight your inner demons vigorously, but take a calmer approach toward the outside forces that stand in your way. This chapter examines each of these points in turn:

Personal restraint

- If you don't have to speak, keep your mouth shut.
- Stay upbeat, humble, and as cool as possible.
- Avoid controversy and extreme statements.

Detachment

- Maintain your flexibility to keep up with the times.
- Don't obsess about popularity or margin of victory.
- Don't give a potential rival an inadvertent boost.

Inner demons

- If you have an addiction, battle it fiercely.
- Don't let your temper get the best of you.

Outer forces

- Mollify (or ignore) potential enemies when possible.
- If an enemy attacks, defend yourself vigorously.
- Certain enemies can actually help you advance.

It's a difficult feat, indeed, to reach the summit of your profession if you lack these elements of self-control. It's almost impossible to stay on top—or to build a lasting legacy—without them, as Richard Nixon and Bill Clinton learned to their great unhappiness.

Nixon appeared to be the epitome of a disciplined president, staying cool in public and carefully planning every move. But he was obsessed with the people who opposed him. He ordered his staff to compile an enemies list that ballooned to more than three hundred names. His aim, as aide John Dean explained in a 1971 memo, was to "use the available federal machinery to screw our political enemies" by harassing and spying on them, a vast array of crimes and abuses that would be immortalized under the collective title of Watergate. Even his landslide reelection in 1972 could not diminish Nixon's paranoia. "I guess the Kennedy crowd is just laying in the bushes, waiting to make their move," he groused to Dean after his victory.

Clinton was the great natural politician of his era—amiable and persuasive in public, tough and demanding in private. He waved off rumors that he was an unfaithful husband. "We feel good about where we are, and we believe in our obligation to each other," he said of his wife, Hillary, during his first presidential campaign in 1992. But their marriage, and the country's patience, were tested by the president's affair with a White House intern, Monica Lewinsky. Clinton vehemently denied the allegations at first—"I did not have sexual relations with that woman"—before reluctantly confessing in the face of overwhelming evidence.

Nixon and Clinton were blessed with impressive brainpower and strong capacities for work. But they paid a stiff price for their lack of self-control. Nixon was forced from office because of Watergate. Clinton came close to the same fate because of Lewinsky. Character flaws blunted the effectiveness and damaged the reputations of both men, making them appear weak and untrustworthy. "I did what people do when they do the wrong thing," Clinton admitted ruefully. "I tried to do it when nobody else was looking."

IF YOU DON'T HAVE TO SPEAK, KEEP YOUR MOUTH SHUT

Stephen Douglas needed a fresh idea. The Illinois senator's first presidential campaign in 1852 had not gone well, and he was planning to run again in 1856. He needed a galvanizing issue this time, something that would attract the support he lacked in '52 and set him apart from the other contenders for the Democratic nomination. But what could it be?

The answer dropped into his lap in 1854. A bill to divide Nebraska Territory into two new states, Kansas and Nebraska, was referred to the Senate Committee on Territories, which Douglas chaired. His colleagues looked to him for leadership on the issue, though most of them accepted the fact that slavery would be prohibited in both states, following the guidelines that had been established thirty-four years earlier by the Missouri Compromise.

Douglas, however, suggested a different tack. He proposed that the residents of Kansas and Nebraska be allowed to decide the slavery issue themselves—a concept known as "popular sovereignty." Douglas admitted privately that such a shift in federal policy might raise "a hell of a storm," but he was convinced that its impact could only be positive for his presidential campaign. The bill would increase his popularity in the slaveholding South, he thought, without hurting his Northern base. He doubted that either state would actually endorse slavery in the end.

Popular sovereignty proved to be every bit as controversial as Douglas had anticipated, but he stuck to his plan, masterfully guiding the bill through the Senate. "I passed the Kansas-Nebraska Act myself," he boasted. "I had the authority and power of a dictator throughout the whole controversy in both houses. The speeches were nothing." He sat back and waited for the anticipated uptick in political support.

It never came. Northerners raged that Douglas had opened the door too wide for slavery in the territories. Southerners sputtered that he hadn't opened it far enough. Open warfare broke out between pro- and anti-slavery factions in Kansas. Douglas was stunned by the hostility he faced on his return home in August 1854. "I could travel from Boston to Chicago by the light of my own effigy," he wrote. "I could find my effigy upon every tree we passed." One of his friends said that the senator looked "like a man who sorrows for a misdeed."

Douglas's bold stance on the most controversial issue of the day contrasted with the muffled position taken by another unsuccessful candidate from the previous election. James Buchanan had sailed off to become the American minister to Great Britain after losing the 1852 race for the Democratic nomination. His appointment turned out to be a fortunate one, since it kept him safely in London while Douglas was igniting the Kansas-Nebraska firestorm.

Buchanan, like Douglas, intended to run again in 1856. But John Slidell, a senator from Louisiana, encouraged him to delay his campaign and stay overseas as long as he could. "The political atmosphere at Washington is malarious," Slidell wrote, "and those who are not compelled to inhale it had better keep away." Buchanan accepted his advice, but couldn't resist writing several letters about the growing crisis. Slidell admonished him to remain totally quiet. "You cannot well be in a better position than you are now," he insisted.

Buchanan's friend was right. The Democratic Party had three candidates to choose from in 1856. There was the incumbent, Franklin Pierce, who was widely disliked. There was the Illinois lightning rod, Douglas, who had alienated both sections of the country. And there was the amiable ambassador, Buchanan, whose views on the Kansas-Nebraska Act were unclear.

The Democrats opted for the man with the fewest enemies. Buchanan coasted to the presidency.

Silence can be golden in politics or business. There are times, of course, when you absolutely must make yourself heard, but the ability to remain quiet is a positive attribute for upwardly mobile men and women in any profession. "A certain sphinx-like quality," said Dwight Eisenhower, "will do a lot toward enhancing one's reputation." Here are five rules—accompanied by five cautionary tales—that will help you hold your tongue:

1. Don't stir up an unnecessary ruckus. Ernest Hollings was a colorful senator from South Carolina who sought the Democratic presidential nomination in 1984. His biggest handicap, in fact, was that he was *too* colorful—and too noisy. He had a quote for every occasion and a taunt for every opponent.

Hollings called the eventual Democratic nominee, Walter Mondale, a "lap dog" who would "lick the hand of everyone in sight." He proposed to end the war in Lebanon by "putting all the striped-pants diplomats at the end of the runway." Giving aid to Latin America, he said, was like "delivering lettuce by way of a rabbit." How could the economy be improved? "Shoot all the economists," he suggested.

One of his friends expressed concern that Hollings's "big mouth and loose tongue" would ruin his chances of reaching the White House. Those worries became reality after the early primaries.

2. Don't tell cruel jokes. Humor is usually an appealing quality, but it can backfire if it comes at the expense of a segment of society. Bob Kerrey, a senator from Nebraska, paid the price for telling an off-color joke to a fellow contender for the 1992 Democratic nomination, Bill Clinton. Kerrey thought that he and Clinton were having a private conversation prior to a public event in New Hampshire, but a boom microphone was dangling over his head. It caught him spinning an unprintable tale involving another Democratic hopeful, Jerry Brown, and a couple of lesbians.

An uproar ensued. Kerrey had previously earned a high rating from the National Gay and Lesbian Task Force, but it no longer counted for much. Liberal groups that had applauded his legislative record were now picketing his public appearances. "It boggles the mind," said Gregory King of the

Human Rights Campaign Fund, "that a man thinks he's smart enough to be president of the United States, but is not smart enough to know that bigotry is not a joke." Kerrey was one of the race's early casualties.

3. Don't make excuses. The Depression struck a few months after Herbert Hoover assumed the presidency in 1929. The sudden collapse wasn't expressly his fault, though he *had* been influential in shaping the nation's economic policy as a Republican cabinet member since 1921.

But Hoover didn't want to shoulder any of the blame himself, nor did he think the Republicans should be held responsible. He pointed overseas, insisting that the Depression had started in "the great storm center ... in Europe," even though most economists believed that domestic factors had played a key role. He eventually took aim at the opposition party, too, warning that "grass would grow in the streets of America" if a Democrat were elected to replace him. He later characterized Franklin Roosevelt's anti-Depression measures in early 1933 as "Roosevelt hysteria."

Average Americans grew tired of Hoover's excuses and blame-shifting. They went too far the other way, saddling him with total responsibility. Rickety towns of shacks and tents, occupied by the homeless and the unemployed, had sprung up across the American landscape. These sad places came to be known as "Hoovervilles."

4. Don't whine. Henry Clay earned widespread acclaim in the era before the Civil War. He held several important offices—speaker of the House, senator, secretary of state. But he never won the presidency, despite mounting five campaigns between 1824 and 1848.

Clay attained success at a young age because of his charming personality and his grace and power as a public speaker. But his reputation began to take on a negative tinge after 1840, when William Henry Harrison defeated him for the Whig Party's nomination. "I am the most unfortunate man in the history of parties," he wailed, "always run by my friends when sure to be defeated, and now betrayed for a nomination when I, or anyone, would be sure of election." His whining intensified during the final twelve years of his life, as he fell short with two more presidential campaigns in 1844 and 1848. Clay frequently asked, "Was ever man before treated as I have been and am now?" This recurring lament did nothing to increase his popularity.

5. Don't cry. Edmund Muskie entered the 1972 campaign as the acknowledged frontrunner for the Democratic nomination. The senator from Maine was tall, imposing, and very lucky that the year's initial primary was scheduled for neighboring New Hampshire, where he seemed certain to win.

But the New Hampshire campaign proved to be tougher than expected, largely because the right-wing publisher of the state's largest newspaper, William Loeb, was attacking Muskie on a daily basis, even singling out the candidate's wife in one column. Muskie's advisers assured him that the primary was well in hand. Don't waste your breath on Loeb, they told him, but the senator was determined to defend his wife's honor. He stood outside the newspaper's offices on a cold, snowy day to deliver a stinging rebuke.

It did not have the desired effect. Muskie appeared to be crying as he lashed back at Loeb. He insisted that snowflakes were melting and trickling down his cheeks—"there wasn't a tear on my face"—but his image was ruined. The stories coming out of New Hampshire insinuated that Muskie had no self-control, that he wasn't strong enough to be president. "I was just goddamned mad and choked up over my anger," he later admitted. The erstwhile frontrunner was forced to abandon his campaign shortly after the arrival of spring.

STAY UPBEAT, HUMBLE, AND AS COOL AS POSSIBLE

Knives were quickly pulled from their sheaths when the battle for the Democratic presidential nomination began in 2004.

Howard Dean, a former governor of Vermont, surprised almost everyone by emerging as the frontrunner before the first contest of the year, the Iowa caucuses. His rapid ascent threatened John Kerry and Richard Gephardt— both of whom were banking heavily on Iowa—and they reacted as candidates who lack momentum typically do. They started to slash ferociously at the leader. Dean was too liberal, too inexperienced, too offbeat, they asserted. Dean sliced back with equal fervor. Kerry and Gephardt were too cautious, too jaded, too predictable, he insisted.

One candidate stayed aloof from this clash of political cutlery. John Edwards, a little-known senator from North Carolina, had pledged to run a positive campaign. "I came here a year ago with a belief that we could change this country," he told audiences in Iowa, "with a belief that the politics of what was possible, the politics of hope, could overcome the politics of cynicism." Edwards occasionally unloaded on the Republican president, George W. Bush—"a man who only values wealth and money"—but he refused to say anything negative about his fellow Democrats.

His upbeat approach impressed Pam Kulczyk, a thirty-six-year-old Iowa voter who was disgusted by the other Democratic contenders and their swordplay. "The East Coast tough-guy thing doesn't go over with me," she told a reporter. Kulczyk decided to vote for Edwards because he was the rare candidate who offered an affirmative vision. "That," she said, "was huge for me."

Thousands of Iowans agreed. Kerry fought his way to victory in the caucuses and, a few months later, took the nomination, too. But the other combatants, Dean and Gephardt, did poorly in Iowa. It was Edwards who scored the real breakthrough, finishing a strong second and establishing himself as a rising political star. Kerry would choose Edwards as his running mate later in the year.

The lesson of Iowa, in Edwards's opinion, was that most voters prefer "a positive, uplifting message to change America." His contention is backed by scientific evidence. Two psychologists from the University of Pennsylvania sifted through convention speeches delivered by every presidential nominee between 1948 and 1984. They discovered that the candidate with the most optimistic outlook won nine of those ten elections. "People tend to vote for the candidate who makes them feel more hopeful about the country's future," concluded Harold Zullow, a co-author of the study.

Modern politicians ignore this simple truth, opting instead to wallow in the mud. Bush and Kerry had surprisingly little to say about public policy during the 2004 campaign. They seemed to prefer bickering about each other's military record. The Gallup Poll asked voters if they were paying much attention to the endless stream of charges and countercharges about Bush's stint in the National Guard and Kerry's tour in Vietnam. Relatively few were.

That's because people are best motivated by hope, not fear. Real leaders don't emphasize the negative; they accentuate the positive. They radiate confidence and optimism. "To stir people, you must give voice to their own deep desires, inspiring them to believe they can climb mountains they always thought were too high," said David Gergen, who shaped the speeches of four presidents from Richard Nixon to Bill Clinton.

Franklin Roosevelt was a master at communicating an upbeat message. The Depression and World War II were daunting obstacles, but he convinced his fellow Americans that both could be conquered. Roosevelt always seemed cool and confident, even if the latest economic report was gloomy or the current battle was turning against the Allies. Ronald Reagan, whose philosophy as president was the polar opposite of Roosevelt's, expressed unbounded admiration for FDR's leadership skills. "He gave confidence to the people," Reagan marveled. "He never lost faith in this country for one minute. I must say I think he was a great war leader."

Nor was Reagan a slouch. His sunny optimism contrasted with the hand-wringing of the man he replaced in the White House. Jimmy Carter worried publicly that America was suffering from malaise and had reached the limits of its power. Reagan opted for a direct, confident approach. "America's best days are ahead of her," he insisted, and the nation rallied behind him.

Humility was another of Reagan's attributes. Critics sniped that he had much to be humble about, but even they found him to be charming. Reagan disarmed them by joking about his advanced age or his faulty memory, and by routinely deflecting praise. A sign on his desk succinctly captured his style. "There is no limit to what a man can do or where he can go," it read, "if he doesn't mind who gets the credit."

That's a rare sentiment in business, politics, or any sphere of life. Ours is an egocentric world, and self-absorbed personalities can be found in abundance. Many of them, however, eventually learn that arrogance can be a dangerously expensive flaw.

Consider the extreme example of Huey Long, a rude, vulgar, larger-than-life senator from Louisiana who was commonly known as "the Kingfish." Long earned national publicity with his repeated claims that Franklin Roosevelt—whom he mocked as "Prince Franklin"—wasn't doing enough to help poor and hungry Americans. Reporters asked Long if he planned on being a presidential candidate himself in 1936. "Sure to be," he replied. "And I think we will sweep the country." Roosevelt's advisers fretted that Long might siphon away as many as six million votes.

But the Kingfish was making thousands of enemies, too. He routinely arranged to have his Louisiana critics beaten or jailed. He mercilessly ridiculed his colleagues in the Senate. He refused to compromise with anybody who disagreed with him. "That didn't work, and now I'm a dynamiter. I dynamite them out of my path," he boasted. Yet he was aware of the hatred that his imperious ways were stirring up. "I may not be back here. This may be my swan song, for all I know," he predicted as the Senate neared adjournment in 1935. His foreshadowing was accurate. A political foe's son-in-law assassinated Long that September.

"We Were Laughing about It Just This Morning"

It is far safer—and considerably more productive—to be self-effacing, rather than bombastic and confrontational. "My experience has been that putting myself down—humility is attractive—is the best kind of humor," wrote Morris Udall, a longtime congressman from Arizona. "It creates empathy, humanizes any message, and puts people at ease."

Udall always liked telling a story about his 1976 presidential campaign. His driver got stuck in the snow on the way to a speaking engagement in New Hampshire. It was going to take several minutes to shovel out the car, so a staff member urged Udall to pass the time by meeting a few voters. The candidate ducked into a nearby barbershop and announced, "Mo Udall. I'm running for president."

"Yeah, I know," replied the barber. "We were laughing about it just this morning."

AVOID CONTROVERSY AND EXTREME STATEMENTS

Robert La Follette exuded an air of danger. He seemed a bit wild, occasionally on the verge of losing control.

Personal appearance had something to do with it—La Follette's hair remained wiry and untamed into his sixties—and combativeness enhanced the image. The man known as "Fighting Bob" attacked his foes with blunt, forceful words. He accused the nation's business leaders of being a "gang of corporation knaves." He blasted federal policies that favored the rich. "The supreme issue," he declared, "is the encroachment of the powerful few upon the rights of the many."

Many of La Follette's Senate colleagues believed him to be a dangerous extremist. His vote against entering World War I struck them as downright unpatriotic. A fellow senator sneered that La Follette belonged either in

Germany or in jail. Woodrow Wilson scorned him as the leader of the "little group of willful men" that opposed the war.

Yet La Follette stood firm, accusing his critics of misinterpreting his career. He was no wild-eyed agitator, no fringe politician. The voters of Wisconsin had elected him to three terms as governor before promoting him to the Senate, where he would serve for nineteen years. If he had to be labeled, La Follette preferred to be called progressive. He bristled at any suggestion that he was subversive. "I'm radical, but not too darned radical," he snapped. "Just enough to make the farmers and the laborers high-paid people."

La Follette's point was well-taken. He was extremely popular in Wisconsin and remarkably successful at his job, two conventional indicators of political skill. His reputation was reinforced in 1957, when a committee headed by John Kennedy named the five greatest senators of all time. This elite list included the famed nineteenth-century triumvirate of John Calhoun, Henry Clay, and Daniel Webster, as well as the renowned "Mr. Republican" of the 1940s and early 1950s, Robert Taft. The fifth immortal senator was Bob La Follette.

A person of such courage, intensity, and ability might seem to be a surefire presidential candidate. La Follette certainly thought so. He joined the race in 1912 and again in 1916, but failed to come anywhere close to the Republican nomination. The only way he could qualify for the November ballot was to form his own party, which he did in 1924. He carried just a single state, his native Wisconsin, while the bland Calvin Coolidge swept to victory across the rest of America.

The unhappy truth was that La Follette was too outspoken to reach his ultimate goal. The sharp tongue and emphatic style that served him well in Senate debates had the opposite impact on his presidential hopes, slicing them to pieces. Too many voters outside of Wisconsin considered Fighting Bob to be a divisive influence—yes, an extremist. It was a perception that he never overcame.

The rules haven't changed in the century since La Follette first stepped on the Senate floor. If you consistently adopt controversial positions on high-profile issues, whether in business or politics, your chances of becoming a chief executive will vaporize. Success is reserved for those who occupy the middle ground. Sad to say, but true.

The most dogmatic presidential nominees of the past hundred years were Barry Goldwater, a conservative Republican, and George McGovern, a liberal Democrat. They were polar opposites in political philosophy, yet shared a willingness to embrace unpopular causes. They possessed the smug confidence of true believers.

Goldwater promised voters "a choice, not an echo" in 1964, pledging to dismantle Democratic social programs and unleash the armed forces. He proudly defended his right-wing views. "I would remind you that extremism in the defense of liberty is no vice," he said. "And let me remind you that moderation in the pursuit of justice is no virtue." His slogan was as straight-forward as the candidate himself: "In Your Heart, You Know He's Right." Democrats jeered, "In your guts, you know he's nuts."

McGovern vowed to immediately withdraw American troops from Viet-nam if elected in 1972. His campaign had an isolationist feel that was best expressed by its slogan, "Come Home, America." His stands on social issues were so unabashedly liberal that the Republicans dubbed him the Triple-A candidate, implying that he favored abortion, acid (drugs), and amnesty for Vietnam deserters. Yet McGovern refused to tone down his views. "If the voters agree with me, that's great," he once said, "but if they don't, I'm not going to pull back."

The people who voted for Goldwater or McGovern were vastly different in political orientation, but much alike in their fierce, even fanatical, loyalty. They were excited about supporting a candidate who didn't flinch from expressing extreme opinions, who didn't worry about being controversial, who didn't back down under intense pressure. Such a politician, they rejoiced, was rare and refreshing.

But there was a problem. Candidates who venture outside the mainstream are virtually certain to lose in the end. Goldwater and McGovern captured the hearts of hardcore supporters, but were unable to expand their political bases. Moderate voters—the middle-of-the-road Americans who form the nation's silent majority—had no interest in voting for extremists of any stripe.

They made their views clear on election day. Lyndon Johnson received 61.1 percent of the votes cast in 1964, dwarfing Goldwater's 38.5 percent. LBJ's margin of 22.6 percentage points was the largest since Franklin Roose-velt's pasting of Alfred Landon in 1936. But Johnson's achievement was eclipsed eight years later in 1972, when Richard Nixon rolled up a margin of 23.2 percentage points over McGovern. "The election was decided the day McGovern was nominated," Nixon said. "The question after that was only how much. McGovern did to his party what Goldwater did."

An ancient Roman proverb recommended "moderation in all things." That's good advice for life in general and career-building in particular. It's possible to establish a reputation through immoderate means—by immersing yourself in controversy and saying whatever you feel. But that's certainly no way to achieve a lasting position of respectability and power.

Goldwater, at least, had a sense of humor about his failure. Losing didn't upset him too much. "No, no. Not when it was over," he mused at his Ari-zona home a quarter-century later. "It didn't even cause me great unhappi-ness. I just came up here on the hill with [wife] Peggy, sat out there watching the sunset, and whistled 'Hail to the Chief.'"

He welcomed McGovern to the club in 1972. A newspaper cartoonist lam-pooned the two landslide losers, inserting them as the dominant characters in an imitation of Grant Wood's painting, *American Gothic*—"like Grandpa and Granny," as McGovern recalled it. Goldwater gleefully clipped the cartoon out of the paper, jotting a quick note on the front before slipping it into the mail.

"George," he wrote, "if you must lose, lose big."

MAINTAIN YOUR FLEXIBILITY TO KEEP UP WITH THE TIMES

"I like movement and change," William Gibbs McAdoo often said, and his career proved it. He frequently switched jobs—beginning as a speculator in Tennessee, then becoming a lawyer in New York City, a cabinet secretary in Washington, D.C., and a senator from California.

McAdoo's first move was born of necessity. His Chattanooga streetcar venture plunged into bankruptcy, dragging him to the same status. New York seemed the best place to earn the enormous sum of money he needed to pay his creditors, so the native of a small Georgia town packed for America's biggest metropolis in 1892. "I was glad to be there," he would later write. "The stir and bustle of the place suited me perfectly. I felt like a born New Yorker."

McAdoo, who often crossed the Hudson River on business, grew increasingly irritated by the costly twenty-minute ferry trip that was the only connection between the city and New Jersey. He organized a company that built the first Holland Tunnel in 1904, cutting twelve minutes off the passage and making him wealthier than he had dreamed.

Life was going well. Politics was the furthest thing from McAdoo's mind until a chance meeting with a future president, Woodrow Wilson, on a train platform in 1909. He would become Wilson's adviser, treasury secretary, son-in-law, and potential successor in the White House.

That last role required great dexterity. A formidable opponent for the Democratic presidential nomination in 1920 and again in 1924 was Alfred Smith, the popular governor of New York and boss of Tammany Hall, the city's Democratic machine. McAdoo knew that his adopted hometown would never support him against its beloved native son, so he abruptly switched sides. He moved to California in 1922 and reinvented himself as the champion of rural America. New York City, he charged, was "the citadel of privilege." It was "reactionary, sinister, unscrupulous, mercenary, and sordid."

This stunning transformation nearly worked. McAdoo undoubtedly would have failed as a minor candidate from New York, but his reincarnation drew enough southern and western votes to tie up the 1924 Democratic convention for ninety-nine ballots before he and Smith quit the race in exhaustion. McAdoo publicly insisted that his swift change of heart had been genuine, but he privately hinted at political motivation. "You can't imagine the distrust the country at large has of a New York candidate identified with and acceptable to Tammany," he wrote a friend. "In fact, there is a wide distrust of New York anyway. That may be unjust, but it is a fact which must be considered."

Politicians rarely shift positions as dramatically as McAdoo did, but they do understand the value of elasticity. Everett Dirksen, an Illinois senator who achieved national fame in the 1950s and 1960s, ranked it among the greatest of political virtues. "I am a man of principle," Dirksen rumbled in his gravelly voice, "and my first principle is flexibility."

It's essential that you develop a positive reputation, as we've noted in earlier chapters. But it's equally important that you leave yourself some wiggle room. American history offers countless tales of political and business leaders whose careers ended in failure because of their inability to adapt. You need to stay flexible to keep up with the times—and with your opponents.

Some of the most dramatic shifts by national candidates have been undeniably heartfelt. James Birney, once an Alabama slaveholder, grew to be the Liberty Party's presidential nominee in 1844, vowing to abolish slavery everywhere in America. John Bidwell, once a California vineyard owner, was nominated as the Prohibition Party's candidate in 1892, dedicated to banning alcohol in all forms.

But Birney and Bidwell were ideologues who ran on minor-party tickets and enjoyed the luxury of stands that their contemporaries considered extreme. Their aim was to make a point, not to assume the practical responsibilities of government. Each received just 2 percent of the votes cast.

Mainstream politicians—and executives, for that matter—must handle their conversions more subtly, following the lead of Abraham Lincoln, a master at riding the political tides. Lincoln arrived at the White House in 1861 with a single overriding goal. "My paramount object in this struggle is to save the Union," he wrote, "and is not either to save or to destroy slavery." He promised Southerners that he would leave slavery undisturbed if they remained loyal to the federal government. But his position had evolved by the fall of 1862, when he signed the Emancipation Proclamation, freeing slaves in every state still in rebellion as of New Year's Day 1863. He soon endorsed the complete abolition of slavery.

This abrupt change was driven not by moral concerns, but by Lincoln's belief that it would bring victory in the Civil War. He hoped it would rally antislavery activists to the Union's cause and encourage blacks to enlist in the federal army. Military success was his objective, and he willingly altered his philosophy to achieve it. "I claim not to have controlled events," Lincoln later admitted, "but confess plainly that events have controlled me."

Franklin Roosevelt was equally flexible. FDR was a great believer in experimentation. He had no qualms about discarding programs that weren't working. "I have no expectation of making a hit every time I come to bat," he said. The important thing was to keep swinging.

The federal budget was the object of one of Roosevelt's notable course changes. He delivered a major address in Pittsburgh during the 1932 campaign, promising to bring the budget into balance. Yet he did the opposite in office. His New Deal programs proved to be much more expensive than anticipated, driving the deficit to depths previously unplumbed.

Roosevelt was scheduled to return to Pittsburgh for another speech in 1936, a prospect he dreaded because of the budget-related questions that were sure to come. FDR instructed his speechwriter, Samuel Rosenman, to cobble together "a good and convincing explanation" of what he had said four years earlier. Rosenman reread the previous address, combed through the budget, and notified the president that he had arrived at an answer.

FDR eagerly replied, "Fine. What sort?"

"Mr. President," said Rosenman, "the only thing you can say about the 1932 speech is to deny categorically that you ever made it."

Today's historians rank Lincoln and Roosevelt among the three greatest presidents of all time, joining George Washington. Each is credited with impressive accomplishments—Lincoln with saving the Union and freeing the slaves, Roosevelt with overcoming the Depression and winning World War II. If they had been rigid fanatics instead of adaptable leaders, it's unlikely that they could have achieved such success.

Flexibility, in fact, can sometimes be the key to an entire career.

Several Republican icons were critical of the elder George Bush, believing that he lacked a guiding philosophy or a backbone. Richard Nixon muttered that his father, Prescott Bush, a senator from Connecticut, had been "tough as nails, with that ramrod, erect posture, but I just don't know what's happened to George." Columnist George Will dismissed Prescott's son as a "lap dog."

But George H.W. Bush rose in the Republican hierarchy, landing a series of high-level appointments in the Nixon and Ford administrations. He considered himself ready for the White House by 1980, when he entered the race for the Republican nomination.

The early returns were positive. Bush shocked the pundits by winning the first contest on that year's calendar, the Iowa caucuses. He bounded eagerly toward the New Hampshire primary, where he expected to deal Ronald Reagan's candidacy a mortal blow. The moderate Bush mocked Reagan's conservative proposals as "voodoo economics," a barbed phrase that chilled the relations between the two candidates. But so what? Bush crowed that he had "Big Mo," his pet phrase for momentum, firmly on his side. He was certain to win.

It was a serious miscalculation. Reagan easily took New Hampshire, as well as twenty-eight primaries that followed, draining every drop of Big Mo from Bush's tank. Columnists began suggesting that Bush's best hope was to become Reagan's running mate, though the odds were against it. The two men seemed personally incompatible and politically out of tune. It was difficult to imagine Bush being comfortable with Reagan's right-wing platform.

The Republican convention went as expected, with Reagan winning easily on the first ballot. His choice of a vice-presidential candidate stirred up the only suspense. Bush was relaxing in his hotel suite when the call came. It was a crossroads in his life. Would he spurn the man whose economic philosophy he had ridiculed? Or would he accept the role of understudy in the hope that he might reach the main stage himself one day?

An excessively proud and rigid person would have rejected the second spot in an instant, but Bush had no such problem. He broke into a big grin.

"Why, yes sir," he told Reagan on the phone. "I think you can say I support the platform—wholeheartedly!" He had taken the initial step toward becoming president himself in eight years.

DON'T OBSESS ABOUT POPULARITY OR MARGIN OF VICTORY

Rutherford Hayes launched his political career with the slimmest of victories. He ran for the post of solicitor in Cincinnati—chief lawyer for the city government—in 1858. The final decision fell to the city council, which chose Hayes by the margin of a single vote. No one considered his win to be auspicious or even particularly noteworthy.

Hayes moved on to bigger jobs, though he never distinguished himself in a major way. He served as a Civil War general and a congressman, then was elected to three terms as governor of Ohio, winning by the skin of his teeth each time. His combined margin in those three elections was just 16,000 votes, decidedly unimpressive in a state as large as Ohio.

It was during his final race for governor in 1875 that Republican strategists began measuring Hayes as a possible candidate for the White House. He was baffled at first, believing that his record didn't warrant such consideration. "Several suggest that if elected governor now, I will stand well for the presidency next year," he wrote in his diary. "How wild! What a queer lot we are becoming!"

But the idea grew on him, and he became a candidate for the party's nomination in 1876. The acknowledged frontrunner, James Blaine, was unable to seal the deal at the convention. Hayes, the dark horse from Ohio, squeaked past him by thirty-three votes on the seventh ballot. It remains the tightest margin of victory at any major-party convention in American history.

Hayes's eighteen-year run of luck finally expired in November, or so it seemed. He lost to Samuel Tilden, the Democratic nominee, by 250,000 votes and trailed in the Electoral College as well, though final returns hadn't been certified in Florida, Louisiana, or South Carolina. Hayes accepted defeat—"I bow cheerfully to the result"—but his campaign managers weren't as submissive to the popular will. They cut deals and pulled out all the stops in the three disputed states, making it possible for Hayes to beat Tilden by a single electoral vote. Democrats ridiculed him ever after as "Rutherfraud" and referred to his victory as the "Crime of '76," but they couldn't escape one essential fact. He, not Tilden, was the president of the United States.

There were several points where Hayes could have been derailed, but he always managed to stay on the career track. He won an improbable series of close elections, the first and last by a single vote each. He may never have been hugely popular or highly regarded, but he kept on winning. That was all that counted.

It's futile to seek a lopsided victory in any pursuit, as Hayes's story shows. If you're coaching a team, it doesn't matter if you win by one point or fifty.

If you're submitting a business plan, it doesn't matter if the executive committee approves it unanimously or by a four-to-three vote. If you're seeking a job, it doesn't matter if you're the company's first choice or its remaining option after four people said no. The win, the approval, the job—those are the only objectives that count.

So don't obsess about being popular. Don't worry if some of your colleagues find your ideas unimpressive. Don't run up the score or do crazy things to humiliate your opponents. Stay cool, and keep your eyes on the prize.

It's hard enough, anyway, to succeed at any venture. The size of victory is usually beyond your control, whether you're in a political race or at an actual racetrack. "A large percentage of horse races are won by a small margin," said Steve Asmussen, one of the greatest thoroughbred trainers of all time. "You're lucky if the horse next to yours doesn't act up in the chute, if the horse in front of yours doesn't fall. Luck is getting the right horse and nothing gets in his way to keep him from winning."

Consider it another way. Take a look at the five presidential elections that ended in the biggest landslides, based on the gap in percentage points between the top two finishers. Did these victories reflect the popularity of the winners, or did they stem from circumstances beyond the candidates' control?

1920: Warren Harding (26.1 points)—Circumstances. Harding was a likable man, but his kindly image had nothing to do with his record-setting victory. Journalist William Allen White correctly attributed it to "a barbaric yawp of enraged democracy at the incompetency" of Woodrow Wilson's outgoing administration. The voters wanted a change, simple as that.

1924: Calvin Coolidge (25.3 points)—Circumstances. Coolidge's tart manner made it believable that he had been "weaned on a pickle," as Alice Roosevelt Longworth memorably suggested. He won easily because the opposition was split between two candidates, and America was generally prosperous.

1936: Franklin Roosevelt (24.3 points)—Popularity. Voters overwhelmingly endorsed FDR's ebullient personality and heroic efforts to defeat the Depression. It didn't hurt, however, that challenger Alfred Landon mounted an inept campaign.

1964: Lyndon Johnson (22.6 points)—Circumstances. Few voters warmed to Johnson, who was a corny, heavy-handed campaigner. But they found his ultraconservative opponent, Barry Goldwater, considerably less appealing.

1972: Richard Nixon (23.2 points)—Circumstances. Few voters warmed to Nixon, who was a stiff, humorless campaigner. But they found his ultraliberal opponent, George McGovern, considerably less appealing.

Only one of these five landslides could be interpreted as a personal endorsement. The other four were clearly dictated by external circumstances. Nothing could better demonstrate that no link exists between popularity and success.

Nor, you might have noted, is there any connection between greatness and margin of victory. Harding, who was elected by the biggest landslide in American history, is considered by many historians to have been the worst president ever. Coolidge and Nixon don't fare too well in those rankings either, and Johnson never rises above the middle of the pack.

Politicians and business executives often forget these lessons. They yearn to be loved by all, incorrectly believing that popularity is the key to success.

Woodrow Wilson, whose self-confidence often showed itself as arrogance, temporarily lost his nerve when the feisty Theodore Roosevelt entered the 1912 race on a third-party ticket. "He is a real, vivid person, whom they have seen and shouted themselves hoarse for and voted for, millions strong," Wilson wrote. "I am a vague, conjectural personality, more made up of opinions and academic prepossessions than of human traits and red corpuscles." He worried that Roosevelt's mass appeal would carry the day.

Wilson ignored the fact that TR and the incumbent president, William Howard Taft, were both Republicans. They would be splitting the Republican vote, virtually guaranteeing a Democratic victory. Roosevelt undoubtedly was more popular, but the "vague, conjectural" Wilson went on to win the election by fourteen percentage points, a true landslide indeed.

DON'T GIVE A POTENTIAL RIVAL AN INADVERTENT BOOST

Winfield Scott was hailed as a military hero for most of his life. His bravery during the War of 1812 earned him the brevet rank of major general before the age of thirty, starting him toward the army's ultimate post, general-in-chief, which he held during the Mexican War and into the first months of the Civil War. He was one of the most distinguished soldiers in American history.

But being a hero wasn't good enough for Scott. The White House was his ultimate goal. He had long coveted the presidency, first seeking the Whig Party's nomination in 1840, only to be crushed by the steamroller known as William Henry Harrison.

Scott's big break came six years later. President James Polk fanned a border dispute with Mexico into a full-fledged war. His general-in-chief set to work, conceiving a bold thrust to the enemy's heart. He would land his troops at the port city of Veracruz on the Gulf of Mexico, then fight his way inland to the capital, Mexico City. His plans—breathtaking in their audacity—seemed certain to bring Mexico to its knees and to win Scott the presidency.

That left one minor detail. Scott needed someone to tie up the Mexican forces along the disputed border in the northern theater of action, while he maneuvered far to the south. He assigned this subordinate role to a little-known general, Zachary Taylor. It seemed a safe, if unimaginative, choice. Taylor had served in virtual anonymity since joining the infantry way back in 1808.

Scott's campaign had the desired result. His troops may have been green and his supplies inadequate, yet he battled his way from Veracruz to Mexico City in six months and secured his objective. The United States, thanks to his efforts, won the war. "His campaign was unsurpassed in military annals. He is the greatest living soldier," gushed the Duke of Wellington, whose own victories over Napoleon gave him claim to that title himself.

But it was Taylor who reaped the political benefits. He had managed to score two quick wins along the Rio Grande in 1846—while Scott was preparing for his complicated southern operations—and then pushed into Mexico and pulled off a decisive victory at Buena Vista, wrapping up the action in the northern theater.

Taylor's wins were insignificant next to Scott's, but they were America's first successes in Mexico, so their impact back home was powerful. He became an instant hero, though an obscure one, to be sure. Congress authorized a medal for Taylor, yet no portrait or likeness could be found anywhere in Washington. An artist had to be sent to his camp in Mexico.

Journalists and political leaders inevitably began to talk about Taylor's political future. He had never voted, had never expressed himself on the issues of the day, and could have walked down any street in America without fear of recognition, yet he was suddenly being mentioned as a presidential contender. He found the whole thing laughable, writing that a campaign for the White House had "never entered my head, nor is it likely to enter the head of any sane person."

Taylor eventually changed his mind and ran for the Whig nomination in 1848 against Henry Clay, Daniel Webster, and the man to whom he owed his sudden national prominence, Winfield Scott. This newcomer to politics seemed out of his league. Clay and Webster were legislative wizards and impressive public speakers, truly legends in their own time. And Scott, after all, was the hero of Mexico City.

But it was Taylor who won the nomination and the presidency, thanks to an important advantage over his three opponents. He was popularly hailed, yet was essentially a blank canvas. His views on slavery were dimly known, a good thing in that volatile period only a decade or so before the Civil War. His political inexperience meant that he had no political enemies.

Winfield Scott learned an important lesson that year. If you're nearing the summit of your career, be very sure about the ambitions and loyalty of the people who are tied onto your rope. Don't give a boost to anyone who could conceivably become your competitor. Even a seemingly innocuous appointment has the potential to be troublesome.

If Scott needed further proof, the same point was driven home again in 1852 when he launched his third presidential campaign. He seemed to possess all of the advantages that year—experience, fame, adulation—yet the results were depressingly familiar. He lost to another unknown officer who had served under him in Mexico, Franklin Pierce.

"This Young Man Had Passed Him By"

Adlai Stevenson, who had been the Democratic presidential nominee in 1952, was poised to win the same honor in 1956.

He asked a freshman senator, John Kennedy of Massachusetts, to deliver the speech formally placing his name before the convention, and also gave serious thought to selecting Kennedy as his running mate. Stevenson eventually decided to throw the process open, letting the delegates choose any vice-presidential nominee they wished. JFK surprised the party's insiders by coming within nineteen votes of winning the second spot on the ticket.

That 1956 convention was Kennedy's coming-out party, instantly establishing his reputation as a young, attractive candidate and whetting his appetite for national office. Stevenson always claimed responsibility for this transformation. Wasn't he the one who had tapped Kennedy to deliver an important address on national television, and hadn't he set the stage for the excitement surrounding the vice-presidential balloting?

Fast forward to 1960. Stevenson toyed with running for president a third time, eventually consenting to have his name put before the Democratic convention, but he lost badly to Kennedy. Their roles were suddenly reversed. Kennedy became president, while Stevenson was shunted off as ambassador to the United Nations. It was no surprise that their relationship was strained, marred by occasional indications of Stevenson's resentment that he was now taking orders from someone he had helped so much. "The age difference was one of the greatest obstacles," Stevenson's son, Adlai III, would recall. "This young man had risen so rapidly and passed him by."

IF YOU HAVE AN ADDICTION, BATTLE IT FIERCELY

This one is fairly obvious, isn't it? Any addiction—alcohol, drugs, sex, whatever—is likely to sap your energy, erode your skills, and ruin your reputation.

But it won't necessarily destroy your career.

Franklin Pierce represented New Hampshire as a senator between 1837 and 1842. He didn't author any significant bills or deliver any memorable speeches. His biographer, demonstrating a deft rhetorical touch, concluded that Pierce made little headway in Washington because "he was too easily a prey to the jovial and reckless life of the politicians." That's a nice way of saying that he bordered on being an out-and-out alcoholic.

Pierce's wife demanded that he resign his Senate seat and return home, far from the liquid attractions of the nation's capital. It seemed that his once-promising political career was over. He would live out his days quietly as a New Hampshire lawyer.

The Mexican War altered his fate. Pierce served with no particular distinction in the attack on Mexico City, suffering a painful injury when he fell off his horse. (He was hurt "in that portion of a man's anatomy that is least tolerant of suffering," as historian David Bruce delicately put it.) But the American army *did* score a smashing victory, and Pierce *did* wear the single star of a brigadier general, a combination that appealed to the Democratic Party. It turned his way in 1852, choosing him as a compromise nominee for president after the frontrunners deadlocked at the convention.

The Whigs—the other major party at the time—saw no reason for concern. Their nominee was that bona fide hero we met a couple of pages ago, Winfield Scott, who had been Pierce's commanding officer during the drive on Mexico City and who sternly disapproved of drunkenness. The Whigs gleefully distributed a book, *The Military Services of General Pierce*, which was an inch tall and half an inch wide. It ridiculed the Democratic candidate as the "hero of many a well-fought bottle."

Pierce—to his wife's great shock and perhaps even his own—won the election.

John Kennedy was another addict who made his way to the White House. Women were his obsession. He confessed to Harold Macmillan, the British prime minister, that if he didn't have sex at least once every three days, he suffered from terrible headaches.

Kennedy rarely needed aspirin. He conducted affairs with dozens of women during his short stay in the Oval Office, among them his wife's press secretary, two White House secretaries (known to insiders as Fiddle and Faddle), a nineteen-year-old White House intern, a woman with Mafia connections (Judith Campbell Exner), and an array of Hollywood stars and hangers-on.

The president understood the risks involved. He went to great lengths to keep his liaisons secret. Ben Bradlee, a Kennedy friend who wrote for *Newsweek* and later became editor of the *Washington Post*, insisted that he knew nothing of JFK's affairs at the time, even one that involved Bradlee's own sister-in-law. "I can only repeat my ignorance of Kennedy's sex life, and state that I am appalled by the details that have emerged, appalled by the recklessness, by the subterfuge that must have been involved," he wrote decades later.

That, of course, is a key point. Americans don't look kindly on addictions or on people who lack self-control. Pierce was an inept president by most accounts, but his problems with alcohol made things worse, transforming his life story into low comedy. Kennedy's womanizing tarnished the gleaming image of Camelot that his wife had hoped would be his lasting legacy.

And don't forget that these two men were exceptions to the rule. For every Pierce and Kennedy who beat the odds, there have been dozens of politicians whose White House dreams were destroyed by internal demons. (Does the name of Gary Hart ring a bell?)

It's a cliché that addictions can't be easily defeated. If there were a simple solution, we wouldn't need all the substance-abuse centers and counselors that we have today. But you must make every possible effort. You're not likely to be as lucky as Franklin Pierce. The odds are that an addiction, if left unchecked, will not only sidetrack your career, but will severely damage your life.

It's equally clear that swinging the pendulum to the other extreme is just as dangerous. Work itself can become an addiction, as Morris Udall discovered by observing the obsessive behavior of several opponents for the 1976 Democratic nomination.

"Beware of the presidential candidate who has no friends his own age and confidantes who can tell him to go to hell, who has no hobbies and outside interests," Udall said. "God help us from presidents who can't be a little bit gentle, and who don't have a sense of humor, and who can't gather friends around and play poker and climb a mountain. You know, these intense workaholics really worry me."

DON'T LET YOUR TEMPER GET THE BEST OF YOU

Several presidents, from the birth of the republic to the present day, have battled to keep oversized tempers in check.

George Washington was prone to sudden bursts of anger that occasionally became violent, as we noted at the beginning of this chapter. His successor, John Adams, commonly exploded in the face of adversity. Alexander Hamilton accused Adams of having an "ungovernable temper" that left him "liable to paroxysms of anger." Hamilton's charge might have been dismissed as the rhetoric of a political foe, had a family member not offered corroboration. "His anger, when thoroughly roused, was, for a time, extremely violent," Charles Francis Adams said of his famous grandfather, "but when it subsided, it left no trace of malevolence behind."

A recent president has been similarly characterized as amiable in public, yet volatile behind closed doors. "Bill Clinton getting mad is like Mount Vesuvius erupting," recalled former aide David Gergen. "At the White House, he would usually blow at least once in the morning and straight into the face of (presidential adviser) George Stephanopoulos."

Executive consultants and leadership manuals typically warn against public displays of anger. Temper tantrums can demoralize your workforce and derail your company, they insist. But the evidence doesn't always agree. Several highly successful executives have been labeled as "great intimidators" by Roderick Kramer, a professor at the Stanford University Graduate School of Business. "They're rough, loud, and in your face," he said of famous twenty-first century CEOs like Rupert Murdoch, Andy Grove, Larry Ellison, and Steve Jobs.

"The great intimidators see a possible path through the thicket, and they're impatient to clear it," wrote Kramer. "They chafe at impediments, even those that are human. They don't suffer from doubt or timidity. They've got a disdain for constraints imposed by others." And, he might have added, they're not afraid to express their negative feelings.

Intimidators know that anger can be a remarkably powerful motivational tool. Andrew Jackson was renowned for his temper—he once killed a man in a duel, after all—but he invariably exhibited a charming, gracious personality in social settings, behaving like an aristocrat, not a backwoodsman. He confessed that he loved to surprise people who "were prepared to see me with a tomahawk in one hand and a scalping knife in the other."

Yet everybody—opponents and allies alike—remained wary. If they crossed Jackson or displeased him in any way, they knew that his hard-bitten alter ego could appear in an instant. "He could hate with a biblical fury," wrote biographer Robert Remini, and Jackson himself admitted to being harshly inflexible. "I have an opinion of my own on all subjects," he declared, "and when that opinion is formed, I pursue it publicly, regardless of who goes with me." Anybody who dared to deviate from Old Hickory's line ran the risk of incurring his wrath, either genuine or simulated. Historian George Bancroft suspected that the latter description often applied. Jackson, he concluded, was "mild by nature and (put) himself into a rage only when it would serve his purpose."

That's where it gets tricky. Not everyone can manipulate his or her emotions so easily. "I can lose it, or I can use it, either way," boasted Edmund Muskie about his fabled temper. Political commentator Chris Matthews, who once served on Muskie's senatorial staff, agreed that his former boss made effective use of his anger. "Muskie was the best of them all, the absolute best, because nobody wanted to tangle with the guy," Matthews said. "You know, why tangle with the guy? Why ruin your day? A bad temper is a very powerful political tool because most people don't like confrontation."

But Muskie's temper eventually proved to be his undoing. He established a positive reputation after the Democrats nominated him for the vice presidency in 1968. James Reston, the famed *New York Times* columnist, hailed him as a calm, reasonable man, "the most refreshing figure in the American campaign." But the consensus changed drastically after Muskie's crying episode in New Hampshire in 1972, which we discussed a few pages back. Reporters suddenly agreed that he was high-strung and temperamental, definitely not presidential material.

It may be easier said than done, but your wisest course is to control yourself as well as you possibly can. If you have a fiery temper, try to limit its exposure. The fewer the explosions, and the more private the circumstances in which they occur, the better off you'll be. An occasional outburst may work to your benefit, it's true, but don't flatter yourself that you can turn your anger on and off at will. You're more likely to be an Ed Muskie than an Andy Jackson.

Never forget that a single public tirade can have devastating consequences, as Joseph Biden learned to his unhappiness. His 1988 presidential campaign was crippled, though not destroyed, by allegations that he had plagiarized a British politician's speech. His advisers believed he could weather the negative publicity, but their hopes sank after a damaging videotape was made public. It showed Biden reacting angrily—and inaccurately—when a voter started asking questions about his academic record.

This seemingly innocuous episode doomed Biden's campaign. He came off as snappish, untruthful, and very much out of control, confirming the negative perceptions created by the earlier charges of plagiarism. He dropped out of the race soon thereafter. "I can remember my dear mother, God bless her, telling me ever since I can remember, 'Joey Biden, some day your temper is going to get you in real trouble,'" he later recalled. "And boy, did it."

MOLLIFY (OR IGNORE) POTENTIAL ENEMIES WHEN POSSIBLE

It began innocently in 1866. A routine bill came before the House of Representatives, a funding request from the office of the army's provost marshal general. A quick unanimous vote, and the matter would be settled. Who could possibly object?

Roscoe Conkling did. The congressman from upstate New York was a powerfully built, arrogant man who hated easily. He intensely disliked the current provost marshal general, James Barnet Fry, so he insisted that Fry's office, instead of being given more money, should be abolished immediately.

A representative from Maine, James Blaine, rose to speak. He was suave and charming, Conkling's opposite in personality. Fry was an "honorable and high-toned officer," Blaine said soothingly. Surely his department could be funded for the coming year.

Conkling would not be swayed. The two men, their tempers slowly rising, went back and forth on the issue for a week. Blaine finally assembled a point-by-point rebuttal that took him more than an hour to lay before the House. He was certain it would be the final word on the Fry controversy.

But Conkling was unimpressed. He asked for the floor and turned directly toward Blaine. "If the member from Maine had the least idea how profoundly indifferent I am to his opinion upon the subject which he has been discussing, or upon any other subject personal to me," he sneered, "I think he would hardly take the trouble to rise here and express his opinion."

Blaine jumped to his feet. "The contempt of that large-minded gentleman is so wilting," he sarcastically began. He went on to ridicule Conkling's "haughty disdain, his grandiloquent swell, his majestic, supereminent, overpowering, turkey-gobbler strut." The hatred both men exuded was palpable. Members of the House watched their rhetorical duel with fascinated horror.

Aftershocks from that 1866 confrontation would be felt for a generation. The Republican Party would eventually split into factions because of it—the Stalwarts supporting Conkling, the Half-Breeds backing Blaine. The leaders of these rival bands would wage three titanic battles for the presidency between 1876 and 1884, but neither would ever win the ultimate prize.

Blaine, the more popular of the two men, surged ahead as the frontrunner for the Republican nomination in 1876. He felt confident enough to mock his enemy's candidacy as "an absurdity." But Conkling enjoyed the year's last laugh. It became clear that he couldn't win himself, so he shepherded his supporters to Rutherford Hayes at the party's convention, making it possible for Hayes to eke out a victory over Blaine on the seventh ballot.

The roles were reversed four years later. Conkling didn't run in 1880, opting to mastermind the campaign of a former president, Ulysses Grant, who wished to return to the White House. Grant and Blaine slugged it out for thirty-five ballots at the Republican convention, neither able to secure a majority. Blaine broke the deadlock on the thirty-sixth roll call by endorsing an old friend, James Garfield, whom the weary delegates gladly nominated.

Even some of the Stalwarts had come to admire Blaine's tenacity by 1884. Thomas Platt, a former New York senator who was one of Conkling's closest allies, voted for the Half-Breed leader at the convention, "believing as I do that his turn has come." Blaine secured the nomination with relative ease. He was convinced that one last element was needed to bring him the presidency itself, and that was Conkling's endorsement. "It would be an immense thing for us," he eagerly wrote his campaign manager. "How can he be induced to do it?"

The only thing to do was ask, a delicate task that was assigned to a committee of leading Republicans. They traveled to Conkling's law office in New York, hopeful that Platt's reversal signaled a similar change of heart in the fiercest Stalwart of all.

Conkling stripped them of their illusions. "Gentlemen," he thundered, "you have been misinformed. I have given up criminal practice." The Republican boss of New York refused to lift a finger to help his rival. His inactivity loomed large on election night, as it became evident that whichever candidate carried New York would reach the White House. Blaine ended up losing the state to Grover Cleveland by just 1,047 votes.

Conkling and Blaine, ironically enough, held similar views on most issues. If they hadn't wasted their energies on their long-simmering feud, each might have fulfilled his political dreams. Conkling might have emerged as the power behind the throne in a new Grant administration and Blaine almost certainly would have been elected president. Their careers ended instead in great disappointment, unhappy legacies of the long-forgotten James Barnet Fry.

Making an enemy is rarely an advantageous move. (There *can* be exceptions, which we'll discuss a few pages ahead.) Successful politicians and executives are the ones who work effectively with people of varying personalities and viewpoints. They keep their friends close and their enemies closer, as the Chinese warrior, Sun Tzu, advised more than two millenniums ago.

Why cut yourself off from someone who might provide valuable information or perform an invaluable favor someday? Why push away a rival who could be observed more easily when near at hand? Why alienate somebody who might have the power to deny you a key promotion years (or even decades) down the road?

Estes Kefauver failed to understand the value of wooing his potential enemies. He built his political career by defying the powers-that-be in Tennessee. He ran for the Senate in 1948 against the handpicked candidate of the state's Democratic boss, Edward Crump, who charged that Kefauver was as deceptive as a pet raccoon. "I may be a pet coon," Kefauver shot back, "but I ain't Mr. Crump's pet coon." He adopted a coonskin cap as his symbol, winning the Senate seat in an upset.

Bucking the establishment had paid off for Kefauver at the state level, so he expanded his strategy nationally. He began laying the groundwork for a presidential campaign, unconcerned about the powerful enemies he was making. He exasperated his fellow white Southerners by taking a liberal stand on civil rights, then angered Northern party leaders by spearheading a Senate investigation into organized crime in fourteen cities, most of them run by those very same political bosses.

Kefauver entered the race for the 1952 Democratic presidential nomination with a devil-may-care attitude. "The boys in the smoke-filled rooms," he chuckled, "have never taken very well to me." He assembled a strong team and hit the campaign trail, winning the New Hampshire primary and eleven that followed. "He's doing pretty well with his operation," said a worried Richard Russell, leader of the Senate's Old Guard. "I read where he has twelve rooms in a hotel four blocks from the White House. I hope that's as close as he gets."

It was. Southern senators like Russell had virtually nothing in common with the ethnic politicians who ran the North's major cities, but both sides agreed that Kefauver had to be stopped. They blocked his every move at the Democratic convention and drafted Adlai Stevenson as a more suitable nominee. Kefauver tried to bow out gracefully and formally endorse Stevenson, but his enemies spurned even that courtesy. The convention's chairman, Sam Rayburn of Texas, coldly ignored his requests to speak.

Kefauver's mistake was in ignoring his enemies, but it can be equally dangerous to become preoccupied with them. Woodrow Wilson, much to his own misfortune, allowed his contempt for Henry Cabot Lodge and other conservative Republicans to color his handling of the peace treaty after World War I.

"If I said what I think about those fellows in Congress," the president spat, "it would take a piece of asbestos two inches thick to hold it." Wilson focused more on settling the score with his foes than on achieving his objective. He refused to compromise with Lodge and his fellow Senate Republicans, setting the stage for rejection of the treaty and the destruction of Wilson's own reputation.

> ## "Those Who Hate You Don't Win Unless You Hate Them"
>
> Richard Nixon compiled an encyclopedic list of his enemies, then systematically harassed and spied on them, ruining his own career in the process. The stupidity of his obsession became clear as he sank in the morass of Watergate. "Always remember," he said on the day he left the White House, "others may hate you, but those who hate you don't win unless you hate them, and then you destroy yourself."
>
> Nixon's mentor, Dwight Eisenhower, never spent much time worrying about his rivals. The idea of listing them and plotting against them would have struck him as absurd. Conciliation and discipline, he always said, were key components of leadership. Those high standards could be met only by taking a calm, reasonable approach that mollified most potential enemies. Getting even with the few who remained was out of the question.
>
> Eisenhower had a much simpler system for dealing with people who annoyed him. It required only three steps, as he recounted. Ike would "write (the miscreant's) name on a piece of paper, put it in my lower desk drawer, and shut the drawer." And then he would turn his attention to things that really mattered.

IF AN ENEMY ATTACKS, DEFEND YOURSELF VIGOROUSLY

Ten-year-old Peter Roberts faced a challenging assignment, and he wasn't sure how to proceed. It was October 1988, just a few days before the presidential election. Peter had been chosen to portray the Democratic candidate, Michael Dukakis, in a fifth-grade debate.

The young man had a decent grasp of the issues. He could mimic Dukakis's positions on health care, defense policy, and other matters of public interest. But he worried about the negative aspects of politics. What should he do if his Republican opponent, a boy playing George H.W. Bush, went on the attack?

Luck was on his side. The Dukakis campaign rolled into Peter's hometown, a Philadelphia suburb, shortly before the mock debate was scheduled. Arrangements were made, and the young surrogate was given a chance to ask the real-life candidate for advice.

"Respond to the attacks immediately," Dukakis told him emphatically. "Don't let them get away with a thing."

Dukakis had learned this lesson the hard way. He had been showered with negative television commercials since midsummer. Bush's ads insinuated that Dukakis was soft on violent crime, unconcerned about pollution, even hostile toward the Pledge of Allegiance. "I thought we should answer immediately," his running mate, Lloyd Bentsen, recalled. "But my friend Mike Dukakis was incredulous. He just didn't believe these kinds of charges would stick."

But stick they did. Dukakis took a healthy lead over Bush in pre-Labor Day polls, but his support disintegrated under the ceaseless bombardment. Democratic advisers pleaded with him to refute Bush's accusations and launch a counterattack. "There were lots of conference phone calls. Nothing happened," Democratic pollster Stanley Greenberg recalled with disgust. Dukakis insisted on waging the campaign on his terms, talking about *his* favorite issues, not Bush's. He didn't approve a retaliatory strike until he had fallen far behind. It was way too late. Dukakis was buried in a November landslide, carrying just ten states and the District of Columbia.

The desirable course in business or politics, as we discussed in the previous section, is to follow your own agenda. It's always preferable to stay upbeat, stress your attributes, emphasize your opinions, and do whatever you can to avoid unproductive confrontations. But the rules change when a rival deliberately misrepresents your record or your intentions. If you remain mute in the face of such an attack, the outcome is not likely to be good, as the 1988 campaign proved. "In Dukakis," a top-level Republican consultant said in astonishment, "you have a candidate who, when a match was lit in his vicinity, poured gasoline all over himself."

People believe what they hear. If you can't be bothered to defend yourself, they naturally assume that the allegations or rumors about you must be factual. "In this crazy political business, at least in our times, a lie unanswered becomes the truth within twenty-four hours," observed Willie Brown, who was speaker of the California Assembly and mayor of San Francisco between 1981 and 2004.

This is not a recent phenomenon, despite Brown's qualifying phrase. Leaders have *always* paid a stiff price for inadequate self-defense.

One of the most controversial politicians in the republic's early years was Aaron Burr, who came within a whisker of being elected president in 1800 and subsequently served as Thomas Jefferson's first vice president. He killed longtime rival Alexander Hamilton in a duel in 1804, then fled to the Mississippi Valley, where he allegedly hatched a scheme whose dimensions remain obscure to this day. Some contemporaries contended that Burr was conspiring to seize Mexican land. Others accused him of plotting to form a new nation on American soil. He was hauled to trial in 1807 on a charge of treason, but was acquitted.

That's when the eloquent, free-spirited Burr stepped out of character. He instantly silenced himself. He sailed into self-imposed exile after his trial, remaining in Europe for four years. Rumors swirled furiously in America, yet he spurned all opportunities to swat them down and tell his side of the story. It was a decision he would regret. "I fear I have committed a great error," Burr wrote. "The men who knew their falsity are dead, and the generation who now read them may take them for truths, being uncontradicted." Friends encouraged him to speak out. Better late than never, they said, but he knew his time had passed. "I admit I have committed a capital error," he confessed, "but it is too late to repair it."

Burr was right. If an enemy attacks, you must defend yourself vigorously and immediately. Bill Clinton was determined to avoid the mistakes that Dukakis had made four years earlier, so he assembled a "war room" in 1992. Its name conjured up a high-tech, Pentagon-style command center, but the reality was "a junk-food-strewed lair filled with telephones and TV sets," as one visitor described it. Yet the war room—unimposing though it might have been—served Clinton's purposes perfectly. Dukakis-style passivity was forbidden within its walls. Young staffers monitored attacks by President Bush's campaign and prepared instant responses. "The rule of the campaign is, every assault must have a counter-assault," wrote Joel Achenbach in the *Washington Post*. "Bush hits, Clinton hits back. Did not, did so."

The costs of a fully equipped war room put it far beyond the budgets of most mortals, but you can—and should—adopt the principles on which such an operation is run:

- Time is always of the essence. Respond to an attack as rapidly as you can—if at all possible, on the same day.

- If your rival is lying about you, lay out the facts in a calm, but firm manner. The forums may be different—a politician might use a speech, a business executive a memo—but the goal is the same. Portray yourself as reasonable and totally in the right. Make the liar appear foolish.

- If your rival is making absurd claims, call his or her bluff. James Carville, the blunt, wisecracking consultant who ran Clinton's war room, jumped on Bush's pledge to simultaneously expand federal programs and cut taxes. "Count up anything that costs money," he shouted to his assistants. "The tax cut, health care—wire the economists. The more experts the better. Bush didn't promise the moon, he promised the universe." Clinton's rebuttal, complete with his own cost estimates for Bush's plan, was sent to reporters within hours.

- Reestablish your core message once the attack has been repulsed. Clinton's team harped on the sluggishness of the job market in 1992. Carville hung a sign in the war room—"The Economy, Stupid"—to keep everyone focused on the key issue. "The advertising," he insisted, "should always come back to: 'We can't afford four more years of Bush.'"

- The final rule may be the toughest. Keep your poise. Always give as good as you get, but never become overheated. Be insistent, not belligerent, no matter what your opponent throws at you. "You just have to grow from the licks," Clinton told a group of high-school students during the campaign. "The main thing is never quit, never quit, never quit."

CERTAIN ENEMIES CAN ACTUALLY HELP YOU ADVANCE

It all started because Grover Cleveland was hungry.

The convivial lawyer—a former sheriff of Erie County, New York—wandered into a Buffalo restaurant on a Saturday afternoon in October 1881. He spotted five friends, members of a Democratic Party committee that had been told to find a suitable candidate for mayor. The search wasn't going well— some men had declined the nomination, others had failed to impress the committee—when the portly Cleveland strolled over to say hello. The weary Democrats asked the ex-sheriff if *he* might be willing to run. He thought the idea over and eventually consented.

Cleveland was elected mayor a month later on a pledge to reform Buffalo's government. He refused to do business with companies that jacked up prices for city contracts. He scuttled a costly street-cleaning deal. He scorned old-line politicians from both parties. "Public office is a public trust," he lectured them. Everyday citizens hailed him as the "veto mayor," but Buffalo's business and political leaders couldn't wait for him to leave City Hall.

Their wish was granted in less than a year. Cleveland's battles with the power structure in Buffalo drew statewide publicity, and he capitalized by winning the governorship of New York in 1882. New York City's Democratic machine, Tammany Hall, welcomed the upstate novice, expecting to lead him around by the nose, but it was quickly disillusioned. Cleveland insisted that all appointments be based on merit. Tammany, he decreed, would receive no special favors. The Tammany-dominated State Senate threatened retribution, but Cleveland would not be cowed. "Give me a sheet of paper," the governor barked to his secretary. "I'll tell the people what a set of damned rascals they have upstairs."

A spirit of such strength and independence inevitably attracted national attention. Cleveland emerged as a leading candidate for the 1884 Democratic presidential nomination. His only drawback, it seemed, was an unusual one. The Democratic leaders of his own state—the largest state of all—were violently opposed to him. Their hatred appeared to be an insurmountable negative.

But Cleveland's campaign transformed it into a positive. New York City and its leaders have always aroused strong emotions—a mixture of fascination and revulsion—across the rest of America. It stood to reason that millions of voters would look favorably upon any candidate who had run afoul of Tammany Hall. General Edward Bragg referred to that very group in bringing Cleveland's name before the Democratic convention. "They respect him not only for himself, for his character, for his integrity and judgment and iron will," he declared, "but they love him most of all for the enemies he has made!"

The convention hall roared its approval. A Tammany leader, Thomas Grady, scrambled toward the stage, shouting, "On behalf of his enemies, I accept the sentiment." It was a splendid bit of theater, but Grady found himself in the minority. Cleveland took the nomination and, four months later, the presidency itself.

His ascension had been unbelievably swift. Only three years had elapsed between ex-Sheriff Cleveland's arrival at Dranger's Restaurant and Governor Cleveland's election to the White House. Luck and good timing had played a part, to be sure. But the new president owed an enormous debt to his enemies in Buffalo and New York City. It was they who had established his reputation and boosted his popularity. He truly couldn't have won without them.

That's the delightful secret about opponents. They're almost always a nuisance—mocking your best efforts, blocking your well-intentioned plans. But they *can* serve a worthwhile purpose on occasion, pushing you together with new allies who hate them as much as you do. If you're blessed with the right enemies—the evil, contemptible kind—you might receive as strong a boost as Franklin Roosevelt did.

Roosevelt's qualifications and personality had little to do with his initial victory in a presidential election. The nation would have voted for anyone in 1932 who promised to fight the Depression, anyone not named Herbert Hoover.

But FDR would win an unprecedented four terms in the White House, forming an unanticipated bond with lower- and middle-class Americans. Even the poorest people in the South, the poorest section of the country, felt a kinship with the wealthy Harvard graduate who owned a Hudson Valley estate. A North Carolina mill worker told a reporter that Roosevelt, the New York patrician, was "the only man we ever had in the White House who would understand that my boss is a son of a bitch."

This mystical link was cemented by the enemies that Roosevelt and everyday Americans shared. The forces that opposed FDR's New Deal programs were the same forces that most people blamed for the Depression. Roosevelt called the roll in a famous speech at the close of the 1936 campaign—"business and financial monopoly, speculation, reckless banking ... organized money"—and the audience in Madison Square Garden hooted derisively. "Never before in all our history have these forces been so united against one candidate as they stand today," Roosevelt shouted. "They are unanimous in their hate for me—and I welcome their hatred." The crowd went wild.

FDR was sincere. He knew that his enemies had inadvertently given him tremendous power. He was amused by the intensity of their animosity, relishing a joke about a Wall Street tycoon who would buy the newspaper each morning, scan the front page, curse loudly, and throw it away. A perplexed newsstand operator watched him for weeks before asking why he tossed the paper out so quickly. Why didn't he read the inside pages?

"I'm looking for an obituary," the man snapped.

"But sir," the vendor replied, "you don't find obituaries on the front page. They're toward the back."

Roosevelt liked to pause at this point, setting up the punch line. He leaned forward, a smile playing at his lips, before giving the tycoon's response.

"Son," the millionaire told the newsstand operator, "believe me, the obituary I'm looking for will be on the front page." And Franklin Roosevelt always laughed with uninhibited joy.

6

Maneuvering

It didn't bother Ronald Reagan that the odds—and history—were solidly against him in 1976. He was determined to pursue the Republican presidential nomination, even though it meant running against the incumbent, Gerald Ford, who had the White House's awesome resources at his disposal.

There was every reason to believe that Reagan's insurgency would meet a quick, dismal end. Only four challengers had snatched a nomination away from a sitting president since the beginning of American history, and all four belonged to the distant past. No upstart had succeeded in ninety-two years, not since James Blaine elbowed Chester Arthur aside at the 1884 Republican convention.

But Reagan proved to be a remarkably effective candidate, a chameleon who could alter his image when the situation required. He had served eight years as governor of California, overseeing the largest state bureaucracy in America, yet billed himself as the anti-government candidate in 1976, pledging to destroy "evil incarnate in the buddy system in Washington." He was the foremost advocate of what he called the Eleventh Commandment—"thou shalt not speak ill of a fellow Republican"—yet had no qualms about routinely blasting Ford, whom he accused of having "neither the vision nor the leadership necessary" to be president.

Reagan kept his campaign on track longer than most pundits had anticipated. He won ten of the year's twenty-six primaries, securing the support of more than a thousand delegates to the Republican convention. It was an impressive performance, though not quite good enough. Ford held a slight lead in the delegate count as the convention neared. The president's nomination seemed to be in the bag.

Desperate times call for creative solutions, and Reagan's campaign manager, John Sears, was always able to conjure up a fresh idea in a pinch. His candidate had won the hearts of conservatives, but the nomination was clearly beyond his reach without support from moderate Republicans. If Reagan balanced his ticket with a middle-of-the-road running mate, Sears thought, he might broaden his appeal and lure away enough Ford delegates to eke out a victory at the convention.

It was an unusual proposal. Presidential candidates typically don't waste a minute picking a vice president until the nomination is firmly in hand. Reagan seemed unlikely to buck this time-honored precedent, which contradicted his stated principles. "I don't believe you choose someone of an opposite philosophy in hopes he'll get you some votes you can't get yourself," he had insisted earlier in the year, "because that's being false with the people who vote for you and your philosophy."

But chameleons adapt with great speed. The only alternative was certain defeat, so Reagan cheerfully endorsed Sears's strategy and chose Richard Schweiker, a fairly liberal senator from Pennsylvania, to be his vice-presidential partner. Doctrinaire conservatives howled about Reagan's betrayal, but pragmatic politicians admired his adroitness. "We had to expand the base. We somehow had to get the moderates and the liberals in the tent," said Paul Laxalt, a Nevada senator and key Reagan adviser. An influential California conservative, unnamed in press reports, was effusive in his praise. "Frankly, I think it was a stroke of genius," he told a reporter. "There was really nothing else to do."

Sears's plan had only one flaw. It didn't work. Schweiker attracted a handful of new Reagan delegates, but nowhere near the number required for the nomination.

Time was running out. Sears now faced two stark options—concede defeat or yank another rabbit from his hat. He predictably chose the latter, proposing that *all* candidates be required to name their running mates before the convention selected the nominee. Perhaps Ford would pick an unattractive partner who would drive delegates into Reagan's camp. A Ford backer labeled it the "misery loves company" rule—which it obviously was—while reporters jokingly accused Sears of being an incorrigible troublemaker. "And it's only Monday," he laughed in reply.

But Reagan's team was finally out of tricks. The convention rejected Sears's proposal after a heated debate, then proceeded to nominate Ford for president the following night.

Reagan would go down in history as the loser of the Republican slugfest of '76, but it was an inadequate, unfair characterization. He waged an agile campaign—bobbing and weaving, constantly staying on the move—and came amazingly close to denying a sitting president the nomination of his party, something that no one else accomplished in the twentieth century. The 1976 Republican convention was the second-tightest on record, with the two contenders separated by just five percentage points. Reagan may not have won, but he had performed incredibly well.

Such dexterity has always been an essential component of political success, as reflected in the stories of two unrelated candidates who shared a surname, great maneuvering skill, and little else.

DeWitt Clinton, the mayor of New York City, had the misfortune of being the Federalist Party's presidential nominee when the War of 1812 broke out. Americans usually rally around the flag during the early stages of any armed conflict, which boded well for Clinton's opponent, President James Madison, who was seeking a second term.

But Clinton saw an opening. New Englanders tended to be more skeptical about the war—many were downright hostile toward it—while most southerners and midwesterners were hawks. The challenger tailored his campaign to these regional biases. His pamphlets posed a simple choice to New England voters: "Madison and War! Or Clinton and Peace!" But pro-Clinton literature in the rest of the country promised that the war "shall be prosecuted till every object shall be attained for which we fight."

A campaign so blatantly contradictory wouldn't be possible in our media-saturated age, but it kept the election close in 1812. Clinton lost to the incumbent by just thirty-nine votes in the Electoral College. This was a notable achievement, given that Madison's margin of victory four years earlier had been almost twice as large.

Bill Clinton brought similar skills to the White House nearly two centuries later. He was an exponent of "triangulation," a fancy term for shifting with the political winds. Clinton's foes labeled him a liberal Democrat, yet many of his policies were lifted directly from the conservative Republican playbook. He scaled back the welfare system, endorsed international free trade, supported a ban on same-sex marriages, and declared that "the era of big government is over." His fluidity made it almost impossible for Robert Dole, who opposed him for reelection in 1996, to identify an issue on which they differed. "I think he's being very shrewd," conservative analyst Kevin Phillips said admiringly of Clinton's style, but an exasperated Dole accused the president of "grand theft."

Your chances of success, whether in politics or business, will improve if you develop a similar ability to maneuver. Don't stand flat-footed while your rivals scramble to get ahead. Learn how to alter the way you're perceived by others, maintain your freedom of movement and, yes, wheel and deal when necessary. This chapter will expand on each of these points:

Altering perceptions

- Subtlety and charm are the keys to manipulation.
- If danger lurks, shift the onus to someone else.
- Spin your negatives into positives.
- Tell the truth whenever you can, but lie if you must.

Freedom of movement

- Labels can only weigh you down, so avoid them.
- Cut ties with any ally who becomes a liability.

Wheeling and dealing

- If success hinges on making a deal, make it.
- If the rules are slanted against you, change them.

These recommendations exude an undeniably Machiavellian odor. And why not? The famed sixteenth-century political theorist, Niccolo Machiavelli, was history's foremost proponent of executive maneuvering. He contended that "the ends justify the means" and that leaders "who had little regard for their word and had the craftiness to turn men's minds have accomplished great things."

But there are limits to the effectiveness of Machiavellian tactics, as we'll discuss in this chapter. Shifting the blame to someone else or telling a lie may not be admirable moves, but they often work well on a small scale over the short term. Excessive reliance on blame-shifting or lying, however, can lead only to disaster. Consider the downward spirals of Woodrow Wilson, Lyndon Johnson, Richard Nixon, and Bill Clinton, to name four presidents who pushed their luck too far. Or ponder the more severe cases from the business world, Bernie Ebbers, John Rigas, and Kenneth Lay's Enron gang among them.

The key is to restrain your darker impulses, yet to stay on your toes, regardless of whether you're pursuing a career in the private sector or in politics. "You may be guided by an overarching vision, clear values, and a strategic plan, but what you actually do from moment to moment cannot be scripted. You must respond as events unfold," consultants Ronald Heifetz and Marty Linsky advised budding executives. Their words echo Franklin Roosevelt's comparison of a president to a quarterback. Both signal-callers knew what the next play would be, FDR said, but neither could plan too far ahead because "future plays will depend on how the next one works."

The effective executive, in the final analysis, is the man or woman who can maneuver adroitly to sustain a positive image and a solid base of support, two elements that even Machiavelli—the Prince of Darkness himself—agreed were vital for success. "You will always need the favor of the inhabitants," he wrote. "It is necessary for a prince to possess the friendship of the people."

SUBTLETY AND CHARM ARE THE KEYS TO MANIPULATION

Most contemporaries, even a few dedicated rivals, thoroughly enjoyed the company of Martin Van Buren. Few could resist the New Yorker's sunny, outgoing personality. He seemed to have a smile and a joke for everyone he met, and his refined manners and sparkling wit made him the perfect guest at any dinner party.

But Van Buren was no social butterfly. He established himself as one of America's foremost politicians during the first half of the nineteenth century, attaining a series of major offices—governor of New York, senator, secretary of state, minister to Great Britain, vice president, and finally, the eighth president of the United States.

This glittering résumé baffled many who knew him. Horace Greeley, the famed editor of the *New York Tribune*, found it difficult to pinpoint the dominant reason for his success. It wasn't charisma, to be sure. Van Buren didn't possess the personal magnetism of Andrew Jackson or Henry Clay, nor was he a particularly skilled orator or administrator. "I believe his strength lay in his suavity," Greeley concluded. "He was the reconciler of the estranged, the harmonizer of those who were at feud among his fellow partisans. An adroit and subtle, rather than a great man."

Van Buren was the master political manipulator of his era, as implied by his nicknames, the Little Magician and the Red Fox. He radiated charm and grace, deftly drawing out his colleagues' opinions while quietly guiding them toward the candidate or legislation he favored. He downplayed his own views, speaking in broad generalities to avoid committing himself in any way. A friend jokingly sought to penetrate this obscurity, asking Van Buren to admit at least that the sun rises in the east. "I presume the fact is according to the common impression," the Red Fox replied with a smile, "but as I invariably sleep until after sunrise, I cannot speak from my own knowledge."

Van Buren's bland amiability helped him build alliances and coalitions that advanced his career. He forged his most important link in 1827 with Andrew Jackson, a political marriage of suave easterner and fiery frontiersman that may have seemed strange on the surface, but proved to be mutually beneficial. Van Buren's New York machine worked tirelessly to elect Jackson president in 1828. Old Hickory's subsequent victory, as one congressman saw it, was achieved "directly under the wand of the great magician."

Van Buren missed no opportunity to flatter his new friend. He sent a stream of obsequious letters to the president and sang Jackson's praises in public. Their relationship was cemented when Jackson named Van Buren his secretary of state. "Van Buren glides along as smoothly as oil and as silently as a cat," said Amos Kendall, another member of Jackson's cabinet. "If he is managing at all, it is so adroitly that nobody perceives it."

This was especially true after a domestic squabble disrupted the new administration. A friend of Jackson's, Senator John Eaton of Tennessee, had become romantically involved with the daughter of a Washington innkeeper. Peggy O'Neale was already married, much to her suitor's misfortune, but her husband conveniently died in the Mediterranean while serving on a naval vessel. Rumors swirled that he had committed suicide after learning of his wife's infidelity.

Eaton subsequently married Peggy, and then joined Jackson's team as secretary of war. The wives and daughters of the other cabinet members, incensed at the couple's alleged adultery, refused to recognize the new Mrs. Eaton socially. Their mass rejection stoked Jackson's notorious temper, which burned white-hot after Vice President John Calhoun's wife also snubbed Peggy.

"And Now I Am Going Blind"

Any executive—even one who is blessed with a commanding, larger-than-life persona—can benefit from the skillful use of manipulation. George Washington, more than any other figure in American history, might seem to have been above such grubby tactics. He was, after all, a revered icon, the Father of His Country. But he was also especially gifted in cajoling others to take actions they originally opposed.

Washington's powers of persuasion were severely tested long before his presidency. Congress grew lax about paying the Continental Army as the Revolutionary War drew to a close, an omission that greatly annoyed General Washington's soldiers. A few hotheaded officers suggested marching on Philadelphia, then the nation's capital, to demand their money. The idea gained popularity as the paymaster's absence stretched into subsequent weeks.

Washington urged Congress to release the necessary funds, but his plea was ignored. Rebellion was now in the air. There was a real danger that the young government might be overthrown by the very men who had just won its independence on the battlefield.

The general saw no option but to appeal to his officers' better natures, so he called them together to thank them for their service and to request their forbearance. His audience was angry, certainly in no mood to be appeased with mere words. Washington began to read a prepared statement, then abruptly stopped and began fumbling in his pockets. His men were astonished as he pulled out a pair of reading glasses. They had never seen him wear spectacles.

"I have already grown gray in the service of my country," Washington quietly explained, "and now I am going blind."

It was a poignant moment. Many of the men cried. They spoke no more of rebellion. If Washington could sacrifice the prime years of adulthood—and even his eyesight—for the cause of freedom, they could wait for Congress to dole out their pay in its own sweet time. There would be no march on Philadelphia, no constitutional crisis.

George Washington, by the way, had been wearing reading glasses for years.

Only one cabinet member ignored the boycott. Charming, loyal Martin Van Buren, a widower, had no wife to draw him into the dispute. He befriended and defended both of the Eatons—taking care to treat Peggy with special kindness—and thus won the president's eternal gratitude. It was no coincidence that Jackson dropped the flinty Calhoun as vice president after his first term, choosing his urbane friend from New York as the replacement. Nor was it a surprise when the outgoing president anointed Van Buren as his successor in 1836.

Few people possess subtlety and charm to the degree that Martin Van Buren did, but any aspiring executive can learn from his example. The proper blend of flattery, persuasion, and amiable vagueness can be highly effective, as noted by a Bryant College psychology professor, Ronald Deluga, who studied 150 pairs of supervisors and workers. Subordinates who soothed their bosses with compliments and praise, he found, had a measurably better chance of earning promotions. "This behavior is the icing on the cake," Deluga said. "From a statistical point of view, it adds 5 percent."

Manipulation works best when it's invisible, so take care not to be impatient or heavy-handed. Listen carefully to what the other person has to say, ask questions about his or her position, and wait for an opportunity to respond in a low-key manner. Try to gradually nudge your associate toward your point of view, but don't expect immediate success. If it takes more than one conversation, if it takes weeks or even months, so be it. You can spend the time. Martin Van Buren always did.

IF DANGER LURKS, SHIFT THE ONUS TO SOMEONE ELSE

Robert Fulghum, a retired Unitarian minister, grabbed the nation's attention in 1988 by writing *All I Really Need to Know I Learned in Kindergarten*, a tiny book of modern parables. He suggested that our earliest teachers had imbued us with the very essentials of life. Share everything, they told us. Play fair. Hold hands and stick together. What else was there? Comedians mocked Fulghum's premise—the essence of human existence couldn't *possibly* be so simple—but the last laugh belonged to him. His book became a bestseller.

Many of Fulghum's homilies admittedly had the ring of truth. We *do* understand a great deal about life at a young age. The recommendation in the following paragraph, for example, may not be one the kindly minister would have endorsed, yet most youngsters grasp its effectiveness long before entering kindergarten.

If you make a mistake or if you see a dangerous situation developing, do whatever you can to transfer blame or deflect criticism. Shift the onus to someone else.

It's not the honorable thing, of course, but this strategy is commonly employed by children and adults alike. It's especially favored by politicians who find themselves boxed in a corner. And you know what? It works remarkably well, at least in the short run.

Woodrow Wilson used this tactic to perfection in his 1916 reelection campaign against a formidable Republican challenger, Charles Evans Hughes, whom many considered to be the odds-on favorite.

The United States was drifting closer and closer to becoming involved in World War I, a step that Wilson didn't want to take, especially in an election year. But he knew that it might soon become inevitable. "I can't keep the country out of war," he confessed unhappily to a cabinet member. Admitting the same truth in public, however, would have been political suicide. The Midwest and West, heavily populated by German immigrants, were violently opposed to American military intervention and appeared to hold the balance of power in the election. What to do?

The president's solution was to tar his opponent as a warmonger, even though Hughes had simply called for America to improve its military preparedness while maintaining "a strict and honest neutrality" in the European conflict.

Wilson's campaign slogan—"He Kept Us Out of War"—implied that Hughes would be unable or unwilling to do the same. A Democratic pamphlet sharpened the point: "The lesson is plain: If you want war, vote for Hughes! If you want peace with honor, vote for Wilson!" Democratic speakers tied Hughes to the bellicose rants of fellow Republican Theodore Roosevelt, who lusted to send American troops to the battlefields of Europe. It was an unfair comparison—and Wilson knew it.

The East, the region most inclined to support Great Britain and France, voted solidly against Wilson and his pacifist campaign. But farm states drifted the president's way on the same issue—despite their traditional Republican leanings—bringing him just enough votes to win reelection. Hughes, no matter what he said to the contrary, had become thoroughly associated in the public mind as a pro-war candidate.

Wilson was unable to live up to his slogan in the end. Germany resumed unrestricted submarine attacks in the Atlantic Ocean three months after the election. The president soon did precisely what he had anticipated all along— and what he had accused Hughes of secretly plotting. He asked Congress to declare war in April 1917, less than a month after his second inauguration.

Lyndon Johnson followed Wilson's lead in 1964. Johnson was quietly gearing up to the Vietnam War, securing congressional approval in August for the Tonkin Gulf Resolution, which authorized him to initiate military action to protect any democratic government in Southeast Asia. He believed it was necessary to take a stand against communism in that region, even though polls clearly showed the public to be in no mood for a war candidate in 1964. How could he finesse such a tricky situation?

Johnson went into deflection mode that fall by depicting his opponent, Barry Goldwater, as the man most likely to escalate hostilities in Vietnam. LBJ's most effective television commercial began with a little girl picking daisies, a pastoral scene that was abruptly jarred by a mushrooming nuclear cloud. "These are the stakes," Johnson's voiceover said. "To make a world in which all of God's children can live, or to go into the dark." If there was any doubt about the alleged plans of Goldwater, the candidate of darkness, the president was only too glad to hint at their dimensions. "We don't want our American boys to do the fighting for Asian boys," Johnson said. "We don't want to get tied down in a land war in Asia." He made no mention of the plans being drawn up in his own Pentagon.

Goldwater was an easy target. He had complained that "a craven fear of death is entering the American consciousness," and had jokingly suggested lobbing a nuclear bomb into the men's room of the Kremlin. It was a simple matter to convince Americans to accept Johnson as the peace candidate against such an opponent, paving the way for one of the most lopsided victories in any presidential election. "The whole campaign was run on fear of me," Goldwater would later reflect. "In fact, if I hadn't known Goldwater, I'd have voted against the son of a bitch myself."

The land war in Asia that Johnson warned about, needless to say, became a reality a few months after the 1964 election. But LBJ was safe from the electorate by then, having won a fresh four-year term.

Two important threads run through these parallel stories of Woodrow Wilson and Lyndon Johnson. The first is positive. Each man was successful in the short term, defusing a dangerous situation by shifting the onus to his opponent. Each achieved his objective of reelection.

The darker thread is one that every rising politician and executive should contemplate. Wilson and Johnson both failed badly in the long run, suffering the exposure of their deceptions and deficiencies. Americans were disillusioned by the tawdry peace talks and political bickering that followed World War I and by the mounting death tolls in Vietnam. Wilson and Johnson left the White House with their popularity depleted and their reputations tarnished. Each was replaced by a president from the other party.

And that's the sad truth about dumping your burden on someone else. It's often an effective way to deal with small difficulties or to temporarily hide bigger ones, but it can't make a major problem disappear forever. No strategy can permanently deflect such unhappy news.

Richard Nixon forgot this fact of life when he chose to handle the Watergate crisis in classic political style. His every move was designed to reinforce his purported innocence—"I am not a crook"—while covering up the facts and placing the blame on others. He had his spokesman describe the break-in at Democratic headquarters as a "third-rate burglary attempt," even though he knew that his own campaign workers were involved. He willingly agreed to have the break-in crew take the rap, he helped raise hush money to purchase their silence, and he later forced a few key subordinates out the door. Nineteen presidential aides would eventually go to jail.

Nixon himself was undone by his own tape recordings of conversations with many of those same aides. The tapes unmasked his campaign of blame-shifting, proving that the president was directly involved in criminal activities. Todd Christofferson, then a clerk for John Sirica, the federal judge handling the Watergate case, was among the first to hear the tapes. He later reflected that Nixon had two options when he first received word of the break-in.

"He could have said, 'No, it goes no further. Let the chips fall where they may,'" Christofferson mused. "And he didn't, and it mushroomed. That one failing brought the whole house down."

SPIN YOUR NEGATIVES INTO POSITIVES

John Kerry, a senator from neighboring Massachusetts, easily outdistanced the rest of the Democratic field in the 2004 New Hampshire primary. He drew 38 percent of all votes cast, twelve percentage points better than his closest competitor. This triumph, coupled with Kerry's earlier victory in the Iowa caucuses, established him as the odds-on favorite to win the party's presidential nomination.

Five other Democrats had campaigned against Kerry in New Hampshire, hoping to drag the frontrunner back to the pack, but they failed badly. These men now straggled out to say a few words to the supporters waiting at their respective headquarters. All of them were smiling, seemingly without a care in the world, as if their objective all along had been to finish not in first place, but anywhere between second and sixth. Their remarks were uniformly upbeat, as they claimed moral victories on a night of obvious defeat:

Howard Dean (26 percent): "The people of New Hampshire have allowed our campaign to regain its momentum, and I'm very grateful."

Wesley Clark (12 percent): "Four months ago, we weren't even in this race. Four months later, we came into New Hampshire as one of the elite eight. Tonight, we leave New Hampshire as one of the final four."

John Edwards (also with 12 percent): "In New Hampshire ten days ago, we were twenty points behind General Clark, and look at what we've done."

Joseph Lieberman (9 percent): "I feel like I achieved my goals here, and I'm grateful to the people of New Hampshire. I did better than expected."

Dennis Kucinich (1 percent): "Don't you get the feeling this is just the beginning of something?"

New Hampshire proved to be the beginning of the end for Kucinich and his fellow also-rans, as Kerry proceeded to win the Democratic nomination with ease. But such an outcome was not a foregone conclusion on that gloomy night. The five losers remained hopeful of derailing Kerry in several primaries coming up in the next few weeks. They had no choice but to radiate optimism, occasionally going to absurd lengths to do so. Their only alternative—one they all considered unacceptable—was to quit the race.

Politicians have a name for this act of issuing self-serving interpretations in the face of adversity. They call it "spinning," likening it to the process of spinning public-relations gold from the rankest variety of political straw.

Critics condemn it harshly. "This word 'spinning,'" said Ben Bradlee, former editor of the *Washington Post*, "is a nice uptown way of saying 'lying.'" But that seems uncharitable. Spinning can be considered an expression of optimism, a glass-half-full view of life. A spinner doesn't spread blatant falsehoods, opting instead to offer a selective version of the truth. He or she is engaged in a natural effort to turn a personal negative into a positive.

Skill at this particular maneuver can be useful for anyone seeking to advance in any field. All of us have weaknesses and flaws that can't be hidden. It's useless to lie about them. The logical course is to encourage others to look upon these shortcomings in a tolerant way. It's a matter of putting your best foot forward, no matter how lame that foot might be.

That's not to say that spinning always works. It usually occurs under adverse circumstances—there's no need to spin when you're way ahead in the game—so its batting average isn't the best. John Kerry's five opponents, try as they might, failed to convince the nation's voters that their campaigns were still viable, though John Edwards did earn a nice consolation prize. He performed so impressively that Kerry tapped him to join the Democratic ticket as the vice-presidential nominee.

Some problems are simply too enormous to spin away. John Connally, a former governor of Texas and secretary of the treasury, desperately wanted to run for president in 1980, but he was saddled with an unsavory reputation as a manipulator, a wheeler-dealer. He had been indicted a few years earlier for allegedly accepting a bribe from a group of milk producers. His subsequent acquittal failed to remove the taint.

Connally spun furiously when reporters asked about his penchant for backroom deals. "Well," he said, "if you mean by 'wheeler-dealer' someone who knows how to talk to congressmen and businessmen and political leaders all over the world, who knows how to compromise and horse-trade with them to get things done, who isn't afraid to negotiate and hear the other man's side, well then, I guess I'm a wheeler-dealer." A nice try, to be sure, but ineffective in the end. Connally was forced out of the race long before the Republican convention.

Ronald Reagan was much more accomplished at this political art, ranking among the greatest spinners of all time. He put his remarkable skills to good use during his very first campaign against the two-term governor of California, Pat Brown, in 1966. Reagan billed himself as a "citizen politician," but Brown ridiculed the notion that a movie actor could run a state government as large and complicated as California's. He suggested that Reagan might want to take up flying as a new career. "This is your citizen pilot," Brown said mockingly. "I've never flown a plane before, but don't worry. I've always had a deep interest in aviation."

Inexperience loomed as a potentially damaging issue—one that might destroy Reagan's political career before it had really begun—but the challenger gradually spun it into a powerful attribute. Brown had served in government for a quarter-century, yet was doing a poor job of running the state,

Reagan contended, so perhaps experience wasn't so important after all. "Once in a while, when you come to a tough problem," he said, "you choose someone who doesn't know anything about it because he doesn't know what you can't do." California's voters bought this creative and decidedly unusual argument. They ousted the incumbent by a margin of nearly a million votes—installing Ronald Reagan, citizen politician, as their new governor.

TELL THE TRUTH WHENEVER YOU CAN, BUT LIE IF YOU MUST

We all know the story. Young George Washington impulsively grabs his trusty ax and chops down a cherry tree on his father's property. Dad, suitably enraged, demands to know what happened. "I cannot tell a lie, Pa," George replies. "I did cut it with my hatchet."

It would be a wonderful parable about the sanctity of honor and truth, were it not for a serious flaw. This timeless tale is almost certainly a lie fabricated by Mason Locke Weems, author of an early bestseller about America's first president.

Weems knew a golden opportunity when he saw it. He rushed his book into print in 1800, the year after Washington's death. "Millions are gaping to read something about him," he wrote his publisher. "I am nearly primed and cocked for 'em. It will sell like flax seed at a quarter of a dollar." He knew his audience well. The public snapped up more copies of *The Life and Memorable Actions of George Washington* than any other book but the Bible.

Sales dipped in subsequent years, as they usually do, but the author refused to be complacent. He spiffed up his book by adding several new stories, including the previously unpublished yarn about young George and his hatchet, which Weems credited to an "aged lady who is a distant cousin of Washington." Most historians are convinced that he made up the whole thing.

The real George Washington bore little resemblance to the saint who glided through the pages of Weems's book. He possessed a volcanic temper, a colorful vocabulary, and an inclination to deceive his rivals when absolutely necessary. If he *had* chopped down his father's cherry tree, he very well might have covered his tracks with a little white lie.

Washington, to be *honest* about it, was as human as the typical American today. "Lying has long been a part of everyday life. We couldn't get through the day without being deceptive," contended Leonard Saxe, a polygraph expert and psychology professor at Brandeis University, and there are studies that support his assertion. Researchers at the University of Virginia asked 147 adults to keep a list of every falsehood they told during a given week in the mid-1990s. Participants typically lied once or twice a day, deliberately misleading 30 percent of the people they dealt with on a one-to-one basis. Many of these untruths were innocuous—a compliment for a bad haircut, perhaps—but they were lies nonetheless.

The pressure to deceive becomes more intense as you rise in the spheres of business or politics. "The American people like being lied to. Hence Ronald Reagan," wrote humorist Roy Blount Jr. "But even for a president who is not a professional actor, misrepresentation is part of the job. Commentators who do not bear this in mind are like critics in the audience shouting, 'Tell us what you really think,' at an actor who is trying to bring off a drama." Blount confined his observations to politicians, but he could have included corporate executives under his umbrella, too, as demonstrated by America's recent wave of high-profile business scandals.

A few presidents have done their best to resist the impulse. Abraham Lincoln—"Honest Abe" himself—was compulsive about telling the truth. An 1860 campaign pamphlet bragged that Lincoln enjoyed reading Plutarch, though he was, in fact, unfamiliar with the author's works. He immediately validated the claim by reading Plutarch's *Lives*. Grover Cleveland, who was accused of fathering a child out of wedlock, willingly admitted his responsibility during the 1884 presidential race. "Tell the truth," he advised his astounded campaign team, which would have preferred to dodge the allegation. Theodore Roosevelt sanctimoniously insisted that "under the great law of morality and righteousness," it was just as wrong to lie to voters or reporters as to a court of law.

But even these paragons stumbled on occasion. Critics accused President Lincoln of lying about his true intentions when he initially denied that the Civil War was a crusade against slavery. President Cleveland told the press that two bad teeth of his had been pulled in 1893; surgeons had actually removed a cancerous tumor. The first President Roosevelt either encouraged or engineered a revolution in Panama—it depends on which historian you read—to facilitate construction of the Panama Canal, though he blithely maintained at the time that his hands were clean.

Honesty, to be blunt, is not always the best policy. If you plan on reaching the top, you'll probably need to, well, shade the truth from time to time. A strategically timed falsehood can be a powerful tool, extricating you from an uncomfortable confrontation or an embarrassing alliance. David Gergen, who worked closely with four presidents from Richard Nixon to Bill Clinton, found his bosses generally willing to fib. "In my experience over the past thirty years, every White House—save one—has on occasion willfully misled or lied to the press. Some have done it promiscuously," Gergen wrote. The honest exception, in his opinion, was Gerald Ford, who, it must be noted, lost the 1976 election to Jimmy Carter.

Don't get the wrong impression here. It still makes sense to tell the truth whenever you can. That's the morally preferable course, and it's easier, too. Deceive only when absolutely necessary, and keep your lies small. Big lies inevitably lead to big cover-ups, which lead in turn to big, big trouble.

Recent history offers ample proof of the dangers of indiscriminate lying. Lyndon Johnson's repeated falsehoods about the Vietnam War brought a new phrase, "credibility gap," into the English language and doomed his hopes for reelection. It became simple to determine if LBJ was telling the truth, according to a popular joke in the 1960s. If he pulled his earlobe, he was being straight. The same if he was scratching his chin. But if Johnson moved his lips, you could be certain he was lying.

Richard Nixon's lies about the Watergate affair were so numerous and egregious as to defy belief, notably his bold declaration, "I am not a crook." He denied involvement in the Watergate crimes almost to the moment that he left the White House in disgrace. "I wanted to believe he would do the right thing," recalled John Dean, a onetime Nixon aide who had been involved in the conspiracy himself. "After all, he was the president of the United States. But he didn't, and the rest, as they say, is history."

Bill Clinton's tendency to dance around the truth not only tarnished his reputation, but nearly forced his removal from office. Clinton seemed unable to resist the urge to fib. He insisted that he had smoked marijuana without inhaling. He denied having sex with Monica Lewinsky. He boasted to a group of Iowa farmers, "I am the only president who knew something about agriculture when I got there." Which surely would have surprised Thomas Jefferson and Jimmy Carter, both of whom ran large farms before assuming the presidency.

Johnson, Nixon, and Clinton—skilled politicians all—were undone by their inept deceptions. They lied too clumsily, too obviously, and much too frequently. They lacked the graceful ease of the master deceiver, Franklin Roosevelt, who offset his falsehoods with great charm and an unequaled ability to sense the popular will.

Few politicians could simultaneously maneuver the country into a world war and steadfastly deny they were doing so, but that's precisely the juggling act that Roosevelt maintained in 1940 and 1941. He instituted a military draft, supplied Great Britain with destroyers, and assigned American naval vessels to protect Allied convoys in the Atlantic, even authorizing them to fire on German ships and submarines. Yet he consistently denied that such actions might draw the United States into World War II. "Your president says this country is not going to war," he promised as the 1940 campaign drew to a close, even though he privately assumed that American involvement was inevitable.

This contradiction infuriated Roosevelt's enemies, but they were unable to box him in. Many admitted frankly that they liked him. FDR's first vice president, John Nance Garner, morphed into a bitter foe of his policies, yet was surprisingly muted in his criticisms of the man. Roosevelt "was a charming fellow," Garner said. "But he was a hard man to have an understanding with. He would deviate from the understanding."

Roosevelt delighted in his ability to confuse and mislead. He broke the tedium of one practice session by delivering a speech as if he were Theodore Roosevelt, punching it up precisely as his namesake would have done. Tommy Corcoran, a key aide, was instantly obsequious. "Oh, but Mr. President," he said, "the difference between you and TR is that you never fake." Roosevelt happily disagreed, "Oh, but Tommy, at times I do, I do."

Even FDR's closest advisers and confidants were not immune from his deceptions. Henry Morgenthau, his longtime secretary of the treasury, recalled a pearl of presidential wisdom. "Never let your left hand know what your right is doing," Roosevelt told him.

That set Morgenthau to wondering. "Which hand am I, Mr. President?" he asked.

"My right hand," FDR replied, "but I keep my left under the table."

Morgenthau had to concede it was true. Roosevelt was willing to mislead anyone—even a trusted ally—if it served his purposes. "This is the most frank expression of the real FDR that I ever listened to," Morgenthau later admitted, "and that is the real way he works."

LABELS CAN ONLY WEIGH YOU DOWN, SO AVOID THEM

Salmon Chase was an ambitious man, always calculating, always on the lookout for the main chance. His destiny, he believed, was to become president of the United States—Abraham Lincoln thought him "a little insane" on the subject—and he never lost sight of that exalted fate. He gladly ditched any person, organization, or thing that threatened to deflect him from his goal of reaching the White House.

Chase even thought about getting rid of his name, which he considered "awkward, fishy," and a possible impediment to future success. He pondered two florid alternatives, Spencer de Cheyce or Spencer Payne Cheyce, when he reached his early twenties. "Perhaps you will laugh at this," he wrote a friend, "but I assure you I have suffered no little inconvenience." He debated his options long and hard before reluctantly deciding to swim the political waters as a Salmon.

Labels meant nothing to him. Chase shifted parties whenever it suited his purposes. He belonged to five during his long career—Whig, Liberty, Free Soil, Democratic, and Republican—without forming firm attachments to any. He was not averse to working the angles in two parties simultaneously, as in 1849, when he ran for the Senate as a Free Soiler and cut a surreptitious deal for Democratic support at the same time. "Every act of his was subsidiary to his own ambition," carped an Ohio newspaper. "He talked of the interests of Free Soil. He meant His Own."

Chase won the Senate seat, but inevitably found himself at odds with his new Democratic allies. The emerging Republican Party seemed as good a haven as any, so he switched allegiance again. He was elected the first Republican governor of Ohio in 1855, freely confessing his cavalier attitude toward party affiliations. "I care nothing for names," he said. "All that I ask for is a platform and an issue, not buried out of sight, but palpable and paramount."

Chase believed he had finally punched his ticket for the White House. The Republicans were rapidly becoming a dominant force in the Northern states, and he was considered one of the nation's leading Republicans. Everything seemed nicely in order—that is, until Lincoln snatched the 1860 presidential nomination from his grasp.

It was the great disappointment of Chase's life. He would occupy important positions in the Republican administrations of the 1860s—secretary of the treasury and chief justice—but never got over his defeat at the hands of a relatively unknown frontier lawyer. "If he keeps on with the notion that he is destined to be president of the United States, and which in my judgment he will never be," Lincoln told a senator, "he will never acquire that fame and usefulness as chief justice which he would otherwise certainly attain." But Chase couldn't help himself. He wrapped up his career with an orgy of party-switching, seeking presidential nominations from dissident Republicans in 1864, the Democrats in 1868, and the new Liberal Republican Party in 1872. Nothing panned out.

Chase died a year after his final stab at the White House, convinced that his career had been a failure. He had, in fact, been amazingly successful, winning the two highest offices that Ohio's voters had to offer, then playing a major role on the national stage. His flexibility enabled him to survive and even prosper during the most volatile era of American history. His first three parties dissolved in chaos, but he kept jumping until he landed in the Republican vehicle that carried him to the cabinet and the Supreme Court during the Civil War.

Chase's story is wonderfully instructive, especially if we concentrate on his ascension and ignore the desperation of his final years. You would do well to emulate the way he emphasized his personal qualities and qualifications, not his affiliations. Never make the mistake of tying yourself too closely to someone else's prospects, philosophy, or school of thought.

Leadership guru John Gardner learned during his years in Lyndon Johnson's cabinet how important it is to maintain independence and freedom of movement. "Show me a legislator described as 'the darling of the liberals' or the 'darling of the conservatives,'" he wrote, "and I'll show you a legislator without options." The elder George Bush was succinct in making a similar point. "Labels," he said dismissively, "are for cans."

The same holds true in business. If you become known as the "numbers guy" or the "gal in human resources," it's unlikely that you'll ever advance beyond your narrow field. If you align yourself with a single executive in the corporate hierarchy, you might rise in his trail, or you might join him in the unemployment line after he's deposed by another interoffice faction.

History tells us that plenty of victorious politicians have shunned labels and kept their options open. Two men especially notable for their flexibility ended up as back-to-back residents of the White House.

William McKinley successfully finessed the dominant issue of the 1890s. Should America stick to the gold standard, or should it also allow its currency to be converted into silver? This question, so esoteric to modern ears, was bitterly controversial as the nineteenth century drew to a close. Politicians dreaded the consequences of landing on the wrong side.

Silver appeared to have momentum at first, and McKinley willingly voted for silver legislation in Congress. But he and his political patron, Mark Hanna, sensed that gold had become the ticket to victory by 1896, the year that McKinley secured the Republican presidential nomination. They approved a platform that stood foursquare behind the gold standard, alienating many farmers and laborers who believed they were being victimized by tight money policies. A small group of silver Republicans stalked out of the party's convention in protest. Hanna was among those angrily shouting, "Go! Go! Go!" as the tiny band departed.

McKinley could afford to lose the support of these former allies, since his monetary independence would pay big dividends that November. He lost the silver states of the South and West, but his advocacy of gold allowed him to sweep the two wealthiest and most populous parts of the country, the East and the Midwest, and win the 1896 election in a walk.

McKinley's successor, Theodore Roosevelt, was equally good at maintaining his freedom of movement. TR vowed to be a "trustbuster," his era's phrase for any government official who vigorously prosecuted corporate abuses. He hauled several business giants into court during his first years in the White House, but seemed to lose enthusiasm as the 1904 election approached.

Word got out that a newly enlightened Roosevelt was seeking well-heeled friends in the business community. The *New York World* caustically asked the president if the corporations "that are pouring money into your campaign chests assume that they are buying protection?" The Democratic nominee, Alton Parker, likened these generous contributions to blackmail. Such an accusation was "a wicked falsehood," Roosevelt snapped, but his new pro-business stance benefited him tremendously. He raised 2.2 million dollars in all, an awe-inspiring sum in 1904 and the equivalent of fifty million in 2007.

Roosevelt buried Parker by nineteen percentage points, one of the largest landslides ever, and reverted to form immediately thereafter. Seventy-two percent of his campaign funds had come from industrialists, but several of those same corporate benefactors suddenly found themselves facing new federal lawsuits. The old trust-busting Roosevelt had returned.

The nation's business leaders were angered at TR's betrayal, but even more, they were embarrassed by the ease with which he had hoodwinked them. Their efforts to pin the president down had failed miserably.

"We bought the son of a bitch," moaned an exasperated steel magnate, Henry Clay Frick, "and then he did not stay bought."

CUT TIES WITH ANY ALLY WHO BECOMES A LIABILITY

Hubert Humphrey played not one, but *two* prominent parts in 1968's political drama. He served throughout the year as Lyndon Johnson's vice president, a job that required him to be a dutiful subordinate. He added a second identity in August when the Democratic Party named him its presidential nominee, a position that called for a dynamic leader.

Humphrey juggled these conflicting roles during the fall campaign against the Republican candidate, Richard Nixon, and an independent who proved to be a surprisingly strong contender, George Wallace. His task was made doubly difficult by the Vietnam War, which Johnson was prosecuting vigorously despite widespread public opposition. The president's popularity ratings were lagging below 50 percent.

Defusing the issue of the war appeared to be Humphrey's best option. He decided to call for an immediate end to the American bombing of North Vietnam. It was a middle-of-the-road policy, not the military escalation favored by hawks, nor the troop withdrawal desired by doves. It would be a subtle signal of his intention to carefully extricate the country from Johnson's war.

Candidate Humphrey prepared a speech announcing his departure from the president's Vietnam strategy, but Vice President Humphrey loyally decided to give his boss a preview. He was surprised by the vehemence of Johnson's opposition. "You can get a headline with this, Hubert, and it will please you and some of your friends," the president snapped. "But if you just let me work for peace, you'll have a better chance for election than by any speech you're going to make."

Humphrey was in a quandary. He knew it was essential to establish himself as his own man, yet he feared the consequences of angering Johnson. "If I announced this," he told an aide, "he'd destroy me for the presidency." Supporters pleaded with him to make a clean break with Johnson—the sooner, the better—but he refused. Patience seemed to be his only option.

The campaign, however, was going badly. Polls showed Humphrey trailing Nixon by fifteen percentage points as September slipped away. Nixon, who kept hinting that he had a secret plan to end the war, lashed Humphrey as "the most articulate and the most uncompromising defender of the Johnson administration." It was a devastatingly effective attack.

The bleakness of his situation convinced Humphrey, at long last, to make a break. His first attempt was tentative: "Come January, it's a new ballgame." He went considerably further by the end of September: "As president, I would stop the bombing of North Vietnam as an acceptable risk for peace." He notified Johnson in advance of the latter speech, but his call was simply a courtesy. "I gather you're not asking my advice," the president grumbled.

Relations deteriorated between the two men. Johnson groused that Humphrey was "weak and disloyal," and that Nixon might make a better president. He ordered the FBI to tap the vice president's phones. Humphrey sought a meeting to smooth over the split, but was turned away. "That bastard Johnson," Humphrey sputtered to an aide, "I saw him sitting in his office."

Humphrey may have found the dispute personally unpleasant, but it turned out to be politically beneficial. Voters began to perceive him as a candidate with a spine and a mind of his own. Liberal Democrats applauded his new stand on Vietnam. Crowds swelled at his public appearances. Campaign contributions increased, and best of all, his poll numbers rebounded dramatically. He pulled into a virtual dead heat with Nixon as time ran out. He lost by the barest of margins in November, seven-tenths of a percentage point.

It was an agonizing defeat, so close that dozens of factors could have been blamed. His worst error, Humphrey decided, was suppressing "some of my personal identity and personal forcefulness" for much of the year. "It would have been better had I stood my ground and remembered that I was fighting for the highest office in the land," he concluded. "I ought not to have let a man who was going to be a former president dictate my future."

Lyndon Johnson had been a valuable friend when both men served in the Senate in the 1950s. He had given Humphrey's career a boost of immeasurable importance by selecting him as vice president in 1964. But allies can evolve into liabilities, as Humphrey learned in 1968, and when they do, they *must* be cut free.

This principle works in either direction, up or down. If your mentor becomes more of a hindrance than a help, break off the relationship, no matter how painful it may be to cut the cord. If a previously helpful subordinate threatens to sidetrack your career, the same rule applies.

Franklin Roosevelt faced the latter dilemma in 1944. FDR had no worries about winning a record fourth presidential nomination from the Democratic Party—it was in the bag—but he faced a potential revolt over his desire to retain Vice President Henry Wallace (no relation to the George Wallace mentioned above). Southerners hated Wallace because of his fervent support for civil rights. Nuts-and-bolts party leaders were put off by his dreamy idealism. Other Democrats simply found him strange. Wallace dabbled in mysticism and religions outside the mainstream, not the common interests of political leaders.

Roosevelt liked Wallace personally and led him to believe he would be renominated. But practical considerations won out. If Southern and big-city Democrats sat on their hands because of their antipathy toward the vice president, it was conceivable that Roosevelt could lose the election.

Whole books have been written about FDR's byzantine maneuvers to replace Wallace with the politically safe Harry Truman, a senator from Missouri. The denouement occurred in a Chicago hotel room, where Robert Hannegan and other Democratic chieftains pressured Truman to take the job. He was still resisting when the phone rang. Hannegan picked up the receiver and held it away from his ear so everyone could hear.

Roosevelt's booming voice came through. "Bob," he asked, "have you got that fellow lined up yet?"

"No, Mr. President," Hannegan replied. "He's the contrariest Missouri mule I've ever dealt with."

"Well, you tell him that if he wants to break up the Democratic Party in the middle of a war, that's his responsibility."

The president hung up. Truman grudgingly consented to his commander-in-chief's wishes, and Wallace was successfully jettisoned. Mission accomplished.

A note of caution: It's not always easy to determine whether you should cut ties with an ally. Weigh your alternatives with extreme care before making an irreversible decision.

Bill Clinton's vice president and heir apparent, Al Gore, struggled to find the right path in 2000. Clinton's popularity ratings remained high—hovering in the range of 65 percent—but his image had been sullied by the Monica Lewinsky scandal. Would he be an asset to Gore's presidential campaign against George W. Bush, or would he be a harmful distraction? That was the crucial question.

Gore believed the latter was the likely answer. He eased away from Clinton, making scant use of the president as a surrogate campaigner. Gore freely condemned Clinton's sexual misbehavior, beginning with the speech announcing his candidacy. "I say to every parent in America: It is our own lives we must master if we are to have the moral authority to guide our children," Gore insisted. He was more explicit in a later chat with reporters. "I felt what the president did, especially as a parent, was inexcusable," he said. The two men, who had once bragged of being so close, now went weeks at a time without seeing each other.

Not everyone agreed with Gore's standoffish strategy. The president was still popular, the economy was strong, and the nation was at peace. Several leading Democrats, including Clinton himself, believed that Gore's best option was to tie himself as tightly as possible to Clinton's record, not run from it.

This subject came up in an oblique way during one of the rare meetings between president and vice president in 2000. Clinton reiterated his willingness to help in any way he could. He jokingly offered to allow Gore to "lash me with a bullwhip" on the front steps of the *Washington Post* if the vice president thought it might help.

Gore feigned interest. He had, after all, once admitted to being a "finger in the wind" type of politician. He could only imagine how a focus group might react when confronted with Clinton's proposal. "Maybe we ought to poll that," Gore laughed.

It was all in fun, of course. There would be no poll, no bullwhipping on the steps of the *Post*, and no high-profile role for Bill Clinton in the 2000 campaign. Al Gore clung to his self-reliant strategy to the very end, losing one of the closest presidential elections in American history.

IF SUCCESS HINGES ON MAKING A DEAL, MAKE IT

Benjamin Harrison wasn't a terribly effective politician. "I was born to be a drudge, I think," he wrote a friend, and his career seemed to confirm it. His chilly personality made it difficult to draw votes and create alliances.

Harrison ran twice for governor of Indiana, losing both times. He reversed his fortunes by winning a Senate seat, yet couldn't hold it. His bid for reelection failed.

But Harrison *did* have a few factors in his favor, beginning with his name. He was the grandson of a president, William Henry Harrison. Timing was on his side, too. The 1888 Republican convention passed over the better-known candidates, looking for a fresh face. Harrison was its surprising choice to do battle with the Democratic president, Grover Cleveland.

Matthew Quay, the Republican national chairman, raised three million dollars (the equivalent of sixty-seven million in 2007) and deployed an army of campaigners across the country on Harrison's behalf. They promised federal jobs, endorsed local projects, passed cash under the table, even blatantly bought votes in a few states. Quay muttered that the candidate himself "would never know how close a number of men were compelled to approach the gates of the penitentiary to make him president."

These massive efforts turned the trick, though just barely. Harrison lost to Cleveland by 90,000 votes in the popular count—a respectable showing against an incumbent—but he won where it really mattered, 233 to 168 in the Electoral College. The president-elect, astonished by his unexpected triumph, jubilantly exclaimed, "Providence has given us the victory!"

Quay viewed Harrison's elation with the jaundiced eye of a backroom politician, a hardened veteran who had cut hundreds of deals in cities all across America. "Think of the man," he fumed. "He ought to know that Providence hadn't a damn thing to do with it!"

It was true. Cleveland, to be fair, had never been an especially popular president, and his 1888 campaign was notably lifeless and prone to error. But Quay and his men still made the difference. If not for their clandestine activities, Cleveland most likely would have been reelected.

Astute deal making elevated Benjamin Harrison from obscurity to the presidency, yet his story was hardly unique. Politicians have been compromising, finagling, and trading for public office since the birth of the republic, and not all of them have been run-of-the-mill hacks desperate for a government paycheck. Many of America's high-profile presidents—including some of the greatest of all time—never could have called the White House home without the help of a timely arrangement or two.

If you want to propel your career into an upward arc, you'll need skill, of course, as well as organizational ability and a polished style. But plenty of other people are skillful, organized, and polished. You may well be required to engage in good old-fashioned horse-trading to get an edge on your rivals. Don't violate your moral standards, and don't tiptoe past the penitentiary as some of Quay's men did. But if success hangs in the balance, and if the deal you've worked out passes the ethical and legal tests, don't hesitate. Shake hands and seal it.

John Quincy Adams followed this rule when it mattered most. Adams was always fussy about politics, refusing to "exhibit" himself to the American people or to travel around the country "like a Methodist preacher" seeking support. He was, nonetheless, an ambitious man, so he joined three other candidates in running for the presidency in 1824.

Andrew Jackson drew the most votes, but failed to reach a majority in the Electoral College. The task of choosing the next president fell to the House of Representatives, which was required to pick Jackson, Adams, or William Crawford. The contender in fourth place, Henry Clay, was eliminated according to constitutional provisions.

A scramble immediately began for Clay's support. Adams overcame his political queasiness and engaged in earnest conversation with his former rival. Adams refused to give any details to colleagues or reporters, while Clay said only that their three-hour chat was "exploratory of the past and prospective of the future."

It soon became clear that the two men had reached an understanding. Clay, who was the speaker of the House, publicly endorsed Adams and pulled strings to secure his victory. Adams announced, after a decorous interval, that Clay would be his secretary of state, then considered the best position from which to launch a future presidential campaign.

The deal swung by Adams was highly effective in the short run—he probably couldn't have become president without it—but its aftereffect was harmful. Jackson was already angry about the House's decision, since he, not Adams, had finished on top in the initial election. But Clay's ascension to the cabinet pushed his fury to the highest possible level. "So you see," he sputtered, "the Judas of the West has closed the contract and will receive the thirty pieces of silver." Jackson vowed to seek revenge for his opponents' "corrupt bargain." He tossed Adams and Clay out of office at the earliest opportunity, easily winning the 1828 election.

Rutherford Hayes faced a similar situation in 1876. He trailed Samuel Tilden by 250,000 votes on election night, causing the *New York Tribune* to declare Tilden the president-elect. But Hayes retained an outside chance of victory. The results in three southern states were still unclear. If he carried all three—admittedly the longest of long shots—he could defeat Tilden by a single vote in the Electoral College.

A four-month drama ensued, featuring the creation of a special commission to determine which candidate really won Florida, Louisiana, and South Carolina, former Confederate states that were still occupied by federal troops. Both parties maneuvered ceaselessly to get the upper hand, but Hayes was ultimately successful. Republicans landed eight of the fifteen seats on the commission, and they proceeded to allocate every single disputed electoral vote to their man.

Southern Democrats erupted in outrage. They vowed to prevent Congress from certifying the commission's verdict. Some adopted the slogan of "Tilden or blood," bitterly threatening to reignite the Civil War. Hayes found himself in a dangerous predicament. It was doubtful that he could assume the presidency in such a supercharged political climate. "I would like to get support from good men of the South, late rebels," he admitted in his diary. "How to do it is the question."

His solution was to deal directly with southern leaders. He pledged to withdraw the army from the former Confederate states, restoring governmental power to the whites who had ruled before the war. He also promised to appoint a Southern Democrat to his cabinet and to greatly increase federal aid to the region.

This package had the desired effect. William Levy, a congressman from Louisiana, announced on the floor of the House of Representatives that he had "solemn, earnest, and I believe, truthful assurances" from Hayes of "a policy of conciliation toward the southern states." Levy urged his colleagues to take the deal and cease their delaying tactics, which they did with little time to spare. Hayes's victory was officially certified at 4:10 A.M. on March 2, 1877, just two days before he took the oath of office.

Few political agreements have been as momentous as the ones fashioned by John Quincy Adams and Rutherford Hayes. Most deals are straightforward and painless, as when a candidate agrees to support specific legislation in exchange for an endorsement. Others are a bit harder to swallow, yet

---

"Lincoln Ain't Here"

William Seward was the frontrunner as the 1860 Republican convention convened in Chicago, while Salmon Chase and Edward Bates were formidable contenders. Abraham Lincoln had attracted a respectable level of support, but it seemed unlikely he could defeat such well-known men for the nomination.

His team met the challenge with dexterity and hard work. "I did not, the whole week I was there, sleep two hours a night," claimed one of his friends. Lincoln's campaign manager, David Davis, sent feelers out to almost every state delegation. Some historians contend that he promised a cabinet post to Caleb Smith if Smith's state, Indiana, backed Lincoln. He almost certainly made such a pledge to Simon Cameron of Pennsylvania, who had famously defined an honest politician as "a man who, when he's bought, stays bought."

Word of Davis's wheeling and dealing reached the candidate himself, who was waiting impatiently back home in Springfield. "I authorize no bargains and will be bound by none," Lincoln wired.

Davis briefly pondered the telegram. "Lincoln ain't here and don't know what we have to meet," he rasped, "so we will go ahead as if we hadn't heard from him, and he must ratify it." And he turned back to the task of sewing up the nomination.

undeniably important, perhaps involving the trade of a powerless office like the vice presidency.

Franklin Roosevelt might have vanished without a trace had he not made the latter type of deal. FDR drew a clear majority on the first ballot at the 1932 Democratic convention, but fell far short of the two-thirds vote the party then required. He pushed hard on subsequent ballots, making little progress. Some of his delegates began to waver.

Roosevelt's advisers thought they had reached a do-or-die moment. They believed their man would either win the nomination on the fourth ballot or begin a slow fade. The only apparent solution was to offer the vice presidency to John Nance Garner, a Texas congressman who was running a distant third in the presidential balloting. The two men had little in common—Roosevelt a northern liberal, Garner a southern conservative—but they made common cause. "Hell, I'll do anything to see the Democrats win one more national election," Garner said after sealing the deal that clinched FDR's nomination. The payoff was enormous, as Roosevelt went on to become one of the three best presidents ever, based on a consensus of today's historians.

IF THE RULES ARE SLANTED AGAINST YOU, CHANGE THEM

George McGovern's first presidential campaign wasn't well organized or successful. It was cobbled together at the last minute in 1968, seeking to fill the void left by Robert Kennedy's assassination. McGovern finished far behind the leading contenders, Hubert Humphrey and Eugene McCarthy, at the Democratic convention.

The next time, he resolved, would be different.

The Democratic Party gave McGovern an inadvertent boost with an important assignment in 1969. The previous year's convention had been a disaster. Young antiwar protestors clogged the streets outside the Chicago arena, while women and blacks angrily complained that the proceedings were dominated by white, middle-aged men. McGovern was handed the task of drafting new rules to guarantee that future conventions would be more representative and open.

The commission that he headed—and others that followed—did a thorough job. McGovern's panel required state delegations to include more women, more minorities, and more young people. It restricted the power that old-line bosses wielded in the nomination process, putting a greater emphasis instead on primary elections. And it adopted a myriad of lesser changes, even abandoning (temporarily, as it turned out) the traditional alphabetical roll call of the states.

These modifications disturbed the Democratic Party's kingpins. "The McGovern-O'Hara-Fraser commissions reformed us out of the presidency, and now they're trying to reform us out of a party," moaned Wayne Hays, a powerful congressman from Ohio. New York City's mayor, John Lindsay, chimed in, "This party seems to have an instinct for suicide."

McGovern paid no attention to the naysayers. The game had changed, as he knew better than anyone. The 1972 Democratic presidential nomination would go to the candidate who best understood and manipulated the new rules, and he intended to be that person. "I thought that if we started early," he said later, "and organized at the grass roots, and got the women, the young people, the antiwar crowd, some from labor, the environmentalists, there was enough to win the nomination."

Most of these groups had been ignored when the bosses controlled the process, and other Democratic presidential candidates still paid them little attention in 1972. McGovern knew better. He targeted the blocs that had been disenfranchised for so long. The result was a surprisingly easy victory at the national convention.

Rewriting the rules is perhaps the ultimate maneuver in politics or business. Opportunities for such handiwork don't come often, so it's essential that you seize them as McGovern did. He was an ineffective candidate under the Democratic Party's old system, but he prospered in a new framework of his own design. Be sure to take advantage in the same way of any chance to establish new guidelines, whether for a small interoffice committee or a large corporate division. It's an excellent way to improve your visibility—and your odds of future success.

The founding fathers certainly weren't averse to changing the rules. They felt politically and economically stifled by Great Britain, so they did what came naturally, breaking away from their colonial parent. "A little rebellion now and then is a good thing," insisted Thomas Jefferson, "and as necessary in the political world as storms in the physical."

Jefferson went on to become the new nation's third president in 1801, though his ascension was unexpectedly difficult. The Constitution required each member of the Electoral College to vote twice on the same ballot—once for president, once for vice president—without stipulating which candidate should be slotted in which office. The person drawing the most votes was awarded the top job; the runner-up was named his understudy. This system was ripe for the disaster that occurred in 1800, when Jefferson and his running mate, Aaron Burr, received precisely the same number of votes. It took the House of Representatives thirty-six ballots to unravel the mess, finally electing Jefferson to the position that was supposed to be his all along.

The new president wasted no time in changing the convoluted procedure that had nearly barred him from the White House. He made certain that the Twelfth Amendment, requiring separate votes for the nation's two highest offices, was enacted before he ran for reelection in 1804.

Jefferson literally rewrote federal law in this instance, substituting an updated regulation for an older version. But it's more common for a candidate to modify one of the *unwritten* rules of politics, as John Kennedy did in 1960.

Kennedy was determined to run for president, even though most Democratic leaders considered him a risky option. He was too young and too independent for their taste, and he was Catholic to boot. Harry Truman, titular head of the Old Guard, called on Kennedy to withdraw in favor of "someone with the greatest possible maturity and experience." Truman and his fellow Democratic elders preferred a more seasoned, more predictable, and 100 percent Protestant nominee. Several candidates fit their bill—chief among them, Lyndon Johnson, Stuart Symington, and Adlai Stevenson.

The bosses called the shots, as everybody knew, and their disdain did not bode well for Kennedy. A few states conducted primary elections, but they were belittled as political beauty pageants. Estes Kefauver had done surprisingly well in the 1952 primaries, though the leaders couldn't have cared less. They crushed Kefauver at convention time, drafting Stevenson for the nomination with Truman's blessing, even though the new nominee hadn't run in a single primary.

So Kennedy faced a tough choice. He could drop out of the 1960 campaign as gracefully as possible, or he could defy Truman, the other Democratic chieftains, and political customs that dated back to the early nineteenth century.

He chose the latter route, entering all of the major primaries as Kefauver had, but bringing much more firepower to bear. "He had to prove to (the bosses) that he could win," Kennedy's close aide, Theodore Sorensen, later explained. "And to prove that to them, he'd have to fight hard to make them give it to him. He couldn't negotiate it. If the convention ever went into the back rooms, he'd never emerge from those back rooms." Kennedy spent money freely, saturated the airwaves with TV commercials, and never missed an opportunity for national publicity. He sought to create an air of inevitability, forcing the party's leaders to bow before his political power and accept him as the nominee.

"It has to come up seven every time," he said as he rolled the dice in the first primary state, New Hampshire, where he won easily. But Wisconsin proved to be much tougher, with Kennedy barely squeaking past Hubert Humphrey. "It means that we've got to go to West Virginia in the morning and do it all over again," he said. "And then we've got to go on to Maryland and Indiana and Oregon and win all of them."

It was an audacious contract, but Kennedy fulfilled it, driven by a sense of destiny. Johnson, Symington, and Stevenson avoided the primaries, expecting to receive the nomination the old-fashioned way. They were oblivious to the fact that JFK was changing the political world as they knew it. "My time is now," he insisted, and the bosses eventually came to believe him. Many of them drifted to Kennedy's side as he swept through the primaries. They provided the necessary votes to clinch his nomination and, in so doing, changed the way the Democratic Party picked its presidential candidates.

The game would never be played the same way again.

7

Succeeding

Pierre du Pont IV appeared to have the necessary ingredients for a serious run at the Republican presidential nomination in 1988.

The obvious one was name recognition. He was one of *the* du Ponts. Who hadn't heard of the famous family that controlled the even-more-famous international chemical corporation? Money was another powerful attribute. Du Pont possessed a personal fortune, and he had the connections to raise any additional cash required to get his message out.

The best part was that he wasn't a political neophyte like Steve Forbes and Ross Perot, other wealthy men who would soon catch the presidential bug. Pete du Pont had served six years in the House of Representatives and eight years as governor of Delaware. He knew how to prepare a budget and run a government. And he knew how to connect with voters, too. "He is, and always has been, very sensitive to the fact that one's knee-jerk reaction to someone named Pete du Pont is going to be, 'Oh, I wonder what kind of snob this guy is,'" said Dave Swayze, the governor's chief of staff. "That's why he's always the one to walk up to somebody, rather than waiting for them to walk up to him."

It was with considerable optimism that du Pont gathered his campaign team in the spring of 1986 to plot his route to the White House. The bulk of their meeting was devoted to nuts-and-bolts topics, such as du Pont's formal announcement. Where should he deliver the first speech of his campaign? And what should he say?

One of the candidate's key aides, Frank Ursomarso, seemed peculiarly uninterested. He gazed out the window and fidgeted, contributing nothing to the conversation. Du Pont, unable to contain his irritation, finally asked Ursomarso what his problem was. Didn't he care about the announcement?

No, the aide replied bluntly, he really didn't. The way he saw it, what du Pont said when he jumped into the race was of little consequence. What really mattered was his statement of withdrawal, the speech he delivered when he *dropped out.*

Du Pont was taken aback by this combination of impertinence and pessimism. Here he was, ready to launch the campaign of his life, and one of his closest assistants already wanted to talk about quitting.

But that was the point, Ursomarso interjected. It's not uncommon for a presidential candidate to run two or three times before snagging a nomination or even—if the fates are especially kind—going all the way to the White House. Du Pont was unlikely to win his first time out. He needed to work hard, make a positive impression, and leave the race gracefully when the time came. He had to set the stage for ultimate success four years out—or maybe four years after that.

Du Pont scoffed at Ursomarso's theory in 1986, but he became a believer by 1988. Running for president was harder than he had expected and nastier than anything he had experienced in tiny Delaware. Vice President George Bush, the frontrunner for the Republican nomination, called him Pierre, not Pete, a not-so-subtle gibe about his inherited wealth, an especially annoying crack because Bush was a rich man's son himself. Other rivals insinuated that du Pont was dangerously conservative, perhaps plotting secretly to do away with Social Security.

The end came more quickly and less gloriously than most participants had envisioned at the first staff meeting. Du Pont did poorly in 1988's first two contests—Iowa and New Hampshire—and soon found himself delivering that all-important withdrawal speech. He departed with good cheer, already thinking about giving it another try in 1992, but it was not to be. Bush won the presidency in November, preempting other Republicans from the field for eight years.

What really struck du Pont about the whole experience was Frank Ursomarso's accuracy as a forecaster. Everything seems to be stacked against you when you seek a top-level job, as Ursomarso was aware. Your rivals are crafty and ruthless. Time is tight and fleeting. Luck is elusive and quite often bad. The person most likely to succeed in such a hostile environment is one who is blessed with incredible self-confidence and persistence.

Ulysses Grant had those qualities in abundance, which is why he persevered through an undistinguished stint in the military and periods of outright failure as a farmer and businessman. His tenacity paid dramatic dividends after he rejoined the army when the Civil War broke out. He soared to the position of general-in-chief within three years and was elected president just four years after that.

"One of my superstitions," Grant wrote in explanation, "had always been when I started to go anywhere or to do anything, not to turn back or stop until the thing intended was accomplished." His troops took heavy losses as they battered their way toward Richmond, but Grant would not be deterred. "I propose to fight it out on this line if it takes all summer," he declared. Abraham Lincoln had been driven to despair by the hesitancy and incompetence of his previous commanders. Grant's fierce determination was a welcome change. "I can't spare this man," Lincoln said. "He fights."

Dozens of famous politicians would have vanished in the mists of history if not for their dogged persistence. Five presidents prior to the Civil War— Thomas Jefferson, James Monroe, Andrew Jackson, William Henry Harrison, and James Buchanan—flopped in their first campaigns for the White House. All succeeded on their second attempts, except for Buchanan, who required a third.

Several of their contemporaries surmounted odds that were even more daunting. James Polk lost the governorship of Tennessee in 1841, launched a comeback bid in 1843, but again was rejected by the voters. "Henceforth, his career will be downwards," crowed a Nashville newspaper. But Polk confounded his enemies—and himself—by rising like a phoenix in 1844 and winning the presidency.

Abraham Lincoln's political rebirth a decade and a half later was equally impressive. Lincoln ran hard for a Senate seat from Illinois in 1854, but lost. He tried again in 1858, daring to challenge the supposedly invincible Stephen Douglas, the Little Giant of the Senate. Lincoln impressed the nation with his eloquence, yet lost the election. His future seemed murky after two successive defeats.

Many politicians would have given up at that point. Lincoln later recalled walking the streets the night after his loss to Douglas. He was profoundly unhappy, but could not surrender his dreams of high office. "The path had been worn pig-backed and was slippery," he said. "My foot slipped from under me, knocking the other out of the way. But I recovered and said to myself, 'It's a slip and not a fall.'" He rebounded to win the presidency— defeating the very same Stephen Douglas—just two years later.

It's almost certain that your career path will prove to be as treacherous as Lincoln's. You'll often find it slippery and hazardous, sometimes completely blocked. The only way to navigate a successful passage is to remain focused on your long-term goal. Approach your journey with pragmatic determination, combining an honest appraisal of your shortcomings with an upbeat view of your future. You must learn to accept life's unhappy truths, to handle adversity when it comes, and to always keep pushing as hard as you can. This chapter will discuss the following points:

Pragmatic determination

- Realistic analysis is always better than blind faith.
- A resilient spirit can overcome any setback.
- You can still reach your goal at an advanced age.

Unhappy truths

- Intelligence and skill do not guarantee success.
- Timing will often be beyond your control.
- Acknowledge the importance of pure, blind luck.

Handling adversity

- Don't fall victim to jealousy and envy.
- Conduct yourself with grace, especially in defeat.

Going as far as possible

- Exult in your success, and do the best job you can.
- Recognize when it's time for you to leave the stage.
- Don't lose track of what's really important in life.

The people who win the top prizes in politics and business—the ones who end up as presidents and CEOs—invariably are confident and tenacious. They have faith in themselves even when others don't. Politicians with higher profiles may have chuckled at the title of Jimmy Carter's autobiography—*Why Not the Best?*—but the obscure Georgia governor denied any accusation of immodesty. If he truly believed that he was the best candidate in 1976's presidential field, Carter reasoned, why should he pretend otherwise?

Winners go after the jobs they want *when* they want, even if critics don't think they should. We've already mentioned the heavy opposition that John Kennedy's 1960 campaign encountered within the Democratic Party, as well as his succinct answer to those who counseled him to wait his turn: "This is my time." Theodore Roosevelt, Woodrow Wilson, and Franklin Roosevelt were told repeatedly that they were too inexperienced to fill the highest office in the land. They ignored the naysayers.

Successful people in every field are distinguished by their refusal to be sidetracked. Ronald Reagan launched a last-ditch campaign for the Republican presidential nomination in 1968, but finished far off the pace. He tried again in 1976—and lost again. Commentators wrote him off. Reagan would be sixty-nine in 1980; it was unthinkable that he might run a third time. He did, of course, and won easily, then repeated the feat in 1984 at the ripe, old age of seventy-three.

The man who pushed Reagan aside in 1968, Richard Nixon, may have been the most persistent politician of his generation. He demonstrated his capacity for hard work as a young man. "I'm scared," he told a classmate at Duke Law School. "I counted thirty-two Phi Beta Kappa keys in my class. I don't believe I can stay up top in that group." But he outworked his more gifted colleagues, graduating third in his class.

Similar diligence (coupled with an unfortunate willingness to cut ethical corners on occasion) propelled Nixon upward in politics—congressman at age thirty-three, senator at thirty-seven, vice president at thirty-nine, presidential nominee at forty-seven.

His ascent came to an abrupt halt in 1960, when he lost the presidential election to Kennedy. Nixon was suddenly off the fast track—and out of a job. He spent his final night as vice president taking one last spin around Washington in his government car, telling his chauffeur to stop at the Capitol, where he walked through the rotunda, continued on to a balcony, and stared at the lights of Washington below. He vowed to return, to win the job that had slipped through his fingers a few weeks earlier.

More setbacks lay ahead—Nixon would lose the governor's race in California two years hence—but he eventually made good on his promise. He came back to the Capitol in 1969 to take the oath of office as president of the United States.

REALISTIC ANALYSIS IS ALWAYS BETTER THAN BLIND FAITH

William Jennings Bryan never doubted himself, not ever. He lost decisively to William McKinley in the 1896 presidential election, dusted himself off, challenged McKinley in 1900, and was soundly thrashed again. A man with less self-assurance might have drifted off to other pursuits, but not Bryan. He launched his third campaign in 1908, still believing the White House was his destiny.

A group of Southern Democrats visited Bryan as he prepared to do battle with the Republican nominee, William Howard Taft. They urged him to tone down the superheated populist rhetoric for which he was famous. A calmer, friendlier approach, they said, might attract the mainstream voters who had spurned him the first two times.

Bryan listened with growing incredulity until he could stand it no more. "That's it! You want to win!" he sputtered. "You would sacrifice principle for success. I would not. I would not desire to be elected if the principles I stood for were not incorporated in the platform. I am not sure that defeat is not better than victory, if victory comes with the sacrifice of principles."

The room fell silent. A senator from Virginia, John Daniel, was the only man who dared to respond. "But some of the things you have stood for in the past have proved wrong," he said to Bryan, "and you may prove wrong again."

This was total heresy. "I have *always* been right," Bryan snapped, and he refused to accept any more unsolicited advice. He would campaign against Taft precisely as he had against McKinley. The results would be equally familiar—a third landslide defeat.

Bryan never learned to assess his career realistically. Winning three Democratic nominations was an impressive accomplishment, to be sure, but he had fallen miserably short of his main objective, the presidency. He glossed over this deficiency as if it were meaningless. "You know, I base my political success on just three things," he confided in 1908 to an ally, Thomas Gore, a senator from Oklahoma. Bryan's friend couldn't recall the three magical keys in later years. "But," Gore added, "I do remember wondering why he thought he was a success."

Bryan was guilty of what Alan Greenspan, the longtime chairman of the Federal Reserve Board, once called "irrational exuberance." The inability to view oneself and one's surroundings in proper perspective is also known as "delusional optimism," a term coined by business analyst Dan Lovallo and psychologist Daniel Kahneman.

This problem, no matter its name, is a widespread one, as demonstrated by a College Board survey of one million students in the 1970s. Seventy percent of the students rated themselves above average in leadership ability, while only 2 percent admitted to being below average. Sixty percent said they were above the norm for athletic ability, compared to 6 percent below it. And 25 percent—fully one-quarter of the study group—placed themselves in the *top 1 percent* in terms of their ability to get along with others. If this survey were repeated in our self-centered decade, there's no reason to believe the results would be any different.

Confidence and persistence, as we've already discussed, are essential qualities for anyone who dreams of becoming a leader one day. But belief and tenacity are insufficient by themselves. They can, in fact, prove to be destructive unless they're tempered with a healthy dose of realism.

It's a fact that mediocrity and outright failure are much more common in everyday life than any of us care to admit. Consider the evidence from a variety of fields: Sixty percent of restaurants shut their doors within three years. Seventy percent of new manufacturing plants close within a decade. About three-quarters of all mergers and acquisitions fail to generate the predicted financial benefits. Most presidential candidates never win a single primary election, let alone the White House. And yes, a majority of college students are average or below average at any given activity, no matter what they might believe.

If you refuse to acknowledge your weaknesses as boldly as you trumpet your strengths, you're certain to be counted in these negative statistics. The political landscape, for example, is littered with the failed hopes of candidates who possessed truly outstanding qualities, but made the fatal mistake of overestimating themselves and underestimating their rivals.

Douglas MacArthur was one of America's greatest generals. Even his harshest critics agreed that he possessed a flair for the dramatic that paid off with decisive victories on the battlefields of World War I, World War II, and the Korean War. But the same qualities that served him well as a commander—unbridled arrogance, disregard for his critics, contempt for his opponents—destroyed his presidential dreams.

MacArthur alienated so many politicians and everyday Americans during his lengthy military career that it was unrealistic to imagine him winning a civilian election, yet he tried in 1944 and again in 1948. Democrats and moderate Republicans mobilized to stop him. Disgruntled former soldiers formed Veterans Against MacArthur clubs in a dozen major cities. He expected to win the 1948 Republican primary in Wisconsin, nominally his home state, but was rebuffed even there. "The general is as low as a rug and very disappointed," his chief of staff warned a visitor to his headquarters the next day.

Yet MacArthur still didn't get the message. The Republican Party invited him to deliver the keynote address at its 1952 convention. He eagerly accepted, sensing a final opportunity to snatch a presidential nomination. The general considered himself a dynamic public speaker—another serious misperception—and was certain he could rally the delegates to his cause. His ponderous, cliché-saturated speech had the opposite effect. "He said nothing but sheer baloney," recalled a reporter, C. L. Sulzberger. "One could feel the electricity gradually running out of the room."

MacArthur never admitted that his military skills were unsuited for the political arena, that other Republicans were better prepared for the presidency than he was, that he had made too many enemies, or that he was a poor speaker and an even worse campaigner. He believed it was America's misfortune that he never moved into the White House. "I should have lived here," he said in 1961 to John Kennedy, the young man who actually did.

It's possible, of course, to hire outsiders to provide a realistic analysis of your strong and weak points, but Harry Truman was always skeptical of such consultants and their market research. "I wonder how far Moses would have gone if he had taken a poll in Egypt," he liked to say. The pollsters wrote Truman off in 1948, insisting that he had no chance of securing another term as president. They guaranteed that the challenger, Thomas Dewey, would win by a sizable margin.

The Republicans believed them. Dewey had made his name as a combative prosecutor and feisty governor, but he campaigned blandly in 1948, lulled by the favorable polls. He delivered platitudinous speeches that didn't stir up even the slightest of controversies. "Governor Dewey is acting like a man who has already been elected and is merely marking time, waiting to take office," a *New York Times* reporter observed in late September.

Dewey began to have doubts about his cautious strategy as election day neared. He read in the newspapers that Truman's crowds were getting louder and more boisterous. His, he felt, were dwindling. Calls were placed to the ninety-six members of the Republican National Committee, seeking their advice. Harry Darby of Kansas said it was time for Dewey to take the gloves off. The other ninety-five voted to stay on the high road. "I can't go against the entire Republican Party," the candidate shrugged, and he continued to pull his punches.

It seemed a wise decision in light of *Newsweek*'s election preview issue. "Fifty Political Experts Unanimously Predict a Dewey Victory," screamed the headline. The *Newsweek* forecast had been eagerly awaited by both campaigns, and a member of Truman's staff jumped off the train to buy a copy on publication day. He was depressed by what he read, and tried to hide the magazine from the president.

Truman knew what was afoot. He demanded to see the issue, scanned the bad news, and then broke into a wide grin. "Oh, those damned fellows, they're always wrong anyway," he said. "Forget it, boys, and let's get on with the job." He beat Dewey with surprising ease a few days later.

"Don't Pay Any Attention to the Polls"

Politicians and business executives alike have become addicted to market research, many to an unhealthy extreme. Bill Clinton, for instance, reportedly spent almost two million dollars on polls during his first year as president. It's helpful to know what the public thinks about you and your products, but too much data can breed either complacency or despair—two equally potent enemies of constructive action.

"Don't pay any attention to the polls," Michael Dukakis would advise his campaign workers in 1988. He said the same thing when the surveys showed him far ahead of George H. W. Bush in late summer, and well behind in the final days. If his staffers got too high or too low, Dukakis knew, they would be distracted from the job at hand. He always reminded them that early polls had shown him fifty percentage points ahead in the race for governor of Massachusetts a decade earlier, yet he had lost. "There are very few politicians in America who have the skill and ability to do that," Dukakis always said. "But I was one of them."

A RESILIENT SPIRIT CAN OVERCOME ANY SETBACK

Bill Clinton liked to call himself the Comeback Kid. It was an appropriate nickname, reflecting his impressive ability to bounce back from adversity. "His critics punch him silly, knock him down, and he always gets off the canvas," marveled a former aide, David Gergen. "He may be disoriented for a moment, but he is still fighting."

Clinton revived his career four times in two decades. If not for the first three comebacks, he never would have become president. If not for the fourth, he would have departed the White House prematurely. His tenacity in overcoming significant obstacles can be taken as an object lesson in resilience:

1980: Reelection defeat—Clinton became the nation's youngest governor in 1978, winning Arkansas's top job at the age of thirty-two. But the voters quickly became disillusioned, finding their new chief executive too liberal and too patronizing. They registered their unhappiness by tossing him out of office two years later, something they almost never did to an incumbent Democrat.

"God, I'm an idiot," Clinton moaned. "I should have seen it coming. How could I be so dumb?" He seemed destined to be quickly forgotten, a mere footnote to Arkansas's history. But he resolved to do whatever it took to regain his job.

Clinton altered his style, morphing into a moderate, humble politician who talked less and listened more. He had never given his stepfather cause to whip him twice for making the same mistake, he told audiences around the state, and he promised not to repeat his previous errors if given another chance as governor. "I think he learned his lessons too well from that defeat," said John Brummett, a political columnist who first met Clinton in 1975. "He became stronger, harder to beat, for sure, but I think he also became too cautious and too willing to compromise."

The end result, though, was precisely what Clinton wanted. He was elected governor again in 1982. His career was back on track.

1988: Disastrous speech—Clinton received a big break at the 1988 Democratic convention, where he was tapped to deliver the nominating address for Michael Dukakis. But he blew the opportunity. His long, monotonous speech was ignored by delegates and ridiculed by commentators. Deborah Norville and Tom Pettit joked about Clinton the next morning on NBC's *Today* program. Norville asked how the governor ever could have been considered an up-and-coming politician. "Now we know better," Pettit replied dismissively.

Clinton responded to this damaging episode with humor and hard work. He appeared on Johnny Carson's *Tonight Show* and other TV programs to laugh at himself and show off his engaging personality. And he made certain that his future speeches were written more smoothly—and delivered with more punch.

1992: Primary setback—It seemed likely that Clinton's first presidential campaign would end badly. He simply had too many skeletons in his closet. He had been accused of dodging the military draft and committing adultery with Gennifer Flowers and several other women. His media advisers put their own spin on both stories, with marginal success.

The year's first primary was unpromising. Clinton lost New Hampshire to Paul Tsongas by nine percentage points. Tsongas immediately declared himself the frontrunner for the Democratic nomination, while Clinton decided to brazen out his personal problems.

It was in New Hampshire that he dubbed himself the Comeback Kid, claiming to have whittled a twenty-point Tsongas lead in half during the final week of campaigning. He also contended that he deserved credit, not criticism, for being engulfed in controversy. "Any president faces far greater pressure than what I've been through," Clinton said. "I think I showed how I'd handle it. People will say, okay, that guy's not going to roll over. He's not going to roll up in a ball."

Most reporters bought his line. They filed stories from New Hampshire about Clinton's resurgent campaign, providing him with urgently needed momentum.

1998: Impeachment—The Monica Lewinsky affair showed Clinton at his worst. His infidelities and lies triggered his impeachment by the House of Representatives. There was a very real possibility that the Senate would remove him from office.

What saved Clinton was his record. The nation was at peace and enjoying an economic boom. Polls showed that most Americans assumed he had lied about his relationship with Lewinsky, yet they wanted him to remain at the nation's helm. "I believed all of it—Gennifer Flowers, Paula Jones (who filed a sexual-harassment suit against Clinton)," an anonymous voter told a *Washington Post* reporter, "and I voted for him twice." The Senate complied with the wishes of the majority and declined to convict the president.

Clinton employed a variety of tactics—transformation, humor, diligence, bravado—to resuscitate his career at critical moments. Any rising politician or executive would be wise to study his strategies for self-revival. "More than education, more than experience, more than training, a person's level of resilience will determine who succeeds and who fails. That's true in the cancer ward, it's true in the Olympics, and it's true in the boardroom," said Dean Becker, the CEO of Adaptiv Learning Systems, a company that specializes in resilience training.

Historian Richard Tedlow reached the same conclusion after studying the dominant business leaders of the past. "Titans don't look back," he wrote. "When they suffer a failure, they get over it. Most know the valleys as well as the peaks—but they never perceive a chasm, no matter how daunting, to be the Valley of Death. They don't ruminate. They are incapable of being discouraged."

Optimism is indeed a key component of resilience, as are self-confidence and the ability to think creatively under pressure. Both major-party nominees in the 1960 presidential election displayed these traits—and both eventually reached the White House.

John Kennedy led a charmed political life, winning his first four elections to the House and Senate. He finally felt the sting of defeat in 1956, when he actively sought the Democratic Party's vice-presidential nomination. Estes Kefauver snatched the prize from him in an open vote at the convention.

Kennedy came to view his loss as a valuable experience. "Someone once said you don't understand politics until you've been defeated," he said. "Then all the mysteries become apparent." His drive for the vice presidency had been hastily planned. It taught him the importance of preparation and organization. It also convinced him to aim higher the next time. "I'm against vice in all forms," he quipped.

Kennedy regained his winning form in 1960, squeaking past Richard Nixon by two-tenths of a percentage point. It was the beginning of what Nixon called his "wilderness years," an eight-year hiatus from public office. The former vice president practiced law, ran for governor of California (and lost), wrote a book, and did plenty of thinking. "I found that some of my most valuable years," he wrote, "were those between the vice presidency and the presidency, when I was able to step back from the center of events and look in a most measured way at the past and the future."

Nixon modified his approach to politics during this fallow period. He hadn't done well in spontaneous settings—losing his televised debates with Kennedy in 1960, ranting to California reporters two years later that he was in the midst of his "last press conference." So he and his advisers resolved to keep a tight rein in 1968, limiting his public appearances and making maximum use of television. They staged their own talk shows with audiences that had been carefully screened. It was a safe, low-risk strategy—and it proved to be highly effective. Reporters began writing about the self-assured "New Nixon," a man of presidential quality. He defeated Hubert Humphrey in the November election.

Nixon was justifiably proud of his resilience. He had revived his career after most pundits pronounced it dead. (ABC had even produced a documentary, *The Political Obituary of Richard Nixon*, in late 1962.) He returned to this theme in a rambling, yet poignant way during his farewell speech as president: "We think sometimes when things happen that don't go the right way; we think that when you don't pass the bar exam the first time—I happened to, but I was just lucky; I mean, my writing was so poor the bar examiner said, 'We have just got to let the guy through'—we think that when someone dear to us dies, we think that when we lose an election, we think that when we suffer a defeat, that all is ended. . . . Not true. It is only a beginning, always."

YOU CAN STILL REACH YOUR GOAL AT AN ADVANCED AGE

William Seward had been a politician of great promise. He won the governorship of New York at the tender age of thirty-seven, then ascended to the Senate a decade later. The presidency was to be the crowning glory of his career. He appeared to have the 1860 Republican nomination locked up—that is, until a prairie lawyer named Abraham Lincoln emerged unexpectedly.

Seward was left with the consolation prize of being Lincoln's secretary of state. He comforted himself that, as the most experienced member of the new Cabinet, he would be pulling strings from behind the curtain. "It seems to me," he wrote, "that if I am absent only three days, this administration, the Congress, and the district would fall into consternation and despair."

Lincoln saw things differently. He quickly made it clear that he intended to be the master of his own White House. Seward, now sixty years of age, had to reconcile himself to a supporting role, his presidential dreams unfulfilled. "What is the use of growing old?" he lamented. "You learn something of men and things, but never until too late to use it."

America has always been a youth-oriented country, forever ready to push its William Sewards to the sidelines whenever a younger, fresher candidate comes along. This is by no means a recent phenomenon. Stephen Douglas, a famous contemporary of Lincoln and Seward, ran for president in 1852 as the self-proclaimed candidate of "Young America." The thirty-nine-year-old Douglas contemptuously dismissed his opponents as "old fogies," introducing an enduring phrase to the English language. He came surprisingly close to winning the Democratic nomination.

The same youthful trend is evident in modern business, as researchers Peter Cappelli and Monika Hamori found when they compared the men and women who held one thousand top executive positions at America's one hundred largest companies in 1980 and 2001.

The typical executive in 2001 was four years younger than his or her 1980 counterpart. "They're also making their way to the top more quickly," Cappelli and Hamori wrote. "They're taking fewer jobs along the way, and they increasingly move from one company to the next as their careers unfold." The image was that of a swiftly advancing battalion of young managers, ruthlessly overrunning the sluggish old-timers who dared to get in their way.

So William Seward was right, wasn't he? If you're a senior executive, you have no hope of getting ahead. Time is your unbeatable foe.

Well, no. Seward came close in 1860, finishing second at the convention, and he might have won if he had been more vigilant and had campaigned more effectively. You, too, can still attain success at an advanced age, provided you meet your challenges with persistence, creativity, and intelligence. Ignore the fact that the odds are slanted against you, and remember that experience always has the power to trump youth.

Ronald Reagan first sought the presidency in 1968, just two years after winning his first political office, governor of California. His was a feeble, last-minute campaign, and he finished a weak third at the Republican convention behind Richard Nixon and Nelson Rockefeller.

Reagan was ready again in 1976. He had served eight years as governor by then, and he believed he was prepared for greater responsibilities. But there were two strikes against him: He would need to defeat the incumbent president, Gerald Ford, to win the Republican nomination, a tall challenge indeed. And he was sixty-five years old.

Reagan lost, not by much, but he lost. "The future role of Ronald Reagan is clearly defined," an esteemed political columnist, Marquis Childs, declared that summer. "Now in his sixty-sixth year, he will be too old to run for the presidency in 1980." And that, it seemed, was that.

Reagan, of course, defied the conventional wisdom, coming back to score landslide victories in 1980 and 1984, the latter when he was seventy-three. He harbored his energy, campaigned only as much as necessary, and rebuffed his detractors with humor. They accused him of being lazy, of delegating too much authority. "I know hard work never killed anyone," Reagan replied. "But I figure, why take a chance?" They pointed out that he was seventeen years older than his Democratic challenger in 1984, Walter Mondale. "I want you to know that also I will not make age an issue of this campaign," Reagan shot back. "I am not going to exploit for political purposes my opponent's youth and inexperience."

Reagan's lifetime in broadcasting, acting, and politics instilled the poise and self-confidence he needed to deflect the barbs hurled by his younger opponents. It also provided him all the time he required to build the alliances and reputation that would enable him to outmaneuver them. Age, in his case, was a strength, not a weakness.

It was equally beneficial for William Henry Harrison and Dwight Eisenhower, who won presidential elections at the respective ages of sixty-seven and sixty-six. Each made a name for himself as a military hero before turning to politics in his later years.

Harrison stressed his vigor and strong health during the 1840 campaign, though his fellow Whigs worried he might overdo it. "If General Harrison lives, he will be president," Daniel Webster wrote in one private letter. And in another: "His election is certain ... if an all-wise Providence shall spare his life."

Harrison did indeed press his luck, choosing to deliver his inaugural address bareheaded on a blustery day. That might have been a reasonable risk for a man of his advanced years, had he not gone overboard with the longest inaugural speech of all time, droning on for nearly two hours. It wasn't totally a surprise that he contracted pneumonia and died within the month. (Nor did it help that his doctors' idea of health care involved castor oil, an Indian liniment, brandy, opium, and selective bleeding.)

Eisenhower was more like Reagan, emphasizing his strengths as a world figure and minimizing his weaknesses. He made it clear to the Republican National Committee that he had no taste for campaigning, and intended to do as little of it as possible. That was especially true in the fall of 1956, as he recovered from a heart attack the previous year and a summer operation for ileitis. Ike was fortunate that his reelection didn't require much of his attention.

Many enlightened employers have come to realize that age can be a positive attribute. "We looked at the demographic risk of losing significant partners. The firm was vulnerable. We've been dealing with it," said Douglas McCracken, the managing director of Deloitte Consulting, which has instituted a program to encourage older partners to put off retirement. It's a sign that corporations have begun to recognize the value of experience, according to William Byham, the president of Development Dimensions International, a human-resources firm. "There's a knowledge problem in organizations," he warned. "All the history is going out the door."

Abraham Lincoln intuitively understood the same point, which is why he welcomed his vanquished rival to his administration. William Seward lamented his fate, but eventually formed a strong partnership with his commander-in-chief. Seward is not recalled today as a young governor or senator or failed presidential candidate. He is remembered for the work he did after the age of sixty—as one of the greatest secretaries of state in American history.

INTELLIGENCE AND SKILL DO NOT GUARANTEE SUCCESS

Most self-help books offer a blend of advice and Darwinian philosophy. They boil Charles Darwin's complex theories of evolution down to "survival of the fittest"—a phrase that Darwin didn't coin—and use this shopworn concept to explain the intricacies of modern corporate life. If you hope to be a successful executive, according to your trusty guidebook, you should behave as if you're in the jungle. Eat or be eaten. Triumph or die.

That's not really the way things work.

It's true, as *this* book has stressed from the beginning, that you must diligently prepare for any opportunities that might come your way. But hard work won't guarantee anything. Intelligence and skill, unfortunately, do not automatically bring success. People with strong minds and impressive abilities often find themselves working for intellectual inferiors. The fittest don't always survive, and the feeble don't always perish.

This is, indeed, an unhappy truth, and you have no choice but to accept it. Keep dreaming your dreams, keep pushing toward your goals, but also make sure that you understand the ways of the world. Consider these examples from the sphere of politics, where the chasm between Darwinian philosophy and reality is as wide as anywhere.

George Weeks, a seasoned reporter, columnist, and gubernatorial aide in Michigan, compiled a list of the ten best governors of the twentieth century. His rankings admittedly represent only one man's opinion, but Neal Peirce, himself a longtime observer of state politics, has applauded them as "exceptionally well crafted." These were Weeks's choices:

- Reubin Askew, Florida, 1971–1979
- Thomas Dewey, New York, 1943–1955
- Daniel Evans, Washington, 1965–1977
- Robert La Follette, Wisconsin, 1901–1906
- Huey Long, Louisiana, 1928–1932
- Nelson Rockefeller, New York, 1959–1973
- Terry Sanford, North Carolina, 1961–1965
- Alfred Smith, New York, 1919–1921 and 1923–1929
- Earl Warren, California, 1943–1953
- Woodrow Wilson, New Jersey, 1911–1913

These ten men not only were supremely successful as governors, but also were exceedingly ambitious. Most were nationally famous in their day. It's only logical to assume that they would have made excellent presidents.

They were interested in the job, that's for sure. Eight of them ran for the White House at least once. Smith was the most persistent, offering himself as a candidate in all four presidential elections between 1920 and 1932. Dewey and La Follette tossed their hats in the ring three times each. Long, one of the two holdouts, almost certainly would have run in 1936, if not for his assassination the year before. The only top-ten governor to resist the White House bug was Evans, who eventually reached Washington, D.C., as a senator, but never tried to go higher.

These elite politicians mounted a grand total of nineteen presidential campaigns, but their collective record was abysmal. They secured just five nominations between them—two each for Dewey and Wilson, one for Smith. Only one of the men listed above reached the White House—Woodrow Wilson—and he failed to draw a majority of the votes in either of the elections he won.

What about another leading source of presidential candidates, the Senate? It took upon itself the task of identifying its greatest members half a century ago. John Kennedy, a Massachusetts senator who had recently written a book about political bravery, *Profiles in Courage*, was put in charge of the project. His committee sifted through the records of sixty-five senatorial giants, finally choosing twenty as worthy of honor in 1957.

The senators at the very top of the list—dubbed the "Famous Five"—received an immediate reward. Portraits of John Calhoun, Henry Clay, Robert La Follette, Robert Taft, and Daniel Webster were placed on permanent display in the Capitol. The other fifteen honorees were to be recognized in some way in the future, though Kennedy's panel was short on specifics. (Not much progress has been made. The Senate decided in 2004 to hang portraits of two members of this second tier, Arthur Vandenberg and Robert Wagner.)

The outstanding senators were even less successful than the best governors when it came to pursuing the presidency. Fifteen of the twenty senators demonstrated a strong interest in the White House. They launched a total of twenty-eight presidential campaigns (taking their full careers into account, encompassing their years in the Senate and in other positions). They also drew support at thirteen conventions when they weren't officially running. All of this activity brought them just three nominations—two for Clay, one for Stephen Douglas—and no general-election victories. Not a single one.

The incongruity between skill and success troubled the Famous Five, who fell short with all sixteen of their campaigns for the White House:

- Calhoun ran for the presidency just twice—1824 and 1844—and withdrew from both races in their early stages. Yet he maneuvered for the job all of his adult life and reacted bitterly to his failure. "I am the last man that can be elected in the present condition of the country," he grumbled. "I am too honest and patriotic to be the choice of anything like a majority."

- Clay was a perpetual candidate, taking the plunge five times between 1824 and 1848. He tried to mask his losses with a noble, oft-quoted remark, "I would rather be right than be president." But he dropped the guise with friends. "I expressed that sentiment to which you refer that I would rather be right than be president," he wrote to one, "but it has been applauded beyond its merit."

- La Follette was excellence personified, the only outstanding senator to also be a top-ten governor. Yet his campaigns for the Republican nomination in 1912 and 1916 were notably unsuccessful. He went the third-party route in 1924, winning the electoral votes of only one state, his native Wisconsin.

- Taft—himself the son of a president, William Howard Taft—sought the job three times on his own. But Thomas Dewey always seemed to be in his way, competing with him for the Republican nomination in 1940 and 1948, then backing the victorious Dwight Eisenhower in 1952. Taft angrily blamed his 1952 defeat on "the New York financial interests," on businessmen "subject to New York influence," and on Dewey, who just happened to be the governor of New York.

- Webster ran three campaigns for the White House, always finishing back in the pack. His final effort in 1852—the year he would die at the age of seventy— was better than the others, yet he still received just 10 percent of the delegate votes at the Whig convention. He despaired at his weak performance that year, wailing, "How will this look in history?"

Only two presidents have been elected directly from the Senate, Warren Harding and John Kennedy. Neither had much in common with the Famous Five. Their senatorial records could best be called undistinguished.

Kennedy's eight years in the Senate were notable for his frequent absences, some caused by his fragile health, others by the demands of his 1960 presidential campaign. He was handsome, glib, and obviously bright, yet he never drafted a significant piece of legislation or delivered a truly memorable speech. His chief accomplishment may have been dodging the controversy that surrounded Joe McCarthy's Communist witch hunts.

McCarthy posed a real problem. He was a friend of the Kennedy family, yet was anathema to the liberals who formed JFK's core constituency. The hospitalized senator from Massachusetts was absent when his colleagues voted to censure McCarthy, and he never took a clear public stand on the matter. It was the way he straddled the McCarthy issue that caused Eleanor Roosevelt to sigh that the White House should not go to "someone who understands what courage is and admires it, but has not quite the independence to have it."

Harding looked like a president, with his thick head of white hair, his classic Roman nose, and his impeccable wardrobe. He sounded like one, too, thanks to his deep, resonant voice. But his weak mind and indiscriminate friendships should have disqualified him, and he knew it. "I should really be ashamed to presume myself fitted to reach out for a place of such responsibility," he admitted in a moment of honesty. Harding wanted to stay in the Senate ("a very pleasant place"), but his ambitious wife and greedy acquaintances nudged him forward and—miracle of miracles—he was elected in 1920.

Connecticut Senator Frank Brandegee was instrumental in pushing Harding toward the White House. He understood better than most that intelligence and skill are wonderful attributes, but aren't always required for success. "There ain't any first-raters this year," Brandegee rasped. "We've got a lot of second-raters, and Warren Harding is the best of the second-raters."

TIMING WILL OFTEN BE BEYOND YOUR CONTROL

Buy low, sell high. That's the Number One rule of investing, yet it's not quite as simple as it sounds.

How can you be sure a stock has bottomed out? How can you tell when it's at its peak? Market timers believe they know the answers. They do extensive research, pay close attention to trends, and jump in and out of the market in—they claim—the nick of time.

There's only one problem. Their results aren't very good. "About one out of five timers are able to do it over the long term. Eighty percent fail," said Mark Hulbert, editor of the *Hulbert Financial Digest*, a newsletter that tracks the performances of stock analysts and investors. Even that estimate was too high for John Bogle, founder of the Vanguard Group, one of the world's largest mutual funds. "After nearly fifty years in the business, I don't know of anybody who has done it successfully and consistently," he said of market timers. "I don't even know anybody who knows anybody who has done it successfully and consistently."

The fact is that nobody has a perfect sense of timing, whether in the stock market or any other facet of life. Even those people who are accustomed to success will occasionally make the wrong move at the wrong moment. William Shakespeare had this conundrum in mind when he wrote *Julius Caesar*: "There is a tide in the affairs of men,/Which, taken at the flood, leads on to fortune;/Omitted, all the voyage of their life/Is bound in shallows and in miseries."

The trick is to recognize when the tide is at flood stage, and to catch it before it recedes. Your record, sorry to say, is bound to be like everyone else's—a good bit short of perfect.

Nelson Rockefeller was rich, charismatic, and the governor of New York, a perfect formula for a presidential candidate. His timing, however, was atrocious. He toyed with entering the race in 1960, even though Richard Nixon had already locked up the Republican nomination. He *did* run in 1964, despite a divorce and remarriage that stirred up too much damaging controversy. He waffled in 1968—seemingly an ideal year for him—jumping in only after Nixon had once again established himself as the frontrunner.

Rockefeller was incapable of determining the best times to make his move or stay on the sidelines. William Crawford had a different problem. He saw his opportunity clearly in 1816, but decided to delay it, much to his later misfortune.

Crawford was a hearty, outgoing politician from Georgia who was highly popular within the Democratic-Republican Party. He served as a senator and minister to France before joining James Madison's cabinet as secretary of war in 1815. His blend of personality and experience made him a leading contender for the party's presidential nomination in 1816, an appealing alternative to Madison's candidate, the colorless James Monroe.

But Crawford backed off, announcing that he didn't want to be "among the number of those from whom the selection ought to be made." He decided to bide his time while Monroe ran the country, confident that his turn would eventually come. Crawford was forty-four years old, fourteen years younger than Monroe. He felt he could afford to wait.

Crawford's friends were less patient. They defied his wishes and presented his name to the party's congressional caucus—the 1816 version of a nominating convention—where he lost by just eleven votes. It was obvious that he could have won if he had been willing to try.

No matter. Crawford stuck to his plan and aimed toward 1824, when Monroe would wrap up his second term. But fate intervened. Crawford suffered a stroke in late 1823, then relapsed in May 1824. His supporters tried to cover up his condition, but it became known that he was paralyzed and nearly blind. His recovery was slow and incomplete. He ran for the presidency anyway, finishing a weak third behind John Quincy Adams and Andrew Jackson, then disappeared from the national political scene entirely.

Timing, quite frankly, will often be beyond your control. Your chance may pop up without warning, as it did for Grover Cleveland, who vaulted from mayor of Buffalo to governor of New York to president of the United States in three short years. Or it might take decades to arrive, as it did for William Henry Harrison, who enjoyed his share of successes, but also lost races for governor of Ohio and the presidency before finally reaching the White House at the age of sixty-seven.

There's little you can do to alter the whimsical schedule of life. Your best strategy is to always be prepared, vigilant, and—above all—ready to seize your opportunity the moment it appears.

"Thanks, But You Know What It's Worth"

John Davis's time came in 1924, when the Democratic convention selected him on its 103rd ballot. The party was so bitterly divided that whomever it nominated for president was certain to lose the general election. Davis, however, willingly accepted the challenge. It was far from ideal, but he knew it was his one and only shot. He was determined to take it, though he was realistic about the odds. "Thanks," he told a well-wisher after his nomination, "but you know what it's worth."

Davis gave it his all. He waged a strenuous campaign against Calvin Coolidge that fall, always acting as if he expected to move into the White House after the votes were counted. Coolidge crushed him by twenty-five percentage points, the second-worst landslide in history. Davis returned to his law practice, confident that he had made the best of his limited opportunity—and he was well aware of how limited it had been. "I went around the country telling people I was going to be elected," he would later joke, "and I knew I hadn't any more chance than a snowball in hell."

ACKNOWLEDGE THE IMPORTANCE OF PURE, BLIND LUCK

Mario Cuomo was a successful politician by anyone's standards. He won three terms as governor of New York, earned national fame for his oratorical

skills, and was frequently touted for the presidency, though he never officially sought the job.

But Cuomo wasn't comfortable with the plaudits that came his way. Many
of his achievements, he felt, could be attributed to happenstance. "My
mind," he wrote, "tells me that 'success' is little more than good luck
attached to efforts you make that aren't much different from the efforts of
many others who don't get touched by the good luck."

Cuomo wasn't unique in that belief. Countless studies and first-person tes-
timonials have confirmed that pure, blind luck can be powerful indeed:

- Successful scientists need to be intelligent and highly trained, but their greatest
  accomplishments sometimes result as much from good fortune as skill. Sociol-
  ogist Robert Merton conducted extensive research into serendipity—happy
  accidents—and encountered a Nobel Prize winner who put his award in that
  classification. "I got it for a purely accidental discovery. Anybody could have
  done that," said the Nobel laureate, whom Merton did not identify.

- Making a profit on the stock market can be the consequence of shrewd investing—or a purely random occurrence. Burton Malkiel, a Princeton University
  economist, studied analysts' reports on specific stocks, and found many to be
  essentially worthless. The future value of stocks, he contended, frequently
  hinges on events that can't be predicted—a scandal, a natural disaster, an international incident. Malkiel concluded that an investor could often do just as
  well by ignoring the analysts and flipping a coin.

- Business titans would have us believe that success is a byproduct of their clear
  vision and dynamic leadership. One of the honest exceptions was Katharine
  Graham, who oversaw the *Washington Post*'s expansion into a media behe-
  moth between 1963 and 2001. "When I look back over my long life," she
  wrote, "if there is one thing that leaps out at me, it is the role of luck and
  chance in our lives."

- Good fortune is equally important in the arts. Many critics considered Katharine Hepburn the greatest actress of the twentieth century. She was nominated
  for twelve Academy Awards, winning four. What was the key to her lengthy,
  productive career? "I think I have a lucky nature," she said. "I think I was
  born at the right time, and suited the atmosphere that I was born into."

- Upward mobility, of course, is no different in politics than in any other field.
  Fate is often the determining factor. Theodore Roosevelt said of his offspring
  as young adults: "Each of my sons is doing and has done better than I was
  doing and had done at his age—and I had done well." The logical assumption
  was that they, too, might be presidential material someday, but the Old Rough
  Rider backed off from that suggestion. "I don't mean that any of you will be
  president," he wrote his eldest son. "As regards the extraordinary prizes, the
  element of luck is the determining factor."

Most self-help manuals gingerly avoid this subject, and now you know
why. Our litany of examples and quotations may have left you feeling a bit
helpless. If your career is subject to the whims of fortune, why devote year
upon year to developing your mind, polishing your skills, organizing,

maneuvering, and following the other steps we've discussed in preceding pages? Why bother to do anything at all?

There are three reasons why this subject is worth your time:

You're a grown person. You should be able to face the fact that luck is a significant factor in career development. Not the *only* factor, but an *important* one, just as developing, polishing, etc., etc., are important. Some people in your company might show great promise, yet become mired in dead-end jobs. Others may be less skilled than you, but whiz past on the fast track. Get over it—and get back to work.

You must learn to accept bad luck gracefully. Business analyst Dan Lovallo and psychologist Daniel Kahneman studied the letters written by CEOs to shareholders in the annual reports of selected companies. They found that corporate leaders usually attributed successes to strategic decisions or research-and-development programs—things the CEO could control and take credit for. But unfavorable outcomes were more likely to be blamed on factors beyond their control, like weather or inflation. Such tactics are transparently self-serving, and have the potential to make you look weak or foolish. Avoid them.

You *can* shape your own luck, at least partially. The renowned chemist and biologist Louis Pasteur always maintained that "chance favors the prepared mind." Psychologist Richard Wiseman came to agree after interviewing hundreds of people who characterized themselves as fortunate or unfortunate. "We found lucky and unlucky people have no insight into why they're lucky or not," he said. "But the lucky ones would tell us, 'I went to this party and chatted up these people.' The fact that they went to the party and explored commonalities, people they both knew, created opportunities for luck. They get out and meet people. They schmooze. They frequently change the patterns of their lives."

So look on the bright side. There's no reason why you can't fit among the lucky people of the world. You could even become as supremely fortunate as Calvin Coolidge, who was transformed by a series of unlikely events from lieutenant governor of Massachusetts to president of the United States in less than five years.

Coolidge moved up to the governorship, the pinnacle of his ambition, in November 1918. He won the statewide election by a narrow margin, and settled in for a quiet term. The new governor made it clear that his favorite action was inaction. "If one will only exercise the patience to wait, his wants are likely to be fulfilled," he often said. And: "If you see ten troubles coming down the road, you can be sure that nine will run into the ditch before they reach you."

A particularly menacing trouble headed Coolidge's way in September 1919. Boston's policemen formed a union, and they demanded that government officials meet with them to hammer out a pay increase. The police chief not only refused to negotiate, but he also suspended the union leaders.

The policemen had cause to be unhappy. They worked seventy-two hours a week, for which they were paid a maximum of fourteen hundred dollars a year, the equivalent of $16,660 in 2007. They were required to pay for their own uniforms out of that magnificent sum, and even had to purchase their own bullets.

Three-quarters of the police walked off the job after the chief announced his suspensions. There were reports of rowdyism during the early hours of the strike. Pedestrians were harassed by roving gangs. Looters and robbers took to the streets. Shots were fired, with three deaths resulting.

Coolidge reacted in predictable fashion, leaving it to Boston's mayor and the police chief to handle the crisis. President Woodrow Wilson condemned the strike in no uncertain terms—"a crime against civilization"—yet the governor stayed mute. He didn't stir until the mayor dismissed the chief and hinted that it might be time to negotiate with the strikers. That was too much for the conservative Coolidge, who called out the State Guard, reinstated the chief, and took control of the police force himself. The strike was swiftly broken.

It was at this point, after any danger had passed, that Coolidge received a telegram from Samuel Gompers, the president of the American Federation of Labor. Gompers asserted that the policemen had legitimate grievances, and he recommended that the governor deal leniently with them. Coolidge wired back, "There is no right to strike against the public safety by anybody, anywhere, any time."

Those fifteen words galvanized the nation. Coolidge, much to his own amazement, was suddenly considered to be presidential material. The *New York World* praised the cautious, quiet governor's "courage and plain speech" and suggested he would be a perfect fit for the White House. He eventually agreed to make a run for the 1920 Republican nomination, but finished far behind the eventual nominee, Warren Harding.

Coolidge's luck appeared to have run out, yet it resurfaced with great speed. The Republican bosses tapped Irvine Lenroot, a senator from Wisconsin, to be Harding's running mate. Conventions typically rubber-stamp such decisions, but the delegates spontaneously revolted in 1920, ditching Lenroot for the Hero of Boston. "Calvin Coolidge was the first vice president in a hundred years who was not wished on the country," marveled the *Boston Globe*. "The country wished him on the Republican Party."

H. L. Mencken, the famed columnist for the *Baltimore Sun*, wandered out of the convention hall after this bizarre turn of events. He ran into a colleague, a Boston reporter, who was unable to contain his agitation.

"To my astonishment," Mencken wrote, "I found that he was offering to bet all comers that Harding, if elected, would be assassinated before he served half his term. Someone in the crowd remonstrated gently, saying that any talk of assassination was unwise and might be misunderstood."

The reporter refused to be quieted. "I don't give a damn what you say," he howled. "I am simply telling you what I know. I know Cal Coolidge inside and out. He is the luckiest son of a bitch in the whole world!"

It happened almost as the reporter predicted. Harding died of a stroke or heart attack—the cause was never determined—while visiting San Francisco in August 1923. Coolidge, the new president, was awakened at his father's home in Vermont. He took the startling news with great aplomb, as if it were perfectly natural to have America's most powerful job drop into his lap. "I believe I can swing it," he said.

Then he went back to bed.

DON'T FALL VICTIM TO JEALOUSY AND ENVY

Franklin Roosevelt owed his career to Alfred Smith. There was no doubt about that at all.

The two New Yorkers achieved prominence in the Democratic Party at roughly the same time. Smith won the governorship in 1918, and Roosevelt was tapped for the party's vice-presidential nomination two years later. Smith pushed on to become a serious contender for the White House, but FDR quickly dropped from sight. A polio attack in 1921 left him unable to walk, or even to stand without braces. It was assumed that his public career had come to an end.

Roosevelt, however, clung to his dreams of political glory, throwing himself into years of strenuous, painful therapy. Only a handful of his colleagues believed he could mount a comeback. Foremost among them was Governor Smith, who single-handedly kept FDR in the spotlight. He asked Roosevelt to deliver his presidential nominating speeches at the 1924 and 1928 Democratic conventions, and then to succeed him as governor in the latter year.

Cynics scoffed at the suggestion that a wheelchair-bound administrator—even one as dynamic as Roosevelt—could run a state as large and diverse as New York. Smith rose to his defense, insisting that physical mobility was not an issue. "We do not elect him for his ability to do a double backflip or a handspring," he snapped. Roosevelt won the governorship by the thinnest of margins—twenty-five thousand votes out of more than four million cast. He couldn't have done it without his benefactor, as he was well aware.

But their friendship soon came under strain. Smith was at loose ends, having lost the 1928 presidential election. He hinted that Roosevelt should take it easy, perhaps even head to Warm Springs, Georgia, for more therapy. The new governor could retain Smith's experienced aides, trusting them to do the heavy lifting. They would send out correspondence under Roosevelt's name and oversee his legislative program. Smith even offered to hang around Albany to lend them a hand.

"Honestly," Roosevelt later reflected, "I think he did this in complete good faith, but at the same time with the rather definite thought that he himself would continue to run the governorship." That wasn't what FDR had in mind. He hired his own assistants, drafted his own legislation, and made it clear that Smith could head back home whenever he wished. "It had become pretty evident," Roosevelt said, "that I was going to be my own governor."

Relations between the two men were never the same. They squared off for the 1932 Democratic presidential nomination, which Roosevelt won. Smith grew bitterer and more conservative as his protégé became more successful.

He professed to see little difference between FDR's New Deal and communism. "It's all right with me if they want to disguise themselves as Karl Marx or Lenin or any of the rest of that bunch," Smith sneered, "but I won't stand for allowing them to march under the banner of (Andrew) Jackson or (Grover) Cleveland."

Roosevelt claimed to be mystified. "All the things we've done in the federal government are like the things Al Smith did as governor of New York," he said. "They're the things he would have done as president. What in the world is the matter?"

The answer was obvious to author Emil Ludwig, who visited Smith in his office in the Empire State Building. The ex-governor exhibited unvarnished contempt for the new president. "Smith lacks, in age and defeat, that inner equilibrium which alone can save a disappointed man," Ludwig decided. The politician once known as the Happy Warrior had been consumed by jealousy and envy.

It's inevitable that opponents will pull ahead of you in the race for professional advancement. They may roar in front for a short spell before dropping back to the pack, or they might grab the lead for good. If you react in either case with bitterness and hatred, you won't slow your rivals at all. But you *will* damage your own chances severely.

Consider the heavy price paid by Al Smith. He should have become the elder statesman of the Roosevelt administration, a revered icon of the Democratic Party. But his harsh, resentful attitude turned his former supporters against him, permanently soiling his reputation and foreclosing any future opportunities within the party. A generation of Democrats remembered him not as an energetic, fearless governor, but as an angry, frustrated cynic. They happily transferred their loyalties to Roosevelt.

Several other high-profile political careers have been destroyed in this manner. The final years of the other presidential Roosevelt may offer the best case history of the toxic powers of jealousy and envy.

Theodore Roosevelt, of course, reached his goal at a tender age, becoming president shortly before his forty-third birthday in 1901. He turned the White House over to his handpicked successor, William Howard Taft, seven and a half years later. Roosevelt pronounced himself satisfied—"Taft will carry on the work substantially as I have carried it on"—but his friends doubted that a vibrant man of fifty could enjoy retirement. Nicholas Murray Butler, the president of Columbia University, predicted, "It will be a lot harder for you, Theodore, to be an ex-president than president."

Taft, despite his conservative leanings, faithfully pursued many of his mentor's policies, often surpassing the previous standards. He proved, for example, to be a better "trustbuster," filing more antitrust lawsuits against major corporations in one term than Roosevelt had in two. TR nonetheless began to find fault with his successor—mildly at first, then with increasing vehemence. He eventually came to ridicule Taft as a "fathead" and a "puzzlewit," and to run against him for the Republican nomination in 1912.

The incumbent president was baffled by Roosevelt's transformation. "I think he occupies his leisure time in finding reasons why he is justified in not supporting me," Taft said. TR's close friends could only agree. Elihu Root, who had served as secretary of state and secretary of war under Roosevelt, thought his former boss was desperate to return to the White House—so desperate, in fact, that he was willing to attack old friends and to advocate policies that he had once scorned, if that's what it took. "He has merely picked up certain popular ideas which were at hand," Root said, "as one might pick up a poker or chair with which to strike."

Taft was strong enough to defeat Roosevelt for the nomination, which should have settled the matter. But TR couldn't quit. He immediately announced that he would run as a third-party candidate in the fall, essentially guaranteeing Woodrow Wilson's election and Taft's defeat. "When he gets into a fight," Root observed, "he is completely dominated by the desire to destroy his adversary completely."

The Taft-Roosevelt battle badly weakened the Republican Party for nearly a decade to come. It cleared the way for Wilson to win a second term in 1916, despite his lack of personal popularity. He became the first Democratic president to be reelected since Andrew Jackson eighty-four years earlier.

The whole story could have been much different. If TR had curbed his jealousy and acted with patience and restraint, Taft most likely would have been reelected in 1912. Roosevelt then would have emerged as the frontrunner in 1916, poised for a triumphant return to the White House he missed so badly.

It was not to be. The Old Rough Rider spent the rest of his life on the sidelines, eventually coming to hate Wilson even more than Taft. The cause of Roosevelt's indiscriminate passion was clear to historian H.W. Brands. It had nothing to do with issues or even personalities. It was simply, as Brands put it, "the resentment of one used to the limelight for whoever steals it."

CONDUCT YOURSELF WITH GRACE, ESPECIALLY IN DEFEAT

Senate colleagues—fellow Republicans and opposing Democrats alike—found Robert Dole to be an angry, self-absorbed man during his early years in Washington. They used several unattractive clichés to describe him. He was an attack dog, they said. He was a hatchet man. He would run over his grandmother with a tank, if that's what it took to get elected.

"His ambition was perceived to be his only dimension," recalled Bill Hoch, a media consultant who had interned in Dole's office. "He was perceived as extremely nasty. The perception was that he was one mean SOB."

That image was buttressed by Dole's first reelection campaign in Kansas. It took place in 1974, the year of Watergate indictments and Richard Nixon's resignation, a terrible year for Republican candidates. The Democratic challenger, a doctor named William Roy, was poised to snatch away Dole's Senate seat until a rumor swept the state that Roy had performed abortions. The operations were perfectly legal—and also were undeniably controversial. Dole denied any role in spreading the story, yet he benefited greatly. He erased a ten-point deficit in the final couple of weeks, aided by a flood of anti-abortion literature, and squeaked past Roy by thirteen thousand votes.

Gerald Ford faced a much greater challenge two years later, when the early presidential polls put him nearly thirty percentage points behind Jimmy Carter. What Ford needed, his advisers said, was a hard-driving running mate, someone willing to grab the Democrats by the throat and hang on for dear life. Who better than Bob Dole?

Ford made a remarkable comeback, pulling almost dead-even with Carter by November. His vice-presidential candidate, however, didn't deserve much credit. Dole's only memorable contribution was a notorious gaffe during his nationally televised debate with Carter's running mate, Walter Mondale. All wars of the twentieth century, Dole declared, were "Democrat wars," started and run by Democrats. That included World War II, which had begun for the United States when Japan launched a sneak attack on Pearl Harbor. Most voters were shocked by his naked partisanship, but his senatorial colleagues shrugged their shoulders. That's Bob, they said.

Dole went on to run for the presidency three times. Reporters occasionally wrote that he was mellowing, a change they credited to his second wife, Elizabeth, who would eventually become a senator and presidential candidate herself. But the old attack dog never lost his bark entirely, as he proved with a resounding howl in 1988.

Dole and George H.W. Bush were the two leading contenders for the Republican nomination that year. They reached New Hampshire at roughly equal strength, both knowing that the winner of that critical primary would emerge as the frontrunner—and most likely the eventual nominee. NBC's Tom Brokaw arranged a joint interview in New Hampshire. Dole sat next to him, while Bush was seen on a remote hookup. The anchorman broke the ice by asking the senator if he had any message for his rival. Dole didn't waste time with innocuous greetings. "Stop lying about my record," he snarled at Bush.

That campaign ended badly, as did 1996, when Dole finally won the Republican nomination on his third try, yet was subsequently buried by Bill Clinton in the general election. What amazed so many observers was the calm, gracious way he accepted this career-ending defeat. "It was no big deal for me," he said later. "I moved along pretty quickly."

Dole made a conscious decision to stow away his anger and sarcasm. "I didn't want to be remembered as I was in New Hampshire in 1988," he admitted. Reporters pestered him to analyze his latest losing campaign, but he declined. "If I do that," he said, "I'm going to get into the details of what happened, whose fault was it, da-da, da-da. I don't want to do all that." He chose a different route, accepting invitations to appear on *Saturday Night Live* and the late-night television shows of David Letterman and Jay Leno, where he cracked jokes at his own expense.

Dole accomplished his objective, effectively rehabilitating his image. "Some people may have expected me to be depressed or bitter or whatever you are after you lose. And I wasn't happy," he said. "But I put on a happy face and had a good time."

It *is* possible to achieve success despite boorish behavior. Richard Nixon's diatribe after losing the governorship of California in 1962—"you won't have Nixon to kick around anymore"—was so bitter that it reverberated throughout the remainder of his career. Yet he was able to rebound and win the presidency six years later.

The preferable alternative, of course, is to always conduct yourself with grace, especially when you lose. It makes tactical sense, for one thing. "How you exit is important, especially if you're thinking of coming back," said Dan Quayle, the vice-presidential half of the losing Republican ticket in 1992. His cheerful demeanor during the transition from the outgoing Bush administration to the incoming Clinton team helped keep his future options open, though when he finally ran for the Republican presidential nomination in 2000, he still fell woefully short.

Adopting a positive attitude in the face of defeat can be beneficial in other ways:

- It can confound your enemies. Martin Van Buren, denied reelection by William Henry Harrison in 1840, wrote privately that he had resolved to show his opponents "abundant evidence" that he was still in good spirits. He invited Harrison to the White House for a dinner party, and even offered to move out early so that Harrison could get settled. The president-elect declined.

- It can foster stability. Al Gore conceded the 2000 election to George W. Bush with grace and dignity, even though the Supreme Court had just halted a recount that might have awarded him the electoral votes of Florida and, with them, the presidency. Some advisers suggested that Gore dig in his heels. He might seek other legal remedies, they said, or perhaps he could try to delay the congressional certification of Bush's victory. Gore refused to disrupt the nation that way. "While I strongly disagree with the court's decision," he told reporters, "I accept it."

- And, as Bob Dole learned, it can enhance your image. Dwight Eisenhower routed Adlai Stevenson in the 1952 presidential election, carrying thirty-nine of the forty-eight states. But Stevenson charmed the nation with his concession speech in Springfield, Illinois, cementing a reputation for humor, eloquence, and good sportsmanship. "Someone asked me, as I came in down on the street, how I felt," he said that night, "and I was reminded of a story that a fellow townsman of ours used to tell—Abraham Lincoln. They asked him how he felt once after an unsuccessful election. He said he felt like a little boy who had stubbed his toe in the dark. He said that he was too old to cry, but it hurt too much to laugh."

Admirers crowded around after Stevenson's speech. It didn't matter that he had lost to Eisenhower, they assured him, because his future in the Democratic

Party was still bright. And, indeed, he would win the party's nomination again in 1956—only to lose to Eisenhower again in the general election.

But a second race for the White House was a distant prospect on that bittersweet night in November 1952, as the compliments kept flowing. One woman told Stevenson that he deserved to be proud. "Governor," she said, "you educated the country with your great campaign."

The defeated candidate smiled wanly. "But," he replied, "a lot of people flunked the course."

EXULT IN YOUR SUCCESS, AND DO THE BEST JOB YOU CAN

Robert Redford never ran for public office, though he certainly had the potential to do well. He was a political consultant's dream—articulate, self-assured, deeply interested in public issues, and, yes, movie-star handsome.

The closest Redford came to campaigning was a 1972 movie, *The Candidate*, in which he played Bill McKay, a young lawyer seeking a Senate seat in California. The fictional McKay didn't have a political record, but he was the son of a popular former governor, which made his name instantly recognizable. Marvin Lucas, a savvy manager played by Peter Boyle, guided the McKay campaign, plotting a strategy that was long on image and short on content. He advised his candidate to speak in sound bites, avoid controversial issues, and let his television commercials carry the burden.

It worked. McKay upset the Republican incumbent, Crocker Jarmon, and achieved his improbable goal of becoming a United States senator. His headquarters erupted in a joyous celebration, but the young winner was troubled. He looked frantically for his manager.

"Marvin," he asked, "what do we do now?" Lucas had no quick answer—he knew how to run for the Senate, not how to be a senator—and McKay was swept away by friends and supporters before the two men could speak.

If your hard work and maneuvering pay off, the day will come when you'll confront the same question that bothered Senator-elect McKay. There you'll be, the new CEO of your company, finally occupying the corner office of your dreams.

What do you do now?

Your first priority should be to savor the moment. Americans have no patience for dour, weary winners. If you reach your goal, don't be obnoxious about it, but don't suppress your feelings, either. Exult in your success.

Enjoy the fact that people suddenly respect you as the symbol of a large, powerful organization. "I'm no longer Bill Clinton," marveled the forty-second commander-in-chief. "And I'm not really even the president. You just become the United States."

Enjoy the fact that people actually listen when you speak. "I am charged with being a preacher," Theodore Roosevelt admitted. "Well, I suppose I am. I have such a bully pulpit."

Enjoy the fact that you get to do interesting things, travel to interesting places, and make the acquaintance of interesting strangers. "I love to meet people," said Warren Harding. "It is the most pleasant thing I do. It is really the only fun I have. It doesn't tax me, and it seems to be a very great pleasure to them."

But don't forget that victory is never the end. It is only the beginning.

Richard Nixon believed that presidential candidates could be divided into two categories, as we noted in the first chapter. Some men and women want to do big things, Nixon said, and others only want to be big. The latter pursue the White House merely for the ego gratification that comes with winning a national election. "They are doomed to failure, because the presidency is one office you can't go into assuming it will guide you; you must know what you desire and attempt to guide it," contended Peggy Noonan, a former presidential speechwriter. The same point holds true for the top job in any organization, whether in the public or private sector.

Nixon entered the Oval Office with a thick sheaf of plans and proposals. He opened the diplomatic door to China, stabilized relations with the Soviet Union, slowly wound down the Vietnam War, and established several new government agencies, including the Drug Enforcement Administration and the Environmental Protection Agency. He might have been remembered as one of America's best presidents, if not for the streak of anger and cynicism that triggered the Watergate crisis and forced his eventual resignation.

But Nixon's observations about leadership remain valid, regardless of his personal failure. You *must* aspire to do big things, not merely to be big. You should establish a few clear goals upon assuming office, and then channel your energy into accomplishing those objectives. That's the best way to build a strong organization—and to establish a legacy that will endure long after you've moved on to other things.

James Polk wasted no time in setting his goals. His inaugural parade was still under way on March 4, 1845, when Polk confided to George Bancroft, his new secretary of the navy, that he planned four "great measures" in the coming four years:

1. He would lower the tariff, in order to boost the purchasing power of farmers and laborers.

2. He would establish an independent treasury, making it possible for the federal government to control its own funds, rather than keeping them in private banks.

3. He would acquire Oregon, where the United States and England had competing claims.

4. He would acquire California, which was then part of Mexico.

A few historians have questioned Bancroft's story. They wonder why the new president would have whispered his goals to a cabinet member, rather than trumpeting them to the world. His inaugural address, after all, contained just a single reference to Oregon and none at all to California. Skeptics insist that Bancroft fabricated his boss's to-do list with the benefit of hindsight.

But these aspersions have had little impact on Polk's legacy. Most historians care only that he met all four of his purported goals. His success wasn't total (the final version of the tariff was a compromise), nor did it come as easily as he wished (it took a war with Mexico to acquire California). But Polk is remembered nonetheless as Mr. Four-for-Four, a man of action and accomplishment. "He knew how to get things done, which is the first necessity of government, and he knew what he wanted done, which is the second," wrote Bernard De Voto, a renowned historian. Polk was rated as one of America's ten greatest presidents by a *Wall Street Journal* panel of 132 professors in 2000.

Another member of that top-ten list, Ronald Reagan, also understood the importance of building a solid record. Tip O'Neill and other Democratic leaders ridiculed him as a conservative ideologue, but Reagan proved to be as pragmatic as Polk. He knew the value of patience and compromise. "I'm willing to take what I can get," he said. "You have to take what you can get and go out and get some more next year. That's what the opposition has been doing for years." Reagan didn't accomplish everything he wanted, but he pushed the nation much further in a conservative direction than the Democrats thought possible. He made his mark.

It's an intoxicating experience to be in command and do big things. Many leaders complain that their jobs are burdensome, yet few surrender the reins voluntarily. Richard Nixon resigned in 1974, the lone president to quit, but he left only because Congress was on the verge of tossing him out. The last president who was eligible to run for reelection, yet declined to do so, was Lyndon Johnson in 1968. The last president who departed the White House of his own free will after a single four-year term was Rutherford Hayes, who said goodbye in 1881.

The natural temptation is to hang on to power as long as possible. Theodore Roosevelt was saddened by his approaching farewell in 1909. "I will confess to you that I like my job. The burdens will be laid aside with a good deal of regret," he told William Jennings Bryan. Five ex-presidents—Roosevelt among them—tried to regain the job after leaving the White House. The only one who made a successful comeback was Grover Cleveland.

But longevity doesn't guarantee productivity. The window of opportunity rarely stays open for long. Leaders are most effective during their early years in command, when their images are unsullied and their plans seem fresh. Polk attained his four objectives in four years. Most of the so-called "Reagan revolution" was completed before Ronald Reagan's first term ended. Abraham Lincoln, often ranked as the greatest president of all, served just four years and forty-two days.

Modern presidents always seek reelection. Their work isn't done, they say. They need another term to accomplish everything they want to do.

But they're wrong. Presidents often run out of gas after four years. Consider this simple game of word association, linking recent presidents with the dominant events of their second terms: Lyndon Johnson—Vietnam. Richard

Nixon—Watergate. Ronald Reagan—Iran-Contra. Bill Clinton—Impeachment. George W. Bush—Iraq. It's enough to make you wonder why Americans ever reelect any president.

The obvious lesson is that you must strike while the iron is hot. Establish your goals as soon as you're promoted to a leadership position, and set out immediately to fulfill them. Time is very precious and very limited, as the diligent James Polk was well aware. "In truth, though I occupy a very high position," he once said, "I am the hardest working man in this country."

Follow Polk's example and get to work. There's no time to waste.

RECOGNIZE WHEN IT'S TIME FOR YOU TO LEAVE THE STAGE

Young Harold Stassen was a golden boy, always basking in the sunshine of success. He graduated from high school at fourteen, zipped through college, and picked up a law degree soon after his twenty-second birthday. He collected a string of awards along the way, ranging from the rifle championship of the English-speaking world to the top prize in an intercollegiate public-speaking competition.

Stassen shifted into overdrive when he reached adulthood. "To be effective," he liked to say, "you have to lay it on the line." Modest goals weren't his style. He took direct aim at the governorship of Minnesota, hit the bull's-eye in 1938 at the callow age of thirty-one, and was twice reelected.

The United States plunged into World War II while Stassen was governor, and he was eager to join the fight. His advisers were opposed. It would be easier to tend to his political base if he stayed home, they pointed out, and besides, he was exempt from the military draft. Stassen ignored their recommendations, resigned the governorship, and enlisted in the navy. He rose to the post of assistant chief of staff for Admiral William "Bull" Halsey, commander of the Third Fleet.

The war ended in 1945, leaving Stassen in a predictably restless mood. He toured Europe and wrote a book, but felt the need for something bigger. He announced his candidacy for the Republican presidential nomination in 1948 and did remarkably well during the campaign's early stages, arriving in Oregon as the frontrunner. But he lost that state's primary to Thomas Dewey and never regained his momentum.

Defeat was an unusual experience for Stassen, yet it didn't seem to bother him. He was confident that something good would turn up. "I literally don't do what I consider for an individual of my position a waste of time, of going over (events) to try to recast," he once said. "I appreciate the importance of historians trying to analyze those things, but I don't live that way." He simply pushed on to the next challenge, accepting the presidency of the University of Pennsylvania at the age of forty-one, while preparing for a second assault on the White House.

His timing, for once, was bad. Two heavyweights—Dwight Eisenhower and Robert Taft—squared off for the Republican nomination in 1952. Stassen wasn't in their league, yet still made the best of the situation. He abandoned his candidacy, jumped on Eisenhower's bandwagon, and was rewarded with a high-level State Department appointment. His chances of ever being elected president were fading, but his overall prospects remained promising. He was on track to become a foreign-policy expert within the Republican Party, perhaps even the secretary of state someday.

Miscalculations and bad luck, however, would soon trigger a change in Stassen's fortunes. He took time off from his government job in 1956 to launch a bizarre campaign to dump Vice President Richard Nixon from the Republican ticket. Eisenhower ignored him and kept Nixon around. Stassen then ran for governor again—not in Minnesota, where he was still highly regarded, but in Pennsylvania, where he had few roots. Another defeat followed.

A new pattern established itself. The Golden Boy no longer stood front and center. He was now upstaged by the Born Loser.

Stassen ran for mayor of Philadelphia—and lost. Senator from Minnesota—and lost. President in 1964—and lost. The same in 1968 and in five subsequent presidential campaigns up to 1992. The once-promising governor, naval officer, and university president became a national laughingstock. "There's one thing about Harold E. Stassen," wrote the *Washington Evening Star*. "He likes to go down with his ship, and he doesn't care how many times it's sunk."

Stassen's striking quality was a refusal to acknowledge his metamorphosis from prodigy to absurdity. He was notable, in the opinion of Washington journalist William White, for having "the most profound absence of a sense of humor in American politics." Reporters loved to gibe Stassen by asking if he planned to retire from politics. His deadly serious reply never varied. "When God ends my life," he would say, "that's when my career will end."

This book, of course, has emphasized the steps that will help you achieve professional success. If you follow the examples of America's great presidents and presidential candidates, there's a good chance that you'll do well in business or politics.

But failure is always an option, too. It's possible to do most things right and still miss your goal. If you repeatedly fall short, you'll confront the same situation that Harold Stassen once faced. He made the wrong choice, deciding to ignore the facts and doggedly pursue his lifelong ambition, the White House, even at the cost of his dignity and reputation.

Tenacity is an admirable quality, but so are realism and flexibility. If the time ever comes to leave the stage, you should accept the inevitable—or at least be happy with a supporting role. Your career, even if you never become a business or political leader, can still be stimulating and rewarding.

Bill Bradley served three terms as a senator from New Jersey. Most pundits believed he could remain in the Senate forever if he wished, yet he walked away in 1996. Bradley ran for president four years later, but scuttled his campaign when he did badly in the early primaries. His inner voice suggested in both instances that it was time to leave—from the Senate because it had become routine, and from his presidential campaign because it had no chance of succeeding. "Reflecting on what you've done has a way of completing the experience," he said. "For me, it's never enough just to do it. I have to reflect on how I've done it, why, and what I've learned. Then when I put down those reflections on paper, that closes the experience for me."

Samuel Tilden and Al Gore lost two of the closest presidential elections in American history. Each received more popular votes than his opponent, but was defeated by a narrow (and hotly disputed) margin in the Electoral College—Tilden by a single electoral vote in 1876, Gore by five in 2000.

Each man declined to seek the presidency again, even though he would have been a heavy favorite for the Democratic nomination in the upcoming election. Both chose, instead, to make a clean break with politics. Their hearts and minds told them it was time to enter a new phase of life.

Tilden, who would turn sixty-six in 1880, was philosophical about his misfortune. He calmly accepted the results and decided to take it easy. "I can retire to private life," he joked, "with the consciousness that I shall receive from posterity the credit of having been elected to the highest position in the gift of the people, without any of the cares and responsibilities of the office." Friends protested that his odds of reaching the White House were still good. "But I am out of politics," he replied. "I have nothing more to do with it." He quietly lived out his years at his New York country estate.

"He's More Popular Now Than He Ever Was"

Al Gore, whose quest for the presidency had begun in 1988, chose to strike out in a new direction after his 2000 loss to George W. Bush, committing himself to the environmental movement. His documentary about global warming, *An Inconvenient Truth*, won two Academy Awards in 2007 and was a key factor in his selection for the Nobel Peace Prize later that same year.

The movie business appealed to Gore as a means of expression—"I'm trying to reach out to people in every effective way that I can find"—but it rehabilitated his image, too. He was widely hailed as a public-spirited citizen who was doing important work—a pleasant change from the harsh rhetoric of politics, as well as a reward for his willingness to take a risk and change careers. "He's more popular now than he ever was in office," admitted one of the movie's co-producers, Laurie David. "And he knows it. He's a superhero now."

DON'T LOSE TRACK OF WHAT'S REALLY IMPORTANT IN LIFE

Franklin Roosevelt never forgot the thrill of visiting the White House as a young boy. He was five years old when his father took him to meet President

Grover Cleveland, then in the midst of his first term. Cleveland, alas, dampened the spirits of the occasion. "I'm making a strange wish for you, little man, a wish I suppose no one else would make," he said as he shook young FDR's hand. "I wish for you that you may never be president of the United States."

Cleveland had been a convivial sort when he practiced law in Buffalo, but public office brought out his inner drudge. He routinely worked from dawn to midnight in the White House, then joked thinly about having put in "half a day." More than a decade of pursuing or holding the presidency left him weary and dispirited. He gladly departed when his second term expired in 1897.

Roosevelt, of course, would grow up to become America's longest-serving president. He lived in the White House for a dozen years—four more than Cleveland—and faced problems much larger than the older man could have imagined. Yet FDR never lost his zest for the job, not even in the midst of a worldwide depression or World War II. If he had ever seen fit to give advice to a five-year-old boy or girl, he would have heartily recommended the presidency.

People react differently to power and responsibility. Many love to be in charge. Ulysses Grant enjoyed being president so much that he and his wife dawdled in the White House for several hours after the inauguration of his successor, Rutherford Hayes. Some people wondered if the Grants would ever leave. Bill Clinton was another person who thrived in the presidency— and sought to retain his influence thereafter. "I left the White House, but I'm still here. We're not going anywhere," he told reporters after George W. Bush was sworn in.

But others couldn't get away from Washington, D.C., quickly enough. They schemed for years—often for decades—to attain the presidency, then were disillusioned to find the job burdensome and oppressive. Many of them regretted ever reaching their goal.

Thomas Jefferson is ranked among America's greatest presidents, but he happily bade the job farewell in 1809. "Never did a prisoner, released from his chains, feel such relief as I shall on shaking off the shackles of power," he said two days before his departure. Jefferson's epitaph, which he wrote himself, cited his authorship of the Declaration of Independence and the Virginia Statute for Religious Freedom, as well as his role in founding the University of Virginia. It said nothing about his years as commander-in-chief.

Another highly rated president, James Polk, served only one term, yet was eager to wash his hands of its cares. "I am sure I shall be a happier man in my retirement than I have been during the four years I have filled the highest office in the gift of my countrymen," he said as the end neared. It proved to be a poor prediction. Polk died from cholera three months after leaving office.

Men of lesser skills denounced the job more vehemently than Jefferson or Polk ever did. "The office of president of the United States is not fit for a gentleman to hold," sputtered James Buchanan. "I'm in jail, and I can't get out," moaned Warren Harding. "This office is a compound hell," raged Herbert Hoover.

A few chief executives split the difference. They enjoyed their high-powered political careers until fate altered their priorities and stripped the presidency of its satisfactions.

Humans typically focus on issues of personal comfort or prestige—such as the type of car they drive or the way they're perceived at work—until weightier matters intervene, as noted by Daniel Kahneman, a Nobel Prize–winning psychologist. "Suppose you're driving in your car with your spouse, and you're quarreling," he said. "Are you better off if you're driving an Escort or a Lexus?" The quality of a person's car becomes irrelevant when his or her personal life is disrupted, even in such a tiny way.

The same effect is greatly magnified when tragedy is involved, as Franklin Pierce learned to his misfortune. Pierce believed the presidency would beautifully cap his political career, bringing him eternal glory and perfect happiness. It did neither.

Pierce's reputation, far from being enhanced, was damaged beyond repair when sectional tensions escalated during his administration in the mid-1850s. Historians rank him among the five worst presidents of all time, blaming him for allowing America to drift toward the Civil War. One of the men who occupied the White House after Pierce, Theodore Roosevelt, ridiculed him as "a small politician, of low capacity and mean surroundings."

The personal toll was even greater. Pierce's wife, Jane, was certain their family life would be destroyed if Franklin was elected in 1852—a belief so strong that she secretly prayed for his defeat. The couple had already lost two young sons. She worried about their remaining boy, eleven-year-old Benjamin, as well as her husband's recurring problems with alcohol.

Her premonition came true in horrible fashion. Franklin won the November election, and Benjamin died in a railroad accident the following January, just forty-seven days before his father's inauguration. Jane never overcame her grief, making only a handful of public appearances as first lady. She grew to believe that Benjamin's death was divine retribution for Franklin's intense ambition. The couple's Washington years, haunted by these professional and personal tribulations, were grim indeed.

Life was no better back home in New Hampshire. Jane died six years after Franklin's term ended. The barrage of disasters drove the ex-president back to the bottle. "After the White House," he reportedly asked, "what is there to do but drink?" Pierce died in 1869, still only sixty-four years old. Cirrhosis of the liver was listed as the cause of death.

Family tragedies placed political power in unhappy perspective for Benjamin Harrison and Calvin Coolidge, too. Harrison's wife died a few weeks before the 1892 election, which he lost to Grover Cleveland. "For me, there is no sting in it," the outgoing president said of his defeat. "Indeed, after the heavy blow the death of my wife dealt me, I do not think I could have stood the strain a reelection would have brought." Coolidge's sixteen-year-old son developed a blister on his right toe while playing on the White House tennis courts in 1924. He died a few days later of blood poisoning. "When he went," his heartbroken father wrote, "the power and the glory of the presidency went with him."

This litany of desperation and sorrow may seem a strange way to end an upbeat book that's dedicated to advancing your career and improving your life. Why end a positive story on such a negative note?

Consider this section to be a final reality check. Professional success is an admirable and desirable destination, to be sure. But, as the stories above make clear, you need to keep these two caveats firmly in mind:

Know yourself. Make certain that you're temperamentally suited to fill an executive position. If you decide that you aren't, find another way to express your creativity and achieve professional fulfillment.

And enjoy the journey. The path that takes you to a leadership position is bound to be a long one. Don't ignore the important features—family, friends, community—that will enrich your life along the way.

Benjamin Franklin was as industrious and self-motivated as anyone in American history. He tackled several professions simultaneously—printer, inventor, scientist, humorist, diplomat, philosopher—and strove to be excellent at each. Many of his famous aphorisms reflected his belief in hard work and high aspirations: "God helps them that help themselves." "Lost time is never found again." "Early to bed and early to rise, makes a man healthy, wealthy, and wise."

Yet Franklin also understood the importance of self-knowledge and a well-balanced life. Happiness, he wrote, "is produced not so much by great pieces of good fortune that seldom happen, as by little advantages that occur every day."

Modern researchers agree. A 1995 study by the University of Illinois discovered that one-third of the nation's wealthiest citizens were less happy than average Americans were. The Gallup Poll reported in 2007 that married people in the lowest income bracket tended to be happier than unmarried men and women in the highest bracket. And the Grant Study of Adult Development—a project that tracked the lives of Harvard University graduates from the early 1940s—concluded that people with stable marriages and strong friendships were more likely to be successful at work, too. "There's no question that conventional lives statistically are the happiest," said George Vaillant, the study's director. "Stopping smoking, exercising, working hard, eating breakfast, and not getting divorced—all these humdrum things correlate directly with happiness."

So, by all means, aim for the top. Achievement and success are important ingredients for a vital, fulfilling life. But don't forget that many other components are equally essential.

The greatest presidents understood this point intuitively. They were aware that single-minded preoccupation with work could be counterproductive.

They knew that perspective, spirit, and serenity were—and always will be—the keys to professional and personal joy.

Abraham Lincoln never lost his sense of perspective, not even after achieving the goal that had enticed him for decades. His friends in Springfield, Illinois, assumed that his departure for the White House in 1861 would mark the end of their association. He was moving to a higher league. That was nonsense, Lincoln said. He would always be one of them. He would do his duty in Washington and then return home. "If I live," he told his law partner, William Herndon, "I'm coming back sometime, and then we'll go right on practicing law as if nothing had ever happened." Lincoln still remained true to that philosophy on his fateful night in Ford's Theatre.

Theodore Roosevelt approached work and play with the same intensity of spirit—running the country, charging up San Juan Hill, hunting wild game, struggling to control his six children. ("I can be president of the United States, or I can attend to Alice," he once said of his free-spirited daughter. "I cannot possibly do both.") TR advocated the "strenuous life," and he lived his advice. A critic complained about his "knack of doing things, and doing them noisily, clamorously; while he is in the neighborhood, the public can no more look the other way than the small boy can turn his head away from a circus parade followed by a steam calliope." But it was this same boisterous style that endeared Roosevelt to the American public, and that gave him so much personal enjoyment. "A mere life of ease," he concluded, "is not a very satisfactory life."

The final quality that will serve you well is serenity—the quiet belief that the pursuit of excellence is worth your while, and that even if you don't achieve your primary objective, you can still lead a life of great value to your family, friends, and the wider community, not to mention yourself.

Such unwavering faith will give you the strength to grow and thrive—to reach your full potential—no matter what challenges may lie ahead. Franklin Roosevelt wasn't the smartest president America ever had, or the most energetic, or the most consistent. But his serene, almost mystical self-confidence was unsurpassed. It was the true secret of his greatness.

"I'll tell you," FDR once said, "at night, when I lay my head on my pillow, and it is often pretty late, and I think of the things that have come before me during the day and the decisions that I have made, I say to myself—well, I have done the best I could, and turn over and go to sleep."

Notes

The sources for this book are noted below, grouped according to subject headings in bold type. Citations generally follow the order in which their corresponding material appears in the text. If a single source was used more than once for a given subject, all page numbers are combined in a single reference.

Book citations consist of the author's last name and appropriate page numbers. If the bibliography includes two or more books by the same author—or books by two authors with the same surname—the specific title is noted, too.

Magazine and newspaper articles are cited by the periodical's name and publication date. Authors, headlines, or page numbers are not provided.

Broadcast or speech transcripts are linked with the program, network, station, or venue, followed by the date.

Websites are noted without their addresses, which can be found in the bibliography. Detailed listings of all other sources can be found in the bibliography, as well.

PREFACE

Introduction
> **Ivins:** *The News With Brian Williams*, MSNBC (February 17, 2000). **Gardner:** Gardner, *On Leadership*, 103.

Lessons that are universal
> **Truman:** Barber, 312. **Smith:** Sherman, 191–198. **Jackson:** Goldman and Fuller, 180.

The seven steps
> **Udall:** *Washington Post* (February 16, 1988). **Herndon:** Hofstadter, 125. **Theodore Roosevelt on education:** Adler, 94. **Churchill:** Gergen, 210. **Reagan:**

Harvard Business Review (January 2003). **Clark:** Caro, *The Path to Power*, 363. **Stevenson:** Martin, *Adlai Stevenson and the World*, 507. **Blount:** *Atlantic Monthly* (February 2001). **Goldwater:** *Current Biography* (1978). **Theodore Roosevelt on luck:** Wead, 298. **Franklin Roosevelt:** Wilson, *Character Above All*, 13.

Learning from the best teachers
   Harding: Sinclair, 74. **Connally:** *Washington Post* (July 8, 1979).

1. DECIDING

Introduction
   Bryan: Schlesinger and Israel, 1894, 1911; Koenig, 167; Olasky, 165. **Carter:** Stroud, 148; Jimmy Carter Library and Museum website; Wooten, 301; Bourne, 232; Germond and Witcover, 52.
Ambition, when under control, is a good impulse
   Bates: Goodwin, *Team of Rivals*, 25. **Lincoln:** Hofstadter, 121, 125; Thomas, *Abraham Lincoln*, 153. **Hayes:** Davison, 19. **Nixon:** Wilson, *Character Above All*, 203. **McCain and Chafee:** *New York Times* (February 18, 1995). **Hartke:** Peirce and Hagstrom, 290; *Chicago Tribune* (January 17, 1993). **Carter:** Thomas, *The Pursuit of the White House*, 163. **Chase:** Donald, *Inside Lincoln's Cabinet*, 5. **Blaine:** Summers, 61–62. **Cuomo:** *USA Today* (October 27, 1995). **Mondale:** *Washington Post* (January 8, 1984); Witcover, *Marathon*, 365.
There's nothing wrong with wanting recognition
   McGovern: *Washington Post* (January 14, 1984). **Fels:** *Harvard Business Review* (April 2004). **Harris:** *Chicago Tribune* (January 17, 1993).
"As long as God gives me breath"
   Stassen: *Washington Post* (December 8, 1978, and April 15, 1988).
A healthy ego is fine, but egomania is dangerous
   Anderson: *Washington Post* (January 20, 1980). **Wilson:** Olasky, 197. **Johnson:** Wilson, *Character Above All*, 112. **Blunders:** Associated Press wire service (February 18, 2006).
"He has been acting strangely"
   Butler: Marrin, 31–33.
Don't shape your career to please someone else
   Adams: Wead, 297; Bellow, 295–296; Associated Press wire service (September 17, 2000); Bemis, 304. **Taft:** Anderson, 4; Chace, 27. **Harding:** Russell, 346–347, 485. **Seymour:** Schlesinger and Israel, 1256; Mitchell, 430.
Excessive caution can destroy your chances
   Gore: Milbank, 19–20; *Washington Post* (November 12, 1987, and November 28, 1993); *Los Angeles Times* (May 2, 1988); Harris, 388; *Newsweek* (December 25, 2000). **Scranton:** Wolf, 61; White, *The Making of the President 1964*, 142–147. **Buchanan:** Taranto and Leo, 78; McConnell Center website.
Your competitors are only human, so don't be awed
   Johnson: Thomas, *The Pursuit of the White House*, 242; Olin, 97; *American Heritage* (August 1969); Russell, 383. **Carter:** *Congressional Quarterly Almanac* (1976); Stroud, 22–23; Bourne, 232.
Women must work harder and be tougher
   Smith: *Washington Post* (October 8, 1983, August 4, 1986, and May 30, 1995); Sherman, 177–200. **Statistics:** Center for American Women and Politics

website; United States Bureau of Labor Statistics website; *Fortune* (April 17, 2006). **Studies:** *Harvard Business Review* (April 2004 and March 2005). **Chisholm:** Chisholm, 2, 31–32. **Braun:** *Washington Post* (November 12, 2003). **Schroeder:** *Washington Post* (September 29, 1987). **Butterfield:** *Psychology Today* (December 1987). **Stennis:** *Washington Post* (August 4, 1986).

Minorities must work harder and be tougher

Chisholm: *New York Times* (June 25, 1972); *Current Biography* (1969); Chisholm, 2, 31–32; *Washington Post* (January 4, 2005). **Jackson:** *Washington Post* (February 22, 2004); *Playboy* (June 1984). **Easter:** *Washington Post* (February 22, 2004). **Obama:** *USA Today* (January 4, 2005). **Private sector:** *Fortune* (August 22, 2005); *Business Week* (July 25, 2005).

Health problems don't have to be impediments

Roosevelt: Goodwin, *No Ordinary Time*, 16–17; Franklin and Eleanor Roosevelt Institute website; Olasky, 217–219; Goldberg, 108; Wilson, *Character Above All*, 15. **Church:** *Current Biography* (1978). **Biden:** *Washington Post* (February 23, 1988, and September 8, 1988).

It doesn't really matter where you grew up

Glass: Smith and Beasley, 276–277. **Virginia:** Schlesinger and Israel, 304. **Ohio:** Sinclair, 25. **Corporate headquarters:** *Fortune* (April 17, 2006). **Presidential birthplaces:** DeGregorio, *passim*; Infoplease website; Author's analysis of United States Census Bureau data. **Clinton:** Thomas, *The United States of Suburbia*, 30.

If you want the top job, make the top effort

Arthur: Morgan, 94–95; Ackerman, 128–129; Taranto and Leo, 109. **Morton:** Barzman, 136. **Kerry:** *Washington Post* (December 5, 2003, and December 28, 2003). **Bradley:** *Washington Post* (March 4, 2000). **Adams:** *American Heritage* (February/March 1984); Bemis, 138, 304; Taranto and Leo, 40–41.

"Every job I've had is bigger than I am"

Johnson: Califano, 27–29; Barber, 79.

2. DEVELOPING

Introduction

Kennedy as campaigner: Dallek, *An Unfinished Life*, 249; *New York Times* (July 3, 1960, and July 5, 1960). **Center for Creative Leadership study:** *Harvard Business Review* (December 2002). **Kennedy as president:** Stacks, 3–4. **Clinton:** Thomas, *The United States of Suburbia*, 83–87; Gergen, 338. **Ages of winners:** Author's analysis. **Dewey:** Smith, *Thomas E. Dewey and His Times*, 216, 643; Thomas, *The Pursuit of the White House*, 125. **McClellan:** Catton, 53, 56; Goodwin, *Team of Rivals*, 476.

A college education (Ivy League or not) is essential

Roosevelt: Adler, 94. **Education and wages:** United States Census Bureau website. **Truman:** Ross, 20–22; Barber, 309–312. **Biden:** Cramer, 501. **Graduation statistics:** *Harvard Business Review* (January 2005); *USA Today* (June 7, 2005). **Johnson:** Goldman, *The Tragedy of Lyndon Johnson*, 23; Dallek, *Flawed Giant*, 88; Caro, *The Path to Power*, 668.

Emotional intelligence is as important as IQ

Adams: McCullough, *John Adams*, 390. **Bennis:** *Boston Globe* (November 26, 1999). **Holmes:** *New York Times* (August 20, 1989). **Reagan:** Associated Press

wire service (June 1, 2006); *Washington Post* (August 20, 1987); Gergen, 200.
Bush and Kerry: *National Post* (November 6, 2004); *Chicago Tribune* (June 8, 2005). **Caperton:** *Boston Globe* (November 26, 1999). **Goleman:** *Harvard Business Review* (January 2004). **Wilson:** Chace, 245; *Washington Post* (November 4, 2001); Sinclair, 174–175.

"I don't know what to do or where to turn"
Harding: Barber, 212; United Press International wire service (October 19, 2000).

Get out and experience all that life has to offer
Population gains: United States Census Bureau website. **Hayes:** *Dictionary of American Biography*, 8:446–451; DeGregorio, 282. **Coolidge:** *Dictionary of American Biography*, 21:191–198; Russell, 381. **Gardner:** Gardner, *On Leadership*, 159. **Roosevelt:** Taranto and Leo, 126; Hofstadter, 271–272; Brands, 173, 214–215, 357; Schlesinger and Israel, 1888–1889. **Washington:** DeGregorio, 5–7. **Lincoln:** DeGregorio, 230–233; *Harvard Business Review* (August 2003); *Weekly Standard* (February 16, 2004).

Develop and demonstrate leadership qualities
1984 poll: Roper Center for Public Opinion Research website. **Tyler:** Peterson, 268. **Taylor:** Remini, *Henry Clay, Statesman for the Union*, 711. **Fillmore:** DeGregorio, 194. **Pierce:** DeGregorio, 207. **Buchanan:** Seigenthaler, 153. **Gardner:** Gardner, *On Leadership*, 33. **Lincoln:** Goodwin, *Team of Rivals,* 206. **Roosevelt:** Gelderman, 12.

Don't become a dull and dreary workaholic
Adams: McCullough, *John Adams*, 259, 364, 549; *Dictionary of American Biography*, 1:81; Barzman, 8; Wead, 297. **Jefferson:** Hofstadter, 28–29. **Garfield:** Leech and Brown, 182–184. **Churchill:** Wilson, *Character Above All*, 22–23. **Cleveland:** Summers, 118. **Polk:** Seigenthaler, 103, 153. **Carter:** Stroud, 148; Bourne, 422. **Clinton:** Gergen, 262.

Learn the blessings of patience
Adams: McCullough, *John Adams*, 364. **Eisenhower:** Wilson, *Character Above All*, 78; Gardner, *On Leadership*, 100. **Lincoln:** Goodwin, *Team of Rivals*, 164, 502; Thomas, *Abraham Lincoln*, 182; Wellman, 414.

If your family gives you a leg up, say thanks
Allan: *Washington Post* (November 17, 2002). **Burns:** *Leadership Quarterly* (Spring 2001). **Roosevelts:** Bellow, 380–381, 395; *Weekly Standard* (August 25, 2003). **Kennedys:** Bellow, 419, 448; Schlesinger, *A Thousand Days*, 142; *Weekly Standard* (August 25, 2003); *Current Biography* (1978); Galbraith, 125. **Hightower:** Bellow, 2.

"It made my life"
Bushes: *Current Biography* (1983); Wead, 4.

Personal wealth can certainly come in handy
Gephardt: *Los Angeles Times* (May 2, 1988). **Forbes:** *Washington Post* (November 12, 1999). **Richest presidents:** *Forbes* (February 14, 2003, and October 29, 2004). **Humphrey and Kennedy:** Bellow, 438–439.

Assume jobs of greater and greater responsibility
Johnson: Caro, *The Path to Power*, 442, 535; Witcover, *Crapshoot*, 147–152. **Charan:** *Harvard Business Review* (February 2005). **Gardner:** Gardner, *On Leadership*, 127. **Eisenhower:** Wilson, *Character Above All*, 66. **Johnson**

telegram: Witcover, *Crapshoot*, 150–152. **Jobs held by nominees:** Author's analysis. **Reagan:** *Chicago Sun-Times* (June 6, 2004). **Garner:** Roberts, *First Rough Draft*, 268. **Marshall:** Feinberg, 9. **Eisenhower:** *Washington Post* (February 28, 1992). **Conkling:** Jordan, 231. **Bradley:** *Psychology Today* (March 1996).

Always keep your bandwagon on the move

> **Perot:** National Press Club transcript (January 15, 1998). **Bush:** Germond and Witcover, 119. **McCain:** *Washington Post* (February 6, 2000). **Hart:** *Washington Post* (April 16, 1984). **Kennedy:** Dallek, *An Unfinished Life*, 368.

3. POLISHING

Introduction

> **Truman:** *Kansas City Star* (April 13, 2005); DeGregorio, 513; Gardner, *On Leadership*, 43, 160–161; Ross, 22; Gergen, 328; Thomas, *The Pursuit of the White House*, 129; Manchester, *The Glory and the Dream*, 449–455. **Simon:** *Washington Post* (November 23, 1987). **Abelson:** *Psychology Today* (November 1988). **Taft:** Wead, 204–205; Patterson, 343. **Dewey:** *Washington Post* (February 21, 1980); Smith, *Thomas E. Dewey and His Times*, 512–515, 545; Gunther, 533.

Break out of your shell, but don't go too far

> **McGovern:** *Washington Post* (January 14, 1984, and February 20, 2005). **Filson:** *Crain's New York Business* (June 27, 2005). **Polk:** Sellers, 276–277. **Coolidge:** Miller, *New World Coming*, 130; White House website. **Blaine:** Jordan, 72; Summers, 61–62; Sievers, 206–218.

"People tire of seeing the same name"

> **Roosevelt:** Wilson, *Character Above All*, 32; Manchester, *The Glory and the Dream*, 117.

A good (or bad) speech makes a lasting impression

> **Carrick:** *Washington Post* (September 10, 2004). **Clay:** Olasky, 67. **Webster on King:** *Dictionary of American Biography*, 10:400. **Lincoln:** Thomas, *Abraham Lincoln*, 200–206; Holzer, 157; Donald, *Lincoln*, 238–240. **Bryan:** *Dictionary of American Biography*, 3:191–197; Koenig, 199. **Reagan:** *Congressional Quarterly* (September 20, 1980); Thomas, *The Pursuit of the White House*, 166–167. **Clinton:** Maraniss, 446–447; *Washington Post* (November 24, 1991). **Gallup Poll:** *USA Today* (March 26, 2001). **Babbitt:** *Washington Post* (January 11, 1988). **Nixon:** Gergen, 54. **Roosevelt:** Wilson, *Character Above All*, 30. **Churchill:** Gergen, 210. **Stevenson:** Martin, *Adlai Stevenson of Illinois*, 764.

Invigorate your career with a touch of stagecraft

> **Roosevelt and Welles:** *Harvard Business Review* (January 2003). **Lodge:** Miller, *Henry Cabot Lodge*, 328. **Reagan:** Gergen, 212. **Carter:** Wilson, *Character Above All*, 185. **MacArthur and Eisenhower:** Manchester, *American Caesar*, 150–166, 309.

Reach people through their funny bones

> **Udall:** Udall, xiv-xv, 30; Witcover, *Marathon*, 284; *New York Times* (February 1, 1976). **Gitomer:** *Business First* (June 17, 2005). **Reed:** Olasky, 180; *American Heritage* (December 1962). **Udall again:** Udall, ix, 192, 199.

"Oh, excuse me, Jerry"

    Jackson: *Newsweek* (February 16, 1976); Udall, 192.

Don't be shy about blowing your own horn

    Charan: *Harvard Business Review* (February 2005). **Pfeffer:** *Fortune* (October 27, 1997). **Lewis and Cuomo:** *Fortune* (April 18, 1994). **Franklin:** *Philadelphia* (December 2005). **Jefferson:** Olasky, 32; *Presidential Studies Quarterly* (Autumn 2006). **Deaver:** Gelderman, 99. **Eisenhower:** Manchester, *The Glory and the Dream*, 330; Dwight Eisenhower Presidential Library website. **Roosevelt:** DeGregorio, 389; *Christian Science Monitor* (November 21, 2001).

Write for publication, or have someone do it for you

    Kennedy: Olasky, 233–234; Dallek, *An Unfinished Life*, 62–65, 199–210. **Books by recent candidates:** *Slate* (November 23, 1999); *Washington Post* (December 3, 2003). **Madison:** Brant, 192–197.

Looks do matter, so spiff up your appearance

    Federal Reserve study: *USA Today* (July 20, 2005). **Todorov:** *New Yorker* (July 25, 2005). **Keating:** *Psychology Today* (May 2004). **Height:** *Psychology Today* (May 2004); *USA Today* (July 20, 2005). **Muskie:** *Newsweek* (May 26, 1980). **Firestone:** *USA Today* (October 26, 2005). **Carter:** Gergen, 167; *Washington Post* (March 2, 1996). **Wood:** Lane, 238. **Jackson:** *Washington Post* (September 13, 1987). **Gephardt:** *Washington Post* (February 2, 1988). **Douglas:** Wellman, 292–293; Donald, *Lincoln*, 214–215.

Establish a positive reputation, and keep it

    Babbitt: *Washington Post* (February 8, 1988, and February 19, 1988). **Gitomer:** *Business First* (August 20, 2004). **Washington:** Flexner, 170–180. **Jackson:** Wellman, 11–12; DeGregorio, 118. **Grant:** DeGregorio, 274. **Roosevelt:** Manchester, *The Glory and the Dream*, 80, 83. **Wilson:** Olasky, 202. **Hoover:** Hofstadter, 370–371; Burner, 151. **Johnson:** Barber, 77. **Hoover again:** Lyons, 325.

If you want to be a leader, you must exude strength

    Johnson: Caro, *Means of Ascent*, 37; *Washington Post* (July 13, 2003); Barber, 25; *Psychology Today* (October 1988). **Roosevelt:** Chace, 230–233; Olasky, 183. **Reagan:** Gergen, 175–176. **Nixon:** Martin, *Adlai Stevenson of Illinois*, 692–693; Gergen, 40. **George H.W. Bush:** *Psychology Today* (October 1988). **Dukakis:** *Washington Post* (July 13, 2003). **Dewey:** Gunther, 528–530; Smith, *Thomas E. Dewey and His Times*, 30.

"Tell the truth"

    Cleveland: DeGregorio, 323; Olasky, 153; Thomas, *The Pursuit of the White House*, 54.

4. ORGANIZING

Introduction

    Willkie: Neal, *Dark Horse*, 46–51, 70–76, 108–109, 116; Schlesinger and Israel, 2938–2939; Parmet and Hecht, 122; Johnson, 64. **Garfield:** DeGregorio, 293; Ackerman, 110; Morgan, 65; Leech and Brown, 203–208. **Trippi:** *Providence Journal-Bulletin* (January 18, 2004). **Kennedy:** Sorensen, 392. **Lincoln:** Goodwin, *Team of Rivals*, 89–90. **Chase:** Goodwin, *Team of Rivals*, 219.

Find somebody who can teach you the ropes

    Mondale: *Current Biography* (1978); *Washington Post* (February 17, 1980, and January 8, 1984); *Congressional Quarterly* (October 8, 1983). **Bennis:**

Harvard Business Review (January 2004). **Van Buren:** Niven, *Martin Van Buren: The Romantic Age of American Politics*, 397. **Taft:** Anderson, 4, 40; *Dictionary of American Biography*, 18:269.

Hire the best staff you can, and get out of its way

    Shrum: *New York Observer* (November 21, 2005); Witcover, *Marathon*, 319–321; *Washington Post* (September 10, 2004, and September 17, 2004). **Rafshoon:** *Washington Post* (September 10, 2004). **Brown:** *Playboy* (August 1992). **Coolidge:** Taranto and Leo, 148. **Gergen:** Gergen, 184. **Johnson:** Califano, 123–124. **Gardner:** Gardner, *On Leadership*, 151. **Glenn:** *Washington Post* (March 17, 1984); Glenn, 348–349. **McGovern:** Thomas, *The Pursuit of the White House*, 163; *Congressional Quarterly* (December 24, 1983).

Expect your loved ones to work alongside you

    Bush and Kerry: *Washington Post* (October 19, 2004). **Wead:** Wead, 29. **Dean:** *Washington Post* (February 3, 2004). **Coolidge:** Miller, *New World Coming*, 139. **Taft:** Gunther, 432. **Theodore Roosevelt:** Olasky, 173. **Franklin Roosevelt:** Manchester, *The Glory and the Dream*, 92–93. **Clinton family:** Klein, *The Natural*, 117; Maraniss, 442–443.

"You sort of step outside yourself"

    Reagan children: *Washington Post* (July 18, 1980).

Count on friends for help and a fresh perspective

    Gracian: ThinkExist website. **McKinley:** DeGregorio, 355; Phillips, 68; Gould, 6–8. **Bradlee:** *Washington Post* (December 8, 1997). **Friendship study:** *USA Today* (June 23, 2006). **Wilson:** Olasky, 195; Hofstadter, 309–310. **Nixon:** Strober and Strober, 34; Wilson, *Character Above All*, 139. **Harding:** Miller, *New World Coming*, 105–107; Russell, 560.

Keep expanding your professional network

    Farley: Neal, *Happy Days Are Here Again*, 28–29. **Wilson:** McAdoo, 143. **McGovern:** *Washington Post* (February 20, 2005); Peirce and Hagstrom, 563. **Bush:** Cramer, 151–153, 417.

Collect chits from anyone you can

    Nixon: *Current Biography* (1969); Ambrose, *Nixon: The Triumph of a Politician, 1962–1972*, 11–12, 26, 56, 60–61, 69, 100. **Lincoln:** Donald, *Lincoln*, 179.

"He must have spent a fortune on flowers"

    Carter: Bourne, 242–247; Witcover, *Marathon*, 117–118.

Make alliances with anybody who can help you

    Heifetz and Linsky: *Harvard Business Review* (June 2002). **Johnson:** Taranto and Leo, 174; Barber, 117; Caro, *Means of Ascent*, 124; Caro, *The Path to Power*, 363; Califano, 122, 337.

5. CONTROLLING

Introduction

    Greeley: *Dictionary of American Biography*, 7:530; Stoddard, 80–93, 290; Maihafer, 28, 104, 240; Thomas, *Abraham Lincoln*, 442; Schlesinger and Israel, 1316–1317; Thomas, *The Pursuit of the White House*, 48. **Washington:** McCullough, *1776*, 212; Flexner, 135, 295, 367. **Lincoln:** DeGregorio, 226; Goodwin, *Team of Rivals*, 102–103, 665. **Nixon:** White, *Breach of Faith*, 152; Barber, 163. **Clinton:** Maraniss, 461; Harris, 340.

If you don't have to speak, keep your mouth shut

> **Douglas:** Klein, *President James Buchanan*, 286–287; Johannsen, 434. **Buchanan:** *Dictionary of American Biography*, 3:207–214; Klein, *President James Buchanan*, 251. **Eisenhower:** Greenstein, 67. **Hollings:** *Washington Post* (January 10, 1984). **Kerrey:** *Washington Post* (November 20, 1991). **Hoover:** Fausold, 78, 210, 240. **Clay:** Thomas, *The Pursuit of the White House*, 22; Remini, *Henry Clay, Statesman for the Union*, 583. **Muskie:** *Washington Post* (March 16, 1994, and January 21, 2004); White, *The Making of the President 1972*, 82.

Stay upbeat, humble, and as cool as possible

> **Edwards and Iowa:** *Washington Post* (October 22, 2003, and January 20, 2004); *Providence Journal-Bulletin* (January 18, 2004). **University of Pennsylvania study:** *Psychology Today* (November 1988). **Gallup Poll:** Gallup Organization website. **Gergen:** *Harvard Business Review* (January 2003). **Reagan:** Gergen, 183, 201; Taranto and Leo, 197. **Long:** Manchester, *The Glory and the Dream*, 113–116.

"We were laughing about it just this morning"

> **Udall:** Udall, 194–195.

Avoid controversy and extreme statements

> **La Follette:** Thomas, *The Pursuit of the White House*, 248–249; La Follette, 760; Schlesinger and Israel, 2479–2480; United States Senate website. **Goldwater:** *Current Biography* (1978); Schlesinger and Israel, 3669. **McGovern:** *Washington Post* (January 14, 1984); *New York Observer* (November 21, 2005). **Nixon:** White, *The Making of the President 1972*, 11. **Goldwater again:** *Washington Post* (August 14, 1988, and February 20, 2005).

Maintain your flexibility to keep up with the times

> **McAdoo:** *Dictionary of American Biography*, Supplement 3:482; Thomas, *The Pursuit of the White House*, 255; McAdoo, 53; Neal, *Happy Days Are Here Again*, 125–126. **Dirksen:** Udall, 122. **Birney:** Fladeland, 19–31. **Bidwell:** Hunt, 322. **Lincoln:** *National Review* (March 19, 1999); Hofstadter, 171. **Roosevelt:** Gergen, 207; Schlesinger, *The Politics of Upheaval*, 621. **Bush:** Wilson, *Character Above All*, 235; *Washington Post* (August 18, 1988); Witcover, *Crapshoot*, 314, 332.

Don't obsess about popularity or margin of victory

> **Hayes:** Davison, 8; *Dictionary of American Biography*, 8:448; Schlesinger and Israel, 1379–1435. **Asmussen:** *Dallas Morning News* (June 13, 2003). **Popular margins:** Thomas, *The Pursuit of the White House*, *passim*. **White on Harding:** Sinclair, 174–175. **Longworth on Coolidge:** Russell, 622. **Wilson:** Link, *Wilson: The Road to the White House*, 475.

Don't give a potential rival an inadvertent boost

> **Scott:** Smith, *Old Fuss and Feathers*, 244–251. **Taylor:** *Dictionary of American Biography*, 18:349–354; Dyer, 185–193; Schlesinger and Israel, 867.

"This young man had passed him by"

> **Stevenson:** Martin, *Adlai Stevenson and the World*, 349–351, 507.

If you have an addiction, battle it fiercely

> **Pierce:** Nichols, 106; Discovering Lewis & Clark website; Taranto and Leo, 73. **Kennedy:** Dallek, *An Unfinished Life*, 475–477. **Udall:** *Washington Post* (April 24, 1991).

Don't let your temper get the best of you

> **Adams:** McCullough, *John Adams*, 549; *Dictionary of American Biography*, 1:81. **Clinton:** Gergen, 273. **Kramer:** *Harvard Business Review* (February

2006). **Jackson:** DeGregorio, 105–106; Hofstadter, 59; Wellman, 87. **Muskie:** *Washington Post* (March 16, 1994); *Harvard Business Review* (February 2006); *Current Biography* (1968). **Biden:** *Washington Post* (September 25, 1987).

Mollify (or ignore) potential enemies when possible

    Conkling and Blaine: Ackerman, 1–15, 74, 110; Jordan, 421; Thomas, *The Pursuit of the White House*, 49–54; Summers, 273. **Kefauver:** *Dictionary of American Biography*, Supplement 7:415–416; Thomas, *The Pursuit of the White House*, 244–245; Gorman, 139–143. **Wilson:** Smith, *When the Cheering Stopped*, 55–56.

"Those who hate you don't win unless you hate them"

    Nixon: Ambrose, *Nixon: Ruin and Recovery, 1973–1990*, 444. **Eisenhower:** Gardner, *On Leadership*, 100; Gergen, 135; Barber, 180.

If an enemy attacks, defend yourself vigorously

    Dukakis: *Washington Post* (October 28, 1988, and November 6, 1988). **Brown:** *New York Times* (October 31, 1988). **Burr:** *Dictionary of American Biography*, 3:313–320; Kennedy, *Burr, Hamilton, and Jefferson*, 8, 349–350. **Clinton's war room:** *Washington Post* (October 2, 1992, and November 7, 1993); *Newsweek* (November/December 1992 special issue); *Boston Globe* (November 5, 1992).

Certain enemies can actually help you advance

    Cleveland: *Western New York Life* (Fall 2006); *Harvard Business Review* (March/April 1985); DeGregorio, 323–324; Summers, 118–119; Graff, 52. **Roosevelt:** Tindall, 607; Manchester, *The Glory and the Dream*, 143–144; Udall, 205.

6. MANEUVERING

Introduction

    Reagan: Thomas, *The Pursuit of the White House*, 164; Witcover, *Marathon*, 401, 456–458, 479. **DeWitt Clinton:** Thomas, *The Pursuit of the White House*, 9. **Bill Clinton:** Thomas, *The United States of Suburbia*, 88; *Philadelphia Inquirer* (May 26, 1996). **Machiavelli:** *Leadership Quarterly* (Autumn 2001). **Heifetz and Linsky:** *Harvard Business Review* (June 2002). **Roosevelt:** Hofstadter, 432. **Machiavelli again:** Gardner, *On Leadership*, 2.

Subtlety and charm are the keys to manipulation

    Van Buren: Schlesinger and Israel, 580; DeGregorio, 123; Wilson, *The Presidency of Martin Van Buren*, 25, 30–31; Thomas, *The Pursuit of the White House*, 282; Witcover, *Crapshoot*, 31. **Deluga:** *Baltimore Sun* (October 24, 1994).

"And now I am going blind"

    Washington: *Harvard Business Review* (January 2003); Gergen, 244.

If danger lurks, shift the onus to someone else

    Hughes: DeGregorio, 418. **Wilson:** Link, *Wilson: Campaigns for Progressivism and Peace*, 111; Olasky, 202. **Johnson:** Goldman, *The Tragedy of Lyndon Johnson*, 235; Dallek, *Flawed Giant*, 175–176. **Goldwater:** White, *The Making of the President 1964*, 300; *Washington Post* (May 13, 1990, and May 30, 1998); *Current Biography* (1978). **Nixon:** *Washington Post* (June 14, 1992, and February 24, 2003).

Spin your negatives into positives

2004 candidates: *Washington Post* (January 29, 2004). **Bradlee:** Gergen, 336. **Connally:** Reston, 579. **Reagan and Brown:** Boyarsky, 6, 34; Thomas, *The Pursuit of the White House*, 267–268.

Tell the truth whenever you can, but lie if you must

Washington: *American Heritage* (February 1990); *Washingtonian* (February 2006). **Studies on lying:** *Psychology Today* (May 1997). **Blount:** *Atlantic Monthly* (February 2001). **Lincoln:** Hofstadter, 119. **Cleveland:** Nevins, 163; Graff, 115–116. **Theodore Roosevelt:** Olasky, 176. **Gergen:** Gergen, 140. **Johnson:** Wilson, *Character Above All*, 121. **Nixon:** *Washington Monthly* (November 2004). **Clinton:** Taranto and Leo, 206; Harris, 147. **Franklin Roosevelt:** Alterman, 17; Caro, *The Path to Power*, 559; Schlesinger, *The Coming of the New Deal*, 583–584.

Labels can only weigh you down, so avoid them

Chase: Donald, *Inside Lincoln's Cabinet*, 5; Goodwin, *Team of Rivals*, 41, 134–136, 752; Niven, *Salmon P. Chase*, 374. **Gardner:** Gardner, *On Leadership*, 31. **Bush:** Wilson, *Character Above All*, 229. **McKinley:** Thomas, *The Pursuit of the White House*, 58–59. **Roosevelt:** Pringle, 355–357; Schlesinger and Israel, 1992.

Cut ties with any ally who becomes a liability

Humphrey: Witcover, *Crapshoot*, 204–205; Dallek, *Flawed Giant*, 571–579, 592; Schlesinger and Israel, 3746; Solberg, 407. **Roosevelt and Wallace:** Wilson, *Character Above All*, 242; Schapsmeier and Schapsmeier, 75–76; Barber, 301. **Gore:** Harris, 386–389.

If success hinges on making a deal, make it

Harrison: Sievers, 290, 426; Thomas, *The Pursuit of the White House*, 54–56, 233. **Adams:** Bemis, 304; *American Heritage* (February/March 1984); Remini, *Henry Clay, Statesman for the Union*, 258; Wellman, 66; Remini, *Andrew Jackson and the Course of American Freedom, 1822–1832*, 96–98. **Hayes:** Thomas, *The Pursuit of the White House*, 49–51; Woodward, 169, 201; Randall and Donald, 695–701. **Roosevelt:** Manchester, *The Glory and the Dream*, 48–49; Freidel, *Franklin D. Roosevelt: The Triumph*, 308.

"Lincoln ain't here"

Lincoln: Goodwin, *Team of Rivals*, 244–246; Wellman, 434; DeGregorio, 237; Schlesinger and Israel, 1115.

If the rules are slanted against you, change them

McGovern: White, *The Making of the President 1972*, 161–178; *Washington Post* (September 2, 1991); Strober and Strober, 262. **Jefferson:** Hofstadter, 33; Thomas, *The Pursuit of the White House*, 7. **Kennedy:** *New York Times* (July 3, 1960); White, *The Making of the President 1960*, 55, 69; Dallek, *An Unfinished Life*, 249, 251.

7. SUCCEEDING

Introduction

Du Pont: *Washington Post* (February 2, 1988, and May 15, 1988). **Grant:** Vidal, 711; Hesseltine, 41–47. **Polk:** Sellers, 492. **Lincoln:** Wellman, 414. **Carter:** *U.S. News and World Report* (July 19, 1976). **Kennedy:** Dallek, *An Unfinished Life*, 249. **Nixon:** Barber, 135; Ambrose, *Nixon: The Triumph of a Politician, 1962–1972*, 608.

Realistic analysis is always better than blind faith
Bryan: Koenig, 426; Vidal, 724. **Delusions and failure:** *Washington Post* (December 7, 1996); *Harvard Business Review* (July 2003); *USA Today* (May 7, 2004). **MacArthur:** Manchester, *American Caesar,* 524–525, 684–686, 701. **Truman and Dewey:** Wilson, *Character Above All,* 52; Manchester, *The Glory and the Dream,* 461–463; Smith, *Thomas E. Dewey and His Times,* 536.

"Don't pay any attention to the polls"
Clinton and polls: Gergen, 331. **Dukakis:** *Los Angeles Times* (May 2, 1988).

A resilient spirit can overcome any setback
Clinton: Gergen, 318; Thomas, *The United States of Suburbia,* 87–88; Maraniss, 385, 398–399; *Washington Post* (February 20, 1992, February 21, 1992, and February 19, 1999). **Becker:** *Harvard Business Review* (May 2002). **Tedlow:** *Harvard Business Review* (December 2001). **Kennedy:** Maraniss, 387; *Newsweek* (November 28, 1983). **Nixon:** Gergen, 31; Ambrose, *Nixon: The Triumph of a Politician, 1962–1972,* 138–139; White, *Breach of Faith,* 72; Ambrose, *Nixon: Ruin and Recovery, 1973–1990,* 443.

You can still reach your goal at an advanced age
Seward: DeGregorio, 237, 252; Goodwin, *Team of Rivals,* 480. **Douglas:** Thomas, *The Pursuit of the White House,* 26–27. **Study of 1980 and 2001 executives:** *Harvard Business Review* (January 2005). **Reagan:** *Washington Post* (August 24, 1976); Goldman and Fuller, 354–355; Wilson, *Character Above All,* 218; *Newsweek* (November/December 1984 special issue). **Harrison:** Peterson, 28, 41; Witcover, *Crapshoot,* 35–36; Green, 398–399. **Eisenhower:** Ambrose, *Nixon: The Triumph of a Politician, 1962–1972,* 400. **Deloitte:** *Business Week* (September 20, 1999).

Intelligence and skill do not guarantee success
Best governors: Peirce and Hagstrom, 840–841; Thomas, *The Pursuit of the White House, passim.* **Best senators:** United States Senate website; *New York Times* (April 14, 1957); Thomas, *The Pursuit of the White House, passim.* **Calhoun:** Schlesinger and Israel, 756. **Clay:** Eaton, 171. **Taft:** Smith, *Thomas E. Dewey and His Times,* 598. **Webster:** Rayback, 361. **Kennedy:** O'Neill, 14. **Harding:** Russell, 314; Thomas, *The Pursuit of the White House,* 94.

Timing will often be beyond your control
Market timing: *USA Today* (September 19, 2005); *Washington Post* (November 11, 2001). **Rockefeller:** *Current Biography* (1979). **Crawford:** Mooney, 213–220; Thomas, *The Pursuit of the White House,* 17.

"Thanks, but you know what it's worth"
Davis: Harbaugh, 221, 250.

Acknowledge the importance of pure, blind luck
Cuomo: McElvaine, 402. **Merton:** *Boston Globe* (February 1, 2004). **Malkiel:** *Saturday Evening Post* (January 2005). **Graham:** *Fortune* (March 21, 2005). **Hepburn:** *Hartford Courant* (June 30, 2003). **Roosevelt:** Wead, 298. **Lovallo and Kahneman study:** *Harvard Business Review* (July 2003). **Pasteur:** *Boston Globe* (February 1, 2004). **Wiseman:** *Dallas Morning News* (June 13, 2003). **Coolidge:** *U.S. News and World Report* (July 9, 1984); Sobel, 127–144, 188–190; White, *A Puritan in Babylon,* 241.

Don't fall victim to jealousy and envy
Smith and Franklin Roosevelt: Goldberg, 108; Freidel, *Franklin D. Roosevelt: A Rendezvous With Destiny,* 55–57; Schlesinger, *The Politics of Upheaval,*

518–520; Josephson and Josephson, 457. **Taft and Theodore Roosevelt:** Brands, 632, 674, 706–707, 736; Gardner, *Departing Glory*, 233–234; Anderson, 177; Chace, 108.

Conduct yourself with grace, especially in defeat

Dole: *Washington Post* (November 9, 1987, April 29, 1997, and February 20, 2005); *Time* (August 30, 1976); Witcover, *Marathon*, 614; Witcover, *Crapshoot*, 336. **Nixon:** *Current Biography* (1969). **Quayle:** *Washington Post* (April 28, 1994). **Van Buren:** Wilson, *The Presidency of Martin Van Buren*, 209–210. **Gore:** *Washington Post* (December 14, 2000). **Stevenson:** Martin, *Adlai Stevenson of Illinois*, 759.

Exult in your success, and do the best job you can

Redford and *The Candidate*: *Washington Post* (February 8, 1988); *New York Times* (October 6, 1988). **Clinton:** *Washington Post* (February 19, 1996). **Roosevelt:** *Washington Post* (January 2, 2007). **Harding:** Barber, 215. **Nixon and Noonan:** Wilson, *Character Above All*, 203. **Polk:** Seigenthaler, 102–103; McCoy, *Polk and the Presidency*, 6; Taranto and Leo, 11–12. **Reagan:** *Washington Post* (June 6, 2004). **Roosevelt again:** Pringle, 476–477. **Polk again:** McCoy, *Polk and the Presidency*, 73.

Recognize when it's time for you to leave the stage

Stassen: *Current Biography* (1948); *Washington Post* (March 5, 2001, and March 7, 2001); Truman Presidential Museum and Library website; *Esquire* (August 1967); Ambrose, *Nixon: The Education of a Politician, 1913–1962*, 402. **Bradley:** *Psychology Today* (March 1996). **Tilden:** Stone, 210; Morgan, 77.

"He's more popular now than he ever was"

Gore: *Washington Post* (February 25, 2007).

Don't lose track of what's really important in life

Cleveland and Roosevelt: Olasky, 210; Summers, 118. **Grant:** Smith, *Lee and Grant*, 334. **Clinton:** *Washington Post* (January 28, 2001). **Jefferson:** Taranto and Leo, 29. **Polk:** DeGregorio, 171. **Buchanan:** Wellman, 428. **Harding:** Russell, 485. **Hoover:** Hofstadter, 382. **Kahneman:** *Psychology Today* (January 2005). **Pierce:** DeGregorio, 207; Wead, 87–88; *Time* (August 22, 1969). **Harrison:** Sievers, 250. **Coolidge:** White, *A Puritan in Babylon*, 308. **Franklin:** *Philadelphia* (December 2005); *Futurist* (September 1997). **Studies on happiness:** *Psychology Today* (July 1995); Gallup Organization website; *Forbes* (October 17, 1988). **Lincoln:** Goodwin, *Team of Rivals*, 306. **Theodore Roosevelt:** *Time* (July 3, 2006); Gelderman, 2; Taranto and Leo, 126. **Franklin Roosevelt:** Wilson, *Character Above All*, 13.

Bibliography

BOOKS

Ackerman, Kenneth. *Dark Horse*. New York: Carroll & Graf, 2003.

Adler, Bill. *Presidential Wit*. New York: Trident, 1966.

Alterman, Eric. *When Presidents Lie*. New York: Viking, 2004.

Ambrose, Stephen. *Eisenhower, 1890–1952*. New York: Simon & Schuster, 1983.

———. *Nixon: The Education of a Politician, 1913–1962*. New York: Simon & Schuster, 1987.

———. *Nixon: Ruin and Recovery, 1973–1990*. New York: Simon & Schuster, 1991.

———. *Nixon: The Triumph of a Politician, 1962–1972*. New York: Simon & Schuster, 1989.

Anderson, Donald. *William Howard Taft*. Ithaca, New York: Cornell University Press, 1968.

Bain, Richard, and Judith Parris. *Convention Decisions and Voting Records*. Washington: Brookings Institution, 1973.

Baker, Jean. *The Stevensons*. New York: W.W. Norton & Co., 1996.

Barber, James David. *The Presidential Character*. Englewood Cliffs, New Jersey: Prentice Hall, 1992.

Barrows, Robert, and Shirley McCord, editors. *Their Infinite Variety: Essays on Indiana Politicians*. Indianapolis: Indiana Historical Bureau, 1981.

Bartlett, Irving. *John C. Calhoun*. New York: W.W. Norton & Co., 1993.

Barzman, Sol. *Madmen and Geniuses*. Chicago: Follett, 1974.

Bellow, Adam. *In Praise of Nepotism*. New York: Doubleday, 2003.

Bemis, Samuel Flagg. *John Quincy Adams and the Union*. New York: Alfred A. Knopf, 1956.

Bennett, David. *Demagogues in the Depression*. New Brunswick, New Jersey: Rutgers University Press, 1969.

Boller, Paul. *Presidential Campaigns*. New York: Oxford University Press, 1984.

Bourne, Peter. *Jimmy Carter*. New York: Scribner, 1997.

Boyarsky, Bill. *Ronald Reagan*. New York: Random House, 1981.

Brands, H.W. *T.R.: The Last Romantic*. New York: Basic Books, 1997.

Brant, Irving. *The Fourth President: A Life of James Madison*. Indianapolis: Bobbs-Merrill, 1970.

Burner, David. *Herbert Hoover*. New York: Alfred A. Knopf, 1979.

Burns, James MacGregor. *Edward Kennedy and the Camelot Legacy*. New York: W.W. Norton & Co., 1976.

————. *John Kennedy*. New York: Harcourt, Brace, & World, 1961.

————. *Roosevelt: The Lion and the Fox*. New York: Harcourt, Brace, & Co., 1956.

————. *Roosevelt: The Soldier of Freedom*. New York: Harcourt, Brace, Jovanovich, 1970.

Califano, Joseph Jr. *The Triumph and Tragedy of Lyndon Johnson*. New York: Simon & Schuster, 1991.

Caro, Robert. *Means of Ascent*. New York: Vintage, 1991.

————. *The Path to Power*. New York: Alfred A. Knopf, 1982.

Catton, Bruce. *Mr. Lincoln's Army*. Garden City, New York: Doubleday & Co., 1951.

Chace, James. *1912*. New York: Simon & Schuster, 2004.

Chisholm, Shirley. *The Good Fight*. New York: Harper & Row, 1973.

Clark, Champ. *My Quarter Century of American Politics*. New York: Harper & Brothers, 1920.

Clifford, Clark. *Counsel to the President*. New York: Random House, 1991.

Coben, Stanley. *A. Mitchell Palmer: Politician*. New York: Columbia University Press, 1963.

Cole, Donald. *Jacksonian Democracy in New Hampshire, 1800–1851*. Cambridge, Massachusetts: Harvard University Press, 1970.

Cox, James. *Journey Through My Years*. New York: Simon & Schuster, 1946.

Cramer, Richard Ben. *What It Takes*. New York: Vintage, 1993.

Crissey, Forrest. *Theodore E. Burton, American Statesman*. Cleveland: World Publishing Co., 1956.

Dallek, Robert. *Flawed Giant*. New York: Oxford University Press, 1998.

————. *An Unfinished Life*. Boston: Little, Brown, & Co., 2003.

Davison, Kenneth. *The Presidency of Rutherford B. Hayes*. Westport, Connecticut: Greenwood Press, 1972.

DeGregorio, William. *The Complete Book of U.S. Presidents*. New York: Dembner, 1984.

Depew, Chauncey. *My Memories of Eighty Years*. New York: Charles Scribner's Sons, 1922.

Dictionary of American Biography (thirty volumes). New York: Charles Scribner's Sons, 1927–1995.

Donald, David. *Lincoln*. New York: Simon & Schuster, 1995.

————, editor. *Inside Lincoln's Cabinet*. New York: Longmans, Green, & Co., 1954.

Dyer, Brainerd. *Zachary Taylor*. Baton Rouge: Louisiana State University Press, 1946.

Eaton, Clement. *Henry Clay and the Art of American Politics*. Boston: Little, Brown, & Co., 1957.

Ernst, Robert. *Rufus King: American Federalist*. Chapel Hill: University of North Carolina Press, 1968.

Ewy, Marvin. *Charles Curtis of Kansas*. Emporia, Kansas: Emporia State Research Studies, 1961.

Fausold, Martin. *The Presidency of Herbert C. Hoover*. Lawrence: University Press of Kansas, 1985.

Feinberg, Barbara Silberdick. *Next in Line*. New York: Franklin Watts, 1996.

Ferrell, Robert. *Truman: A Centenary Remembrance*. New York: Viking Press, 1984.

Fladeland, Betty. *James Gillespie Birney: Slaveholder to Abolitionist*. Ithaca, New York: Cornell University Press, 1955.

Flexner, James Thomas. *Washington: The Indispensable Man*. Boston: Little, Brown, & Co., 1974.

Freeman, Douglas Southall. *George Washington: Volume Six*. New York: Charles Scribner's Sons, 1954.

Freidel, Frank. *Franklin D. Roosevelt: A Rendezvous With Destiny*. Boston: Little, Brown, & Co., 1990.

————. *Franklin D. Roosevelt: The Triumph*. Boston: Little, Brown, & Co., 1956.

Galbraith, John Kenneth. *Name-Dropping*. Boston: Houghton Mifflin, 1999.

Gardner, John. *On Leadership*. New York: Free Press, 1990.

Gardner, Joseph. *Departing Glory*. New York: Charles Scribner's Sons, 1973.

Gelderman, Carol. *All the Presidents' Words*. New York: Walker & Co., 1997.

Gergen, David. *Eyewitness to Power*. New York: Simon & Schuster, 2000.

Germond, Jack, and Jules Witcover. *Blue Smoke and Mirrors*. New York: Viking Press, 1981.

Glenn, John. *John Glenn: A Memoir*. New York: Bantam, 1999.

Goldberg, Richard Thayer. *The Making of Franklin D. Roosevelt*. Cambridge, Massachusetts: Abt Books, 1981.

Goldman, Eric. *The Tragedy of Lyndon Johnson*. New York: Alfred A. Knopf, 1969.

Goldman, Peter, and Tony Fuller. *The Quest for the Presidency 1984*. New York: Bantam, 1985.

Goldwater, Barry. *With No Apologies*. New York: William Morrow & Co., 1979.

Goodwin, Doris Kearns. *No Ordinary Time*. New York: Touchstone, 1994.

————. *Team of Rivals*. New York: Simon & Schuster, 2005.

Gorman, Joseph. *Kefauver*. New York: Oxford University Press, 1971.

Gould, Lewis. *The Presidency of William McKinley*. Lawrence: The Regents Press of Kansas, 1980.

Graff, Henry. *Grover Cleveland*. New York: Henry Holt & Co., 2002.

Green, James. *William Henry Harrison, His Life and Times*. Richmond, Virginia: Garrett & Massie, 1941.

Greenstein, Fred. *The Hidden-Hand Presidency*. New York: Basic Books, 1982.

Gunderson, Robert. *The Log Cabin Campaign*. Lexington: University of Kentucky Press, 1957.

Gunther, John. *Inside U.S.A.* London: Hamish Hamilton, 1948.

Hancock, Almira. *Reminiscences of Winfield Scott Hancock*. New York: Charles L. Webster & Co., 1887.

Harbaugh, William. *Lawyer's Lawyer*. New York: Oxford University Press, 1973.

Harris, John. *The Survivor*. New York: Random House, 2005.

Helmes, Winifred. *John A. Johnson: The People's Governor*. Minneapolis: University of Minnesota Press, 1949.

Hesseltine, William. *Ulysses Grant, Politician*. New York: Frederick Ungar Publishing Co., 1957.

Hofstadter, Richard. *The American Political Tradition*. New York: Vintage, 1974.

Holzer, Harold. *Lincoln at Cooper Union*. New York: Simon & Schuster, 2004.

Hoover, Herbert. *The Memoirs of Herbert Hoover: The Cabinet and the Presidency*. New York: Macmillan, 1952.

Hughes, Emmet John. *The Ordeal of Power*. New York: Atheneum, 1963.

Hunt, Rockwell. *John Bidwell, Prince of California Pioneers*. Caldwell, Idaho: Caxton Printers, 1942.

James, Marquis. *The Life of Andrew Jackson*. Indianapolis: Bobbs-Merrill, 1938.

———. *Mr. Garner of Texas*. Indianapolis: Bobbs-Merrill, 1939.

Johannsen, Robert. *Stephen A. Douglas*. New York: Oxford University Press, 1973.

Johnson, Donald. *The Republican Party and Wendell Willkie*. Westport, Connecticut: Greenwood Press, 1960.

Jordan, David. *Roscoe Conkling of New York*. Ithaca, New York: Cornell University Press, 1971.

Josephson, Matthew, and Hannah Josephson. *Al Smith: Hero of the Cities*. London: Thames & Hudson, 1969.

Kennedy, John. *Public Papers of the Presidents of the United States, 1962*. Washington: United States Government Printing Office, 1963.

Kennedy, Roger. *Burr, Hamilton, and Jefferson*. New York: Oxford University Press, 2000.

Klein, Joe. *The Natural*. New York: Doubleday, 2002.

Klein, Philip. *President James Buchanan*. University Park: Pennsylvania State University Press, 1962.

Koenig, Louis. *Bryan*. New York: G. P. Putnam's Sons, 1971.

La Follette, Robert. *A Personal Narrative of Political Experiences*. Madison, Wisconsin: La Follette Co., 1913.

Lane, Jack. *Armed Progressive*. San Rafael, California: Presidio Press, 1978.

Leech, Margaret, and Harry Brown. *The Garfield Orbit*. New York: Harper & Row, 1978.

Link, Arthur. *Wilson: Campaigns for Progressivism and Peace*. Princeton, New Jersey: Princeton University Press, 1965.

———. *Wilson: The Road to the White House*. Princeton, New Jersey: Princeton University Press, 1947.

Lippman, Theo Jr. *Senator Ted Kennedy*. New York: W.W. Norton & Co., 1976.

Lomask, Milton. *Aaron Burr: The Years From Princeton to Vice President*. New York: Farrar, Straus, Giroux, 1979.

Lurie, Leonard. *Party Politics*. New York: Stein & Day, 1980.

Luthin, Reinhard. *The First Lincoln Campaign*. Gloucester, Massachusetts: Peter Smith, 1964.

Lyons, Eugene. *Herbert Hoover*. Garden City, New York: Doubleday & Co., 1964.

Maihafer, Harry. *The General and the Journalists*. Washington: Brassey's, 2001.

Malone, Dumas. *Jefferson and the Ordeal of Liberty*. Boston: Little, Brown, & Co., 1962.

Manchester, William. *American Caesar*. Boston: Little, Brown, & Co., 1978.

———. *The Glory and the Dream*. Boston: Little, Brown, & Co., 1973.

Maraniss, David. *First in His Class*. New York: Simon & Schuster, 1995.

Marrin, Albert. *Nicholas Murray Butler*. Boston: Twayne Publishers, 1976.

Martin, John Bartlow. *Adlai Stevenson of Illinois*. Garden City, New York: Doubleday & Co., 1976.

———. *Adlai Stevenson and the World*. Garden City, New York: Doubleday & Co., 1977.

McAdoo, William Gibbs. *Crowded Years*. Boston: Houghton Mifflin, 1931.

McCoy, Charles. *Polk and the Presidency*. Austin: University of Texas Press, 1960.

McCoy, Donald. *Landon of Kansas*. Lincoln: University of Nebraska Press, 1966.

McCullough, David. *1776*. New York: Simon & Schuster, 2005.

———. *John Adams*. New York: Simon & Schuster, 2001.

McElvaine, Robert. *Mario Cuomo*. New York: Charles Scribner's Sons, 1988.

McKenna, Marian. *Borah*. Ann Arbor: University of Michigan Press, 1961.

Milbank, Dana. *Smashmouth*. New York: Basic Books, 2001.

Miller, Merle. *Lyndon: An Oral Biography*. New York: G. P. Putnam's Sons, 1980.

Miller, Nathan. *New World Coming*. New York: Scribner, 2003.

Miller, William. *Henry Cabot Lodge*. New York: James H. Heineman Inc., 1967.

Mitchell, Stewart. *Horatio Seymour of New York*. New York: Da Capo Press, 1938.

Mooney, Chase. *William H. Crawford*. Lexington: University Press of Kentucky, 1974.

Morgan, H. Wayne. *From Hayes to McKinley: National Party Politics, 1877–1896*. Syracuse, New York: Syracuse University Press, 1969.

Murray, Robert. *The 103rd Ballot*. New York: Harper & Row, 1976.

———. *Red Scare*. Minneapolis: University of Minnesota Press, 1955.

Muzzey, David. *James G. Blaine: A Political Idol of Other Days*. New York: Dodd, Mead, & Co., 1934.

Neal, Steve. *Dark Horse*. Garden City, New York: Doubleday & Co., 1984.

———. *Happy Days Are Here Again*. New York: William Morrow, 2004.

Nevins, Allan. *Grover Cleveland: A Study in Courage*. New York: Dodd, Mead, & Co., 1933.

Nichols, Roy. *Franklin Pierce*. Philadelphia: University of Pennsylvania Press, 1931.

Niven, John. *Martin Van Buren: The Romantic Age of American Politics*. New York: Oxford University Press, 1983.

———. *Salmon P. Chase*. New York: Oxford University Press, 1995.

Olasky, Marvin. *The American Leadership Tradition*. New York: Free Press, 1999.

Olin, Spencer. *California's Prodigal Sons*. Berkeley: University of California Press, 1968.

O'Neill, William. *Coming Apart*. New York: Times Books, 1971.

Pack, Robert. *Jerry Brown: The Philosopher-Prince*. New York: Stein & Day, 1978.

Parmet, Herbert, and Marie Hecht. *Never Again: A President Runs for a Third Term*. New York: Macmillan, 1968.

Patterson, James. *Mr. Republican*. Boston: Houghton Mifflin, 1972.

Peirce, Neal, and Jerry Hagstrom. *The Book of America*. New York: W.W. Norton & Co., 1983.

Peskin, Allan. *Garfield*. Kent, Ohio: Kent State University Press, 1978.

Peterson, Norma. *The Presidencies of William Henry Harrison and John Tyler*. Lawrence: University Press of Kansas, 1989.

Phillips, Kevin. *William McKinley*. New York: Henry Holt & Co., 2003.

Pringle, Henry. *Theodore Roosevelt*. New York: Harcourt, Brace, & Co., 1931.

Pusey, Merlo. *Charles Evans Hughes*. New York: Macmillan, 1951.

Randall, J. G., and David Donald. *The Civil War and Reconstruction*. Lexington, Massachusetts: D. C. Heath & Co., 1969.

Rayback, Robert. *Millard Fillmore*. Buffalo: Henry Stewart, 1959.

Remini, Robert. *Andrew Jackson and the Course of American Freedom, 1822–1832*. New York: Harper & Row, 1981.

———. *Henry Clay, Statesman for the Union*. New York: W.W. Norton & Co., 1991.

Reston, James Jr. *The Lone Star*. New York: Harper & Row, 1989.

Reynolds, Barbara. *Jesse Jackson: The Man, The Movement, The Myth*. Chicago: Nelson-Hall, 1975.

Roberts, Chalmers. *First Rough Draft*. New York: Praeger, 1973.

———. *The Washington Post: The First 100 Years*. Boston: Houghton Mifflin, 1977.

Ross, Irwin. *The Loneliest Campaign*. New York: New American Library, 1968.

Russell, Francis. *The Shadow of Blooming Grove*. New York: McGraw-Hill, 1968.

Salinger, Pierre. *With Kennedy*. Garden City, New York: Doubleday & Co., 1966.

Salvatore, Nick. *Eugene V. Debs, Citizen and Socialist*. Urbana: University of Illinois Press, 1982.

Schapsmeier, Edward, and Frederick Schapsmeier. *Prophet in Politics: Henry A. Wallace and the War Years*. Ames: Iowa State University Press, 1970.

Schlesinger, Arthur Jr. *A Thousand Days*. Boston: Houghton Mifflin, 1965.

———. *The Coming of the New Deal*. Boston: Houghton Mifflin, 1959.

———. *The Politics of Upheaval*. Boston: Houghton Mifflin, 1960.

———, and Fred Israel, editors. *History of American Presidential Elections, 1789–1968*. New York: Chelsea House, 1971.

Seigenthaler, John. *James K. Polk*. New York: Henry Holt & Co., 2003.

Sellers, Charles. *James K. Polk: Jacksonian*. Princeton, New Jersey: Princeton University Press, 1957.

Sherman, Janann. *No Place for a Woman*. New Brunswick, New Jersey: Rutgers University Press, 2000.

Sievers, Harry. *Benjamin Harrison: Hoosier Statesman, 1865–1888*. New York: University Publishers, 1959.

Sinclair, Andrew. *The Available Man*. New York: Macmillan, 1965.

Smith, Arthur. *Old Fuss and Feathers*. New York: Greystone Press, 1937.

Smith, Gene. *Lee and Grant*. New York: McGraw-Hill, 1984.

———. *When the Cheering Stopped*. New York: William Morrow & Co., 1964.

Smith, Page. *John Adams*. Garden City, New York: Doubleday & Co., 1962.

Smith, Richard Norton. *Thomas E. Dewey and His Times*. New York: Simon & Schuster, 1982.

Smith, Rixey, and Norman Beasley. *Carter Glass*. New York: Longmans, Green, & Co., 1939.

Sobel, Robert. *Coolidge: An American Enigma*. Washington: Regnery, 1998.

Solberg, Carl. *Hubert Humphrey*. New York: W.W. Norton & Co., 1984.

Sorensen, Theodore. *Kennedy*. New York: Harper & Row, 1965.

Spaulding, E. Wilder. *His Excellency George Clinton*. New York: Macmillan, 1938.

Spencer, Ivor. *The Victor and the Spoils*. Providence, Rhode Island: Brown University Press, 1959.

Stacks, John. *Scotty*. Boston: Little, Brown, & Co., 2003.

Stoddard, Henry. *Horace Greeley*. New York: G. P. Putnam's Sons, 1946.

Stone, Irving. *They Also Ran*. Garden City, New York: Doubleday, Doran, & Co., 1943.

Stout, Richard. *People*. New York: Harper & Row, 1970.

Strober, Gerald, and Deborah Hart Strober. *Nixon*. New York: HarperCollins, 1994.

Stroud, Kandy. *How Jimmy Won*. New York: William Morrow & Co., 1977.

Summers, Mark. *Rum, Romanism, and Rebellion*. Chapel Hill: University of North Carolina Press, 2000.

Swanberg, W. A. *Norman Thomas: The Last Idealist*. New York: Charles Scribner's Sons, 1976.

Tansill, Charles Callan. *The Congressional Career of Thomas Francis Bayard*. Washington: Georgetown University Press, 1946.

Taranto, James, and Leonard Leo, editors. *Presidential Leadership*. New York: Free Press, 2004.

Thomas, Benjamin. *Abraham Lincoln*. New York: Alfred A. Knopf, 1952.

Thomas, G. Scott. *The Pursuit of the White House*. Westport, Connecticut: Greenwood Press, 1987.

————. *The United States of Suburbia*. Amherst, New York: Prometheus, 1998.

Tindall, George. *The Emergence of the New South*. Baton Rouge: Louisiana State University Press, 1967.

Truman, Harry. *Memoirs: Years of Trial and Hope*. Garden City, New York: Doubleday & Co., 1956.

Udall, Morris. *Too Funny to Be President*. New York: Henry Holt & Co., 1988.

Van Deusen, Glyndon. *The Life of Henry Clay*. Boston: Little, Brown, & Co., 1937.

————. *William Henry Seward*. New York: Oxford University Press, 1967.

Vidal, Gore. *United States*. New York: Random House, 1993.

Wead, Doug. *All the Presidents' Children*. New York: Atria, 2003.

Wellman, Paul. *The House Divides*. Garden City, New York: Doubleday & Co., 1966.

White, Theodore. *Breach of Faith*. New York: Atheneum, 1975.

————. *The Making of the President 1960*. New York: Atheneum, 1961.

————. *The Making of the President 1964*. New York: Atheneum, 1965.

————. *The Making of the President 1968*. New York: Atheneum, 1969.

————. *The Making of the President 1972*. New York: Atheneum, 1973.

White, William Allen. *A Puritan in Babylon*. New York: Macmillan, 1939.

Wilson, Major. *The Presidency of Martin Van Buren*. Lawrence: University Press of Kansas, 1984.

Wilson, Robert, editor. *Character Above All*. New York: Simon & Schuster, 1995.

Witcover, Jules. *Crapshoot*. New York: Crown, 1992.

————. *Marathon*. New York: Viking Press, 1977.

Wolf, George. *William Warren Scranton*. University Park, Pennsylvania: Keystone, 1981.

Woodford, Frank. *Lewis Cass: The Last Jeffersonian*. New Brunswick, New Jersey: Rutgers University Press, 1950.

Woodward, C. Vann. *Reunion and Reaction*. Boston: Little, Brown, & Co., 1966.

Wooten, James. *Dasher*. New York: Summit, 1978.
Zahniser, Marvin. *Charles Cotesworth Pinckney, Founding Father*. Chapel Hill: University of North Carolina Press, 1967.

BROADCAST AND SPEECH TRANSCRIPTS

All Things Considered, National Public Radio.
American Public Power Association
Good Morning America, ABC.
National Press Club
The News With Brian Williams, MSNBC.

MAGAZINES AND JOURNALS

American Heritage
Atlantic Monthly
Business Week
Congressional Quarterly
Current Biography
Economic Perspectives
Esquire
Forbes
Fortune
Futurist
Harvard Business Review
Journal of Management Development
Leadership Quarterly
Nation
National Journal
National Review
Newsweek
New Yorker
Outlook
Philadelphia
Playboy
Presidential Studies Quarterly
Psychology Today
Regardie's
Saturday Evening Post
Science
Slate
Social Forces
Time
U.S. News and World Report
Washingtonian
Washington Monthly

Weekly Standard
Western New York Life

NEWSPAPERS, NEWSLETTERS, AND WIRE SERVICES

Associated Press wire service
Atlanta Journal and Constitution
Baltimore Sun
Boston Globe
Business First
Chicago Sun-Times
Chicago Tribune
Christian Science Monitor
Crain's New York Business
Dallas Morning News
Denver Post
Fort Lauderdale Sun-Sentinel
Hartford Courant
Hotline
Indianapolis Star
Kansas City Star
Los Angeles Times
National Post
New York Observer
New York Times
Orange County Register
Philadelphia Inquirer
Providence Journal-Bulletin
Richmond Times-Dispatch
Seattle Post-Intelligencer
United Press International wire service
USA Today
Washington Post

WEBSITES

Biographical Directory of the United States Congress, http://bioguide.congress.gov.
Center for American Women and Politics, http://www.cawp.rutgers.edu.
Discovering Lewis & Clark, http://www.lewis-clark.org.
Dwight Eisenhower Presidential Library, http://www.eisenhower.archives.gov.
Franklin and Eleanor Roosevelt Institute, http://www.feri.org.
Gallup Organization, http://www.gallup.com.
Infoplease, http://www.infoplease.com.
Jimmy Carter Library and Museum, http://www.jimmycarterlibrary.org.
McConnell Center, http://www.mcconnellcenter.org.
National Center for Education Statistics, http://nces.ed.gov.
Roper Center for Public Opinion Research, http://www.ropercenter.uconn.edu.

ThinkExist, http://www.thinkexist.com.
Truman Presidential Museum and Library, http://www.trumanlibrary.org.
United States Bureau of Labor Statistics, http://www.bls.gov.
United States Census Bureau, http://www.census.gov.
United States Senate, http://www.senate.gov.
White House, http://www.whitehouse.gov.

Index

About the Author

G. SCOTT THOMAS has been a journalist for over thirty years, specializing in stories about business and demographics. The author of over one hundred articles for national magazines like *American Demographics*, *Savvy*, and the *Wall Street Journal*, he has also written seven books, including *The Rating Guide to Life in America's Small Cities*, *Leveling the Field*, and *The Pursuit of the White House* (Greenwood).